A Reader in Marketing Communications

A Reader in Marketing Communications is an international and multidisciplinary collection of papers and commentary that reflects the complex and diverse range of information available on marketing communications today.

Features include:

- Editors' analysis and commentary
- Case vignettes
- Discussion questions
- Each chapter is dedicated to a key element of the promotional mix.

The Editors provide pathways of understanding to enable readers to develop their knowledge and comprehension of the various tools, concepts and practice of marketing communications.

Engaging and illuminating, the editors have created a wonderful resource that spans this complex and important subject, offering a thoughtful analysis and explanation that will prove invaluable to anybody with an interest in marketing communications.

Philip J. Kitchen holds the Chair in Strategic Marketing at Hull University Business School, UK.

Patrick de Pelsmacker is Professor of Marketing at the University of Antwerp Management School, Belgium.

Lynne Eagle is Professor of Marketing at Middlesex University, UK.

Don E. Schultz is Professor Emeritus-in-Service of Integrated Marketing Communications at the Medill School of Journalism, Northwestern University, USA.

A Reader in Marketing Communications

Edited by

Philip J. Kitchen, Patrick de Pelsmacker, Lynne Eagle and Don E. Schultz

LONDON AND NEW YORK

First published 2005
by Routledge
2 Park Square, Milton Park, Abingdon, Oxon OX14 4RN

Simultaneously published in the USA and Canada
by Routledge
270 Madison Ave, New York, NY 10016

Routledge is an imprint of the Taylor & Francis Group

Typeset in Perpetua and Bell Gothic by
RefineCatch Ltd, Bungay, Suffolk
Printed and bound in Great Britain by
TJ International Ltd, Padstow, Cornwall

British Library Cataloguing in Publication Data
A catalogue record for this book is available from the British Library

Library of Congress Cataloging in Publication Data
A catalog record for this book has been requested

ISBN 0–415–35648–2 (hbk)
ISBN 0–415–35649–0 (pbk)

To all those who assisted in the preparation of this book and to the authors and publishers of the papers we have selected.

Contents

List of illustrations

List of tables

About the editors

Philip J. Kitchen holds the Chair in Strategic Marketing at Hull University Business School. At Hull he teaches and carries out research in marketing management, marketing communications, corporate communications, promotion management and international communications management. Prior to academe he worked as a regional manager for a national firm before entering higher education as a mature student. A graduate of the CNAA (B.A. [Hons]) initially, he received Master's degrees in marketing from UMIST (M.Sc.) and Manchester Business School (M.B.Sc.) respectively, and his Ph.D. from Keele University. Since 1984 he has been active in teaching and research in the communications domain. He is Founding Editor of the *Journal of Marketing Communications* (Routledge Journals, 1995). He has published ten books, the most recent of which are: *Marketing Mind Prints (2004), A Primer on Integrated Marketing Communications* (with Patrick de Pelsmacker, 2004), *Communicating Globally: an Integrated Marketing Approach* (with Don Schultz, 2004, in Russian). Dr Kitchen has contributed to such journals as the *International Journal of Advertising, Journal of Advertising Research, Journal of Marketing Management, European Journal of Marketing, Marketing Intelligence and Planning, Journal of Marketing Communications, ADMAP, Journal of Nonprofit and Public Sector Marketing, International Journal of Bank Marketing, Journal of Corporate Communications, Small Business and Enterprise Development, Creativity and Innovation Management, Journal of Business Ethics* and numerous practitioner journals. He founded, organized and chaired the first International Conference on Marketing and Corporate Communications and was editor of the Proceedings (Keele 1996, Strathclyde 1998). This conference is now an annual event (Antwerp, Belgium, 1997; Glasgow, Scotland 1998; Salford, England, 1999; Erasmus Universiteit, the Netherlands, 2000; Northwestern University, USA, 2001). Dr Kitchen serves on the Editorial Advisory Board of the *Journal of Marketing Management* and is a Review

Board member for *Marketing Intelligence and Planning* and *Corporate Communications: an International Journal*. He has given papers on marketing management, corporate or marketing communications in England, Scotland, the Czech Republic, Estonia, France, Germany, Belgium, Portugal, Australia, New Zealand, Spain, the Republic of Ireland, Northern Ireland, Israel and in the United States. He is Visiting Professor at Massey University, New Zealand, the Norwegian School of Management, Norway, Intercollege, Cyprus and ESC Rouen, France.

Patrick de Pelsmacker is Professor of Marketing at the University of Antwerp and Ghent. Previously he was Dean of the Universiteit Antwerpen Management School (University of Antwerp). He also teaches and carries out research on Marketing Research and Marketing Communications at the University of Antwerp and the University of Ghent. He is co-author of, among others, a textbook in Dutch on Marketing Research Techniques (1994, 1996, 1999, 2002) and a book on Marketing Communications, (2001, 2004), and has written chapters in various books on advertising, marketing and management. He has published articles on marketing, marketing communications in general and advertising in particular, consumer behaviour and various other subjects in, among others, *Applied Economics, International Journal of Research in Marketing, Advances in Consumer Research, Journal of Advertising, International Journal of Advertising, Journal of Marketing Communications, International Marketing Review, Psychology and Marketing, Educational and Psychological Measurement, Psychological Reports, Operations Research Insights, Review of Econometrics, Journal of International Consumer Marketing, Journal of Business Ethics* and *AMS Review*. He has given papers, courses and lectures on marketing, marketing research and marketing communications in conferences and seminars in England, the Netherlands, France, Italy, Sweden, Poland, the Czech Republic, Hungary, Romania, Norway, Germany, the United States, Thailand, the Philippines, Indonesia and Vietnam. He is involved in executive training programmes for various companies and organizations on a regular basis.

Lynne Eagle is Professor of Marketing at Middlesex University, UK, where she teaches marketing communications and consumer behaviour. She has an extensive industry background, having worked for multinational advertising agencies prior to entering academia in 1987. Her research interests centre on advertising effects and effectiveness, and include integrated marketing communication, the impact of advertising on children and the impact marketing communication has on perceptions and the use of medications. She has published in a range of academic journals, including *European Journal of Marketing, Journal of Marketing Management, International Journal of Advertising, Corporate Communications International Journal, Journal of Marketing Communications, International Journal of Advertising and Marketing to Children, International Journal of Medical Marketing* and the *Marketing Intelligence and Planning Journal*. She has also contributed chapters to books on advertising management and other related subjects. Dr Eagle has presented research papers at conferences in England, Scotland, Ireland, Belgium, France, the United States and Australia as well as her native New Zealand. She has also acted as a judge for a number of advertising effectiveness awards and was convenor of judges for the inaugural New Zealand Advertising Effectiveness Awards (now Effies). She also provides consultancy advice for key industry groups regarding the interface between marketing communication and sensitive public policy areas.

Don E. Schultz is Professor Emeritus-in-Service of Integrated Marketing Communications at the Medill School of Journalism, Northwestern University. He is also president of the consulting firm Agora Inc., both located in Evanston, IL. Additionally, he is a Visiting Professor at Cranfield School of Management, Bedfordshire, UK, Adjunct Professor at Queensland University of Technology, Brisbane, Australia, and Visiting Professor, Tsinghua University, Beijing, China. Following his graduation from the University of Oklahoma with a degree in Marketing/Journalism, Schultz began his career as a sales promotion writer for trade magazine publishers in Dallas. From there, he moved into publication sales and management, and was advertising director of a daily newspaper in Texas. He then joined Tracy-Locke Advertising and Public Relations in Dallas in 1965. He was with the agency for almost ten years in its Dallas, New York and Columbus, OH, offices as branch manager. In 1974 Schultz resigned as senior vice-president of Tracy-Locke to launch a career in academia. He obtained a Master's degree in Advertising and a Ph.D. in Mass Media from Michigan State University while also teaching in the MSU Department of Advertising. He joined Northwestern in 1977. Schultz has consulted, lectured and held seminars on integrated marketing communication, marketing, advertising, sales promotion, brands and branding and communication management in Europe, South America, Asia, the Middle East, Australia and North America. His articles have appeared in numerous professional trade publications and academic journals, including *Advertising Age*, *Journal of Advertising Research*, *Journal of Advertising*, *Marketing News*, *Interactive Marketing*, *Journal of Consumer Behavior* and *Journal of International Advertising*. Professor Schultz was the founding editor of the *Journal of Direct Marketing*. He has served as the Associate Editor of the *Journal of Marketing Communications*, and on the editorial review board for a number of trade and scholarly publications. He is also a regular columnist for *Marketing News* and *Marketing Management*. He is author/co-author of fifteen books, *Strategic Advertising Campaigns* (now in its fifth edition), *Essentials of Advertising Strategy* (now in its third edition), *Essentials of Sales Promotion* (now in its third edition), *Sales Promotion Management*, *Strategic Newspaper Marketing* and *Measuring Brand Communication ROI*. His book, *Integrated Marketing Communications* was the first text in this emerging field. Schultz's recent books include *Communicating Globally* (2000) and *Raising the Corporate Umbrella* (2001). In 2003 he and his wife Heidi co-authored an update of the seminal text on IMC, *IMC: Next Generation*, as well as *Brand Babble: Sense and Nonsense about Brands and Branding*. His latest text is 'How to Sell More Stuff' (2004). Schultz is former director of the Promotion Marketing Association of America and past chairman, Accrediting Committee, Accrediting Council in Journalism and Mass Communications. He has also served as Director, Institute of Advanced Advertising Studies and as public member on the National Advertising Review Board and was a founding member of the Board of

Directors of the Virginia Commonwealth University's Ad Center. He is also co-chair of the IMC Committee of the Advertising Research Foundation. He was selected the first Direct Marketing Educator of the Year by the Direct Marketing Educational Foundation. He was named Educator of the Year by the Chicago chapter, Sales and Marketing Executives Association. American Advertising Federation named him Distinguished Advertising Educator of the Year. *Sales and Marketing Management* magazine named Schultz one of the 'Eighty Most Influential People in Sales and Marketing'. He is a member of the American Marketing Association, American Academy of Advertising, Advertising Research Foundation, Association for Consumer Research, Business Marketing Association, Direct Marketing Association and International Advertising Association. He is past chairman, Communications Committee, Illinois Division, of the American Cancer Society. Schultz has served on the board of directors of a number of corporations, including Penton Media, Cleveland, the Simon Richards Group, Melbourne, Australia, Brand Finance plc, London, Insignia Systems, Minneapolis and dunnhumby associates, London. Schultz resides in Evanston with his wife and business partner, Heidi.

Acknowledgements

The editors and publishers wish to thank and acknowledge the various authors, journals, and publishers that have assisted us in allowing materials to be cited and shared, particularly:

- Glen L. Nowak and Joseph Phelps, for their paper in *Journal of Current Issues in Research in Advertising*.
- Rajesh K. Chandy, Gerard J. Tellis, Deborah J. MacInnis and Pattana Thaivanich for their paper in *Journal of Marketing Research*.
- Kusum L. Alawadi, Scott A. Nelsin and Karen Gedenk for their paper in *Journal of Marketing*.
- *Direct Marketing* for their Special Reports on Stan Rapp and Tom Collins's book *The Great Marketing Turnaround*.
- Philip J. Kitchen and Ioanna Papasolomou for their paper in *Marketing Intelligence and Planning*.
- Julie Verity for her paper in *European Business Journal*.
- Nigel Piercy and Nikala Lane for their paper in *Marketing Review*.
- Ritu Lohtia, Naveen Donthu and Edmund K. Hershberger for their paper in *Journal of Advertising Research*.
- Christian Grönroos for his paper in *Journal of Marketing Management*.

Also, we thank the many practitioners and students who via their questions and comments have helped shape and focus this work. To all of you, thank you for your help, guidance, assistance and permissions given as we offer this work on marketing communications.

Every effort has been made to trace and acknowledge all the copyright holders of material used and cited here, but if any have been inadvertently overlooked, the publishers will be pleased to make the necessary arrangement at the first opportunity.

P.J.K.
P.P.
L.E.
D.E.S.

Chapter 1

Philip J. Kitchen

MARKETING COMMUNICATIONS

OVER THE PAST FIFTEEN years the marketing communications landscape has changed massively and irrevocably. The traditional craft disciplines such as advertising, sales promotion, direct marketing, and marketing public relations have moved from named and labelled agencies (i.e. 'advertising' and 'PR' agencies) to become 'integrated' agencies from which clients seek solutions to marketing and communication problems. Undoubtedly, developments in communication and information technology have contributed to growth in the overall marketing communications sector. Thus old-style distinctions between above, through and below the line have blurred. Simultaneously, mass markets have de-massified and fragmented into smaller and smaller units, and the mechanisms for evaluation are under the microscope of reconsideration and needed re-evaluation. Consumers, for so long forced into marketer-developed attitudinal boxes, are being rediscovered in terms of what they want to see, hear, feel, and how and when they wish to be exposed to various forms of marketing communication. New ways of communicating, e.g. – SMS text messaging to teenagers, event marketing to students, and many other non-traditional methods, have become exciting and innovative creative battlegrounds.

Yet there is still no single coherent model as to what integrated approaches are, nor indeed how they should operate in practice. Indeed, the actual practice of – rather than theorizing about – communications will be the major research emphasis for the second half of the first decade of the twenty-first century. Here, and in the other texts (see Kitchen and de Pelsmacker, 2004 as an example), IMC is seen as part and parcel of the creative and dynamic processes that have always characterized the communication services industry. Marketing communications is part of a moving tidal frontier that will continue to test the boundaries of existing practice. Yet here, within these pages, we look back to keynote papers of the the past to analyse how and in what ways each functional element of the promotional mix has evolved or is evolving, and to provide directional pointers as to what we consider the crucial contributions to be in those areas. If we know somewhat of the past, this may provide a significant pointer to the future.

Structure

We see marketing communications practice moving inexorably toward inclusive and non-media-determined approaches to finding creatively integrated solutions. While integrated approaches negate campaign thinking and are being replaced by on-going, consistent, interactive communication between buyer and seller, such communication may well extend from individual short-term activities to long-term strategies. Initially we discuss the need for such a move. We give context to this by tracing the trajectory and development of the literature by discussing published work on 'integrated marketing communication' (IMC).

Why is this Important?

The professional communication world is changing and with it are the marketing communications needed to persuade customers to buy. (We use the word 'persuasion' deliberately, though it is rather old-line, traditional thinking. We emphasize that many authors are now focusing on information sharing and reciprocity.) Who would deny the emergence of new channels or shifting viewer media habits? A glance through the range of claimed client service support offered by different agencies in the classified sections of relevant trade magazines, like *PR Week* or *Campaign* (UK, Australia, New Zealand); *Internationalist, AdWeek, Marketing Bulletin* (US); *Marketing Magazine* (UK, US, Pacific rim); *B&T Weekly* (Australia, New Zealand), etc., quickly identifies communication activities that few clients may have even considered let alone employed before 2004: Web presence, webcasts, on-line chat, viral marketing, SMS marketing, event marketing . . . the list goes on. When boundaries are shifting in the communication industry then it stands to reason that new questions are being asked. To address such questions, the character of the communications provided will need to shift.

In this changing environment, challenging and successful marketing communications are developed in relatively new ways. For example, by identifying activities and promotional tools as key parts of marketing communications strategy that would not have appeared in many papers winning awards in the past, activities like guerrilla marketing, fly-posting, brand experiences and ambient media (Durden 2004). Some companies and the agencies who service their needs are adapting to such challenges, but this adaptation may be relatively exceptional or it may be shallow within a business structure or within the communications strategy that they develop and implement (see Jones 2002). Thus the *concept* of integrated marketing communication cannot now be claimed as 'new'; however, integrated *practice* may be (see Kitchen and de Pelsmacker 2004).

Clients and agencies who lack a strategic overview or vision or with a negative view toward transcending promotional mix boundaries – perhaps because of a silo mentality or turf battles – are likely to face threats to their position if they are to retain a significant share of the value communications may create. Recent evolutions within the industry are given some context with a timeline of thought development and reported industry practices connected to integration of promotional elements, at least one major facet of IMC

A Timeline in IMC Development

The concept of IMC had stimulated discussion in the world of marketing and communication for well over a decade before Pickton and Broderick (2001) described it as 'the process of integrating the elements of the marketing communication mix across customer contact points to achieve greater brand coherence'. From the early 1990s, IMC began to be seen as a comparatively new paradigm and was proclaimed as a potential advance within the marketing communication field (Schultz et al. 1994; Kitchen 1999; Schultz and Kitchen 2000; Kitchen and de Pelsmacker 2004). Integration itself is a concept with a much longer marketing heritage.

A timeline in the development of IMC can be traced back to at least the early 1980s when Coulson-Thomas (1983) considered integration was 'not feasible'. By the early 1990s integration was reported as *under the surface* within the advertising industry but not as a clearly defined concept (Caywood et al. 1991). By 1993 Schultz (1993) claimed IMC was a hot topic under debate in the US. Notably, even at this relatively early stage the UK professional marketing body, the Chartered Institute of Marketing (CIM), adopted a standing question on integration within their postgraduate communication examination paper, and indeed shortly afterward changed the title of the paper to 'Integrated Marketing Communication'.

In 1993 Duncan and Everett (1993) reported that agencies were familiar with the term, and Acheson (1993) observed that there was professional and academic interaction over IMC. In an early study to establish client perceptions of attitudes towards IMC and its practice and management in the market place, Duncan and Everett (1993) found the extent to which integration was offered seemed to differ dependent on the agency. Compared to communication agencies labelled as focusing on other promotional functions (like direct response and sales promotion) Duncan and Everett (1993) claimed it was advertising agencies that were significantly more likely to be responsible for multiple aspects of communication. Their findings suggested over half the ad agencies surveyed claimed to offer more than one communication function and a third were willing to take responsibility for three or more functions.

At the time of this early survey (Duncan and Everett 1993) there was a low awareness of the term 'IMC'. Only 59 per cent of clients were familiar with it. However, the findings indicated that among these clients IMC was perceived as an effective and valuable concept and that a substantial number of them were assigning multiple responsibilities for communication functions to a single agency.

Schultz (1995) predicted that as, IMC began to develop in organizations, the value and future role of traditional and predominantly mass-media image advertising would become uncertain. He argued that, while image-building advertising might remain a vital element in many campaigns its contribution to the long-term success of a brand and its investment value in the future remained difficult to measure, making it problematic to understand the true value of much mass-media advertising. Without being specific, some authors claimed the concept of IMC had rapidly diffused within the promotional industry during the 1990s and that it had developed its own individual approach to 'holistic' communication (Moriarty 1994).

By the mid-1990s the term had obtained currency and a range of researchers sought some degree of agreement as to what IMC was and how it could be done. In 1996 Schultz published a comparative study of IMC in the US (1995) in which he predicted IMC was on the verge of becoming a mainstream marketing topic, or at least a more regularly used and useful concept. In consecutive meetings of the Advertising Research Foundation (ARF), Schultz reported that not only had IMC dominated agendas, it had also stimulated interest and support from major marketing organizations; with a drive for adoption of IMC coming from marketing and corporate management, followed by advertising and sales staff (Kitchen and Schultz 1999). Following Schultz (1995), McArthur and Griffin (1997) reported the perspectives of different types of businesses toward IMC. They claimed PR was most popular for spanning different communication activities, often as part of an in-house activity, while a full-service ad agency was the second choice for hosting an IMC approach. Yarbrough (1996), in a sales and marketing management survey, revealed conflicting impressions of IMC. He suggested that IMC was like a new religion, which 'captured the faith of some and made them converts', but others seemed to see it as an alternative rather than an advance in promotional strategy.

McLaughlin (1997) noted that, although aspects of IMC may have been 'offered' by major advertising agencies some twenty-five years earlier, the offer was not readily taken up. Initially clients failed to see a clear cost benefit from combining all communication services within one agency and if the client decided to change agency the transition process would be highly complicated. It has been argued, in any case, that the real work of brand building is done solely by advertising campaigns in combination with other (lesser) promotional mix elements (Weilbacher 2001).

By 1998 Schneider reported a survey where 200 agencies were described, by themselves or the press, as IMC practitioners. The findings revealed that 'IMC agencies' were making significant progress in understanding the concept and implication of IMC, with more than half the agencies developing programmes with clients they reported as successful, while also reducing the overall communication budget (see also McArthur and Griffin 1997).

By 1999 Kitchen and Schultz (1999) claimed IMC had developed as a dynamic and contemporary approach to marketing communication, viewed from a strategic, tactical and planning perspective. At the end of the decade McGoon (1999) claimed to have identified four key stages in the introduction of IMC: *tactical co-ordination; redefining the scope* of marketing communication (e.g. to include internal supply-chain audiences); *blending with IT*, to allow customer data to lead a customer-based strategy; and fourth, *integration with financial and strategic issues,* using estimates of relative returns proportional to different levels of investment in particular functions. How such complexity was managed was not explained, though, perhaps because his work was fundamentally based on earlier work by Schultz and others at the American Productivity Quality Council (APQC).

To further complicate issues, by 1999 Kaye was laying emphasis on the key role of internal marketing communication to assure success, and Schultz and Kitchen (2000) were calling for a viewpoint based on the value that communication activities added (as they reported on a cross-national study of IMC practice covering the US, UK, New Zealand, Australia and India, finding that IMC take-up was more common in smaller agencies).

By the close of the 1990s Shimp (2000) claimed five key elements within IMC:

- A primary goal to *affect behaviour* through communication.
- The need to *work backwards* from the customer's or target's perspective.
- The *use of all forms of communication* and all sources of brand and company context as prospective message sources.
- The requirement to *find synergy through co-ordination.*
- The *focus of building relationships* between brands and customers.

More recently attempts to redefine the issues using terms like 'media-neutral planning' have started to fill the professional trade press (Spickett-Jones et al. 2003). This does not mean, however, that IMC had become a way of life. As Ward (2004: 23) claims, a 'campaign with a single unifying idea executed across multiple media' is still a rare occurrence, largely because of the 'significant interest vested in maintaining the *status quo*'. He claims many large clients have pre-set budgets for aspects like advertising, PR and direct marketing which 'still engage with agencies as discrete entities rather than an holistic group'.

Moving toward the middle of 2004, it is perhaps interesting to note that the syllabus of the CIM's (UK) Professional Postgraduate Diploma in marketing will, in examinations from December 2004, abandon the separate 'Integrated Marketing Communication' paper in favour of an expectation that communication roles should be integrated within the fabric of strategic marketing itself, rather than seen as a separate specialism. One might, therefore, question whether 'integration' has come of age beyond the communication disciplines; and if so, if the professional marketing support services have adequately recognized this yet.

In summary, the pressures on agencies for higher efficiencies and better competitive competence may be reflected in a growth in claims by advertising agencies, during the early 1990s, to offer synchronized campaigns. Many started to rebrand themselves as 'total communication agencies' by investing in expertise within areas like public relations, sales promotion and direct marketing (Acheson 1993). In addition, Duncan and Everett (1993) identified that, although the majority of key advertising agencies were diversifying into other communication areas, there were still many clients who were sceptical about setting their entire business under the 'communication umbrella' of a single agency. By the early twenty-first century this had changed dramatically, however (see Cook, 2004; Keller, 2001; Reid, 2003; Zahay et al. 2004). Nonetheless, the early argument focused on whether clients were better to try to employ 'best of breed' practitioners in each communication discipline or seek economies of scale and ease of co-ordination by placing communication services under a single roof but, in so doing, risk relying on a possible mediocre mix of relative competences. No conclusive arguments have yet been offered to support either route, as Keenan (2001) suggested, 'The future of advertising points towards fully integrating marketing communication with measurable results.' By implication, therefore, so do non-advertising aspects of the marketing communication effort.

Overall, the growing literature relating to IMC activities is raising the importance of the debate about the role of IMC and promoting a wider awareness of the concept. A wide range of authors have now reported attempts to grasp the concept and various manifestations of its existence have been discovered within the range of relationships between agencies and clients. However, no single coherent model seems to have yet established what IMC is made up of, or how it should operate in practice. Within the current literature, evidence of any common widespread practice appears to be unreliable. One question to address is, why? Are there perhaps significant barriers to adoption? Or is the concept felt by practitioners to be in some way flawed? One perspective by Kitchen and de Pelsmacker (2004) refers to the 'stages theory of IMC' and suggests that the early and powerful arguments about integrating elements of the promotional mix (the 'one-voice' approach), has actually been fulfilled in large part around the world. Yet this early 'stage' requires no market research, no real focus on customers or consumers, no databases. Further, they suggest that a real barrier to progressing through IMC stages is the substantive organizational investment required to put it together and make it work. A further very real barrier is the lack of progress on the evaluation front. However, this is not just a problem for IMC, but for the whole field of marketing communications. It seems to us that many organizations hold back from implementing IMC for financial, organizational and psychological reasons. The down side to such reticence results in doing things in the old ways.

> The sermon had ended,
> The priest had descended.
> Delighted were they
> But they preferred the old way
> (Anon.)

Conclusion

Integrated marketing communications epitomizes the drive and dynamism surrounding marketing communications in the twentieth and twenty-first centuries. Yet even integrated approaches require tools and techniques. In this reader we have tracked down the papers that we feel make the most significant contribution in each disciplinary area of the promotional mix. We also include keynote papers on the topic of integration, the promotional mix, relationship marketing and measuring outputs. As you work through the text, answering the end-of-chapter questions will help understanding. Yet there is a problem in that when clients call for strategies that will embrace an integrated communication approach, the very tacit nature of the professional codes ingrained in agency modes of working may make it difficult for existing agencies to appreciate the character of change needed within their organization in order to deliver effective integrated campaign solutions. Instead they seem more inclined to reach out for help from other specialists in order to satisfy client demands. In other words, the mercurial nature of the ways agencies and clients have learned to use marketing communications may also be a barrier to them changing this way of working.

True integration may remain out of reach of many agencies by virtue, or vice, of the fact that that their tacit professional practices may not yet have been remodelled to accommodate working practice that moves seamlessly between traditional promotional disciplines. There is some evidence that agencies appear to put their traditional 'standard product' offering ahead of the core strategic service they also report many clients as requesting.

Hopefully this book will contribute something to the awareness and broader understanding of integrated marketing communication and marketing communication in general. Changes taking place in the agency sector, such as the growth in DM agency work, may have encouraged positive attitudes towards integration, and have provided a significant drive in the direction of IMC (Pickton and Broderick 2001). Undoubtedly, the need for integrated approaches is starkly outlined around the world.

Acknowledgement

This chapter acknowledges a huge debt to a paper by *P.J. Kitchen* and J.G. Spickett-Jones entitled 'Moving Goalposts: The integration chimera: barriers to the evolution in agency services in the UK's professional services sector' which is shortly to be submitted for review to an academic journal.

References

Acheson, K. L. (1993) 'Integrated Marketing must bring two Perspectives together', *Marketing News* (Chicago) 27 (17): 4.

Caywood, C., Schultz, D. E. and Wang, P. (1991) 'Integrated Marketing Communication: a Survey of National Goods Advertisers', unpublished report, Evanston IL: Medill School of Journalism, Northwestern University.

Cook, William A. (2004) 'Editorial: IMC's Fuzzy Picture: Breakthrough or Breakdown?' *Journal of Advertising Research* (New York) 44 (March): 1–2.

Coulson-Thomas, C. J. (1983) *Marketing Communication*, Oxford: Butterworth Heinemann.

Duncan, T. R. and Everett, S. E. (1993) 'Client Perceptions of Integrated Communication', *Journal of Advertising Research* (New York) 32 (3): 30–9.

Durden, Frank, WCRS Board Account Director (2004), British Design and Art Direction (D&AD) Xchange conference, London: London School of Fashion, August.

Jones, J. P. (2002) *The Ultimate Secrets of Advertising*, London: Sage.

Kaye, R. L. (1999) 'Companies need to realize Internal Marketing's Potential', *Advertising Age's Business Marketing* (Chicago) 84 (7): 13.

Keenan, W. F. (2001) 'The Right Kind of Advertising', *Credit Card Management* (New York) 14 (8): 66–9.

Keller, Kevin L. (2001) 'Mastering the Marketing Communications Mix: Micro and Macro Perspectives on Integrated Marketing Communication Programs', *Journal of Marketing Management* 17 (7–8): 819–48.

Kitchen, P. J. (1999) *Marketing Communication: Principles and Practice*, London: International Thomson Business Press.

Kitchen, P. J. and de Pelsmacker, P. (2004) *Integrated Marketing Communication: a Primer*, London: Routledge.

Kitchen, P. J. and Schultz, D. E. (1999) 'A Multi-country Comparison of the Drive for IMC', *Journal of Advertising Research* (New York) 39 (1): 21–38.

McArthur, D. N. and Griffin, T. (1997) 'A Marketing Management View of Integrated Marketing Communication', *Journal of Advertising Research* (New York) 37 (5): 19–26.

McGoon, C. (1999) 'Cutting-edge Companies use Integrated Marketing Communication', *Communication World* (San Francisco) 16 (1): 15–19.

McLaughlin, J. P. (1997) 'Why is IMC taking so long? Blame it on the Clients', *Marketing News* (Chicago) 31 (19): 27–30.

Moriarty, S. E. (1994) 'PR and IMC: the Benefits of Integration', *Public Relations Quarterly* (Rhinebeck NY) 39 (3): 38.

Moriarty, S. E. (1997) 'IMC needs PR's Stakeholder Focus', *Marketing News* (Chicago) 31 (11): 7.

Pickton, D. and Broderick, A. (2001) *Integrated Marketing Communication*, Harlow: Pearson.

Reid, Mike (2003) 'IMC–Performance Relationship: Further Insight and Evidence from the Australian Marketplace', *International Journal of Advertising* 22 (3): 227–48.

Schneider, L. (1998) 'Agencies show that IMC can be good for Bottom Line', *Marketing News* (Chicago): 32 (10): 11.

Schultz, D. E. (1993) 'Integration helps you plan Communication from Outside-in', *Marketing News* (Chicago) 27 (6): 12.

Schultz, D. E. (1995) 'Traditional Advertising has Role to play in IMC', *Marketing News* (Chicago) 29 (18): 18.

Schultz, D. E. and Kitchen, P. J. (2000) *Communicating Globally: an Integrated Marketing Approach*, Chicago: NTC; Basingstoke: Palgrave Macmillan.

Schultz, D. E., Tannenbaum, S. I. and Lauterborn, R. F. (1994) *Integrated Marketing Communications: Pulling it Together and Making it Work*, Chicago: NTC.

Shimp, T. A. (2000) *Advertising Promotion: Supplemental Aspects of Integrated Marketing Communication*, 5th edn, Fort Worth TX: Dryden Press Harcourt.

Spickett-Jones, G., Kitchen, P. J. and Brignell, J. (2003) 'The Growing Use of Integration', *Admap* 442 (September): 24–7.

Ward, S. (2004) 'Relationship Building', *Marketing Business*, March, pp. 22–4.

Weilbacher, W. M. (2001) 'Point of View: does Advertising cause a "Hierarchy of Effects"?' *Journal of Advertising Research* (New York) 41 (6): 19–26.

Yarbrough, J. F. (1996) 'Putting the Pieces together', *Sales and Marketing Management* (New York) 148 (9): 68.

Zahay, D., Peltier, J., Schultz, D. E. and Griffin, A. (2004) 'The role of Transactional versus Relational Data in IMC Programs: bringing Customer Data together', *Journal of Advertising Research* (New York) 44 (1): 3–19.

Chapter 2

Don E. Schultz

FROM ADVERTISING TO INTEGRATED MARKETING COMMUNICATIONS

WHEN THE CONCEPT OF integrated marketing communications (IMC) was first articulated by the faculty of the Department of Advertising at Northwestern University in the late 1980s, very little formal academic research had been conducted. Most of the writings were reports or descriptions of marketplace activities being conducted by advertising agencies or marketing organisations. What little formal research that had been conducted was primarily in the form of marketplace surveys of integrating practices and practitioner opinions. Indeed, even the first text in the field, *Integrated Marketing Communication: Putting it Together and Making it Work* (Schultz et al. 1993) was primarily focused on practical applications of various integrating approaches gleaned from personal experience and marketplace applications.

Thus IMC in its early days was challenged by both practitioners and academics alike and rightly so, as being only common sense or, even worse, something that advertising practitioners were already doing and had been doing for a number of years. Thus the Nowak and Phelps article in this chapter, 'Conceptualizing the Integrated Marketing Communications Phenomenon: an Examination of its Impact on Advertising Practices and its Implications for Advertising Research', was one of the first attempts to provide a theoretical base and framework to what was a clearly observable marketplace activity.

As can be seen in the article, the focus of the authors was on relating IMC to existing advertising research. Indeed, this article and the background and experience of the early leaders of IMC had come from advertising. Both Nowak and Phelps were trained advertising academicians. It was only natural for them to compare IMC with what they know best, existing advertising theory. And, since the concept had emanated from another set of advertising professors at Northwestern University, the theoretical base for IMC was *de facto* established from the theoretical base of advertising. Whether the use of an advertising theory base to understand IMC is good or bad is still being debated.

The key contribution of this article is that it develops a comparative framework against which IMC practice at the time could be compared. Since most of the IMC academic research, writing and teaching was occurring in departments or schools of advertising in the US and abroad, the use of advertising theory as the comparative field seemed quite logical. Those active in the field were familiar with the advertising theory and writings and could thus compare and contrast the new thoughts in IMC with the existing literature. Whether that is true today in hindsight is questionable.

The primary contribution that Nowak and Phelps made to the understanding and application of IMC was their rigorous approach to building a conceptual base for the discipline. They did that in three ways:

- Descriptions of how IMC was conceptualized at the time.
- The use of shifts in marketing communication spending to verify that IMC was a legitimate new form of marketing.
- Descriptions of the changed and changing marketing communication strategies and tactics they had observed in the market place.

Using these concepts, they created an 'Integrated Marketing Communications Framework'. This provided a direct comparison of IMC and advertising, something that had been missing in the work of earlier authors and practitioners.

The other relevant innovation in this article is the measurement tools Nowak and Phelps proposed. They advocated and demonstrated the use of changes in consumer behaviours as best methodology to use in determining the effects and impact of IMC. This approach came primarily from direct marketing. It flew directly in the face of most advertising measurement techniques, which used consumer attitudinal change as the basic yardstick for measurement. This made good sense, as the goal of Nowak and Phelps in this article was to determine and define the impact and effect and the relationship of IMC on general advertising and its theoretical base.

There are two interesting elements in this paper that have had a lasting effect on the development of IMC concepts, applications and theory. First, Nowak and Phelps ignored public relations as part of their framework and analysis. Thus, while the article is groundbreaking from an IMC perspective, it has given public relations academics and practitioners fertile ground to argue that their discipline actually includes and is based on integrated and integrating theories. Seemingly, this has widened the gap between IMC and public relations rather than helped to close it.

Second, the use of the advertising theory base as a comparison for IMC has had a major impact on the development of IMC theory. For the most part, researchers and writers have followed the same path as Nowak and Phelps, that is, using advertising theory as the conceptual base for IMC. For the most part, these approaches have proved unsuccessful and have likely limited the development of IMC theory more than they have advanced it.

In my view (Schultz 2005), IMC is a different type of communication concept and the use of externally oriented, outbound messages delivered through various forms of paid media are only one part of IMC. Thus, while the Nowak and Phelps article did provide the first beginnings of a theory for IMC, the article has also had a limiting effect on the field as well.

CONCEPTUALIZING THE INTEGRATED MARKETING COMMUNICATIONS PHENOMENON: AN EXAMINATION OF ITS IMPACT ON ADVERTISING PRACTICES AND ITS IMPLICATIONS FOR ADVERTISING RESEARCH

Glen J. Nowak and Joseph Phelps

An increasing number of marketers are integrating the results-oriented methods of consumer sales promotion and direct response advertising with the image/ awareness capabilities of general advertising. This integration has blurred the boundaries between traditionally independent marketing communication disciplines and, more importantly, fundamentally restructured many of marketing and advertising communication. In hopes of stimulating scholarly interest in the integrated marketing communications phenomenon, this article identifies the underlying tenets of integrated marketing or advertising communication philosophies; offers a conceptual framework for understanding and addressing integrated marketing and advertising communication issues; and delineates the advertising-related research opportunities that exist as a result of the integrated phenomenon. This examination indicates the integrated phenomenon has impacted marketing communications at an advertisement as well as campaign level, and created a need for empirical research and theoretical development in four advertising domains.

Introduction

THE DEMASSIFICATION AND SPLINTERING of consumer markets combined with increased media costs and options have challenged conventional marketing wisdom and traditional marketing communication practices. On the marketing side, the mass merchandising philosophies of major brand and packaged-goods companies are being displaced by technology and market-driven perspectives that employ 'micromarketing,' 'databases,' 'one-to-one targeting,' and 'consumer-initiated' communication (Coogle 1990; Hoke 1990; Podems

---

Journal of Current Issues and Research in Advertising, Vol. 16, No. 1 (spring 1994), pp. 49–66. Reprinted with permission, CTC Press.

Glen J. Nowak, Ph.D., is an Assistant Professor in the Department of Advertising and Public Relations at the College of Journalism, University of Georgia, Athens, Georgia. Joseph Phelps, Ph.D., is an Assistant Professor in the Advertising and Public Relations Department at the College of Communication, University of Alabama, Tuscaloosa, Alabama.

1988; Schlossberg 1992; Walley 1989). These concepts, traditionally associated with mail-order firms, catalogers, and direct marketers, often involve using detailed consumer profiles stored on computers to target customers and prospects in an attempt to maximize selling efforts (Rapp and Collins 1990, 1988). Conversely, many traditional direct marketers are attempting to increase sales and market shares by adopting practices often associated with 'general' (i.e., brand or packaged-goods) advertisers. For some, this has meant expanding distribution into retail stores and other outlets (Rapp and Collins 1988), while for others this has meant paying more attention to long-term image than to short-term sales (Jenkins 1984).

Similar changes have taken place with respect to marketing communications. Growing numbers of marketers, skeptical about the often ambiguous results of mass media advertising, are placing greater emphasis on consumer sales promotion and direct response advertising (Goerne 1992; Landler, Konrad, Schiller and Therrien 1991). Traditional advertising communication models and their emphasis on mediating consumer responses (e.g., awareness, knowledge, or attitudes) are giving way to behavior-oriented models that emphasize audience segmentation, customized persuasion, purchase incentives, and advertising accountability (Light 1990; Nelson 1991; Rapp and Collins 1990, 1988; Roscitt and Parkett 1988). Marketers who rely on behavior-oriented marketing communications, however, are finding that focus has drawbacks also. Many, for instance, have found heavy reliance on direct response advertising or consumer sales promotion dilutes brand equity by making price or purchase incentives the key determinant of brand choice (Goerne 1992; Landler et al. 1991).

Regardless of whether it is brand or packaged-goods advertisers incorporating direct response advertising or consumer sales promotion practices, or direct response advertisers using image or brand advertising techniques, the end result is a fundamental restructuring of the 'rules' of marketing and advertising communication. The walls between the major marketing communication disciplines, namely consumer sales promotion, direct response advertising, and 'brand' or 'image' advertising, are collapsing, and marketers' interest in 'integrated marketing and advertising communications' is expanding (Rapp and Collins 1990, 1988; Roman 1988; Stephenson 1989). There is increased marketer demand for multi-disciplinary campaigns (Clancy 1990; Reilly 1991), for advertising strategies that accomplish communication and behavioral objectives concurrently (Bowman 1987; Kobs 1988; Peltier, Mueller and Rosen 1992), and for creative executions that simultaneously generate awareness, promote market positions, encourage immediate behavioral responses, and build consumer databases that can be used to foster long-term customer relationships (Nelson 1991; Rapp and Collins 1990). Although these developments have prompted two academic institutions (i.e., Northwestern University and the University of Colorado) to begin graduate programs in integrated marketing and advertising communications (Hume 1991b), the advertising world has responded with caution and doubt (Baker 1992; Cohen 1991; Landler et al. 1991). The excitement of some over what has been labelled 'new advertising' (Sloan 1992) has been countered with claims that relatively little has in fact changed (Rotzoll 1991). Similarly, few academic advertising scholars and researchers have taken seriously marketers' interest in integrated marketing or advertising communications. Only one published academic article has explored definitional issues (Peltier, Mueller and Rosen 1992), while the only assessment of consumer responses to advertisements that contain both image and direct response elements is found in Woodside and Motes' (1980, 1979) tourism advertising studies. The tenets of an integrated marketing communications perspective and the advertising research issues associated with such a perspective have yet to be examined.

The purpose of this article is thus two-fold. First, to call advertising scholars' attention to the impact the integrated marketing communications' phenomenon has had on advertising strategies and tactics. Second, to stimulate those involved in the study of advertising and consumer behavior to investigate the theoretical and practical issues that arise from 'integrating' traditionally independent marketing communication disciplines – direct response advertising, consumer sales promotion, and brand/image advertising. To achieve these objectives, this article: (1) identifies the underlying tenets of integrated marketing or advertising communications philosophies; (2) offers a conceptual framework for understanding and addressing integrated marketing and advertising communication issues; and (3) uses the direct response advertising literature to illustrate the advertising-related research opportunities that exist in the integrated marketing communications' arena. Public relations, another discipline employed by marketers, also has influenced and been affected by the integrated marketing communications phenomenon (Haroldsen 1992; Newsom, Carrell and Hussain 1992), but those developments will not be explored here.

Defining Integrated Marketing Communications

Like the advertising industry, academic advertising and consumer behavior theory and research has focused on brand and image-oriented advertising, and tended to ignore other forms of marketing communications on the assumption they are not prominent nor pervasive enough to warrant study (Blattberg 1987). In the case of integrated marketing communications, two perceptions bolster this belief. First, there is little consensus as to what integrated marketing or advertising communication is or means. Second, unlike media advertising, no reliable index exists for tracking advertiser spending on integrated marketing or advertising communications. Understanding the scope and magnitude of the 'integrated' phenomenon thus requires reviewing current conceptualizations as well as identifying the changes in marketing communication spending and strategies that occur when marketers adopt an integrated marketing communications perspective.

Current conceptualizations of integrated marketing communications

Interest in, or even use of, an 'integrated' perspective has not yet answered the question 'What is integrated marketing communications?' The chairperson of Northwestern University's new integrated advertising/marketing communication program, Stanley Tannenbaum, has said:

> I don't think there's any consensus of what integrated marketing is and how it works, but there's a tremendous amount of interest in (the idea) . . . We're going to be searching for a definition of integrated marketing communications that's deeper than just 'speaking with one voice in all communications.
>
> (Hume 1991b)

To date, however, at least three broad conceptualizations are found in the mostly practitioner-based literature: 'one voice' marketing communications; 'integrated' marketing communications (i.e., advertisements); and 'coordinated' marketing communications.

One voice marketing communications. Often characterized as 'seamless' marketing communication, this view suggests that 'integration' involves maintaining a clear and consistent image, position, message and/or theme across all marketing communication disciplines or tools. A common strategy or 'singular identity' is decided upon at the outset of a campaign, and that strategy unifies consumer sales promotion, direct response advertising, brand/image advertising, and even public relations efforts (Reilly 1991). According to Synder (1991), full integration is achieved when all disciplines are involved in creating a 'single positioning concept for the brand that drives all communications' (versus just being asked to coordinate creative executions). Under this perspective, the guiding image, position, message or theme matters more than disciplinary boundaries. In other words, once given the guiding strategy, it would be desirable, but not necessary, for a marketer's advertising, public relations, or sales promotion agencies to work together on implementation. Most likely, each agency would independently develop and implement whatever strategies and tactics it believed necessary to effectively disseminate the overall position or message to target consumers. Often, it is the marketer's responsibility to ensure 'one voice' results.

Integrated communications. This conceptualization is micro-oriented in that it revolves around the notion that marketing communication materials, particularly advertisements, should simultaneously establish or develop an image and directly influence consumer behavior (Kobs 1988; Nelson 1991; Peltier, Mueller and Rosen 1992; Roman 1988). Under this perspective, the advertisements, commercials, and/or creative executions used in a campaign try to simultaneously attain communication and behavioral objectives. In essence, this view emanates from the belief that brand/image advertising, consumer sales promotion, direct response advertising, and public relations are not mutually exclusive disciplines and that incorporating elements of each into communication materials 'may jointly maximize their unique strengths, while minimizing their weaknesses' (Peltier et al. 1992). Brand/image advertising, for example, is often believed to require large budgets and relatively long time frames, while consumer sales promotion and direct response advertising are thought to be relatively ineffective when it comes to establishing a long-term brand image or position (Nelson 1991). This integrated marketing communications perspective, however, would mandate advertisements that strive to include or retain the artistry and flair of brand/image advertising while simultaneously including the response devices (e.g., phone numbers, mail-in forms, explicit offers, purchase incentives or premiums) traditionally found only in consumer sales promotions or direct response advertising (see Peltier et al. 1992 for a detailed review).

Coordinated marketing communication campaigns. The third conceptualization associates. 'integrated' with 'coordinated.' Under this view, integrated marketing communications means coordinating marketing communication disciplines or instituting steps that result in better coordination between advertising, sales promotion, direct response, and public relations functions and/or agencies (Schutlz, Tannenbaum and Lauterborn 1992). Unlike the 'one voice' perspective, the various disciplines are not necessarily working under a single, unifying brand positioning. In fact, multiple positionings based on multiple target audiences are more typically the norm (Rapp and Collins 1990). The emphasis is thus on producing 'wholistic' campaigns that draw upon brand/image advertising, consumer sales promotion, and direct response advertising in order to do 'whatever is necessary to identify, contact, activate, and cultivate individual consumers and increase market share' (Rapp and Collins 1990, p. 41). Marketing communications are therefore 'integrated' to the extent they create a 'synergism' that, at a campaign level, develops awareness, images, or beliefs while boosting behavioral responses beyond those that would be attained with a traditional one-discipline, one-message campaign (Roman 1988).

Impact on Marketing Communication and Advertising Practices

Although the current conceptualizations provide a valuable starting point for assessing the integrated marketing communications phenomenon, they only hint at the changes that accompany an 'integrated' perspective. Regardless of which definition is used, adoption of an integrated marketing communication perspective tangibly affects advertising practices, and in turn, advertising research. Fortunately, the underlying tenets of integrated marketing communications perspectives can be identified by examining recent trends in marketing communications spending and thinking with respect to direct response advertising, consumer sales promotion, and national media advertising. In the process, not only does the perspective's impact become apparent, so does a framework for addressing the integrated marketing communications landscape.

Marketing communications spending

One of the marketing communication practices consistently associated with an integrated perspective is a shift of dollars, primarily by consumer brand and packaged-goods marketers, from mass media advertising to direct response advertising and consumer sales promotion (Goerne 1992; Hume 1992b; Rapp and Collins 1990, 1991; Wylie 1992a).

Direct response advertising. National media expenditures combine direct response and general advertising dollars for most national and local categories (thereby creating discrepancies in direct response advertising estimates), but most estimates suggest that spending on targeted advertising media (i.e., direct mail, direct response, and telemarketing) now equals or exceeds that for mass media advertising. Stevenson (1988), for instance, estimated that half of the $120 billion spent on advertising in 1988 was spent on targeted advertising media, while Smolowe (1990) reported that total expenditures on targeted advertising media exceeds combined magazine, radio, and network television spending. A slightly higher estimate is offered by *Direct Marketing*, an industry trade publication. They calculate that direct response advertising, including yellow pages spending, made up 65 percent of the $126 billion spent on advertising in 1989.

Direct response advertising has also been the fastest growing marketing communication discipline. In line with the above estimates, total direct response advertising expenditures have tripled from about $25 billion in 1981 to around $75 billion in 1990 (Direct Marketing Association; Hoke 1989). Spending on national direct mail went from $8 billion in 1981 to $25 billion in 1991, a 310 percent increase (Landler et al. 1991). Results from recent industry surveys show direct response spending increased even during recent economic downturns. Ad agencies' direct response billings climbed to $4.1 billion in 1991, a 13.4 percent increase that exceeded the overall 2.9 percent increase for all U.S. advertising agencies and the 6.3 percent gain by sales promotion shops (Wylie 1992b). Direct response billings increased 15.2 percent in 1990 and 18.3 percent in 1989 (Wylie 1992a, 1991).

The significance of response-oriented advertising is reflected further in consumer behaviors. A recent industry study estimated that 16.2 billion calls were made to 800-number call centers in 1991, with about 39 billion minutes spent on those calls (an average of 2.4 minutes per call) (Jaffee 1992). According to the Direct Marketing Association (DMA), 96 million Americans purchased at least one item by phone or mail in 1991, the third consecutive year that more than half of American adults bought merchandise or services directly. Catalog, mail, and telephone sales increased 42 percent between 1984 and 1989 (from $115.7 billion to $164.5 billion), while sales involving personal visits by either a seller or buyer only increased 3 percent (*Direct Marketing Magazine*, January 1990, January 1984). Similarly, the DMA, which defines direct response sales as purchases resulting from direct response advertising, estimates over $150 billion worth of goods and services were bought direct in 1991. Although the estimate is based on a formula that assumes direct marketing costs represent one-fifth of gross sales, the DMA's 1987 survey of 399 for-profit member organizations found the $3.3 billion they invested in direct response advertising generated $33.9 billion in sales (Graham 1987).

Consumer sales promotion. Spending on marketing communications that directly stimulate consumer behavior, such as coupons, incentives, rebates, sweep-stakes and contests also has grown at the expense of traditional media advertising. Between 1986 and 1991, promotion not only received a larger share of marketing communication dollars than measured media ($159.9 billion vs. $108.1 billion), it grew at a faster annual rate (6.3 percent vs. 4.6 percent) (Mandese and Donaton 1992). Similarly, sales promotion agencies revenue gross income increased 6.3 percent in 1991 and 14.1 percent in 1990, compared to 2.6 percent and 6.4 percent for the top 500 U.S. advertising agencies (Wylie

1992b, 1991). A Fall 1991 survey of fifty U.S. and Canadian consumer goods marketers found that 64 percent expected to spend more on sales promotion in 1992 than they had spent in 1991 (Hume 1991a). In 1980, 43 percent of marketing communication dollars went to media advertising, while trade and consumer promotions got 57 percent. By 1989, promotion received 66 percent and media advertising's share declined to 34 percent (Bowman 1990). In 1991, 49.5 percent of marketing communication dollars went to trade promotions, with consumer promotion spending equalling that spent on media advertising (25.4 percent vs. 25.1 percent) (Hume 1992c). The trend is expected to continue with consumer promotion spending growing at an annual rate of 8.4 percent between 1991 and 1996, compared to an average annual growth rate of 7.1 percent for ad spending in major media (Hume 1992b).

Brand/image advertising. Media advertising revenues, which are largely dependent on packaged-good and brand advertisers, have not only failed to keep pace with direct response and consumer sale promotion spending, but actually declined in 1991. According to Coen (1992), media advertising revenues were 1.7 percent lower in 1991 than in 1990, the biggest decline since 1942. While some of the reduction can be contributed to economic recession, the decline was not uniform across advertising media. Advertiser spending on traditional advertising media, including newspapers, network television, outdoor, and magazines, declined 4.4 percent, while direct mail and yellow pages were the only major media categories where revenues increased (4.7 percent and 2.8 percent, respectively) (Coen 1992). Similarly, advertising spending by the 200 largest consumer-goods brands in newspapers, magazines, and television dropped another 6.2 percent in the first six months of 1991 (Cohen 1991).

Marketing communications strategies and tactics

Although some have argued the spending shifts are simply a result of economic recession, they reflect an evolution in marketing communication thinking, fostered, in some cases, by economic and technological considerations. A review of the literature indicates there are at least four interrelated changes in marketing communication strategy and tactics that frequently accompany an 'integrated' perspective: reduced faith in the power of mass media advertising; reliance on highly targeted rather than broadly targeted marketing communications; greater utilization of consumer databases; and new expectations for marketing communication suppliers.

Reduced faith in mass media advertising. Consumer goods marketers who adopt an integrated marketing communications' perspective often no longer regard widely disseminated brand/image advertising, particularly that which involves network television, as a major or central component of their marketing communications efforts. As many advertising practitioners have noted, since the 1980s, the sizes of the audiences for television programs have steadily decreased while the costs involved with television advertising have increased faster than the rate of inflation (Landler et al. 1990; Rapp and Collins 1988). Videocassette recorders, remote control channel changers, and a greater number of channel options have further reduced the audience for TV commercials. Meanwhile, economic factors along with supermarket scanner technology have raised questions about mass media advertising's cost and value in general, particularly for established brands (Fahey 1992; Miller 1992).

According to Landler et al. (1991), growing corporate debt (often the result of megamergers) and the 1989–91 recession were two economic factors that caused many marketers to drastically reduce brand/image advertising spending. Debt forced many large brand and packaged-goods companies to focus on quarterly sales and short-term incentives instead of long-term investments in brand images. Product marketers thus distributed a record 292 billion cents-off coupons in 1991 (compared to 210 billion in 1986), with the average face value of redeemed coupons increasing from 49.8 cents in 1990 to 54 cents in 1991 (Hume 1992d). Similarly, economic recession furthered the shift away from higher priced brands. One survey found the percentage of consumers who say they buy only well-known brands dropped from 77 percent in 1977 to 62 percent in 1990, while another study found that 66 percent of consumers said they had traded down to lower-priced brands (Landler et al. 1991). Thus, brand managers' quest to attain sales objectives combined with consumers' need to extend limited purchasing dollars has eroded brand loyalty and fostered the perception that prices and purchase incentives, not brand images, are the ultimate determinant of brand choice.

Analyses of data collected from scanning devices at checkout counters also has reduced marketers' willingness to spend money on advertising. Scanner-based studies, for example, often find consumer promotions have stronger, or more direct, effects on brand purchases than advertising (Kumar and Leone 1988; Tellis 1988). Although that finding may be influenced by the research method (Block and Brezen 1990), scanner data does give marketers the ability to design programs that reward consumer purchases, with the funding often coming from advertising and trade promotion budgets (Manning and Lukas 1990). In 1990 it was estimated that most consumer product companies have at least one-scanner based frequent shopper reward program in test market, while Donnelly's 1989 'Survey of Promotional Practices' found 81 percent of larger companies and 61 percent of smaller companies had some experience with scanner-based frequent shopper programs (Bowman 1990).

In addition to the above, a demand for advertising accountability has persuaded marketers to re-evaluate national brand or image-oriented advertising campaigns. Rapp and Collins (1988) 'Maximarketing Model,' for instance, advocates 'maximized advertising accountability.' Citing the proliferation of media choices and the escalation of media costs, they contend that advertising cost per impression, readership studies, copy tests, and artificial marketplace simulations are relatively ineffective ways to assess advertising effectiveness. Conversely, sales promotion and direct response advertising provide the accountability that mass media advertising lacks. 'Response devices,' such as mail-in promotional offers, 800/900 telephone numbers and coupons, can be used to directly measure the behavioral effects of a marketing communication effort. One consequence is greater use of blended communications, such as brand/image advertisements that include response devices. Another is a further move of marketing communication dollars from advertising to sales promotion and direct response.

Greater reliance on highly targeted communications. For many marketers today, media advertising is a 'shotgun' – a marketing communication tool that relies on a broad-sweeping, scatter-shot approach to hit target consumers (Cohen 1991). Whereas this approach was often justified on the basis of cost effectiveness, it is now perceived as inefficient even for the largest consumer goods marketers. Instead, as marketers gather, store, and assimilate ever increasing amounts of consumer data, they begin looking for 'more personalized and more targeted [marketing communication] approaches and media that define audiences more clearly' (Levin 1991a). This replacement of mass national advertising with customized media and marketing communication plans aimed at narrow market segments has been identified as one of seven fundamental changes influencing advertising worldwide (Light 1990).

One of the primary contributors to the targeting of smaller rather than broader market segments is the belief that it is more important to reach the right people as it is to reach large numbers of people. In fact, supporters of integrated marketing communications typically advocate replacing mass media marketing, 'where one message fits all,' with 'discrete messages targeted according to customer profiles' (Fahey 1992). Although most brand and packaged-goods marketers have probably always believed marketing communication is most effective when customized messages are directed to well-defined audiences through highly targeted media, what's different today is the ability to act upon that belief. Direct mail, special interest magazines, cable television, and alternative media (e.g., televisions placed in schools, stores, or airports) are now able to provide marketers with two significant advantages over mass advertising media: better defined audiences and more efficient delivery of those audiences. In the case of data, most targeted media require consumers to provide information about themselves in exchange for access to the medium. This information, whether contained in purchase records, subscription lists, customer files, mailing lists, registration lists, or public records, gives marketers a better sense of who their messages are reaching. It also allows them to define consumers using a multitude of demographic, geographic, psychographic, and shopping behavior variables (Nowak and Phelps 1992). More importantly, by combining information sources (such as in-house information with data obtained from outside services), marketers can develop detailed consumer profiles, identify market segments, and create customized or even personalized selling messages.

As for audience delivery, the information-intensive nature of targeted media, a proliferation of new media, and advances in technology have facilitated the faith in highly targeted media. The information-intensive nature of targeted media thus enhances marketers' ability to select media vehicles that match the characteristics of their target market. The shotgun is replaced with 'rifles' that allow marketers to reach target consumers without wasting money talking to people who are not interested in the advertised product or service. In many cases, advances in computer, printing, and broadcast technology have contributed to this shift by assisting the development of media vehicles that serve smaller but homogenous audiences. Unlike mass advertising media, these media give marketers access to well-defined audiences that have considerable interest in the editorial or program content, often in a less cluttered advertising environment.

The result is that the customized marketing and highly segmented media approaches once deemed appropriate only for magazine subscriptions, financial services, and other relatively specialized goods and services are now being employed by brand and packaged-goods marketers in such industries as soft drinks, beer and wine, fast food restaurants, bath soap, and cereal (Hume 1992a; Landler et al. 1991; Levin 1992; Rapp and Collins 1990). Automobile manufacturers, in using direct mail, catalogs, special interest magazines, computer diskettes, videocassettes, and toll-free phone numbers to reach consumers now budget 10 percent of all marketing dollars to direct response or targeted media, with some advertising executives predicting this will soon increase to 15 percent (Fannin 1989). Buick, which spent about $20 million on direct response advertising in 1998 estimated it sold 4,000 more Buick Riverias as a result of mailing 500,000 brochures. Similarly, Lincoln-Continental's print advertisements with reply cards generated some 150,000 responses, while Cadillac, which began using direct response in 1985, got a 3 percent response rate in 1988 with an offer for one of its luxury sports cars (Fannin 1989). In perhaps the most extreme application of target marketing, American Isuzu Motors personally addressed each of 9 million subscribers to *Time, Sports Illustrated*, and *People* magazine advertisements. Thanks to advances in printing technology, each ad contained the subscriber's name and location of the nearest dealer (*Washington Post*, January 15, 1990).

Utilization of consumer databases. The increased reliance on targeting and the demand for advertising accountability that have accompanied the integrated marketing communications phenomenon also have spurred greater use of both in-house and computer service bureau consumer databases. Whereas the creation of computer databases once required expensive mainframe computers with teams of programmers and analysts, it is now economically feasible to gather, store, and analyze relatively in-depth consumer and transaction data (Rapp and Collins 1990; Shepard and Associates 1991). These databases, whether developed in-house or maintained by a computer service bureau that combines the files of multiple national data sources, have become 'the absolutely essential new order in the world of marketing' (Bernstein 1991), with a level of prominence that 'advertising agencies can't afford to ignore' (Hume 1992e).

Long used by mail-order firms, catalogue companies, direct mail marketers, and other direct marketers, computerized databases are becoming common tools for brand and packaged-goods marketers, especially those with relatively narrow audiences or whose profitability is highly dependent on consumer loyalty (Block and Brezen 1990; Hume 1992e; Levin 1992, 1991b; Levin and Jones 1992). A survey of 47 major consumer product marketers found 67 percent were compiling and using consumer databases in 1991, compared with 48 percent in 1990 (Hume 1992c). Similar results were found in 1991 surveys involving leading direct response advertising and sales promotion agencies. In the direct response survey, 61 percent of the agencies said that more than half of their clients were maintaining a marketing database of customers, and 86 percent expected clients to broaden database use in 1992 (Levin 1992). One third of the respondents said packaged goods was the fastest growing user category. Meanwhile, 99 percent of the sales promotion agencies indicated database development was a prime growth area, with 72 percent labelling it as having 'high' growth potential (*Advertising Age*, April 29, 1991).

Although many brand and packaged-goods marketers have yet to realize the full potential of marketing databases (Levin and Jones 1992), the ability to gather, store, and manipulate consumer data is thought to improve marketing communication performance in at least three ways. First, databases improve target marketing by giving marketers a better understanding of who their customers are and what media to use to reach them. The detailed information contained in a database typically goes beyond demographic approximations to include names, addresses, individual-level shopping and purchase information (Shepard and Associates 1991). It is therefore possible to isolate and determine the characteristics of 'best' customers, information that can then be used to find new prospects. Second, shopping, purchase, and other lifestyle information contained in databases can provide insight into consumer's buying habits and motivations. Using these insights, marketers can develop creative and media strategies that better match market segments. In related-fashion, databases can track those audiences' responses to different marketing communication strategies and tactics (Burnett 1992; Clancy 1990). Finally, the profiles derived from databases can be used to establish long-term customer relationships and foster repeat buying (thereby attaining market share objectives) (Bodin 1991). Long-term programs, or 'relationship marketing efforts,' are rarer but thought to be more effective contributor to a firm's long-term success and profitability (Dwyer 1989). In this sense, marketing databases serve as an advertising medium that provides direct access to known customers and prospects. According to the survey of direct response agencies, 81 percent said clients were using databases for loyalty or continuity programs, 59 percent to cross-sell other products or services, and 41 percent for coupon mailings or other promotions (Levin 1992).

New demands on marketing communication suppliers. In many respects, the blending of marketing communication disciplines, both strategically and tactically, is the most conspicuous aspect of the integrated marketing communications' phenomenon. It is not unusual, for instance, for the advent of 'integrated marketing communication' to be traced to consumer goods manufacturers' use of sales promotion and direct response advertising tactics to build consumer databases (Nelson 1991; Rapp and Collins 1991) or to direct response advertisers use of brand/image advertising to build product or brand credibility (Kobs 1988; Nash 1986). Thus, examining marketers' relationships with marketing communication suppliers (e.g., outside firms that provide advertising, consumer sales promotion, or direct response advertising services) reveals a fourth set of characteristics associated with an integrated perspective. The examination indicates the switch from national advertising toward highly targeted media, consumer sales promotion, and greater use of marketing databases has both heightened marketers expectations regarding the types of services performed by outside supplies and blurred traditional distinctions between marketing communication disciplines.

Sales promotion, direct response, and general advertising agencies, for example, all are being asked by clients to add direct marketing and database assistance. In a 1991 survey of sales promotion agencies, eighty-four of the 105 respondents indicated that direct marketing would be a major growth area in 1992 (Wylie 1992b). Over half said they were adding direct response advertising to their list of services for the first time. The survey also documented the emergence of a new type of sales promotion agency, one that goes beyond specializing in tactical and executional services by providing marketers with strategic planning and an array of services that include direct and database marketing, direct response advertising, and consumer research (Hume 1992b). Similarly, 60 percent of the respondents in a 1991 survey of direct response advertising agencies said database development had 'high' growth potential for their business (Levin 1992), while large advertising agencies are entering the database arena either by buying direct marketing firms or hiring database specialists (Hume 1992e). On the client side, a 1991 survey of 50 U.S. and Canadian consumer goods marketers found that half planned to increase their sales promotion agencies' involvement in strategic planning and direct marketing (Hume 1991a).

Marketers' interest in behavior-oriented strategies and tactics has not, however, led them to discount the value of company and brand images. Rather, concern about increasing product parity and diminishing brand equity has facilitated the breakdown of boundaries between marketing communication disciplines. Brand/image advertising, consumer sales promotion, and databases all have come to be viewed as useful and necessary for creating an image or identity that clearly distinguishes a brand from its competitors. One of the largest packaged-goods marketers in the U.S. (Kraft General Foods), for example, found direct mail, 800 phone numbers, and consumer sales promotions not only enabled it to build a 30 million name customer database, but improved the communication and sales effectiveness of five brand advertising campaigns (DiBella 1991). Another major consumer goods marketer, Procter & Gamble, in seeking to expand the use of direct marketing beyond product sampling and coupon distribution, recently instructed its general advertising agencies to think of 'direct marketing ideas while developing general advertising strategies' (Levin 1992). Meanwhile, a survey of consumer goods marketing executives found 63 percent believed that 'brand building' was one of the long-term effects of consumer sales promotion (Manning and Lukas 1990). Similarly, when consumer goods marketers decide to create customer databases, general advertising agencies are often called upon to design and execute a campaign that looks more like sales promotion than brand/image advertising (e.g., a mail-in premium offer, sweepstake, trackable coupon, or rebate). In other instances, general and direct response advertising agencies have expanded their responsibilities to encompass sales promotion planning, purchase of promotional media, direct marketing and point-of-purchase displays (Hume 1991a; 1992d), and public relations agencies have, at the behest of clients, branched into consumer sales promotion (Hume and Levin 1991).

An Integrated Marketing Communications Framework

The 'integrated' phenomenon becomes clearer when the integrated marketing communications' conceptualizations are viewed in conjunction with the spending and strategy changes that accompany adoption of an integrated perspective. As Figure 1 shows, the result is a conceptual framework that reduces the confusion regarding what integrated marketing communication is, and what it means for advertising practices. The framework highlights the fact that integrated marketing communications involves utilizing two or more marketing communication disciplines, with public relations and advertising typically associated with the 'image' component and consumer sales promotion and direct response advertising typically associated with 'behavior,' or some type of consumer action. Further, Figure 1 reconciles previous integrated marketing communication conceptualizations by recognizing that 'integration' can occur at a campaign level, at an advertisement level, or both. Combining elements from two or more marketing communication disciplines in a single advertisement, commercial, or other creative execution results in 'integrated advertisements.' When marketing communication disciplines are combined at a campaign level, the result (or in some cases, end goal) is 'coordinated marketing communications campaigns.' This campaign, in turn, can either have 'one voice' or use a variety of messages depending on the target audience. It is even possible to use 'integrated advertisements' as part of a 'coordinated marketing communications campaign.'

Along with providing a way to clarify whether the integration is at the campaign or advertisement level, Figure 1 shows where an integrated perspective directly affects advertising practices. First, and most importantly, it

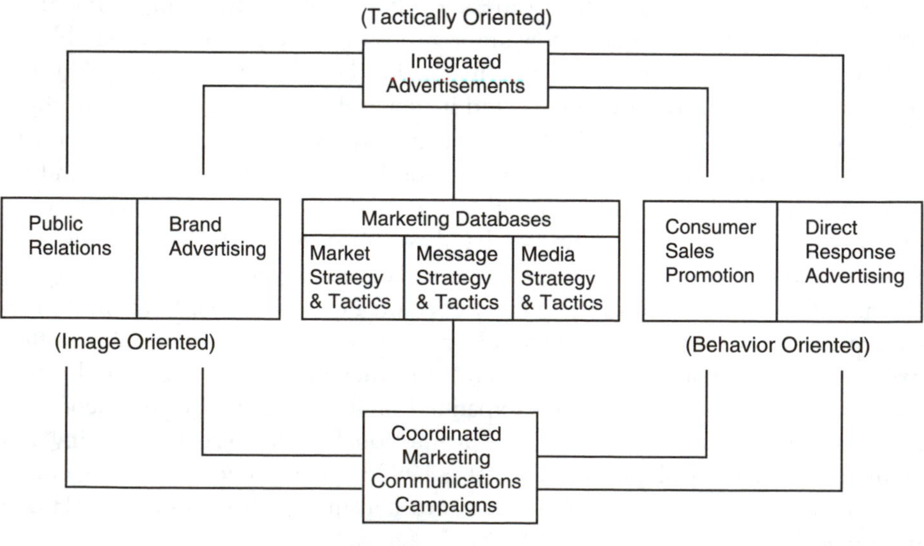

Figure 1 The 'integrated' communications' landscape

recognizes that marketing databases are either the end goal, or an integral component, of an integrated marketing communication perspective. As the review of strategy changes indicated, marketing communication disciplines are often 'integrated,' at either the campaign or advertisement level, in order to create a customer or prospect database. This database, in turn, is used to shape strategy and tactics in three areas: market, message, and media. As previous discussion indicated, this generally means using highly targeted media to direct customized messages to well-defined audiences.

The framework also recognizes that integrated marketing communications' perspectives are dynamic. Information gathered in one campaign, or from responses to integrated advertisements, is fed back into the system (often via the database) and used to direct markets, messages, and media decisions. Information sharing between marketers and agencies thus becomes essential. Although disciplinary (i.e., territorial) disputes represent a potential hurdle (Cohen 1991), integrated marketing communications offer the advantage of greater continuity across campaigns or advertisements. Finally, the framework suggests that 'integrated advertisements' are more likely to be used as a tactic (i.e., one of the many tools used in a campaign), while 'coordinated marketing communication campaigns' are typically part of a marketing strategy.

Implications for Advertising Theory and Research

By affecting advertising practices, the integrated marketing communications' phenomenon has implications for advertising theory and research. As Figure 2 illustrates, the advent of coordinated marketing communications campaigns and integrated advertisements directly affects at least four advertising theory and research domains: receiver, message, media, and social issues. Although each area has been much examined in the general (i.e., brand/image) advertising literature, the applicability of previous efforts is uncertain. First, there has not yet been a concerted effort to extend advertising theory and research into the integrated marketing communications' realm. Second, integrated marketing communications' perspectives introduce, or raise to new levels of prominence, such marketing communication elements as databases, highly targeted media, and customized messages. Finally, much previous research deals with communication effects and effectiveness, whereas the allure of integrated marketing communications is its inclusion of behavioral effects. Theoretical development and empirical research in the integrated marketing communications' arena is thus likely to require incorporating constructs, concepts, and ideas from more behavior-oriented marketing communication disciplines, such as consumer sales promotion, direct marketing and direct response advertising.

The direct response advertising literature, for example, can be used to identify the major advertising research opportunities that exist as a result of the integrated marketing communications' phenomenon. As Table 1 shows, each of the advertising domains affected by the integrated marketing communications' phenomenon has been recently addressed in the direct response advertising literature. The literature outlined in Table 1, while not exhaustive, thus provides a behavior-based foundation for addressing integrated marketing communications issues. More importantly, it helps identify the important, and as yet unanswered, questions the integrated marketing communications' phenomenon raises in each advertising domain.

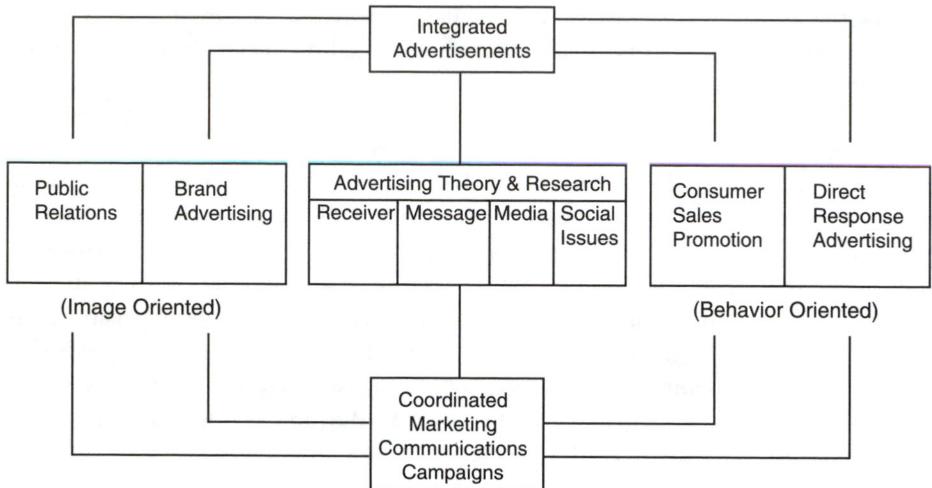

Figure 2 Advertising's changing landscape

Table 1 Identifying research opportunities using the direct-response advertising literature

Research questions	*Relevant research*
1 Receiver	
Information processing: How do consumers process advertisements that simultaneously attempt to achieve communication and behavioral objectives? Do consumers process direct response advertisements differently than brand/image advertisments (e.g., are behavioral learning models more appropriate)? What model(s) would be most appropriate for the processing of integrated advertisements?	**Information processing:** Akhter (1989) Offers a schematic framework for examining consumers' cognitive processes involved in evaluating and making purchase decisions of directly marketed products. Akhter argues that schematic representations of the three elements of direct marketing – source, mode, and response – influence consumers' purchase decisions of directly marketed products.
Does the addition of response devices to brand/image oriented advertisments help or hinder the attainment of communication objectives? Under what circumstances do response devices help communication objectives? When do they hinder communication objectives?	**Types (characteristics of):** Woodside and Motes (1979, 1980) Evaluated travel profiles of general response, direct response, and reader service inquirers from magazine advertising. Results suggested that there were differences among travel profiles and that direct response inquirers were more

Research questions	*Relevant research*
Does the addition of brand/image oriented components to direct response advertisements help or hinder the attainment of behavioral objectives? Under what circumstances do they help attain behavior objectives? When do they hinder behavioral objectives? What role do mental constructs, such as attitude toward the ad and attitude toward the advertiser, play in the processing of integrated advertisements (e.g., does attitude toward the ad influence behavioral responses to integrated advertisements)?	likely to buy the product advertised and produce greater revenue per inquiry compared with magazine reader service and general response inquirers. However, Woodside and Motes (1980) reported that they did not find significant consumer profile (e.g., lifecycle and occupation) differences between image-ad inquirers and direct response-ad inquirers. McCorkle, Planchon, and James (1987) This was a comprehensive review of the in-home shopping studies conducted between 1964 and 1987. The 27 studies published in that period lent only limited support to two relatively 'commensense' notions: (1) that buying from home involves more risk; and (2) the more discretionary income a household has, the more discretionary products it will purchase via direct response advertising.
Types (characteristics of): Are consumer characteristics useful or important for understanding consumer responses to integrated advertisements and coordinated marketing communications campaigns? Which consumer characteristics are most useful for understanding consumer responses to integrated advertisements and coordinated marketing communication campaigns (e.g., which consumer characteristics are reliable predictors of who is likely to respond positively to an integrated advertisment)? Are there differences among consumers who respond to integrated advertisements versus consumers who respond to direct response advertisements or consumer sales promotions that do not emphasize image? What are the relationships between viewer characteristics and viewer responses to integrated advertisements and coordinated marketing communications campaigns (e.g., what role do individual characteristics/traits play in the processing of integrated advertisements)?	Woodside and Soni (1991) This study extended Woodside and Soni's (1988, 1990) research by: (1) profiling consumers who respond to advertising offers of free information based upon their evaluation and use of the information received, and(2) examining the purchase and consumption behavior differences among these groups. They reported that heavy users of requested information buy a greater number of the services advertised, are more prone to buy competing services, and have higher expenditures of the services adverised compared to light and nonusers who also requested the information. Nowak (1992) This study examined the relationships among TV viewers' characteristics and their reactions to direct response TV commercials. The findings suggested:(1) that consumer characteristics are related to viewer reactions to direct response TV commercials:(2) that specific viewer characteristics, rather than broad segmentation categories, have the strongest relationship to viewer responses; and(3) that the strongest relationships are found between viewer characteristics and attitude and intention responses. *Continued*

Table 1 *continued*

Research questions	*Relevant research*
2 Message	
Content:	**Content:**
What are the identifying content characteristics of a coordinated marketing communication campaign? What are the indentifying content characteristics of an integrated advertisement? What types of message strategies and appeals are most commonly used in integrated advertisements? What types of measurement procedures would best measure the amount of brand/image and response components in integrated advertisements? Can creative guidelines be developed for integrating image and direct response tactics which would help the advertiser select the appropriate mix of image and direct response components to include in an integrated advertisement?	LeBourveau, Dwyer, and Kernan (1988) Used Cialdini's taxonomy of communication strategies to content analyze magazine advertisements. Results indicated that while both conventional display and direct response ads rely mostly on friendship/liking strategies, direct response ads use a scarcity theme more than do conventional ads. James and Vanden Bergh (1989) Used and Stern's information scale to the information value of 8,457 full-page 'general' and direct response magazine ads. Overall, the direct response ads out-performed the general ads in amount of information given. Motes, Hilton, and Fielden (1989) Examined the role of communication style (how something is said) and organization (i.e., the sequential positioning of requests). Style and organization were found to have little effect on how readers reacted to the ads. Peltier, Meuller, and Rosen (1992) Outlined the message factors that distinguish image from direct response advertising and proposed a method for determining where a particular message falls on the direct-image continuum.
Effects:	**Effects:**
What are the communication and behavioral effects of integrated advertisements and coordinated marketing communications campaigns? Are marketers better off using an integrated advertisement or simply coordinating the messages sent via various communication disciplines? Should integrated advertisements focus on communication efficiency (i.e., getting the message out to a lot of people) or behavioral effectiveness (i.e., getting a lot of people to respond)? Similarly, what should be the objectives of a coordinated marketing communications campaign?	Woodside and Motes (1980) Examined the revenue generated and cost per inquiry for image advertisement inquirers versus inquires generated from direct response advertisements. Reported no significant difference for revenue, however, the cost per inquiry was significantly lower for the direct response inquirers. Bodenberg and Roberts (1990) Combined marketing research concept testing with the basic in-mail testing approach of direct marketing. The new method would provide behavioral as well as cognitive measures of advertising effectiveness.

Research questions	*Relevant research*
How do you assess the effectiveness of a coordinated marketing communications campaign (e.g., what measures do you use)? What is the appropriate time frame to measure the effects of integrated advertisements? Should the time frame be closer to the few weeks used by direct response advertisers or more like the six to twelve months suggested by general advertisers? How about for coordinated marketing communications campaigns?	Scott, Klein, and Bryant (1990) This study tested the behavioral impact of humorous promotions with a series of three field studies. The humorous promotions significantly increased the attendance for social events, but showed no impact for business events. Weigold, Flusser, and Ferguson (1992) Examined the contributions of price, amount of information, artwork, and individual differences on purchase consideration. Results suggest information has important direct and indirect effects. Other variables, such as risk tendencies and purchase riskiness, appear to contribute little to understanding purchase consideration.
3 Media	
What impact does the advent of integrated advertising and coordinated marketing communications campaigns have on media planning? What role do the media play in coordinated marketing communications campaigns (e.g., what role do media traditionally associated with direct response, such as mailing lists and databases, play in coordinated marketing communications campaigns)? Do message content and presentation style of integrated advertisements differ across the different media? Are integrated advertisements more effective in one medium versus another (e.g., magazine versus television)? Do 'general' advertisers favor placing their integrated advertisements in different media than marketers who have traditionally relied on direct response or consumer sales promotion (e.g., would brand/image oriented marketers favor television while other marketers favor direct mail)?	Schnorbus (1987) This is a descriptive article that chronicles the many media choices available for direct marketers as well as discussing important recent developments relating to each media choice. It also provides information on new media such as interactive TV and videologs. Fanin (1989) Reported the increasing use of direct response and databased advertising used by automobile manufacturers. Discussed the many different media used by auto manufacturers including: direct mail, computer diskettes, video-cassettes, lavish catalogs, magazines, and toll-free phone numbers. Block and Brezen (1990) Although not directly concerned with direct-response advertising, Block and Brezen argue for the use of individual-level information for media planning. They propose using database analysis to segment general media audiences, whereby media planning becomes a process of segmenting audiences based on their historical response patterns.

Continued

Table 1 *continued*

Research questions	*Relevant research*
4 Social issues	
What moral, social, and ethical issues arises as a result of the use of coordinated marketing communications campaigns, integrated advertisements, and consumer information databases? What are consumers' overall perceptions of the appropriateness of marketers' information gathering and use practices (e.g., are they aware of the existence of marketing databases and do they know what information is typically contained in the databases)?	Katz and Tassone (1990) This was a trend analysis of public opinion toward privacy covering the period 19780–1989. Among other findings, results indicated: (1) modest increases in the amount of public concern over privacy during the 80s; and (2) the proportion of people who believe they give up their privacy to participate in a consumer society has grown, as has the proportion who believe they are subjects of computer files being put together for purposes unknown to them.
Should restrictions be placed on marketers information gathering and use practices? If so, what practices should be restricted and who should create or enforce these restrictions?	Harris-Equifax Consumer Privacy Surveys (1990, 1991) Among other findings, these surveys indicated: (1) a much higher level of concern over privacy than did the Katz and Tassone study; (2) a growing concern over having to reveal personal information; (3) a majority of Americans not satisfied with the way some organizations, particularly financial and credit institutions, collect and use information about individuals; and (4) consumer attitudes about direct marketers' use of individual-level information depending on their relationship with direct marketers. Nowak and Phelps (1992) This study examined consumer concern regarding direct marketers' information gathering and use practices as well as consumer knowledge of specific information gathering and use practices. The survey results suggested that (1) consumers are very concerned about privacy, (2) although consumer concern is affected by type of information practice and specificity of information, most respondents were not very knowlegeable about direct marketers' information practices, and (3) most respondents favor restrictions on the gathering and use of personal information.

Receiver issues (information processing). Integrated marketing communications' perspectives raise a number of information processing issues. The questions concern how consumers react to 'integrated advertisements,' whether integrating elements from different disciplines helps or hinders communication effectiveness, and the role, if any, played by mental constructs such as attitudes. Given that brand and packaged-goods advertising has traditionally focused on communication goals (e.g., creating awareness or favorable attitudes), many advertising models suggest that consumers go through a series of hierarchically order steps (Barry 1987). The appropriateness of this assumption for integrated advertisements or coordinated marketing communication campaigns, which often seek to attain communication and behavior effects simultaneously, remains to be seen. Still, answers to processing questions are likely to emanate from the general, rather than direct response, advertising literature. Compared to the brand/image advertising scholars, direct response researchers have ignored information processing issues. One notable exception, however, is Akhter's (1988) framework for examining the cognitive processes used by consumers in responding to, or evaluating, direct marketing communications. His model suggests consumers' schematic representations of the marketers (i.e., the source), the media utilized, and the response alternatives available (e.g., phone or mail) directly influence, and can be used to predict, purchase decisions. His model, however, is yet to be tested.

Receiver issues (characteristics of). As the table shows, a considerable amount of research has examined the characteristics of people who respond behaviorally (i.e., inquire by phone or mail, or purchase) to direct response media or advertising. Beginning with Cox and Rich's (1964) study of telephone shoppers, these studies have operated under the assumption that demographic or psychographic characteristics mediate or explain consumer responses (or lack thereof) to direct marketing efforts. Although early studies often identified age, gender, geography, attitude toward credit, household income, and education as potentially important correlates of in-home shopping (Cox and Rich 1964; Cunningham and Cunningham 1973; Gillet 1970), much of the research is dated or hampered by poor measures, biased sampling designs, or lack of control over other mediating variables (McCorkle, Planchon and James 1987). Still, the idea that consumer characteristics are related to consumer responses appears to have applicability with respect to integrated marketing communications. The addition of response devices to brand/image advertisements, along with the use of computerized databases, for instance, gives researchers the ability to identify, and assess the effects of, a variety of responder characteristics. This information, in turn, can be compared with that describing nonresponders (e.g., census or market data). Nowak's (1992) study, for instance, supports the existence of links between market segmentation variables and responses to 'integrated advertisements.' Further, Woodside and Motes' (1980) study suggests research is needed to identify the circumstances in which integrated advertisements or coordinated marketing communications are most appropriate.

Message content. The integration of direct response advertising or consumer sales promotion devices with brand or image building advertising practices has changed the message strategies and creative executions of both camps. The most visible evidence of this in the consumer goods advertising world is the greater use of mail-in offers, 800/900 numbers, and increased advertising of frequent buyer reward programs. Although anecdotal evidence of these changes is readily available (Rapp and Collins 1990), skepticism about the pervasiveness of integrated marketing communications suggests empirical research is needed to more accurately document the changes that have taken place. Content analyses of direct response advertisements, for instance, have found that these ads contain more information and information cues than brand/image advertisements (James and Vanden Bergh 1989). Direct response ads are also thought to rely more on compliance strategies that involve scarcity or social reciprocation themes (LeBourveau, Dwyer and Kernan 1988), and place greater emphasis on action-oriented creative devices and techniques (Nowak 1989) than brand/image advertisements. Although Peltier. Meuller and Rosen (1992) outlined the factors that distinguish image from direct response ads, and provided a method for evaluating where a particular message falls on the direct-image continuum, their framework has yet to be applied. Thus, basic descriptive studies are needed to document the characteristics of integrated advertisements, the type of appeals used in such ads, and the prevalence of integrated ads relative to other types of advertisements.

Message effects. Another set of integrated marketing communications' research opportunities involves advertising effects and effectiveness. Thanks to the adoption of integrated perspectives, many marketers are trying to develop advertising assessment systems that either determine: (a) communication effects/effectiveness when responses may be as much attitudinal as behavioral (Passavant 1989) or (b) sales effects/effectiveness when behavioral responses are as important as attitudinal responses (Rapp and Collins 1988). As a result, advertising and consumer behavior researchers need to identify the communication and behavioral effects of integrated advertising and coordinated marketing communication campaigns, and develop measures that assess the effectiveness of such ads and campaigns (e.g., what measures best capture the effects of integrated advertisements). A recent example of such an approach was presented by Bodenberg and Roberts (1990). They found that combining market research concept testing with the in-mail testing approach of direct marketing resulted in a measurement system that provides attitude and intention data as well as sales effectiveness measures.

Research is also needed to determine how long it takes for integrated advertisements and coordinated marketing communication campaigns to affect consumers. In other words, what is the appropriate time frame for measuring effects? Direct response advertisers, for instance, typically assess advertising or campaign effects using a relatively short time frame (e.g., minutes or weeks), whereas brand/image advertisers favor six to twelve month time frames. Further complicating matters is the notion of customer lifetime value. This concept, fostered by the integrated advertising perspective, advocates measuring advertising the effectiveness of advertising based on the present value of the expected benefits (e.g., sales) less the costs of servicing and informing customers (Dwyer 1989). The idea is based on the assumption that advertising success requires looking beyond initial ad exposure. Thus, by taking into account customer satisfaction, attitudes, and repeat purchase behavior, campaigns or advertisements that perform poorly on a short-run basis may be judged favorably when repeat purchase behavior is factored in. Although Dwyer has explicated a simple taxonomy of the lifetime value concept, the use of this construct to conceptually capture and operationally calculate the communication and behavioral effects of integrated advertisements or coordinated marketing communication campaigns remains untested. Further, the conceptual sophistication involved in lifetime value calculations means much theoretical development is needed to adapt the idea to integrated advertisements or coordinated campaigns.

Media. Despite the documented shift in media expenditures from mass media toward highly targeted media, many of the media planning questions raised by integrated advertisements and coordinated marketing communication campaigns are unanswered. Thus, research opportunities abound. Basic questions, such as 'How do integrated advertisements and coordinated marketing communication campaigns change media strategy and tactics?' need to be addressed. Research that examines whether traditional media preferences change as a result of integrated ads or coordinated campaigns is also needed. For example, should packaged goods advertisers who adopt an integrated perspective still utilize television as their primary medium, or should they shift dollars elsewhere?

Studies that examine how advertising media have adapted to databases, integrated advertisements, and coordinated marketing communication campaigns are needed. As Katz (1991) showed, media planning departments at major U.S. advertising agencies struggle with a variety of information management and use issues. How marketers and other ad agency departments utilize consumer information remains unexamined. Consumer databases harnessed to technological advances have also led to such identifiable changes as magazines using selective binding techniques to 'personalize' ads and the use of highly customized direct mail (e.g., sending different messages to different market segments or individuals). The communication or sales efficacy of such techniques, however, has received little academic attention.

Social issues. Similar to advertising in general, the number and type of social issues potentially raised by the integrated marketing communications' phenomenon are limited only by researchers' imaginations. Most of social issues, including those related to advertising clutter, regulation, and ethics, are not likely to lose their relevance in a world of integrated advertisements and coordinated marketing communication campaigns. If anything, widespread adoption of 'integrated' perspectives will likely lead to new issues. The most significant recent example involves marketers' information gathering and use practices and consumer privacy. As discussed, integrated ads, marketing databases, and coordinated campaigns escalate the demand for individual-level demographic, lifestyle, and media use information about consumers. Many marketers, for instance, believe the effectiveness of marketing communication strategies and tactics is directly related to the amount and specificity of consumer information (Block and Brezen 1990). A recent Gallup survey, however, found over 78 percent of consumers described themselves as 'very' or 'somewhat' concerned about what marketers know about them (Hume 1991). Similarly, two surveys commissioned by Equifax found 70 percent of the respondents believed consumers 'have lost all control over how personal information about them is used by companies' (Equifax 1991, 1990). A series of questions is thus raised concerning the types, specificity, and amount of information that marketers should be able to gather, store, access, and use. Do consumers have a 'right to privacy' that supersedes marketers information gathering and use practices? Additional questions surround marketers information gathering methods, which vary considerably in terms of conspicuousness or obtrusiveness. For instance, what do consumers perceive as appropriate and inappropriate information gathering practices? How about marketers? Should restrictions be placed on marketers information gathering, storage, or use practices, and who should create or enforce those regulations?

Conclusions

The integrated marketing communications' phenomenon, manifest as integrated advertisements and coordinated marketing communications' campaigns, has impacted the advertising world on a number of levels. First, it is no longer possible for advertising practitioner or scholars to dismiss integrated marketing communications as a temporary aberration from marketing communication norms. As this review has demonstrated, an examination of integrated marketing communications' perspectives reveals a fundamental restructuring of the 'rules' of marketing and advertising communication. Not only have traditional marketing communication disciplinary boundaries been irrevocably blurred, but integrated advertisements and coordinated marketing communication campaigns reflect marketers' expanded capabilities for targeting, reaching, persuading, and cultivating consumers. Second, the changes brought by integrated perspectives call into question many of the widely-held assumptions regarding strategies and tactics in four advertising-related domains: markets, messages, media, and social issues. As the number of marketers employing integrated advertisements and coordinated, multidisciplinary campaigns increases, the need for new marketing and advertising communication models, methods, and theories will become even more apparent. Finally, as the list of advertising research opportunities illustrates, the ramifications of the integrated phenomenon are as of yet uncertain. The only certainty being the existence of a marketing communication environment that offers marketers a wealth of options and provides scholars with a new opportunities for bridging the gaps between advertising and its ultimate communication and behavioral effects.

References

Akhter, Syed H. (1989), 'Schematic Information Processing: Direct Marketing and Purchase Decisions,' *Journal of Direct Marketing*, 3 (2), 31–38.

Baker, Wilder D. (1992), 'Compensation Barrier: It's the Key to an Agency's Culture Change,' *Advertising Age*, February 3, 20.

Barry, Thomas E. (1987). 'The Development of the Hierarchy of Effects: An Historical

Perspective,' in J. Leigh and C.R. Martin (eds.) *Current Issues and Research in Advertising*, Graduate School of Business: University of Michigan, 251–295.

Bernstein, Sid (1991), 'Riding the Database Wave.' *Advertising Age*, May 20, 20.

Blattberg, Robert C. (1987), 'Research Opportunities in Direct Marketing,' *Journal of Direct Marketing*, 1(1), 7–14.

Block, Martin P. and Tamara S. Brezen (1990), 'Using Database Analysis to Segment General Media Audiences.' *Journal of Media Planning*, Spring, 1–14.

Bodenberg, Thomas M. and Mary Lou Roberts (1990), 'Integrating Marketing Research into the Direct Marketing Testing Process,' *Journal of Advertising Research*, 30(October/November), 50–60.

Bodin, Madeline (1991), 'The Future of Database Marketing,' *Inbound/Outbound Magazine*, January, 19–21.

Bowman, Russ (1990), 'Sales Promotion: Annual Report for 1989,' *Marketing and Media Decisions*, 25 (July), 20–21.

—— (1987), 'Different Disciplines, Similar Tactics,' *Marketing and Media Decisions*, 22(October), 99–102.

Burnett, Ed (1992), 'How to Access Mainframe Data With Your PC,' *Direct Marketing News*, June 15, 21–22.

Clancy, Kevin J. (1990), 'The Coming Revolution in Advertising.' *Journal of Advertising Research*, 30 (February/March), 47–52.

Coen, Robert (1992), 'How Bad a Year for Ads was '91? Almost the Worst,' *Advertising Age*, May 4, 1,51.

Cohen, Stanley (1991), 'The Danger's of Today's Media Revolution,' *Advertising Age*, September 30, 18.

Coogle, Joe (1990), 'Data-Base Marketing,' *Marketing and Media Decisions*, 25 (January), 75–77.

Cox, Donald F. and Stuart U. Rich (1964), 'Perceived Risk and Consumer Decision Making – The Case of the Telephone Shopper,' *Journal of Marketing Research*, 1 (November), 32–39.

Cunningham, Isabella C. M. and William H. Cunningham (1973), 'The Urban In-Home Shopper: Socioeconomic and Attitudinal Characteristics,' *Journal of Retailing*, 49 (Fall), 42–50.

DiBella, Lori (1991), 'Not Just For the Little Guys,' *Direct Marketing*, 53 (May), 20–22.

Dwyer, F. Robert (1989), 'Customer Lifetime Valuation to Support Marketing Decision Making,' *Journal of Direct Marketing*, 3(4), 8–15.

Equifax Consumer Privacy Survey (1991), Atlanta, GA: Equifax Inc.

Equifax Report on Consumers in the Information Age (1990), Atlanta, GA: Equifax Inc.

Fahey, Alison (1992), 'TV Faces Transition,' *Advertising Age*, February 3, 29.

Fannin, Rebecca (1989), 'Detroit's Direct Route,' *Marketing and Media Decisions*, 24 (February), 41–44.

Gillet, Peter (1970), 'A Profile of Urban In-Home Shoppers,' *Journal of Marketing*, 34 (July), 40–45.

Goerne, Carrie (1992), 'Direct Mail Spending Rises, but Success May Be Overblown,' *Marketing News*, March 2, 6.

Graham, Judith (1987), 'DMA Members' Ads Hit $3 Billion,' *Advertising Age*, November 2.

Haroldsen, Edwin O. (1992), 'Integrate Advertising and PR?' *Public Relations Update*, July, 5.

Hoke, Henry R. (1990), 'More Bang for the Buck,' *Direct Marketing Magazine*, 52 (January), 49–52.

—— (1989), 'Editorial,' *Direct Marketing Magazine*, 51 (January), 122.

Hume, Scott (1992a), 'Pizza Hut Hungry for Data,' *Advertising Age*, June 22, S-6.

—— (1992b), 'Agency Services Take on Exaggerated Importance for Marketers,' *Advertising Age*, May 4, 29,32.

—— (1992c), 'Trade Promotions Devour Half of All Marketing Dollars,' *Advertising Age*, April 13, 3, 53.

—— (1992d), 'Couponing Reaches Record Clip,' *Advertising Age*, February 3, 1,41.

—— (1992e), 'Shops Scratching to Develop their Database Niche,' *Advertising Age*, January 13, 26, 30.

—— (1991a), 'Promotions Get Boost,' *Advertising Age*, November 18, 30.

—— (1991b), 'Campus Adopts "New Advertising," ' *Advertising Age*, September 23, 17.

—— and Gary Levin (1991), 'PR Agencies Tread Promotion Turf,' *Advertising Age*, November 4, 36.

Jaffee, Larry (1992), '16.2 Billion Called 800 Numbers in 1991: Study,' *Direct Marketing News*, June 8, 13.

James, E. Lincoln and James Vanden Bergh (1989), 'On the Information Content of Advertising.' *Journal of Direct Marketing*, 3(3), 7–15.

Jenkins, Vin (1984), 'Understanding Direct Marketing Concept is Vitally Important,' *Direct Marketing*, 47 (October), 46–75.

Katz, Helen (1991), 'How Major U.S. Advertising Agencies Are Coping with Data Overload,' *Journal of Advertising Research*, 31 (February/March), 7–16.

Katz, James E. and A.R. Tassone (1990), 'Public Opinion Trends: Privacy and Information Technology,' *Public Opinion Quarterly*, 54 (Spring), 125–144.

Kobs, Jim (1988), 'Action Blends with Image-Building,' *Advertising Age*, November 9, 78.

Kumar, V. and Robert Leone (1988), 'Measuring the Effect of Retail Store Promotions on Brand and Store Substitution,' *Journal of Marketing Research*, 25 (May), 178–185.

Landler, M., W. Konrad, Z. Schiller, and L. Therrien (1991), 'What Happened to Advertising,' *Business Week*, Sept. 23, 66–72.

LeBourveau, Carol A., F.B. Dwyer and J.B. Kernan (1988), 'Compliance Strategies in Direct Response Advertising,' *Journal of Direct Marketing*, 2(3), 25–34.

Levin, Gary (1992), 'Database Draws Fevered Interest,' *Advertising Age*, June 8, 31.

—— (1991a), 'Going Direct Route,' *Advertising Age*, November 11, 37.

—— (1991b), 'Databases Loom Large for the '90s,' *Advertising Age*, October 21, 22–24.

—— and T. Jones (1992), 'Recession Not Hurting Database Growth: Exec,' *Advertising Age*, January 13, 25, 30.

Lewis, Herschell Gordon (1988), 'Let Them Integrate With Us,' *Direct Marketing*, November, 52–54.

Light, Larry (1990), 'The Changing Advertising World,' *Journal of Advertising Research*, February/March, 30–35.

Mandese, Joe and Scott Donaton (1992), 'Media, Promotion Gap to Narrow,' *Advertising Age*, June 29, 16.

McCorkle, Denny E., J.M. Planchon and W.L. James (1987), 'In-Home Shopping: A Critical Review and Research Agenda,' *Journal of Direct Marketing*, 1(2), 5–21.

Medney, Clifford R. (1979), 'Premiums that Build Brand Image,' *Marketing Communications*, February, 40–42.

Miller, Cyndee (1992), 'Moves by P&G, Heinz Rekindle Fears that Brands are in Danger,' *Marketing News*, June 8, 1, 15.

Motes, William H., C.B. Hilton and J.S. Fielden (1989), 'Reactions to Creative Variations of a Direct Response Ad,' *Journal of Direct Marketing*, 3(3), 16–26.

Nash, Edward L. (1986), *Direct Marketing: Strategy, Planning, Execution*, 2nd ed., New York: McGraw-Hill.

Nelson, Carol (1991). *The New Road to Advertising Success*, Chicago: Bonus Books.

Newsom, Doug A., B.J. Carrell and S. Hussain (1992), 'The Tower of Babel: A Descriptive Report on Attitudes Toward the Idea of Integrated Communications Programs,' paper presented at the annual convention of the Association for Education in Journalism and Mass Communication, Montreal, August 7.

Nowak, Glen J. (1992), 'TV Viewer Characteristics and "Results Beyond Response,"' *Journal of Direct Marketing*, 6(2), 18–31.

—— (1989), 'Getting Viewers to Respond: Assessing the Impact of Direct Response TV Commercials and their Executional Elements,' *Journal of Direct Marketing*, 3(2), 42–52.

—— and Joseph Phelps (1992), 'Understanding Privacy Concerns: An Assessment of Consumers' Information-related Knowledge and Beliefs,' *Journal of Direct Marketing*, 6(4), 7–16.

Passavant, Pierre (1989), 'What's Ahead in the 1990s?' *Direct Marketing*, 52 (September), 12–19.

Peltier, James W., Barbara Mueller, and Richard G. Rosen (1992), 'Direct Response versus Image Advertising,' *Journal of Direct Marketing*, 6(1), 40–49.

Podems, Ruth (1988), 'What's in Store for the 1990s,' *Target Marketing*, October.

Rapp, Stan and Tom Collins (1990), *The Great Marketing Turnaround: The Age of the Individual and How to Profit From It*, Englewood Cliffs, NJ: Prentice Hall.

—— and —— (1988), *Maximarketing: The New Direction in Advertising, Promotion and Marketing Strategy*, New York: NAL Penguin Books.

Reilly, James C. (1991), 'The Role of Integrated Marketing Communications in Brand Management,' *The Advertiser*, Fall, 32–35.

Roman, Ernan (1988), *Integrated Direct Marketing: Techniques and Strategies for Success*, New York: McGraw-Hill Book Company.

Roscitt, Rick and I. Robert Parket (1988), 'Direct Marketing to Consumers,' *Journal of Consumer Marketing*, 5(1), 5–14.

Rotzoll, Kim B. (1991), 'New Advertising is Old,' *Advertising Age*, September 2, 16.

Schlossberg, Howard (1992), 'Packaged-Goods Expert: Micromarketing the Only Way to Go,' *Marketing News*, July 6, 8.

Schultz, Don E. Stanley Tannenbaum, and Robert Lauterborn (1992), *Integrated Marketing Communications*, Lincolnwood, IL: NTC Business Books.

Schnorbus, Paula (1987), 'New Directions,' *Marketing and Media Decisions*, 50 (October), 83–86.

Scott, Cliff, David M. Klein, and Jennings Bryant (1990), 'Consumer Response to Humor in Advertising: A Series of Field Studies Using Behavioral Observation,' *Journal of Consumer Research*, 16 (March), 498–501.

Shepard and Associates (1990), *The New Direct Marketing*, Homewood, IL: Business One Irwin.

Sloan, Pat (1992), 'James Blasts Promotions,' *Advertising Age*, April 6, 1, 37.

Smolowe, Jill (1990), 'Read This,' *Time Magazine*, November 26, 62–77.

Stephenson, Blair (1989), 'Critical Marketing Strategies for the 1990s,' *Journal of Direct Marketing*, 3(3), 34–41.
Stevenson, John (1988), 'The Ability to Do It: Today's Hottest Product in Direct Marketing,' *Direct Marketing Magazine*, 51(December), 90–91.
Synder, Merrill (1991), 'Rethinking "Integrated,"' *Advertising Age*, October 28, 32.
Tellis, Gerard (1988), 'Advertising Exposure, Loyalty and Brand Purchase: A Two Stage Model of Choice,' *Journal of Marketing Research*, 25 (May), 134–144.
Walley, Wayne (1989), 'Wunderman Touts New Age of TV,' *Advertising Age*, November 6, 50.
Weigold, Michael F., S. Flusser, and M.A. Ferguson (1992), 'Direct Response Advertising: The Contributions of Price, Information, Artwork, and Individual Differences to Purchase Considerations,' *Journal of Direct Marketing*, 6(2), 32–39.
Woodside, Arch G. and William H. Motes (1980), 'Image versus Direct Response Advertising,' *Journal of Advertising Research*, 20(4), 31–37.
—— and—— (1979), 'Evaluating Consumer Profiles of General Response, Direct Response, and Reader Service Inquirers from Magazine Advertising,' *Journal of Advertising*, 8(1), 19–26.
—— and Praveen K. Soni (1991), 'Direct Response Advertising Information: Profiling Heavy, Light, and Nonusers,' *Journal of Advertising Research*, December, 26–36.
Wylie, Kenneth (1992a), 'Direct Billings Hit $4 Billion,' *Advertising Age*, June 8, 29–30.
—— (1992b), 'Heady Growth Days Vaporize for Shops,' *Advertising Age*, May 4, 30.
—— (1991), 'Sales Promotion Income Climbs to $637.7 Million,' *Advertising Age*, April 29, 32, 34.

? Questions

1 Nowak and Phelps, in their framework, use behaviour as their basis for measurement, rather than a consumer attitude-change approach. While this offers greater opportunity to measure the financial impact of marketing communication, it also challenges the use of attitudinal data. Can you think of ways in which behavioural and attitudinal data might be combined to provide a total IMC view of marketing communications?

2 Public relations was ignored by Nowak and Phelps in their approach to building a framework for IMC. Does PR have a role to play in IMC? If so, how might it be included in the Nowak and Phelps framework?

3 In the article, Nowak and Phelps identify three broad conceptualizations of IMC, i.e. (a) one voice, (b) integrated communications and (c) co-ordinated marketing communications campaigns. Which do you believe is the most appropriate conceptualization of IMC? If you do not agree with any of the three, what conceptualization would you propose?

4 Nowak and Phelps use advertising theory as the basis for their discussion of IMC. Over the past few years, this has proved to be a most difficult comparison. What other communication theory base might be used to construct a relevant understanding of IMC?

5 When the Nowak and Phelps article was written, the Internet and World Wide Web were just emerging as marketing communication distribution methods and consumer information sources. What impact and effect do you think these new forms of communication have had on the basic frameworks that Nowak and Phelps propose?
6 Great strides have been made in the development of databases, customer information gathering methodologies and various forms of customer identification and valuation. For example, in Chapter 10 of this book, three new streams of marketing metrics are described, i.e. value added marketing, customer-based equity and marketing return on investment. What impact do you think these new marketing metrics have had or might have on the development of IMC going forward?

Vignette

Since the Nowak and Phelps article appeared, IMC has developed in a number of ways around the world. It has been adopted and adapted by a number of organizations although it is still being debated in academic and professional circles. It is being taught in a number of colleges and universities. But the theoretical base for IMC is still being debated.

Part of the debate is the continuing emphasis by functional specialists such as advertising, sales promotion, direct marketing, public relations, events, sponsorships and a seemingly endless number of other marketing communication forms and formats that this activity should and must be considered separately. Each and every one of these functional specialists generally has little interest or concern for integration, since the combining of various specialties would have a direct impact on their budget, power and position within the marketing organization. Thus, there is little reason for the practitioners of various forms of marketing communication to find ways to integrate and align their activities with those of others within the same marketing organization or the same agency. As a result, while most marketing and marketing communication managers and specialists agree that integration, whether as IMC or under some other rubric, is good, there is little incentive for them to try to develop the concept.

Part of the problem is the manner in which firms are organized. For the most part, all types of organizations are still organized and managed as separate functional units, i.e. at the corporate level, marketing, finance, information technology, human resources and so on. In these functional management schemes there is little incentive and even less practicality for integration of any activity, and certainly not marketing communication. Thus one of the major developments in IMC over the past few years has been the new focus on systems thinking and planning in IMC. That approach, in which horizontal processes or methodologies are used to bring the organization together without disturbing the basic organizational structure, appears to hold great promise for the future.

A second area of organizational development that promises to increase the interest and acceptance of many of the IMC principles is the growing adoption by senior management of quantitative management systems such as Six Sigma, Balanced Scorecards, Economic Value Added and the like. These new cross-organizational systems require marketing and other functional groups to provide solid evidence of the return generated on the marketing and marketing communication investments. Thus to truly understand marketing communications as an organizational investment requires an integrated view. We believe these new senior management tools may do more to drive interest and understanding of IMC than the traditional approaches that have historically been used by middle managers.

Finally, the major factor that will impact IMC going forward is the increasing interest in developing or finding ways for the organization to develop communication programmes from a 'media-neutral' view, that is, that will require starting with a 'blank media slate' rather than building programmes from a television or print view, weighing and evaluating all forms of marketing communication to find the most effective communication delivery system, not just the least expensive. Much work is being done in this area as marketers continue to try and combine traditional media with the new electronic and interactive forms but no clear paths have yet emerged. Clearly, the need for IMC has likely never been greater. But the principles of IMC are still driven by the writings of Nowak and Phelps as they appear in the article.

Reference

Schultz, D. E., Tannenbaum, S. F. and Lauterborn, R. F. (1993) *Integrated Marketing Communications: Pulling it Together and Making it Work*, Chicago: NTC Business Books.

Chapter 3

Patrick de Pelsmacker

ADVERTISING: WHAT TO SAY, WHEN

THE AMBITIOUS QUESTION TACKLED in this paper was 'Which creative or ad cue has the best effect on brand sales, and to what extent does that depend on the age of the market?' The body of research into advertising effectiveness is enormous. Two main research streams can be discerned that are in fact two separate worlds. On the one hand there is the experimental laboratory approach that attempts to measure the effects of advertising content on cognitive, affective and intentional responses. Often this research is based on carefully designed new advertising stimuli for non-existing brands, and the measurement impact stops at the 'intention' stage or self-reported buying behaviour. Effects on actual purchasing behaviour or behavioural responses are seldom measured. On the other hand, there are the econometric studies that focus on the impact of advertising intensity (budgets, GRP, etc.) on sales. They are mostly based on real-life data in relation to existing advertising campaigns. This paper is exceptional and very relevant because it integrates the two approaches by exploring the effects of characteristics of real advertisements in real markets on buying behaviour.

Furthermore the moderating role of the age of the market is investigated. The basic proposition is that the effects of different advertising cues change when markets grow older. The theoretical framework in which the study is embedded is the role of the motivation and ability of consumers to process advertising messages. The study is based on a very detailed and rich database that enables the authors to carry out analyses at the hourly level, thereby having to control for monthly, daily and hourly patterns in advertising responses.

The study is very rich in that it offers links to various well known advertising theories and frameworks. The motivation and ability constructs upon which the hypotheses are built explicitly refer to the Elaboration Likelihood Model. One of the advertising content factors studied is 'appeal mode', i.e. whether the ads are argument-based or emotion-based. This offers links to the ever-growing body of research into the effectiveness of both categories of advertising characteristics and is also very relevant to practice, given the increasing use of emotional appeals in advertising. This study shows that emotional appeals are not the right creative solution in all circumstances.

Two other factors measured are 'prominence' and 'goal framing'. The extent to which an ad stresses selling arguments (prominence) and focuses either upon negative (problem-solving) or positive reasons to buy the product (goal framing) directly relates to the discussion of the role of the strength or level of persuasion cues in advertising and the importance of different types of buying motivations, such as the informational-transformational dimension and the FCB grid. The 'source expertise' factor refers to the role of expert endorsers in advertising. Expert endorsement is a frequently used advertising technique, and this factor provides a direct link to the importance of reference groups in consumer behaviour.

The article studies the impact of market age on the effectiveness of the creative factors measured. The authors convincingly show that the age of the market (i.e. the number of months that the product has been marketed in a certain area) is an important moderating factor. This taps into the idea of the product life cycle, and the fact that marketing strategies and tactics should be adapted to different stages in this cycle. Additionally, the authors find indications of changing advertising effectiveness as markets grow older and have been exposed to advertising campaigns longer, linking to the 'wear in, wear out' principle of advertising exposure. Although the study was carried out in one country (the US) only, the relevance of the basic proposition to international marketing (with 'new' and 'old' markets) can be easily envisaged.

The study is not just a theoretical exercise. It also offers the important basic conclusion that the 'ideal ad' changes as markets grow older, and it provides a number of relevant ideas that can be implemented in day-to-day advertising practice.

WHAT TO SAY WHEN: ADVERTISING APPEALS IN EVOLVING MARKETS

Rajesh K. Chandy, Gerard J. Tellis, Deborah J. MacInnis, and Pattana Thaivanich

The authors study how ad cues affect consumer behavior in new versus well-established markets. The authors use theoretical insights from consumer

---

Journal of Marketing Research, Vol. XXXVIII (November 2001), pp. 399–414.
Rajesh K. Chandy is Assistant Professor of Marketing, Carlson School of Management, University of Minnesota (e-mail: rchandy@csom.umn. edu). Gerard J. Tellis holds the Jerry and Nancy Neely Chair in American Enterprise (e-mail: tellis@usc.edu), and Deborah J. MacInnis is Professor of Marketing (e-mail: macinnis@mizar.usc.edu), Marshall School of Business, University of Southern California. Pattana Thaivanich is Senior Statistical Associate, Custom Research Incorporated, Minneapolis (e-mail: pthaivanich@customresearch.com). The authors appreciate the valuable comments of Ed Blair, Michael Houston, Debbie Roedder John, Partha Krishnamurthy, Joan Meyers-Levy, and participants at a research seminar at the University of Houston and the research assistance of Chris Pruszko and Nicholas Yoong. The authors are also grateful for the helpful feedback from the three anonymous *JMR* reviewers.

information processing to argue that the same ad cues can have different effects on consumer behavior, depending on whether the market is new or old. The authors then test these hypotheses in the context of a toll-free referral service, using a highly disaggregate econometric model of advertising response. The results indicate that argument-based appeals, expert sources, and negatively framed messages are particularly effective in new markets. Emotion-based appeals and positively framed messages are more effective in older markets than in new markets.

DOES ADVERTISING AFFECT BEHAVIOR? If so, which particular creative appeal or ad cue works best? Researchers have tried to answer these questions for several decades. Research to date can be broadly classified into two streams: laboratory studies of the effects of ad cues on cognitions, affect, or intentions and econometric studies of the effects of advertising intensity on purchase behavior. Table 1 lists a sample of articles in these streams.

Laboratory studies have covered a variety of advertising elements, including emotional cues (e.g., Holbrook and Batra 1987; Singh and Cole 1993), types of arguments (Etgar and Goodwin 1982), humor (Sternthal and Craig 1973), and music (e.g., MacInnis and Park 1991; Park and Young 1986). These studies emphasize experimental control and are almost exclusively lab-based (see MacInnis and Jaworski 1989; Meyers-Levy and Malaviya 1999). Dependent variables studied include attitude toward the ad, attitude toward the brand, memory, and purchase intentions (see Stewart and Furse 1986). An important finding

Table 1 Representative studies

	Independent variables	
Dependent variables	*Ad intensity*	*Ad cues*
Attitudes, Memory, Intentions	• Petty and Cacioppo (1979) • Craig, Sternthal, and Leavitt (1976) • Pechmann and Stewart (1988, review)	• Sternthal and Craig (1973) • Holbrook and Batra (1987) • Singh and Cole (1993) • Etgar and Goodwin (1982) • MacInnis and Park (1991) • Park and Young (1986) • Weinberger and Gulas (1992, review)
Behavior	• Raj (1982) • Krishnamurthi, Narayan, and Raj (1986) • Eastlack and Rao (1986, 1989) • Lodish et al. (1995a, b)	• **The present study**

from this research is that the effects of various executional cues often depend on consumers' motivation and/or ability to process ad information.

In contrast, econometric studies focus on the role of advertising intensity on consumer behavior. Typically, researchers measure advertising intensity as dollars; gross rating points; or, more recently, ad exposures. Researchers measure behavior as sales, market share, or consumer choice (for reviews, see Sethuraman and Tellis 1991; Tellis 1998; Vakratsas and Ambler 1999). These studies emphasize the precise modeling of the sales response to advertising and are largely field-based, often in specific empirical contexts such as toilet tissue, laundry detergent, vegetable juice, and other consumer packaged goods (Eastlack and Rao 1986, 1989; Krishnamurthi, Narayan, and Raj 1986; Lodish et al. 1995a, b; Raj 1982; Tellis 1988; Tellis and Weiss 1995). One finding from this research is that a change in the ad used has a stronger effect on sales response than changes in advertising intensity alone (Blair and Rosenburg 1994; Eastlack and Rao 1986; Lodish et al. 1995b; Lodish and Riskey 1997).

Although these two research streams have contributed greatly to the current understanding of advertising, each has focused on different variables and has operated largely in isolation of the other. For example, lab-based studies of consumer behavior focus on the effects of an ad's executional cues on attitudes, intentions, and memory (see Wells 1993; Winer 1999). They rarely examine how or whether these cues affect actual behavior. Many authors suspect that theories of the role of advertising on consumer attitudes and persuasion may also explain consumers' behavioral response to ads. However, other authors suggest that some commonly used measures of attitude and persuasion may not relate to behavior at all (Lodish et al. 1995b). Furthermore, despite extensive econometric modeling of advertising response, little is known about why some ads drive consumer behavior more than others and whether variation in behavioral response to ads relates to specific executional cues of those ads. Therefore, many researchers have called for an integration of these two research streams (e.g., Cook and Kover 1997; Stewart 1992; see also Wells 1993; Winer 1999).

This article addresses this call. It contributes to the literature in three ways. First, it attempts to develop deeper insight into the relationship between the executional cues of ads and consumers' behavioral response to those ads. On the basis of the behavioral literature, we develop a set of hypotheses on how these cues may affect behavior in actual markets. Second, we conduct our tests using data from real ads aired in real markets, a setting that enables us to explore the contextual boundaries of advertising theories. In particular, our data cover executional cues used in ads and actual response to those ads in real markets. The context, medical service, is also different from that typically used in prior research.

Third, we assess consumer response to ads across different levels of market age. *Market age* refers to the length of time a product or service has been available and advertised in a particular market. For a particular product or service, one market is said to be older than another if the product or service has been available and advertised longer in the first market than in the second. Thus, a young market is one where the product or service was introduced only recently;

an old market is one where the product or service has been available and advertised for a long time. We argue that different cues work differently in younger markets than in older ones because of intrinsic differences in consumers' motivation and ability to process information in those markets. Knowledge of these differences can help marketers design ads that are tailored to the age of individual markets.

The remainder of this article is organized as follows. The next two sections present the theory and hypotheses of the study. The following three sections describe the study's empirical context, method, and results. The last two sections discuss the implications and limitations of the research.

How Advertising Cues affect Behavior in Evolving Markets

Many advertising researchers have noted that the effects of advertising change as markets grow older. The empirical evidence suggests that ad elasticities decline significantly in older markets (Parsons 1975; Tellis and Fornell 1988). The focus of the research so far has been on the amount of advertising (in the form of exposures or expenditures); the results indicate that the same amount of advertising is less effective in older markets than in younger ones. But in the quest for higher effectiveness, the marketer has control over more than just the amount of advertising; the marketer also controls the type of ad creative or execution. We focus on the type of advertising execution and ask how different executional cues work at different stages of market evolution.

We organize the theoretical discussion of advertising effects in evolving markets around the theme of consumers' motivation and ability to process ads. In the next section, we first highlight the role of consumer motivation and ability. We then use these constructs to develop hypotheses about the role of various advertising cues in different stages of market evolution.

Consumer motivation and ability to process ads

Considerable research in consumer behavior suggests that consumers' motivation, ability, and opportunity to process information from ads affects their responses to those ads (see MacInnis and Jaworski 1989; Petty and Cacioppo 1986). *Motivation* is typically defined as the extent to which consumers are interested in information in an ad and willing to expend effort to process it, given its relevance to their personal goals. *Ability* relates to the extent of knowledge consumers have about the brand and its usage. *Opportunity* is typically defined as the extent to which situational factors facilitate ad processing. In our discussion of advertising effects, we focus on consumers' motivation and ability. We do not consider opportunity, because it often reflects idiosyncratic factors that vary both within a consumer and across situations.

Researchers often conceptualize motivation and ability as independent factors influencing consumers' responsiveness to marketing communications. However, MacInnis, Moorman, and Jaworski (1991) propose that motivation and ability may be related. For example, consumers who are highly knowledgeable about a product may have such well-developed knowledge structures and extensive product experience that they consider brand information from ads largely irrelevant. Therefore, highly knowledgeable consumers may also lack the motivation to process information from ads. In contrast, consumers who lack prior knowledge may be motivated to acquire knowledge as a way of reducing purchase risk. So one can imagine contexts in which an inverse relationship exists between motivation and ability to process information from ads.

Role of market age

Market age represents an important context in which this inverse relationship between motivation and ability to process ads may be evident. In young markets, consumers are likely to have little information about the product in prior memory. Indeed, because the market is young, few customers are likely to be aware either of the product or its differentiating attributes. Because prior knowledge is limited, consumers are likely to be more motivated to process information about the product from ads when the product and ad represent novel stimuli (Grunert 1996). Furthermore, because the effects of word of mouth are not yet established, consumers may be uncertain about product quality and features. Advertising is therefore a key source of product information. In young markets, consumers' lack of product knowledge, limited prior experience, and limited communication by word of mouth can make the choice of the product risky. This perceived risk, coupled with the inherent novelty of the product and the ad, enhances consumers' motivation to process information about the product. The notion that young markets may be characterized by high motivation and limited ability is consistent with classic models of buyer behavior (Howard 1977; Howard and Sheth 1969) that posit that when decision making is novel (as when markets are new) consumers exhibit considerable motivation to learn about novel product features and benefits about which they have no prior knowledge, and they spend time gathering information to acquire this knowledge. It is further consistent with classic conceptions of advertising decisions over the product life cycle, in which an emphasis is placed on reaching as many members of the target audience as possible to inform them of the existence and features of the product.

In contrast to younger markets, in markets where the product is old and well known, consumers may have had more opportunities to gather and store product knowledge through prior advertising exposures, personal experiences, and word of mouth. However, the very existence of this prior knowledge may reduce consumers' motivation to attend to and process key aspects of an ad. Classical models of buyer behavior are consistent with the notion that consumers may exhibit limited motivation and high ability in older markets. When markets are old, consumers have already acquired product and market information and have completed their decision making, which limits their motivation to evaluate new information. Their decision making may be routinized, characterized by limited information processing and habitual purchasing.

On the basis of this theoretical structure, we focus on how executional cues differentially affect consumer response to advertising in markets at different stages of evolution. Note that within a particular market, different consumers may respond very differently to the same ads (see Cacioppo and Petty 1982). However, this within-market variation is not the focus of this study. Our emphasis is on understanding variation in consumer behavior across markets of different age levels.

Myriad executional cues may interact with market age to affect consumer response. We strive for a balance between breadth in the choice of advertising cues and control over confounding factors (e.g., brand, product category). As such, we focus on a select set of cues that can be classified into four types: (1) appeal mode, (2) appeal prominence, (3) appeal frame, and (4) appeal source. In the context of appeal mode, we study the role of arguments and emotions. In the context of appeal prominence, we study the prominence of key product or service attributes. In the context of appeal frame, we study the role of positive and negative goal framing. In the context of appeal sources, we study the role of expert endorsers. The following discussion presents hypotheses on how the effects of each cue vary by market age.

Within each of these areas, we focus on specific variables that have both a strong theoretical background and adequate variation in our empirical context. For example, there is a large theoretical literature on ad length and on celebrity endorsers. However, we are unable to test the effects of ad length because our data contain only thirty second ads. Similarly, we are unable to test for celebrity endorsers because they are not used in our ads. Therefore, we do not include these variables in the theoretical discussion.

Hypotheses

Appeal mode: the role of argument and emotion

Scholars have long examined the role of arguments relative to emotions in driving behavior (Agres, Edell, and Dubitsky 1990; Cohen and Areni 1991; McGuire 1969; Petty and Wegener 1998). Early research in marketing focused on whether emotional ads are more effective than argument-based ads (Friestad and Thorson 1986; Golden and Johnson 1983; Ray and Batra 1983). This research shows conflicting findings; some authors argue that emotions are more effective (e.g., Edwards 1990; Edwards and von Hippel 1995; Friestad and Thorson 1986), and others argue that arguments are more effective (e.g., Golden and Johnson 1983; Millar and Millar 1990).

More recent research suggests that both emotions and arguments can be effective, but their effectiveness varies by context (see Olson and Zanna 1993; Petty and Wegener 1998; Stayman and Aaker 1988). Specifically, when consumers have little information about a product, they are more motivated to attend to and process arguments in the ads. Then, if ads are to be persuasive, they need to provide compelling arguments that reduce purchase risks and differentiate the product from competitors. Because consumers are motivated to process ads when prior knowledge is lacking, they should find ads more compelling when the ads provide a credible reason for buying the product. However, when consumers are already aware of the product and have preexisting attitudes toward it, they are less motivated to process information about it. Indeed, they may respond negatively to argument-focused ads because of satiation, boredom, or irritation (Batra and Ray 1986; Pechmann and Stewart 1988; Petty and Cacioppo 1979; Rethans, Swasy, and Marks 1986; Schumann, Petty, and Clemons 1990). In the context of market age, this theory suggests that argument-based ads would be more persuasive in younger markets than in older ones, because consumers would be more motivated to process their content.

The opposite effect may hold for emotion-based ads. Such ads rarely convey factual information about a product. Therefore, they may not reduce consumers' perceptions of risk. As such, they may have limited effects on consumers who have limited prior knowledge. Although emotions may convey warm feelings and stimulate favorable brand attitudes, attitudes formed by such processes may not lead to choices of products about which consumers are not well informed. The reason may be that such ads may neither provide a credible reason for buying the product nor change fundamental beliefs about it. Furthermore, when consumers lack product knowledge, emotional ads may distract consumers from critical product content (Moore and Hutchinson 1983). Thus, consumers are less likely to encode or transfer product information to long-term memory.

However, in older markets, where motivation is lacking but product knowledge is present, emotion-laden ads may win consumers' attention and help the retrieval of prior product knowledge from memory. Because such ads make the product more accessible, bringing it to the forefront of consumers' memory, they are likely to affect behavior. Furthermore, emotion-based ads may be more user oriented and therefore more capable of enabling high-knowledge consumers to imagine themselves interacting with the product. This usage-oriented imagery may stimulate consumers to elaborate on the benefits of personal usage, thus motivating behavior.

This logic suggests the following hypotheses:

H_1: Argument-based ads are more effective in younger markets than in older markets.

H_2: Emotion-based ads are more effective in older markets than in younger markets.

Note that we are not equating emotional ads with peripheral cues. Several models of persuasion (e.g., MacInnis and Jaworski 1989; Rossiter and Percy 1987; Vaughn 1980) presume no necessary relationship between ad content (emotional versus rational) and peripheral versus central route processing. Nor are we arguing that emotional and information ads represent two ends of a continuum. Rather, we are conceptualizing them as independent entities. Nor are we comparing emotional to rational arguments. Rather, we argue that ads that contain rational information will be more effective in younger markets than in older markets, whereas ads that contain emotional information will work better in older markets than in younger markets.

Appeal prominence

In young markets, consumers are unfamiliar with the product and its key attributes. Therefore, they are less efficient at assimilating key ad information into memory. Consumers in younger markets may therefore take longer to assimilate key message information than those in older markets. As such, anything that increases attention to and assimilation of message information should facilitate ad effectiveness. One variable that should influence attention and assimilation is appeal or attribute prominence. Attributes and appeals can be prominent by virtue of their size (e.g., a large font versus a small font), their duration on screen, or the number of times they are shown (Stewart and Furse 1986). Indeed, Gardner (1983) finds that consumers pay more attention to and process more deeply attributes that are more prominent than those that are less so. Furthermore, her results indicate that prominence increases consumers' ability to recall attributes. Attributes are also more likely to affect brand attitudes, particularly when consumers consider themselves knowledgeable about the category (Gardner 1983).

Stewart and Furse (1986) find positive relationships between brand prominence in ads and recall, persuasion, and comprehension, but only for products in the early stage of the product life cycle. These results are consistent with the notion that prominence may affect behavior more in younger than in older markets. In older markets, brief prompting may be adequate to access the relevant memory structures. As such, making key information salient by virtue of its prominence may be less critical in older than in younger markets. Thus,

> H_3: Ads in which key attributes are prominent are more effective in younger markets than in older markets.

Appeal frame

Kahneman and Tversky (1979) have stimulated a large literature on the effect of framing on consumer decisions. Although decisions can be framed in many different ways, advertising messages often involve the use of a specific type of frame: goal framing. In this case, advertisers can frame the uses of a product in a positive manner, highlighting the potential of the product to provide gains (or obtain benefits), or a negative manner, highlighting its potential to avoid loss (or solve problems) (see Levin, Schneider, and Gaeth 1998; Meyerowitz and Chaiken 1987). Literature on goals and goal framing is limited in consumer research, as is any research on the efficacy of this cue by market age (see Bagozzi and Dholakia 1999; Roney, Higgins, and Shah 1995). Therefore, our empirical efforts in this regard reflect a unique contribution of the research.

Since many products introduced to a market are initially developed to solve consumption problems, stating how a product or service can avoid or solve a problem (negative goal frame) is likely to be particularly effective in younger than in older markets because the message appeals to those consumers for whom the problem or its potential existence are already a reality. In this case, the problem is already at the top of a consumer's mind, and advertising provides necessary information about how that problem can be avoided or eliminated. Therefore, ads that contain information for avoiding or removing the problem will immediately motivate such consumers to process the message (see Maheswaran and Meyers-Levy 1990; for an exception, see Shiv, Edell, and Payne 1997) and use the service. As the market ages, however, knowledge of how a product or service resolves the problem diffuses through the population. Thus, the pool of those consumers who are motivated by such a message declines. Furthermore, consumers may be irritated by repetition of negatively framed messages (as would occur as markets age) that focus on problem avoidance, because these ads focus on things that are unpleasant to think about (Aaker and Bruzonne 1981). Therefore, negatively framed messages may be more successful in younger markets than in older ones.

In contrast, messages that state positive and appetitive goals may be more successful in older than in younger markets. As consumers become more aware of products' abilities to solve consumption problems, added motivation for product use may be provided by information about how the product fulfills appetitive and positive states. Thus, a cleaning product that focuses on the product's fresh scent may appeal to consumers in older markets who are already aware of and convinced about the product's core cleaning abilities. But when the market is young, such messages may fail to address consumers' concerns with the problem, the brand, or the category. As the market ages and these messages are repeated, consumers' motivation to process the ads declines, but their belief in ad claims that do not explicitly highlight solutions to problems may rise (Hawkins and Hoch 1992). In addition, positively framed messages may be more effective than negatively framed messages in older markets because they contain fewer aversive stimuli that could create wearout.

Given the limited work on goal framing, our hypotheses about its potential interaction with market age are tentative, but they suggest the following:

H_4: Negatively framed ads are more effective in younger markets than in older markets.

H_5: Positively framed ads are more effective in older markets than younger markets.

Appeal source: the role of expertise

Expert sources are characters in an ad whose knowledge or experience with the product category makes them highly knowledgeable about product attributes and their benefits for consumers. The impact of an expert source on behavioral responses at different ages of the market is somewhat difficult to understand. Prior laboratory studies suggest that when consumers' motivation and ability to process the advertised message are low, expert sources enhance the credibility of the ad and thus its persuasive impact. Given their low motivation and/or ability to process the message, consumers rely on source expertise as a peripheral cue. They infer that the brand or service must be good if it is endorsed by the expert (Petty and Cacioppo 1986; Petty, Cacioppo, and Goldman 1981; Ratneshwar and Chaiken 1991; Yalch and Yalch 1984). Other research suggests that expert sources can also be important when motivation and ability to deeply process a message are high. When consumers deeply process a message, they may interpret an expert source as an additional argument in favor of the service (Kahle and Homer 1985; Petty and Cacioppo 1986). This research suggests that an expert is always more valuable than a nonexpert.

However, we expect that source expertise is likely to have a larger impact in younger markets than in older markets. In younger markets, where category and brand knowledge is limited, consumers are likely to rely on the opinions of others. The expert in the ad provides an important source of such information. Prior research suggests that consumers' susceptibility to informational influence is high when the source is regarded as an expert and the consumer lacks expertise (French and Raven 1959; Hovland and Weiss 1951; Park and Lessig 1977) – as would be the case when markets are younger. Furthermore, because consumers in younger markets may be more motivated to process the advertised message, these motivated recipients are likely to scrutinize the entire ad deeply before arriving at a judgment. Expert sources can enhance persuasion for consumers who process a message deeply, because they serve as strong arguments that enhance the persuasion of a deeply processed ad (Homer and Kahle 1990). This logic suggests the following:

H_6: Expert endorsers are more effective in younger markets than in older ones.

Role of market age

All else being equal, do ads become more or less effective as markets age? This section explores the main effects of market age. Two countervailing forces influence the effects of market age: increased consumer reach and product familiarity on the one hand and increased consumer tedium and tapping out on the other.

In young markets, only a fraction of the potential consumer pool is likely to be aware of the product. Furthermore, tedium may not yet have occurred, because consumers may not yet be fully familiar with the product. Thus, ads are likely to increase in effectiveness when the product is first introduced in the market. Subsequent airing of ads, though, leads to fewer consumers who have not yet learned about the product, while increasing the probability of tedium with the product. Therefore, additional advertising about the product becomes less and less effective. Therefore, we propose the following:

H_7: The relationship between market age and ad effectiveness follows an inverted U shape.

The next two sections present the context of the study and the models we use to test these hypotheses.

Research Context

There are at least two approaches to study the effects of ad cues in evolving markets. One approach would be to collect market data from various ads for many brands across categories and code the ads for their executional cues. Such an approach would maximize the number of potential cues. However, it would introduce potential confounds due to variations in brands, marketing mix, and category, whose effects cannot be easily measured or controlled. Another approach would be to examine a set of ads for a single brand over a long period of its history. This approach would eliminate confounds due to brand and category. However, it would limit the number of potential cues. Moreover, it would introduce history as a confound, because the effectiveness of various cues could be due to changes in ads used over time.

Our unique database attempts to maximize the benefits of both approaches while minimizing their negative aspects. The database contains a set of ads that have been used repeatedly, in the absence of marketing variables, to promote one service in several markets at different known stages of market age, in one historical time period. We first explain the service and then elaborate how the unique database enables a strong test of our hypotheses.

The data record consumers' response to ads for a toll-free referral service for a medical service. Consumers watch the ads for the medical service on television and call the toll-free number highlighted in the ads. A service advisor who responds to the calls first queries callers on their needs and preferences. The service advisor then searches through a database of service providers and connects the customer directly with the office of the service provider with the closest match. We use the term 'referral' to define this connection of a consumer to a service provider. The referral is the key variable of interest to the firm. It is the basis for its revenues and profits. The firm also assesses its performance on the basis of referrals. As such, referral is the key dependent variable in this research.

This context controls for many potential confounds. Television advertising is the primary means of marketing, though the firm also advertises a little in radio, billboards, and yellow pages in a few cities. Thus, television advertising is the main trigger for referrals for the firm. Pricing is irrelevant because the referral service is free to consumers. Service providers who sign up for membership in the firm's database pay the firm a fixed monthly amount for a guaranteed minimum number of referrals. Distribution does not affect response, because referrals are made completely over the telephone. Product type does not affect response, because there is only one type of service. Sales promotions do not affect response, because the firm does not use sales promotions. Effects due to the competitive environment are limited, as the firm has virtually no direct competition in the cities in which it operates.

The firm began operations on the West Coast in 1986 and now operates in sixty two markets throughout the United States. A *market* is a well-defined metropolitan area in which the firm solicits clients, advertises to consumers, and processes consumers' responses into referrals to those clients. Our data involve twenty three of these markets (see Table 2). They vary considerably in age, from eight months in Honolulu to 144 months in Los Angeles. Variation in market age at a single point in historical time controls for the effects of history. During the period covered in this research, the firm did not systematically vary the executional cues used in old versus new markets. Therefore, the executional cues used in each market are not confounded with market age.

The firm draws on a library of seventy two different television ads developed over the years. Each ad involves a unique configuration of ad executional cues that we call a 'creative.' Thus, we use the term 'ad' generically and the term 'creative' to refer to a particular ad with unique content. During the period covered in this research, the firm used thirty nine creatives across the twenty three markets. The existence of thirty nine creatives provides sufficient opportunity to find variation on many executional cues, though the set in no way represents the myriad executional cues discussed in the literature. The continued use of the same ads in markets of different ages enables us to determine how

Table 2 Descriptive statistics

Market	Age (Months)	Number of creatives used	Creative coefficients (β_c)	
			Minimum	*Maximum*
Chicago	86	27	−0.010	0.025
Cincinnati	16	19	−0.037	0.048
Cleveland	10	13	−0.024	0.077
Columbus	16	19	−0.008	0.099
Dallas	77	28	−0.014	0.044
Denver	82	30	−0.021	0.033
Detroit	83	28	−0.019	0.034
Fresno	115	26	−0.012	0.063
Honolulu	8	12	−0.024	0.044
Houston	77	30	−0.027	0.049
Kansas City	35	26	−0.033	0.033
Los Angeles	144	28	−0.018	0.013
Miami	81	28	−0.028	0.035
Milwaukee	78	27	−0.031	0.029
Minneapolis-St Paul	16	28	−0.023	0.033
Phoenix	89	32	−0.026	0.023
Portland	81	27	−0.016	0.060
Sacramento	120	27	−0.012	0.028
St. Louis	20	25	−0.043	0.048
San Diego	141	29	−0.015	0.032
San Francisco	143	27	−0.004	0.019
Seattle	86	27	−0.021	0.013
Washington, DC	17	19	−0.015	0.033

market age moderates the effect of the cues. Thus, the study provides a relatively clean test of the hypotheses.

In a recent article, Tellis, Chandy, and Thaivanich (2000) use a small data set from this context to decompose the instantaneous and carryover effect of advertising due to television station, time, and ad repetition. That study focuses on ad scheduling issues, covers only five markets, and considers neither the executional cues of the ads nor the role of market age. In contrast, the current study covers twenty three markets, codes the ads for their executional cues, and uses market age as a moderator.

Coding of Ad Cues

Constructs and operationalization

Table 3 presents the instrument we designed to operationalize each cue. Here, we define each cue and explain its coding.

Appeal mode. Argument-based ads are those that highlight at least one factual benefit, and emotional ads are those that highlight at least one emotional benefit. The greater the number of factual claims made about the service, the more the ad is argument focused. The greater the number of references to emotional benefits or circumstances surrounding use of the service, the more the ad is emotionally focused.

For factual claims, coders were instructed to count the number of times the ad mentioned such factual information as consumers' ability to obtain information (1) that is reliable, trustworthy, and unbiased; (2) that is free of charge; (3) that is thorough, specific, and complete; (4) that has been used by others; (5) that can be accessed in a convenient way; and (6) that they cannot get elsewhere. The firm chose to highlight these arguments because it believed such arguments drive consumer preferences.

For emotional claims, coders were instructed to count the number of times the ad mentioned such emotional benefits or motivators as the service's understanding of (1) consumers' fears, (2) consumers' desire to avoid pain, (3) the discomfort consumers feel in asking for credentials, (4) consumers' desire to have confidence in the service provider, and (5) the feelings consumers will have after they use the service.

Coders were also asked to rate the ad for the type of argument. Superficially, they were asked to rate (0 = 'not present,' 1 = 'present') whether the ad used a refutational appeal, comparative appeal, or unique positioning. An ad is coded as using *a refutational appeal* if it presents a premise or belief and then tries to destroy it with contrary evidence or arguments. The ad uses a *comparative appeal* if it compares the service with another service. The ad uses a *unique positioning* if it attempts to change the criteria of evaluation so consumers would then assess the service more favorably than they did before they saw the ad.

Similarly, the raters rated the ad for the specific emotional appeals it contained. The raters looked for the following specific appeals, which they rated either as present (=1) or not present (=0): love, pride, guilt, and fear. Note that

Table 3 Executional cue variables: their meaning and intercoder reliabilities

	Appeal mode
Emotion Intercoder agreement = 0.80	Count the number of emotional benefits mentioned They understand me: • my fears about this medical service. • my desire to avoid pain (I've got to have pain relief). • my discomfort in asking service provider for credentials. • my desire to have confidence in my service provider. • my desire to find a provider who cares about me (caring, takes time with me, attentive). After using the service I will feel better (e.g., less guilt, happier, healthier, like a better parent).
Argument Intercoder agreement = 0.64	Count the number of factual benefits mentioned I can get information: • that is reliable, trustworthy, and unbiased (list contains referrals from other providers and patients). • for free. • that is thorough, specific, and complete (list contains information on licensing, standing with medical board, education, specialties/special services, who performs new services, insurance provider, financing plans, personal characteristics, length of time as a service provider, hours, pain prevention techniques, days of the week open, location in relation to my work or home). • that has also been used by others (the service refers thousands of people per month to providers). • in a convenient way. • that you can't get elsewhere.
Emotion type	
Love Intercoder agreement = 0.90	The ad shows warmth, care, love: for a dear one. (0 = 'no,' 1 = 'yes')
Pride Intercoder agreement = 0.88	The ad shows pride: in being responsible, of having beautiful features, beautiful children. (0 = 'no,' 1 = 'yes')
Guilt Intercoder agreement = 0.84	The ad suggests guilt: of not being good, caring, dutiful, etc. (0 = 'no,' 1 = 'yes')
Fear Intercoder agreement = 0.89	The ad suggests fear: of consequences of not using service. (0 = 'no,' 1 = 'yes')

Table 3 *continued*

	Appeal mode
Argument type	
Refute	The ad presents any contrary feeling or belief and then tries to assuage or destroy it.
Intercoder agreement = 0.82	(0 = 'no,' 1 = 'yes')
Compare	The ad compares the service to another service.
Intercoder agreement = 0.85	(0 = 'no,' 1 = 'yes')
Unique positioning	The ad restates attributes so as to reposition an existing belief or option.
Intercoder agreement = 0.61	(0 = 'no,' 1 = 'yes')
	Attribute Prominence
800 Visible	Total duration for which 800 number is visible (in seconds) in all appearances.
Intercoder agreement = 0.77	
	Appeal Frame
Negative goal frame	The ad shows how use of the service can avoid or prevent a potential problem, remove or solve an existing problem.
Intercoder agreement = 0.67	(0 = 'no,' 1 = 'yes')
Positive goal frame	The ad shows how using the service enables the consumer to be a better parent, care for others, look more beautiful, gain approval.
Intercoder agreement = 0.55	(0 = 'no,' 1 = 'yes')
	Appeal Source
Service provider	Endorser is a medical service provider.
Intercoder agreement = 0.98	(0 = 'no,' 1 = 'yes')
Service advisor	Endorser is a service advisor.
Intercoder agreement = 0.93	(0 = 'no,' 1 = 'yes')

the appeals are not mutually exclusive; a single ad can include more than one of the appeal types.

Appeal prominence. Appeal prominence is measured here as the length of time, in seconds, the 800 number is visible during an ad exposure. This issue is important, because in our context, the key message text is the 800 number consumers call to request a referral.

Appeal frame. Some ads show how the use of the service could avoid or prevent a potential problem or remove or solve an existing problem. In this case, consumers are shown a problem, and the ad suggests how this problem could be prevented, minimized, or eradicated. Consistent with Maheswaran and Meyers-Levy's (1990) focus on message framing and goals, we call this a negative goal frame because the message focuses on the goal of avoiding or eliminating a negative state (see also Shiv, Edell, and Payne 1997). Other ads show how the service enables the consumer to take a current (and potentially positive) situation and make it even better. For example, some ads suggest that consumers would be better parents, others suggest that they would look better, and still others suggest that the use of the service would evoke social approval. We call this a positive goal frame because the message focuses on the goal of achieving a positive state. Others in the literature (e.g., Rossiter and Percy 1987) refer to this framing of messages in terms of informational (problem solving) versus transformational motives. Coders were instructed to evaluate whether each ad used negative goal framing (0, 1) and/or the extent to which it used positive goal framing (1, 0). Theoretically, these are conceptualized as independent forms of goal framing, because a given ad could focus on one, the other, or both goals.

Appeal source. Service providers and service advisors are two types of experts used in our sample of ads. A *service provider* is a medical service professional who provides the actual medical service. The service provider offers expertise by virtue of his or her ability to perform needed medical services and knowledge of the medical service domain. A *service advisor* is an operator who helps customers identify and access a suitable service provider. The service advisor offers expertise by facilitating a match between the patient and the service provider. Coders were asked to rate whether the ad contained a service provider (0 = 'not present,' 1 = 'present') and whether it contained a service advisor (0 = 'not present,' 1 = 'present').

Coding procedure

Two paid coders familiarized themselves with the bank of seventy two creatives and were trained in coding the content and executional cues of each ad. The coders were first provided with a written description of each cue and then were involved in a more detailed discussion of the meaning of each. Discussion between the authors and the coders ensured that coders understood the meaning of each cue. The two coders then independently watched a set of three ads and coded each. Two authors also viewed and coded these same ads independently. The authors then discussed these ratings of the ads with the coders and refined the instrument. The coders subsequently coded a set of three additional creatives and compared their responses. We discussed disagreements between coders to clarify the meaning of the cues and the ratings of the creatives. After this meeting, the coders independently coded the remaining commercials. We calculated intercoder reliabilities at the levels of the ad and the executional cue. Disagreements between the coders were resolved by discussion.

Two of the seventy two ads have intercoder agreement levels above 90 percent; thirty have intercoder agreement levels between 80 percent and 89 percent; thirty three have intercoder agreement levels between 70 percent and 79 percent; six have intercoder agreement levels between 60 percent and 69 percent. One ad has an intercoder agreement level of 52 percent. The average intercoder agreement across ads is 76 percent.

Intercoder agreements for executional cue variables are shown in Table 3. For the variables that did not involve counts, the intercoder agreement level ranges from a high of 98 percent to a low of 55 percent, with an average of 81 percent. For the variables that involve frequencies and counts (Emotion, Argument, and 800 Visible), the two raters are within one count from each other in 80 percent, 64 percent, and 77 percent of the cases, respectively; the data in Table 3 reflect these figures (for a similar method of assessing intercoder agreement, see Price and Arnould 1999). Lower intercoder reliabilities for goal framing may be attributable to the fact that evaluations of the ad's use of positive or negative goal framing require that coders focus on global aspects of the ad (the ad's theme or focus) as opposed to the more micro-level responses contained in some of the other coding categories. As expected, argument focus and emotional focus appear to be relatively independent, because they are not highly correlated ($r = 0.24$). As expected, positive and negative goal framing also are not highly correlated ($r = -0.12$).

Model Specification

We conduct our analysis at the hourly level, for two reasons. First, this level of analysis enables us to isolate the effects of the ad creative from other variables such as time of the day and the television station on which the ad was aired. Second, research has shown that aggregating temporal data to higher time intervals can upwardly bias the estimated effects of advertising (Clarke 1976; Leone 1995). Analysis at the hourly level is most appropriate, because ads are aired within the hour and consumers are most likely to respond immediately (Tellis, Chandy, and Thaivanich 2000).

To test our hypotheses, we follow a two-step procedure. We first model consumer behavior as a function of advertising. For the sake of consistency, we use the same modeling approach in this step as Tellis, Chandy, and Thaivanich (2000) use. As in their research, our database includes detailed information, at the hourly level, on the ads aired by the referral service, the specific ad creative used, and the specific station used in each market, as well as the number of exposures of each ad, per hour, per television station. We measure behaviour by referrals received and advertising by exposures to a specific ad in an hour in one medium. We use referrals as our dependent variable because this is the variable of interest to the firm's management. All analyses at this stage take place within a market, for each of the twenty three markets. The model provides estimates of the response of each market to each ad.

In the second stage, we model the variation in the ad response coefficients (obtained from the first stage) as a function of ad cues and market age. We describe these stages in detail next. In principle, we can combine the two stages of our model and estimate a single reduced form. However, because of the complexity of our model and the large number of independent variables, such estimation is difficult to execute and interpret (Greene 1997). Therefore, we estimate the equations in each stage separately as explained next.

Stage I: Estimating response to advertising

To allow the advertising response curve to take on a variety of shapes beyond the exponential form, we follow Tellis, Chandy, and Thaivanich (2000) and use a general distributed lag model of the form

$$(1) \qquad R_t = \alpha + \gamma_1 R_{t-1} + \gamma_2 R_{t-2} + \gamma_3 R_{t-3} + \ldots + \beta_0 A_t + \beta_1 A_{t-1} + \beta_2 A_{t-2} + \ldots + \varepsilon_t,$$

where

t = an index for time period,
R = referrals per hour,
α, β, γ = coefficients to be estimated,
A = ads per hour, and
ε = errors.

In this formulation, the number and position of lagged values of advertising affect the duration of the decay. The number and position of lagged values of advertising also affect the shape of the decay (e.g., the presence and shape of humps in the decay).

Advertising at different times of day can have different decay structures. Responses to morning ads may emerge a few hours later than ads at other times, because consumers are frequently rushed in the morning and may therefore take longer to respond to morning ads. To test for this difference, the basic model in Equation 1 also includes a variable for morning advertising and its corresponding decay. Furthermore, to properly isolate the effects of ad creatives from those due to other factors, we include several control variables (described subsequently) in Equation 1.

Control variables. The referral service is closed at night and during part of the weekend. Therefore, we control for the hours when the service is open. Furthermore, we interact hours open with every other explanatory variable in the model, because no other variable can affect calls for referrals unless the service is open. Properly including that variable in the model can account fully for the truncation bias and eliminate the need for more complex models (Amemiya 1985; Judge et al. 1985).

Tellis, Chandy, and Thaivanich (2000) show that medical calls follow typical daily patterns. Calls peak around midday, when consumers have more spare time to make the calls. Calls tend to be lower in the early morning and late evening as consumers attend to other compelling activities. For this reason, we include dummy variables for each hour of the day when the service is open, from 8 a.m. to 9 p.m. Eastern Time. We drop 12 p.m. to serve as the reference level. Calls are higher after a holiday, especially at the beginning of the week, either because of pent-up demand when the service is closed or because consumers are more sensitive to pain when fun ends and work begins. Calls for medical service drop toward the end of the week, perhaps because consumers put off medical help to prepare for or enjoy the weekend. We therefore include dummy variables for each day of the week, excluding Sunday (when the service is closed) and Saturday (the reference level).

On the basis of this discussion, we test the following general model separately in each of the twenty three markets for which we have data. Matrices representing sets of related variables measured by hour are denoted in boldface text.

$$R = \alpha + (\mathbf{R}_{-1}\lambda + \mathbf{A}\beta_A + \mathbf{A}_M\beta_M + \mathbf{S}\beta_S + \mathbf{SH}\beta_{SH} + \mathbf{HD}\beta_{HD} + \mathbf{C}\beta_c +)O + \varepsilon_t, \quad (2)$$

where

- R = a vector of referrals by hour;
- $\mathbf{R}_{-1}$ = a matrix of lagged referrals by hour;
- $\mathbf{A}$ = a matrix of current and lagged ads by hour;
- $\mathbf{A}_M$ = a matrix of current and lagged morning ads by hour;
- $\mathbf{S}$ = a matrix of current and lagged ads on each television station by hour;
- $\mathbf{H}$ = a matrix of dummy variables for time of day by hour;
- $\mathbf{D}$ = a matrix of dummy variables for day of week by hour;
- O = a vector of dummies recording whether the service is open by hour;
- $\mathbf{C}$ = a matrix of dummy variables indicating whether a creative is used in each hour;[1]
- α = constant term to be estimated;
- λ = a vector of coefficients to be estimated for lagged referrals;
- β_i = vectors of coefficients to be estimated; and
- ε_t = a vector of error terms, initially assumed to be i.i.d. normal.

A, the matrix of exposures of a particular ad per hour, and **C**, the matrix of creatives, contain many zeros, because many hours of the day have no advertising. Thus, at the disaggregate hourly level, these variables have limited distribution, almost becoming zero/one variables. With the exception of current and lagged values of referrals, all the other variables are dummies. This characteristic of the independent variables greatly limits the possibility of and need for alternative functional forms (Hanssens, Parsons, and Schultz 1990). In addition, given the large number of independent variables and the inclusion of many of the exogenous influences on the dependent variables, we initially assume that the error terms follow a normal distribution identically and independently. As such, we estimate the model with ordinary least squares. (An empirical test of the model reveals no major deviations from the classical assumptions.)

In this study, our primary interest is in the coefficients (β_c) of the creatives (c) in each market. Note that we include the creatives as dummy variables, indicating whether a creative is used in a particular market for which we estimate Equation 2. We choose to drop the creatives that have an average effectiveness and to include only those that are significantly above or below the average. Thus, the coefficient of a creative in Equation 2 represents the increase or decrease in expected referrals due to that creative relative to the average of creatives in that particular market. This specification has the most practical relevance. Managers are not interested much in a global optimization of the best mix of creatives. Rather, they are interested in making improvements over their strategy in the previous year. For this reason, they seek analyses that highlight the best creatives (to use more often) or the worst creatives (to drop).

Stage 2: Explaining effectiveness across ads

In this stage, we collect the coefficients (β_c) for each creative for each market (m) in which it is used, and explain their variation as a function of creative characteristics and the age of the market in which it ran. H_1–H_7 suggest the following model:

$$
\begin{aligned}
(3)\quad \beta_{c,m} = {} & \varphi_1 \text{Argument}_c + \varphi_2(\text{Argument}_c \times \text{Age}_m) + \varphi_3 \text{Emotion}_c \\
& + \varphi_4(\text{Emotion}_c \times \text{Age}_m) + \varphi_5 800\ \text{Visible}_c \\
& + \varphi_6(800\ \text{Visible}_c \times \text{Age}_m) + \varphi_7 \text{Negative}_c \\
& + \varphi_8(\text{Negative}_c \times \text{Age}_m) + \varphi_9 \text{Positive}_c \\
& + \varphi_{10}(\text{Positive}_c \times \text{Age}_m) + \varphi_{11} \text{Expert}_c \\
& + \varphi_{12}(\text{Expert}_c \times \text{Age}_m) + \varphi_{13} \text{Nonexpert}_c \\
& + \varphi_{14}(\text{Nonexpert}_c \times \text{Age}_m) + \varphi_{15} \text{Age}_m \\
& + \varphi_{16}(\text{Age}_m)^2 + \mathbf{\Gamma}\ \mathbf{Market} + \text{v}
\end{aligned}
$$

where

$\beta_{c,m}$ = coefficients of creative c in market m from Equation 2,
c = index for creative,
Age = market age (number of weeks since the inception of service in the market),
Market = matrix of market dummies,
$\mathbf{\Gamma}$ = vector of market coefficients,
v = vector of errors,

and other variables are as defined in Table 3 or in Equation 2.

Because we do not have a priori hypotheses for different markets, we insert the Market dummies in a stepwise manner, such that only statistically significant dummies are included in the final regression equation.

Results

Our results for the equations estimated in Stage 1 are generally consistent with the results reported by Tellis, Chandy, and Thaivanich (2000). For this reason, and because the hypotheses of interest relate to Equation 3, we focus here on the results of estimating Equation 3. Table 2 provides descriptive statistics on the creative coefficients, β_c, for each market m. These coefficients reflect the expected referrals from the most and least effective creatives in each market relative to the average creatives in that market.

Table 4 provides descriptive statistics for each independent variable of interest. Table 5 provides pooled regression coefficients for Equation 3. The model is statistically significant ($F = 20.52$, $p > 0.0001$) and explains a substantial variation in the dependent variable, referrals ($R^2 = 42.25\%$). We describe the results for each hypothesis subsequently. All reported coefficients reflect standardized values. Because all our hypotheses on ad cues relate to their interactions with market age, we focus only on these interaction effects.

Appeal mode: argument- and emotion-focused ads

H_1 suggests that argument-based ads are likely to be more effective in younger markets than in older markets. The results in Table 5 support this hypothesis.

Table 4 Descriptive statistics

Variable	*Mean*	*Standard deviation*	*Minimum*	*Maximum*
		Appeal mode		
Emotion	.3	0.48	0	2
Argument	1.77	1.79	0	8
Emotion type				
Love	0.12	0.32	0	1
Pride	0.07	0.26	0	1
Guilt	0.17	0.38	0	1
Fear	0.09	0.29	0	1
Argument type				
Refute	0.04	0.19	0	1
Compare	0.12	0.32	0	1
Frame	0.23	0.42	0	1
		Attribute prominence		
800 Visible	6.46	1.8	4	11
		Goal frame		
Negative	0.66	0.47	0	1
Positive	0.34	0.47	0	1
		Appeal source		
Service provider	0.09	0.29	0	1
Service advisor	0.22	0.41	0	1

Table 5 Regression results

Variable	*Standardized coefficient*
Argument	0.25***
Argument × Age	−0.17**
Emotion	−0.17**
Emotion × Age	0.18**
800 Visible	0.26***
800 Visible × Age	−0.21*
Negative	0.25***
Negative × Age	−0.15**
Positive	−0.33***
Positive × Age	0.14*
Service Provider	−0.05
Service Provider × Age	0.00
Service Advisor	0.43***
Service Advisor × Age	−0.18**
Age	0.55**
$(\text{Age})^2$	−0.26**
Columbus (market dummy)	0.26***
Fresno (market dummy)	0.14***
Phoenix (market dummy)	−0.11***
Seattle (market dummy)	−0.10**
R^2	42.25%

* $p < 0.10$. ** $p < 0.05$. *** $p < 0.001$.

The Argument × Age interaction is negative and significant ($\varphi_2 = -0.17$, $p < 0.05$). Thus, argument-based ads become less effective as markets get older.

H_2 argues that emotion-based ads are more effective in older markets than in younger markets. The results in Table 5 also support this hypothesis. The interaction between Emotion and Age is positive and significant ($\varphi_4 = 0.18$, $p < 0.05$). Thus, emotion-based ads become more effective as markets get older.

Figure 1 shows mean referrals for appeal mode by market age. It pictorially highlights the effects of emotion-based versus argument-based appeals in young versus old markets. The y-axis in the graph refers to the β_c values, obtained from Equation 2 and described previously. We dichotomize Age, Emotion, and Argument in Figure 1 using median splits. An overall analysis of variance (ANOVA) indicates a significant interaction between the type of appeal and market age ($F = 6.10$, $p < 0.001$), which also supports H_1 and H_2.

To provide deeper insight into these effects, we identify specific types of argument- and emotion-based appeals (see also Frijda 1986; Russell 1978). As noted previously, the emotional appeals used include love, pride, guilt, and fear. The argument types include refutation, comparison, and unique positioning.

Figure 2 shows mean referrals for different emotional appeals in young versus old markets. Although ANOVAs comparing means across the different cells indicate that the interaction effects are not statistically significant, the effects are in the expected direction. Figure 3 describes the mean referrals for

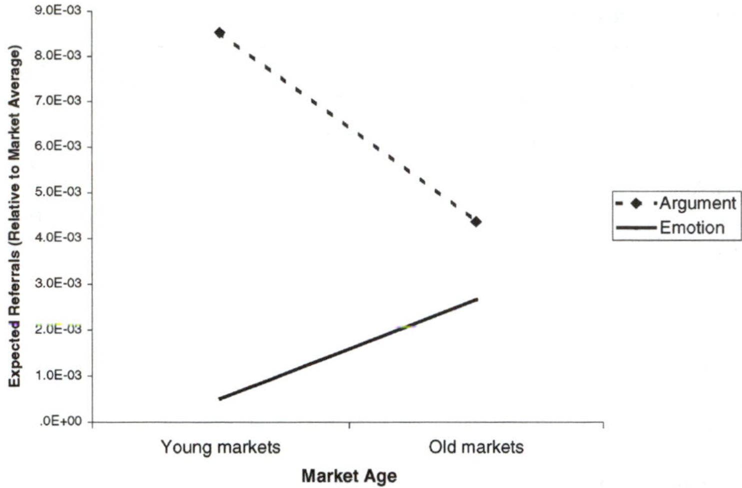

Figure 1 Effects of argument versus emotion by market age

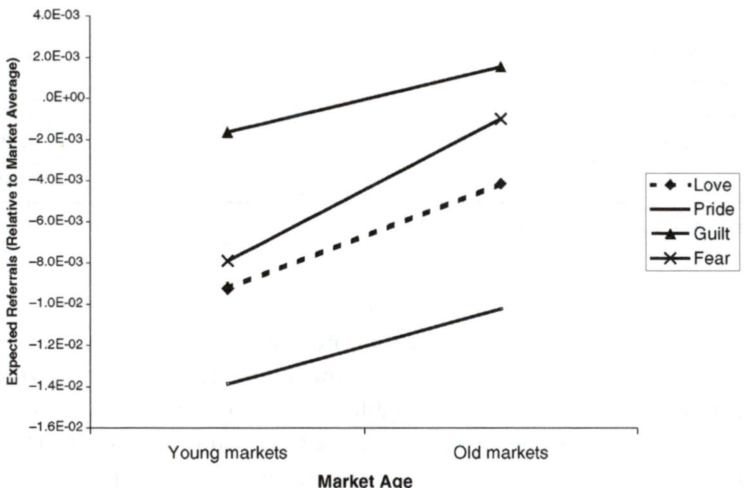

Figure 2 Effects of emotion type by market age

different argument types. An ANOVA comparing differences in means indicates that the interaction of Compare × Market Age in Figure 3 is significant and in the expected direction ($F = 20.84$, $p < 0.001$). However, the interactions of Refute × Position are not statistically significant, though the interaction of Refute × Market Age is in the expected direction.

Appeal prominence

H_3 suggests that ads in which key message text is prominent (here operationalized as being visible on screen for longer periods of time) are more effective in younger than in older markets. The coefficient of the interaction of 800 Visible

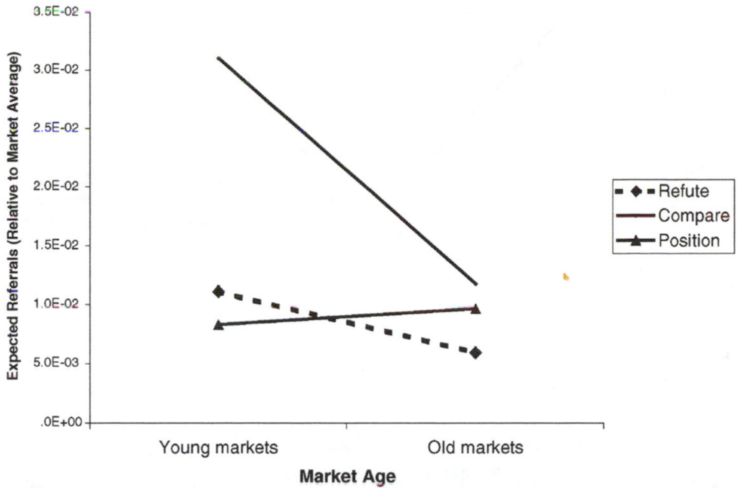

Figure 3 Effects of argument type by market age

× Age in Table 5 is negative and significantly different from zero at the 90% level of significance ($\varphi_6 = -0.21$, $p < 0.10$). The results in Table 5 thus provide some support for H_3.

Figure 4 provides a pictorial description of the effects of the duration of message text in young versus old markets. To create Figure 4, we dichotomize both the 800 Visible variable and the Age variable using a median split. The figure shows that ads in which the key message text is visible for longer than the median number of seconds are much more effective in young markets than in older markets. An overall ANOVA of the dichotomous variables indicates a significant interaction between the duration of message text and market age ($F = 6.22$, $p < 0.001$). Furthermore, the difference in means in older markets between ads with short message text duration and those with longer message text duration is significant at the $p < 0.10$ level ($F = 3.30$, $p < 0.074$).

Appeal frame

H_4 argues that negatively framed ads will be more effective in younger markets than in older markets, and H_5 suggests that positively framed ads will be more effective in older markets than in younger markets. The results in Table 5 support these hypotheses. The Negative × Age interaction is negative and significant ($\varphi_8 = -0.15$, $p < 0.05$). The Positive × Age interaction is positive and significant at the 90% significance level ($\varphi_{10} = -0.14$, $p = 0.10$).

Figure 5 describes the mean referrals for negatively and positively framed ads in young versus old markets. The figure reinforces the regression findings and suggests that negatively framed ads are more effective in young markets than in old markets, whereas positively framed messages tend to be more successful in older than in younger markets. An overall ANOVA indicates a significant interaction between appeal frame and market age ($F = 22.81$, $p < 0.001$).

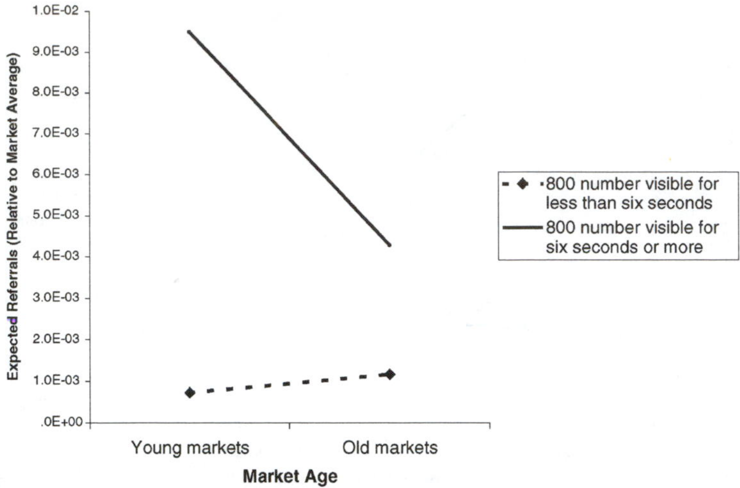

Figure 4 Effects of attribute prominence by market age

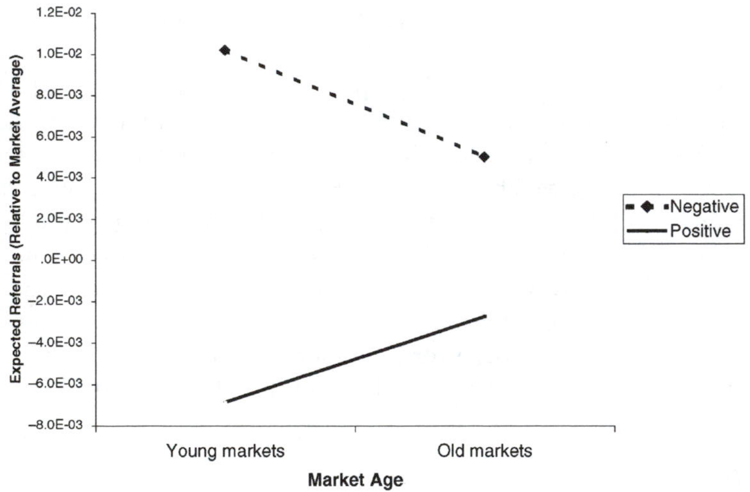

Figure 5 Effects of negative versus positive goal frames by market age

Appeal source

H_6 suggests that expert endorsers are more effective in younger markets than in older markets. In our context, there are two types of expert endorsers: service providers and service advisors. The interaction of Service Provider × Age is not significantly different from zero ($\varphi_{12} = 0.00$, $p > 0.99$). The interaction of Service Advisor × Age, however, is significant and in the expected direction ($\varphi_{14} = -0.18$, $p < 0.05$). H_6 is thus partially supported, indicating that endorsement by a service advisor is more effective in younger markets than in older markets.

Market age

H_7 argues that as a market gets older, opposing forces influence ads' effectiveness. Consumer response would likely increase initially because of increased market reach and growing brand awareness but decrease later because of tedium effects and potential reactance. Therefore, we hypothesized an inverted U-shaped response to the effects of market age. The results in Table 5 support this hypothesis. The Age coefficient is positive and significant ($\varphi_{15} = 0.55$, $p < 0.05$), and the squared Age coefficient is negative and significant ($\varphi_{16} = -0.26$, $p < 0.05$).

Figure 6 represents the effects of Age in graphical form. The model predicts that the diminishing returns to Age arise during the thirteenth year of operation. Note that this inverted-U response does not correspond directly to traditional wearout curves, because those curves generally track the effects due to repeated exposure to the same ads. Figure 6, however, tracks market age, which corresponds to repeated exposure to the service, using a variety of different ads and after controlling for the effects of ad repetition. Therefore, it is not surprising to see the inflection point appear later than is usual in traditional tests of wearout.

Discussion

Summary and contributions

Econometric literature on the real-world effects of advertising is extensive. However, rarely does this work rely on the vast information-processing domain or consider how an ad's creative content affects consumers' behavioral response. Analogously, there is a rich literature on how various executional cues of ads affect consumers' responses at different levels of motivation, ability, and

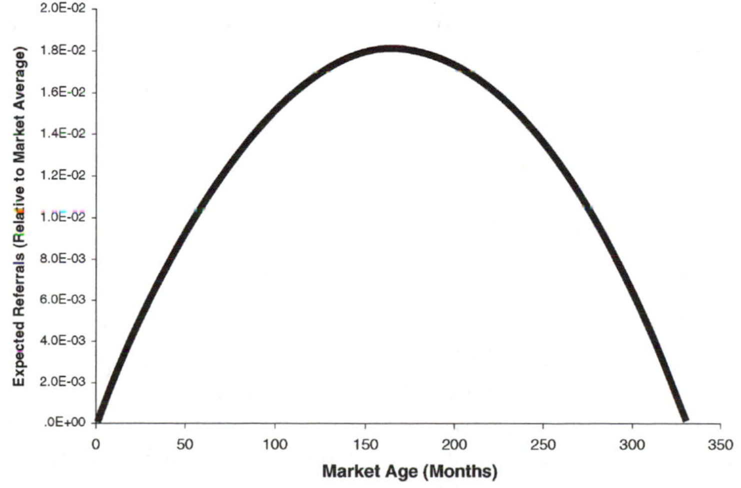

Figure 6 Predicted effect of market age on referrals

opportunity. However, rarely does this work examine the real-world, behavioral impact of ads. The present study is an attempt at bridging these two areas.

Building on work on motivation and ability to process information from ads, we argue that the behavioral impact of various executional cues depends on whether the market is young or old. Marketing researchers who study advertising elasticities have noted that an ad budget that is just right for one stage of product evolution may be inappropriate for another stage (one size does not fit all stages, so to speak; Tellis and Fornell 1988). Our research highlights the point that an ad cue that is just right for one stage of market evolution may be less appropriate for another stage (one style does not fit all stages).

In young markets, consumers' knowledge of a product may be limited, making their ability to process information from ads low and their motivation relatively high. This situation should make them particularly responsive to argument-focused appeals, expert sources, and negatively framed messages. Also, they should have greater capacity to encode and act on message arguments when these arguments are prominent within the ad. In older markets, consumers may have gained knowledge, which reduces their motivation to engage in extensive ad processing. As such, factors that increase their personal involvement in the ad – such as the use of emotion-focused appeals and positively framed messages – may be particularly likely to create a behavioral response. An empirical analysis of a set of ad creatives in real markets supports these predictions. The findings supplement the knowledge about the role of market age in understanding advertising's effects. Just as advertising elasticities vary by market age, so too does the effectiveness of various executional cues.

Our study contains several novel features. Most important, our focus on the behavioral impact of various creative elements by market age is novel. Indeed, a recent summary by Vakratsas and Ambler (1999) of 250 empirical studies of advertising reveals no empirical generalizations regarding this idea. Stewart and Furse's (1986) work is a rare case that examines the efficacy of various executional cues – for new versus established brands. However, those authors do not study ad efficacy using a behavioral measure; their measure of efficacy is based on a persuasion score (similar to a purchase intention measure) provided by respondents who were recruited to view a single exposure of the ads in off-air test sessions (Stewart and Furse 1986, p. 39). Our study is also novel in its focus on a novel product (advertising for medical services). This focus adds to the bulk of work done experimentally and in the field on consumer packaged goods products. Finally, our study adds novel elements to the literature on goal framing. Given the limited work on this executional cue, our results suggest that further study and theory on goal framing and advertising is warranted.

Our study differs from Stewart and Furse's (1986) in several regards. First, we focus on ads for a single brand in markets of different ages (versus many different brands at various stages of the product life cycle). We control for history effects by examining markets of different ages that exist at the same time. Recall that in our context, the same ads aired in new markets as well as in old markets. Second, we examine the behavioral impact of commercials for the service as the market ages. Finally, our model enables us to isolate the behavioral impact of advertising due to creative characteristics from other potentially confounding factors. Perhaps for these reasons, our results appear more robust than those of Stewart and Furse (1986).

Our research on market age also adds to the consumer information-processing literature by suggesting the importance of understanding the potentially negative relationship between motivation and ability to process information from ads (MacInnis, Moorman, and Jaworski 1991). Although traditional information-processing models focus on situations in which motivation and ability are low versus high (MacInnis and Jaworski 1989; Petty and Cacioppo 1986), the fact that in real markets these two factors may be negatively related complicates predictions about advertising's effects. We focus on the efficacy of executional cues when motivation is high and ability low or when motivation is low and ability high. This approach is relatively novel to the consumer information-processing literature.

Our results are particularly relevant for managers dealing with products that involve rollouts over a relatively extended period of time. Examples of such products are plentiful (e.g., digital subscriber lines, cellular telephone services, airlines, as well as toll-free services of the type studied in this article). Extended rollouts are often necessary because of the complexity and expense associated with building a local infrastructure to deliver the product or service in each market (Chandy and Tellis 1998, 2000). The extended rollout results in markets of widely varying ages: some that are quite mature and others that are brand new. Anecdotal evidence suggests that the current practice (except perhaps in cross-national situations) is to show roughly the same set of ads across all markets. Indeed, this was the strategy followed by the firm studied here. Our results suggest the need to tailor ads to fit the age of specific markets and use different ads for different ages.

Limitations and further research

As with any study, our results should be viewed as tentative. This article tests the simple premise that market age moderates the relationship between executional cues in ads and their behavioral impact. One strength of our study is that its narrow context enables us to control for a variety of confounding factors while incorporating real-world advertising and actual consumers. Although this context serves us well in terms of internal validity and extends experimental work done on advertising effects, generalizations would depend on additional work that incorporates competitive effects and uses other products and services, different sets of ads, and a larger body of executional cues.

For example, because we studied a market in which competitive pressures are limited, it is reasonable to determine whether the effects generalize to contexts in which competitive pressures are high. Furthermore, the context we examined was one in which there was limited time between exposure and potential consumer response. Although current models of persuasion (e.g., the theory of reasoned action model or theory of planned behavior) suggest that attitudes are capable of predicting behavior marked by long periods between exposure and behavior (see Sheppard, Hartwick, and Warshaw 1988), it is possible that predicting behavior from advertising will require richer theoretical models that incorporate both competitive effects and exposure-response durations.

Further work could also consider the intervening factors that underline the effects we observed. Although our prediction was that a priori levels of motivation and ability would explain why various cues may or may not be effective, our study did not measure the level of these variables. Work that more directly links these states to advertising outcomes is therefore in order. Also, the bulk of our analysis here is at the market level; there is the potential for heterogeneity biases when aggregating responses from the individual level. Future work with individual-level data can help address this issue.

Future work should also focus on additional process variables that mediate ad effectiveness for products of different market ages. One could expect, for example, that the high motivation level predicted for consumers in young markets would lead to deep processing with support and counterarguments to message claims. This deep processing would make ad claims more salient and render them easier to recall. Because the product is new to the market, recall may be quite important. In contrast, the low motivation but high ability predicted for consumers in older markets would render them susceptible to emotional and approach-based messages that motivate them to imagine positive benefits from product use. Less cognitive response and more emotional response might be observed for consumers in older markets.

Further research should also focus on additional executional cues beyond those studied here. Stewart and Furse's (1986) study provides a rich basis for identifying cues different from those we studied that might vary across markets of different ages. For example, in younger versus older markets, congruence of commercial elements (e.g., the extent to which the brand name reinforces a brand benefit), attributes as the main message, and demonstrations would be more important. These cues would facilitate brand name and attribute learning – important effects when the product is new and consumers are limited in their prior product knowledge. In contrast, when product knowledge is high but motivation low, as would be the case in older markets, the use of humor, comfort appeals, sex appeals, scenic beauty, surrealistic visuals, and aesthetic claims might be effective. These cues might enhance consumers' motivation to process the ad by their appetitive and emotional nature.

Finally, further research should examine the effectiveness of advertising executional cues in other types of product-markets. For example, competition may moderate the effects studied here – the effects of advertising cues in highly competitive markets may well be different from those in the current context. Perceived risk in product purchase or use may be another moderating factor. For a medical service, consumers may perceive risk to be high, making them more susceptible to arguments, negatively framed messages, and expert sources in young markets. The effects may be different when consumers perceive the risk in product purchase or use to be limited.

Note

1 We use C to refer to the matrix of creatives here and c to refer to individual creatives subsequently.

References

Aaker, David A. and Donald E. Bruzonne (1981), 'Viewer Perceptions of Prime-Time Television Advertising,' *Journal of Advertising Research*, 21 (October), 15–23.

Agres, Stuart, Julie A. Edell, and Tony M. Dubitsky (1990), *Emotion in Advertising: Theoretical and Practical Explorations*. New York: Quorum Books.

Amemiya, T. (1985), *Advanced Econometrics*. Cambridge, MA: Harvard University Press.

Bagozzi, Richard P. and Uptal Dholakia (1999), 'Goal Setting and Goal Striving in Consumer Behavior,' *Journal of Marketing*, 63 (Special Issue), 19–32.

Batra, Rajeev and Michael L. Ray (1986), 'Situational Effects of Advertising Repetition: The Moderating Influence of Motivation, Ability and Opportunity to Respond,' *Journal of Consumer Research*, 12 (March), 432–45.

Blair, Margaret and Karl E. Rosenberg (1994), 'Convergent Findings Increase Our Understanding of How Advertising Works,' *Journal of Advertising Research*, 34 (May/June), 35–45.

Cacioppo, John T. and Richard E. Petty (1982), 'The Need for Cognition,' *Journal of Personality and Social Psychology*, 42 (1), 116–31.

Chandy, Rajesh K. and Gerard J. Tellis (1998), 'Organizing for Radical Product Innovation,' *Journal of Marketing Research*, 35 (November), 474–87.

—— and—— (2000) 'The Incumbent's Curse? Incumbency, Size, and Radical Product Innovation,' *Journal of Marketing*, 64 (July), 1–17.

Clarke, Darryl G. (1976), 'Econometric Measurement of the Duration of Advertising Effect on Sales,' *Journal of Marketing Research*, 13 (November), 345–57.

Cohen, Joel B. and Charles S. Areni (1991), 'Affect and Consumer Behavior,' in *Handbook of Consumer Behavior*, Thomas S. Robertson and Harold H. Kassarjian, eds. Englewood Cliffs, NJ: Prentice Hall, 188–240.

Cook, William A. and Arthur J. Kover (1997), 'Research and the Meaning of Advertising Effectiveness: Mutual Misunderstandings,' in *Measuring Advertising Effectiveness*, W. Wells, ed. Hillsdale, NJ: Lawrence Erlbaum Associates, 13–20.

Craig, Samuel, Brian Sternthal, and Clark Leavitt (1976), 'Advertising Wearout: An Experimental Analysis,' *Journal of Marketing Research*, 13(4), 365–72.

Eastlack, Joseph O., Jr., and Ambar G. Rao (1986), 'Modeling Response to Advertising and Pricing Changes for "V-8" Cocktail Vegetable Juice,' *Marketing Science*, 5 (3), 245–59.

—— and —— (1989), 'Advertising Experiments at the Campbell Soup Company,' *Marketing Science*, 8 (Winter), 57–71.

Edwards, Kari (1990), 'The Interplay of Affect and Cognition in Attitude Formation and Change,' *Journal of Personality and Social Psychology*, 59 (2), 202–16.

—— and William von Hippel (1995), 'Hearts and Minds: The Priority of Affective Versus Cognitive Factors in Person Perception,' *Personality and Social Psychology Bulletin*, 21 (October), 996–1011.

Etgar, Michael and Stephen A. Goodwin (1982), 'One-Sided Versus Two-Sided Comparative Message Appeals for New Brand Introductions,' *Journal of Consumer Research*, 8 (March), 460–65.

French, John R. and Bertram Raven (1959), 'The Bases of Social Power,' in *Studies in Social Power*, D. Cartwright, ed. Ann Arbor, MI: Institute for Social Research, 150–67.

Friestad, Marian and Esther Thorson (1986), 'Emotion-Eliciting Advertising: Effect on Long-Term Memory and Judgement,' in *Advances in Consumer Research*, Vol. 13, Richard J. Lutz, ed. Provo, UT: Association for Consumer Research, 111–5.

Frijda, Nico H. (1986), *The Emotions*. Cambridge, UK: Cambridge University Press.

Gardner, Meryl P. (1983), 'Advertising Effects on Attributes Recalled and Criteria Used for Brand Evaluations,' *Journal of Consumer Research*, 10 (December), 310–18.

Golden, Linda L. and K.A. Johnson (1983), 'The Impact of Sensory Preference and Thinking Versus Feeling Appeals on Advertising Effectiveness,' in *Advances in Consumer Research*, Vol. 10, Richard P. Bagozzi and Alice M. Tybout, eds. Ann Arbor, MI: Association for Consumer Research, 203–8.

Greene, William H. (1997), *Econometric Analysis*. Upper Saddle River, NJ: Prentice Hall.

Grunert, Klaus G. (1996), 'Automatic and Strategic Processes in Advertising Effects,' *Journal of Marketing*, 60 (October), 88–101.

Hanssens, Dominique, Leonard J. Parsons, and Randall L. Schultz (1990), *Market Response Models, Econometric and Time Series Analysis*. Norwell, MA: Kluwer Academic Publishers.

Hawkins, Scott A. and Stephen J. Hoch (1992), 'Low Involvement Learning: Memory Without Evaluation,' *Journal of Consumer Research*, 19 (September), 212–25.

Holbrook, Morris B. and Rajeev Batra (1987), 'Assessing the Role of Emotions as Mediators of Consumer Responses to Advertising,' *Journal of Consumer Research*, 14 (December), 404–20.

Homer, Pamela M. and Lynn R. Kahle (1990), 'Source Expertise, Time of Source Identification, and Involvement in Persuasion: An Elaborative Processing Perspective,' *Journal of Advertising*, 19(1), 30–39.

Hovland, C.I. and W. Weiss (1951), 'The Influence of Source Credibility on Communication Effectiveness,' *Public Opinion Quarterly*, 15 (Winter), 635–50.

Howard, John A. (1977), *Consumer Behavior: Application of Theory*. New York: McGraw-Hill.

—— and Jagdish N. Sheth (1969), *The Theory of Buyer Behavior*. New York: John Wiley & Sons.

Judge, George G., W.E. Griffiths, R. Carter Hill, Helmut Lutkepohl, and Tsoung-Chao Lee (1985), *The Theory and Practice of Econometrics*. New York: John Wiley & Sons.

Kahle, Lynn R. and Pamela M. Homer (1985), 'Physical Attractiveness of the Celebrity Endorser: A Social Adaptation Perspective,' *Journal of Consumer Research*, 11 (March), 954–61.

Kahneman, Daniel and Amos Tversky (1979), 'Prospect Theory: An Analysis of Decisions Under Risk,' *Econometrica*, 47, 262–91.

Krishnamurthi, Lakshman, Jack Narayan, and S.P. Raj (1986), 'Intervention Analysis of a Field Experiment to Assess the Buildup Effect of Advertising,' *Journal of Marketing Research*, 23 (November), 337–45.

Leone, Robert P. (1995), 'Generalizing What Is Known About Temporal Aggregation and Advertising Carryover,' *Marketing Science*, 14 (3), G141–G150.

Levin, Irwin P., Sandra L. Schneider, and Gary J. Gaeth (1998), 'All Frames Are Not Created Equal: A Typology and Critical Analysis of Framing Effects,' *Organizational Behavior and Human Decision Processes*, 76 (November), 149–88.

Lodish, Leonard M., Magid Abraham, Stuart Kalmenson, Jeanne Livelsberger, Beth Lubetkin, Bruce Richardson, and Mary Ellen Stevens (1995a), 'How TV Advertising Works: A Meta-Analysis of 389 Real World Split Cable TV Advertising Experiments,' *Journal of Marketing Research*, 32 (May), 125–39.

——, ——, Jeanne Livelsberger, Bruce Richardson, and Mary Ellen Stevens (1995b), 'A Summary of Fifty-Five In-Market Experimental Estimates of the Long-Term Effect of TV Advertising,' *Marketing Science*, 14 (3), 143–40.

—— and Dwight Riskey (1997), 'Making Ads Profitable,' *Marketing Research*, 9 (4), 38–42.

MacInnis, Deborah J. and Bernard J. Jaworski (1989), 'Information Processing from Advertisements: Towards an Integrative Framework,' *Journal of Marketing*, 53 (October), 1–23.

——, Christine Moorman, and Bernard J. Jaworski (1991), 'Enhancing and Measuring Consumers' Motivation, Opportunity, and Ability to Process Brand Information from Ads,' *Journal of Marketing*, 55 (4), 32–54.

—— and C. Whan Park (1991), 'The Differential Role of Characteristics of Music on High-and Low-Involvement Consumers' Processing of Ads,' *Journal of Consumer Research*, 18 (September), 161–73.

Maheswaran, Durairaj and Joan Meyers-Levy (1990), 'The Influence of Message Framing and Issue Involvement,' *Journal of Marketing Research*, 27 (August), 361–7.

McGuire, W.J. (1969), 'The Nature of Attitudes and Attitude Change,' in *Handbook of Social Psychology*, Gardner Lindzey and Elliot Aronson, eds. Reading, MA: Addison Wesley, 136–314.

Meyerowitz, B.E. and Shelley Chaiken (1987), 'The Effect of Message Framing on Breast Self-Examination Attitudes, Intentions and Behavior,' *Journal of Personality and Social Psychology*, 52 (March), 500–510.

Meyers-Levy, Joan and Prashant Malaviya (1999), 'Consumers' Processing of Persuasive of Advertisements: An Integrative Framework of Persuasion Theories,' *Journal of Marketing*, 63 (Special Issue), 45–60.

Millar, Murray G. and Karen U. Millar (1990), 'Attitude Change as a Function of Attitude Type and Argument Type,' *Journal of Personality and Social Psychology*, 52 (2), 217–28.

Moore, Danny L. and J. Wesley Hutchinson (1983), 'The Effects of Ad Affect on Advertising Effectiveness,' in *Advances in Consumer Research*, Vol. 10, Richard P. Bagozzi and Alice M. Tybout, eds. Ann Arbor, MI: Association for Consumer Research, 536–31.

Olson, James M. and Mark P. Zanna (1993), 'Attitudes and Attitude Change,' *Annual Review of Psychology*, 44, 117–55.

Park, C. Whan and Parker Lessig (1977), 'Students and House-wives: Differences in Susceptibility to Reference Group Influence,' *Journal of Consumer Research*, 4 (September), 102–10.

—— and S. Mark Young (1986), 'Consumer Response to Television Commercials: The Impact of Involvement and Background Music on Brand Attitude Formation,' *Journal of Marketing Research*, 23 (January), 11–24.

Parsons, Leonard J. (1975), 'The Product Life-Cycle and Time Varying Advertising Elasticities,' *Journal of Marketing Research*, 12 (November), 476.

Pechmann, Cornelia and David W. Stewart (1988), 'Advertising Repetition: A Critical Review of Wearin and Wearout,' in *Current Issues and Research in Advertising*, James H. Leigh and Claude R. Martin Jr., eds. Ann Arbor, MI: University of Michigan, Division of Research, School of Business Administration, 285–330.

Petty, Richard E. and John T. Cacioppo (1979), 'Effects of Message Repetition and Position on Cognitive Response, Recall, and Persuasion,' *Journal of Personality and Social Psychology*, 37 (January), 97–109.

—— and—— (1986), *Communication and Persuasion: Central and Peripheral Routes to Attitude Change*. New York: Springer-Verlag.

——, ——, and R. Goldman (1981), 'Personal Involvement as a Determinant of Argument-Based Persuasion,' *Journal of Personality and Social Psychology*, 41 (November), 847–55.

—— and Duane T. Wegener (1998), 'Attitude Change: Multiple Roles for Persuasion Variables,' in *The Handbook of Social Psychology*, Daniel T. Gilbert, Susan T. Fiske, and Gardner Lindzey, eds. Boston: McGraw-Hill, 323–90.

Price, Linda L. and Eric J. Arnould (1999), 'Commercial Friendships: Service Provider-Client Relationships in Context,' *Journal of Marketing*, 63 (October), 38–56.

Raj, S.P. (1982), 'The Effects of Advertising on High and Low Loyalty Consumer Segments,' *Journal of Consumer Research*, 9 (June), 77–89.

Ratneshwar, S. and Chaiken Shelly (1991), 'Comprehension's Role in Persuasion: The Case of Its Moderating Effect on the Persuasive Impact of Source Cues,' *Journal of Consumer Research*, 18 (June), 52–62.

Ray, Michael L. and Rajeev Batra (1983), 'Emotion and Persuasion in Advertising: What We Do and Don't Know About Affect,' in *Advances in Consumer Research*, Vol. 10, R.P. Bagozzi and A.M. Tybout, eds. Ann Arbor, MI: Association for Consumer Research, 543–8.

Rethans, Arno J., John L. Swasy, and Lawrence J. Marks (1986), 'Effects of Television Commercials Repetition, Receiver Knowledge, and Commercial Length: A Test of the Two-Factor Model,' *Journal of Marketing Research*, 23 (1), 50–61.

Roney, Christopher, E. Torry Higgins, and James Shah (1995), 'Goals and Framing: How Outcome Focus Influences Motivation and Emotion,' *Personality and Social Psychology Bulletin*, 21 (November), 1151–60.

Rossiter, John R. and Larry Percy (1987), *Advertising and Promotion Management*. New York: McGraw-Hill.

Russell, James A. (1978), 'Evidence of Convergent Validity on the Dimensions of Affect,' *Journal of Personality and Social Psychology*, 36 (10), 1152–68.

Schumann, D.W., Richard E. Petty, and D.S. Clemons (1990), 'Predicting the Effectiveness of Different Strategies of Advertising Variation: A Test of the Repetition-Variation Hypotheses,' *Journal of Consumer Research*, 17 (September), 192–202.

Sethuraman, Raj and Gerard J. Tellis (1991), 'An Analysis of the Tradeoff Between Advertising and Pricing,' *Journal of Marketing Research*, 31 (May), 160–74.

Sheppard, Blair, Jon Hartwick, and Paul R. Warshaw (1988), 'The Theory of Reasoned Action: A Meta-Analysis of Past Research with Recommendations for Modifications and Future Research,' *Journal of Consumer Research*, 15 (December), 325–43.

Shiv, Baba, Julie A. Edell, and John W. Payne (1997), 'Factors Affecting the Impact of Negatively and Positively Framed Ad Messages,' *Journal of Consumer Research*, 24 (3), 285–94.

Singh, Surendra N. and Catherine A. Cole (1993), 'The Effects of Length, Content, and Repetition on Television Commercial Effectiveness,' *Journal of Marketing Research*, 30 (February), 91–104.

Stayman, Douglas M. and David A. Aaker (1988), 'Are All the Effects of Ad-Induced Feelings Mediated by A_{AD}?' *Journal of Consumer Research*, 15 (December), 368–73.

Sternthal, Brian and C. Samuel Craig (1973), 'Humor in Advertising,' *Journal of Marketing*, 37 (October), 12–18.

Stewart, David W. (1992), 'Speculations on the Future of Advertising Research,' *Journal of Advertising*, 21 (September), 1–46.

—— and David H. Furse (1986), *Effective Television Advertising: A Study of 1000 Commercials*. Lexington, MA: Lexington Books.

Tellis, Gerard J. (1988), 'Advertising Exposure, Loyalty, and Brand Purchase: A Two Stage Model of Choice,' *Journal of Marketing Research*, 15 (May), 134–44.

—— (1998), *Advertising and Sales Promotion Strategy*. Reading, MA: Addison Wesley.

——, Rajesh K. Chandy, and Pattana Thaivanich (2000), 'Which Ad Works, When, Where, and How Often? Modeling the Effects of Direct Television Advertising,' *Journal of Marketing Research*, 37 (February), 32–46.

—— and Claes Fornell (1988) 'Advertising and Quality Over the Product Life Cycle: A Contingency Theory,' *Journal of Marketing Research*, 15 (February), 64–71.

—— and Doyle Weiss (1995), 'Does TV Advertising Really Affect Sales?' *Journal of Advertising*, 24(3), 1–12.

Vakratsas, Demetrios and Tim Ambler (1999), 'How Advertising Works: What Do We Really Know?' *Journal of Marketing*, 63 (1), 26–43.

Vaughn, Richard (1980), 'How Advertising Works: A Planning Model,' *Journal of Advertising Research*, 20 (5), 27–33.

Weinberger, Marc C. and Charles S. Gulas (1992), 'The Impact of Humor in Advertising: A Review,' *Journal of Advertising*, 21 (4), 35–59.

Wells, William (1993), 'Discovery-Oriented Consumer Research,' *Journal of Consumer Research*, 19 (March), 489–504.

Winer, Russell S. (1999), 'Experimentation in the 21st Century: The Importance of External Validity,' *Journal of the Academy of Marketing Science*, 27 (Summer), 349–58.

Yalch, Richard F. and Rebecca Elmore-Yalch (1984), 'The Effect of Numbers on the Route to Persuasion,' *Journal of Consumer Research*, 11 (June), 522–7.

? Questions

1 What are the unique contributions of this study?
2 The authors propose a number of hypotheses with regard to the interaction effects between creative ad content and age of the market. Do you think the motivations for their hypotheses are correct and justified? Why or why not?
3 In this study, motivation and ability to process advertising information are discussed at the market level, while in fact they are characteristics of

individuals. How could this have affected the validity of the conclusions? Can you think of alternative ways of studying the subject of the paper, taking individual motivation and ability into account?

4 How were the independent variables of the study defined and measured?
5 The authors claim that, given the characteristics of their data set, the effects modelled can be measured validly. Which characteristics do they refer to? Do you agree with them?
6 What are the advantages and limitations of the data set used in this study?
7 Describe the analytical procedure in this study.
8 Why was the analysis conducted at the hourly level? Redefining the unit of analysis to a daily measurement could lead to what mistakes?
9 Describe the interaction effects found in this study, using Figures 1–5.
10 Why do you think service advisers, in contrast to service providers, in advertising have a significant effect on referrals?
11 An inverted U-shape relation between market age and referrals was found. How does this relate to the wear-in and/or wear-out effect of advertising?
12 What are the limitations (factors that could not be studied or were not studied) of this research?
13 Given the results of this paper, what would an 'ideal ad' for a new market look like? And for an old market?

Vignette

Rebranding GB and launching Carrefour supermarkets in Belgium

Belgium has been called a paradise for shoppers and hell for retailers. With 103 m^2 shop floor per square kilometer of territory Belgium has by far the most dense shop network in Europe (for instance, this ratio is 32 in Italy, 41 in the UK and 74 in Germany). Almost 45 per cent of Belgians regularly visit at least five different supermarkets (as opposed to, for instance, 21 per cent in the UK, 5 per cent in Italy), and the average number of shops regularly visited is 4.2 (3.7 in the UK, 3.2 in France). In this highly competitive food retailing market, GB used to be the market leader, with a market share of almost 32 per cent. And although GB is a famous brand in Belgium (it enjoyed 100 per cent awareness), it suffered from a weak stuck-in-the-middle image. This resulted in less loyal customers than their main competitors. In 2001 about half the GB activities (the MaxiGB's) were taken over by Carrefour, Europe's first and the world's second largest retail group, that mainly owns large-surface hypermarkets and originates from France. Carrefour faced a difficult task, i.e. having to replace one of the most famous Belgian brands by a completely unknown one, and reposition the supermarkets successfully.

The objective of the 2001 launch campaign and the 2002 follow-up campaign was to rebrand the supermarkets without loss of market share, to increase market penetration and to enhance customer loyalty. But first of all, a new 'place in the mind of the customer' had to be established. Carrefour aimed at creating a brand awareness rate of at least that of the 'old' GB, and at establishing a clear position. Worldwide, the positioning of Carrefour is based on four axes: more quality assurance, more discount, more proximity and always first. To that end an integrated communications campaign was launched in which traditional advertising media were supplemented with point-of-sale tools. In the shops, the new situation was explained by means of folders, displays, radio spots and parking lot activities. Billboards were used in the 'customer zones' to create awareness of the new brand. Outdoor advertising on trams guided people to the 'new' Carrefour shops. The campaign also used newspaper advertising extensively. Every Friday a different product was highlighted in all major newspapers. In that way this medium was used to generate knowledge about the product assortment and to create an atmosphere of expectation (every week something new . . .). Newspapers were also used as a tactical tool, to create special buying occasions. To that end, teaser campaigns ('two days to go before . . .') were used. Finally free door-to-door advertising was used to support the campaign further.

The advertising campaign was well remembered and well attributed. For instance, the 2002 campaign resulted in a 26 per cent spontaneous recall score (all food retail adverts: 10 per cent), a recognition score of 76 per cent (all food adverts: 49 per cent), and a correct attribution of the brand to the advertisement of 89 per cent (all food retail adverts: 76 per cent). At the end of 2002 the market share of Carrefour was higher than the market share of MaxiGB in 2000. Also the number of customers, the average ticket and, consequently, total sales increased substantially. Furthermore, the shopping frequency of Carrefour customers was higher than that of MaxiGB customers (on average 6.2 versus 5.6), indicating increased customer loyalty. Total prompted awareness of the Carrefour brand was 100 per cent, and the Carrefour image improved on all major attributes, as compared with the former MaxiGB image.

Sources: www.carrefour.com; A. C. Nielsen Belgium; Belgian Effie Award, 2003.

Chapter 4

Patrick de Pelsmacker

SALES PROMOTION

MANUFACTURERS INCREASINGLY RELY UPON sales promotions to convince consumers to buy their brands. Some sources claim that the advertising/sales promotions expenditure ratio has evolved from 60/40 in the 1980s to 30/70 in 2000. Indeed, individual ads get lost in communications clutter, consumers become less brand loyal and take more buying decisions in the retail outlet, and brand managers increasingly have to be short-term-oriented, and therefore rely upon short-term marketing communications tools such as sales promotions. Moreover, distribution channels have become increasingly powerful, forcing manufacturers to maximize sales and store profits in the short run. Additionally, retailers actively challenge manufacturers by offering store brands or private labels.

Depending upon the country, these brands hold markets shares of 20–45 per cent, and in many product categories pose a serious threat to manufacturers. This is a source of intense channel conflicts, also referred to as 'store wars'. Manufacturers can react to the threat in a number of ways: they can increase the distance between their own brands and store brands by means of innovation or advertising, they can introduce cheap 'flanker brands' themselves, or they can reduce the price gap with store brands by means of sales promotions. In the latter case they apparently decide to compete head-on with the store brands.

This study questions the basic assumption that manufacturer brand promotions in all cases imply direct competition with private labels, by trying to answer the question whether national (manufacturer) brand promotions and store brands attract different value-conscious consumers. The unique contribution of the paper is that it studies both categories of buying behaviour (store brands and promoted manufacturer brands) in one study. Furthermore two different types of promotion (in-store and out-of-store) are compared. The basic theoretical framework starts from hedonic, utilitarian and cost motives and links them to a large number of demographic and psychographic consumer characteristics which, in turn, are assumed to have an impact on store brand and in-store and out-of-store promotion buying. Moreover the authors try to find out to what extent demographic factors have a direct and/or an indirect influence (through their impact on psychographics) on buying behaviour. This is as such an interesting question, because all too often marketers refer to 'easy' demographic variables when segmenting markets, while in fact the basic underlying factors are often psychographic. The model is estimated using data from 319 mall intercept personal interviews.

The study offers an interesting build-up of a comprehensive set of hypotheses a number of which have not been previously tested. Owing to its comprehensive and all-encompassing nature, it also offers many links to well known consumer behaviour and retailing concepts, such as the role of reference groups (peer expectations), brand and store loyalty, personality traits like Need for Cognition, variety-seeker behaviour, price and quality consciousness and many others.

The last part of the study defines four different types of consumer in terms of their value consciousness and their demographic and psychographic characteristics. This typology shows that manufacturers and retailers can indeed opt for a non-promotion (or non-store brand) strategy (focusing upon the use-no-deals consumer), or a head-on price competition (focusing upon the use-all-deals consumer), which are both traditional store wars strategies. However, they can also avoid direct competition by carefully targeting the two different types of consumer that were also identified in this study: the store brand-oriented and the promoted manufacturer brand-oriented consumers. The identification of these two consumer segments and their characteristics is an interesting contribution of the study, with an important strategic significance. Along with the study of the impact of many consumer characteristics in a comprehensive framework, the study also offers challenging insights into, for example, the (lack of) impact of promotions on brand switching, and the role of promotions in customer acquisition and retention.

PURSUING THE VALUE-CONSCIOUS CONSUMER: STORE BRANDS VERSUS NATIONAL BRAND PROMOTIONS

Kusum L. Ailawadi, Scott A. Neslin, and Karen Gedenk

The objective of this article is to determine whether national brand promotions and store brands attract the same value-conscious consumers, which would

Journal of Marketing, Vol. 65 (January 2001), pp. 71–89.
Kusum L. Ailawadi is Associate Professor of Business Administration, and Scott A. Neslin is Albert Wesley Frey Professor of Marketing, Amos Tuck School of Business Administration, Dartmouth College. Karen Gedenk is Professor of Marketing, University of Frankfurt. The authors thank Andrew Hayes for invaluable research computing support and Soenke Albers, Punam Keller, Kevin Keller, Praveen Kopalle, Don Lehmann, Jeannie Newton, Jan-Benedict Steenkamp, and participants at the 1998 INFORMS Marketing Science Conference for their helpful comments. The authors gratefully acknowledge financial support from the Tuck Associates program and the German National Science Foundation (Deutsche Forschungsgemeinschaft) and thank Survey Research & Design Inc., especially Eva Ginsburg, for survey data collection.

aggravate channel conflict between manufacturers and retailers. The authors identify psychographic and demographic traits that potentially drive usage of store brands and national brand promotions. They then develop a framework and structural equation model to study the association of these traits with store brand and national brand promotion usage. The authors find that though demographics do not influence these behaviors directly, they have significant associations with psychographic characteristics and therefore are useful for market targeting. Most important, usage of store brands and usage of promotions, particularly out-of-store promotions, are associated with different psychographics. Store brand use correlates mainly with traits related to economic benefits and costs, whereas the use of out-of-store promotions is associated mainly with traits related to hedonic benefits and costs. These differences result in four well-defined and identifiable consumer segments: deal-focused consumers, store brand-focused consumers, deal and store brand users (use-all), and nonusers of both store brands and deals (use-none). Therefore, manufacturers and retailers have the opportunity to either avoid each other or compete head to head, depending on which segment they target.

SALES PROMOTIONS ACCOUNTED FOR 74 percent of the marketing budget of U.S. packaged goods firms in 1997 (Cox Direct 1998), up from 65 percent in 1984 (Donnelley Marketing Inc. 1995). During this time, the market share of store brands increased in several product categories, accounting for 20 percent of sales overall in 1998 (Dunne and Narasimhan 1999). Although there are many reasons that manufacturers offer promotions and retailers offer store brands, one common motivation is to provide value to the consumer. The average store brand sells for approximately 30 percent less than national brands, and national brand promotions typically deliver discounts of 20–30 percent (Information Resources Inc. 1998; Sethuraman 1992). Given this common motivation for national brand promotions and store brands, the natural question is whether these offerings attract the same consumers. If they do, there is a tug-of-war between manufacturers and retailers for the same market segment, whereas if not, the partitioning of market segments could reduce competition between them (e.g., Moorthy 1988).

The answer to this question is not readily apparent. The common emphasis on delivering value suggests that store brands and national brand promotions attract the same consumers. Consistent with this belief, some researchers have argued that national brand promotions are an effective way to combat the growth of store brands (e.g., Lal 1990; Quelch and Harding 1996). However, national brand promotions and store brands may satisfy different consumer needs, and consumers may incur different costs in using them. For example, promotions provide not only economic but also hedonic benefits, such as exploration and self-expression (Chandon, Wansink, and Laurent 2000), whereas store brands may not provide hedonic benefits to the same extent. Similarly, making use of promotions can require consumers to plan their shopping or shop at different stores, whereas buying store brands may not entail these costs.

Another factor that makes it difficult to determine whether the same consumers use both national brand promotions and store brands is that previous research has mainly focused on one behavior or the other but rarely on both in the same study. Blattberg and Neslin (1990, ch. 3) summarize several studies that characterize the deal-prone consumer in terms of demographics and/or psychographics. Other studies do the same for store brand-prone consumers (e.g., Baltas and Doyle 1998; Cunningham, Hardy, and Imperia 1982; Richardson, Jain, and Dick 1996). However, there is little work that studies both behaviors. Doing so would provide the common basis for comparison, in terms of both the characteristics studied and the method employed, that is necessary for making a definitive judgment on this issue.

The objective of this article is to determine whether deals and store brands attract the same consumers through a study of the demographic and psychographic factors that drive usage of these offerings. Our analysis proceeds in three stages. First, we develop a structural equation model to study the fundamental relationships of psychographics and demographics with deal and store brand usage.[1] Second, we perform a cluster analysis to uncover the usage segments that emerge from these relationships. Third, we develop a predictive model to classify consumers into these segments. The result is a deeper understanding of the drivers of deal and store brand usage, insight on whether deal and store brand users belong to the same market segment, and guidance for how to target the various segments.

This article is unique in three ways. First, we unify and complement previous work that has examined deal use and store brand use separately. Second, we consider two types of promotion – in-store and out-of-store. The first type includes displays, in-store specials, and so forth that are encountered in the store and used opportunistically or passively, whereas the second type includes coupons, in-store flyers, and the like, which are actively considered before the consumer goes shopping (Bucklin and Lattin 1991; Schneider and Currim 1991). Third, we examine both psychographic and demographic characteristics and investigate whether demographics work by determining deal and store brand usage directly or whether they work indirectly through their impact on psychographics (see Mittal 1994; Urbany, Dickson, and Kalapurakal 1996).

We find that national brand promotion usage and store brand usage are distinct behaviors, driven by different psychographics. Store brand users are characterized by psychographics linked largely to economic benefits and costs, whereas out-of-store promotion users are characterized by psychographics linked mainly to hedonic benefits and costs. In-store promotion users differ from out-of-store promotion users on some hedonic benefits and cost-related psychographics. However, users of these two types of promotions also have a lot in common. These findings result in a clearly defined store brand user segment, a national brand promotion segment (combining in-store and out-of-store promotions), and two other segments: one partaking in both store brands and national brand promotions and one partaking in neither. We also find that demographics influence these behaviors primarily through their effect on psychographics rather than directly.

The rest of the article is organized as follows: We present our conceptual framework, structural model, and data in the following section. Next, we describe the results of the structural model and the segmentation analysis. We conclude with a summary of findings and their implications for researchers and managers.

Conceptual Framework and Model

Overview of conceptual framework

In Figure 1, we provide an overview of our conceptual framework. The solid lines represent the structural equation model to be estimated. Although our overall purpose is to distinguish between store brand and deal users, previous research suggests that deal usage may not be a homogeneous construct (Henderson 1984; Lichtenstein, Netemeyer, and Burton 1995). We therefore build on Schneider and Currim's (1991) distinction between active and passive promotions and Bucklin and Lattin's (1991) distinction between planned and opportunistic shopping behavior and divide deal usage into in-store and out-of-store promotions. Thus, the three behaviors we wish to characterize are store brand use, in-store national brand promotion use, and out-of-store national brand promotion use.

Figure 1 proposes that these three behaviors are influenced by consumer psychographic and demographic characteristics. Demographics influence these behaviors not only directly but also indirectly through their effect on psychographics. The motivation for considering this indirect effect is that neither deal proneness nor store brand proneness research has had much success in obtaining consistent and strong associations with demographics. In addition, Mittal's (1994) and Urbany, Dickson, and Kalapurakal's (1996) findings suggest that demographics may be better predictors of psychographics than of deal proneness or store brand proneness per se.

Another important element of our framework is that the consumer's decision whether to use store brands or promotions is driven by economic benefits, hedonic benefits, and costs. This typology has a well-established

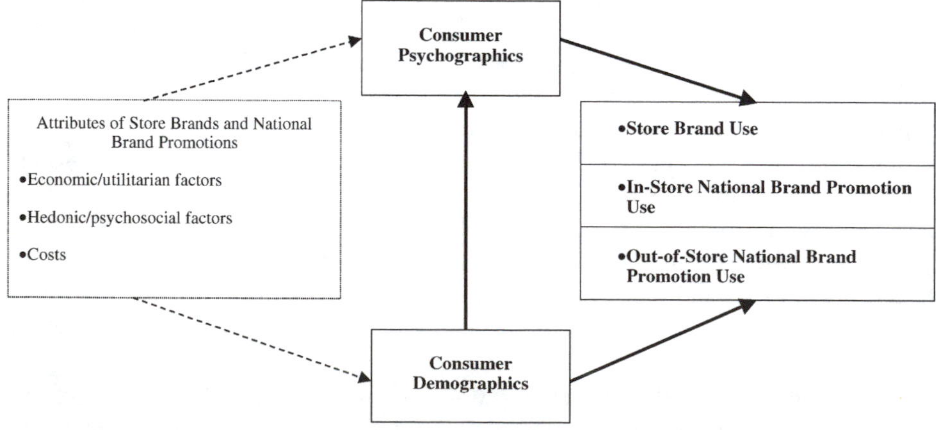

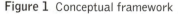

Figure 1 Conceptual framework

tradition in the literature on shopping behavior. Researchers such as Blattberg and colleagues (1978), Narasimhan (1984), and Bawa and Shoemaker (1987) have used economic benefits and costs to characterize the deal prone consumer, whereas others, such as Shimp and Kavas (1984), Price, Feick, and Guskey-Federouch (1988), and Schindler (1989), have focused attention on hedonic benefits. Recent research brings together the economic and hedonic attributes in evaluating deals (e.g., Chandon, Wansink, and Laurent 2000) or studying other aspects of shopping (Mittal 1994; Urbany, Dickson, and Kalapurakal 1996).

Figure 1 also proposes that the benefits and costs of using store brands and promotions create associations between psychographics or demographics and these behaviors. The reason is that particular psychographic or demographic groups will be attracted to particular costs and benefits. This suggests an approach for generating the particular psychographics and demographics we study. We first generate a more specific list of benefits and costs. Then we generate the psychographic and demographic characteristics of consumers that would make them most attracted to these benefits and costs. We do this in Figure 2.

The specific benefits and costs we consider are listed on the left-hand side of Figure 2. The economic benefits are savings and product quality (Chandon, Wansink, and Laurent 2000). The hedonic benefits are entertainment, exploration, and self-expression (Bellizzi et al. 1981; Chandon, Wansink, and Laurent 2000; Schindler 1989). And the costs are switching, search, thinking, and inventory holding costs (Bawa and Shoemaker 1987; Blattberg et al. 1978; Urbany, Dickson, and Kalapurakal 1996).[2]

The right-hand side of Figure 2 shows the psychographic and demographic characteristics that are particularly suggested by each benefit and cost. We discuss these links and use prior theoretical and empirical research to hypothesize how consumers with each psychographic characteristic vary in their usage of store brands or national brand promotions. As we have noted previously, most prior research examines either promotion use or store brand use, but not both. As a result, there are a few variables for which we can specify directional hypotheses with respect to one behavior but not the other. There are also a few variables for which there is strong theoretical support for some role in deal or store brand usage but where evidence from prior research is mixed with respect to the direction of association. Given the integrative nature of our research, we discuss the evidence to date and include these variables in our empirical model even when prior research does not enable us to state unambiguous, directional hypotheses. We note, however, that results for such hypotheses are in that sense exploratory, and it would be valuable for further research to examine the convergent validity of our findings on these variables.

The role of psychographics

Savings. Price savings are relevant to consumers who are price conscious and perceive themselves as having financial constraints. Because both store brands and national brand promotions offer price savings, we expect price consciousness and financial constraints to be positively related to all three behaviors.

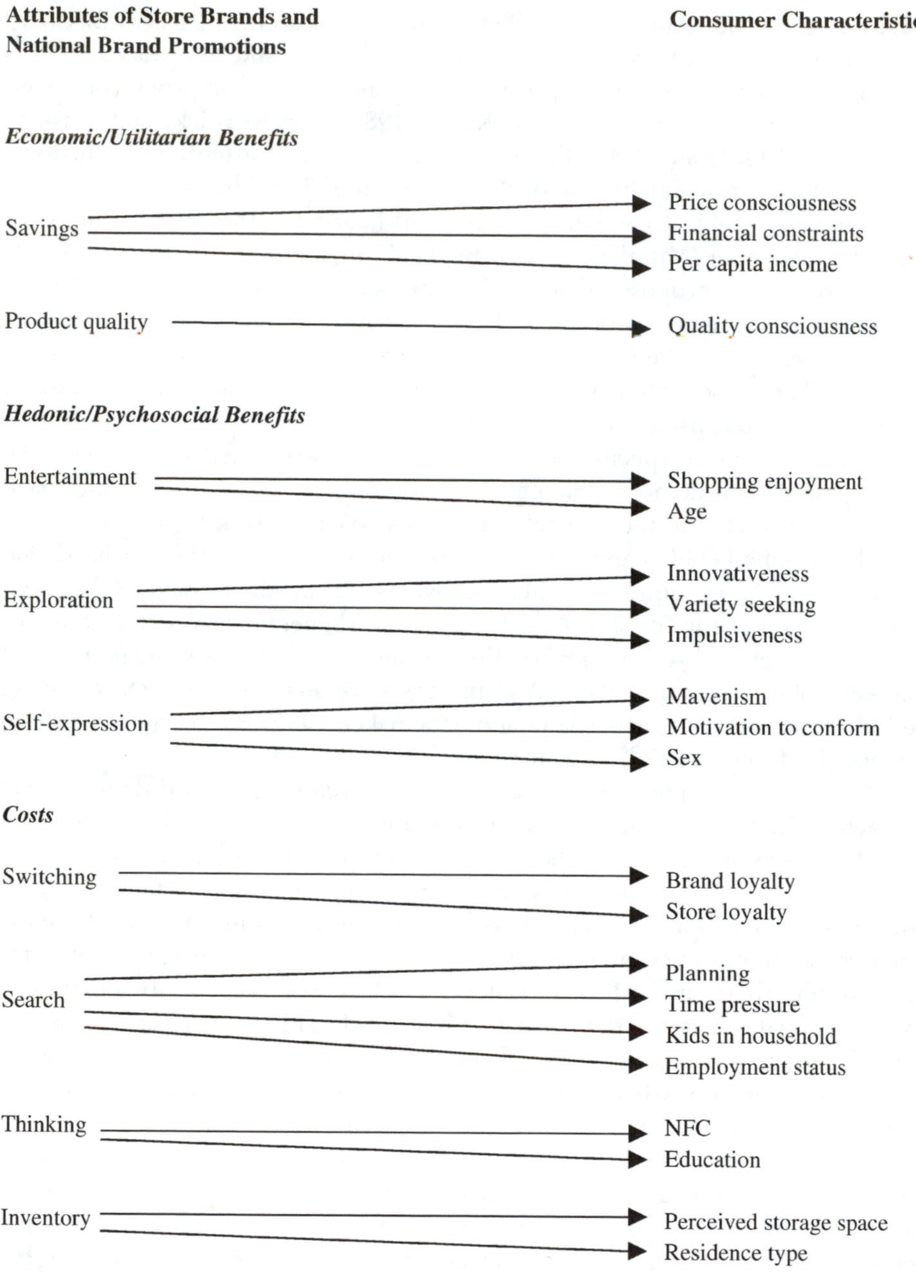

Figure 2 Identifying relevant consumer characteristics

Product quality. Product quality is relevant by definition to quality-conscious consumers. Quality consciousness should deter consumers from using store brands, because such brands are perceived to be inferior in quality (Cunningham, Hardy, and Imperia 1982; Richardson, Dick, and Jain 1994). Quality consciousness should not particularly influence use of in-store or out-of-store promotions for national brands, because the consumer can obtain the quality that these brands deliver without being deal prone.

Entertainment. Entertainment is relevant to people who enjoy shopping. Consumers who enjoy shopping have been found to be heavier users of feature advertising and coupons (Kolodinsky 1990), perhaps because they enjoy making use of marketing information. We therefore expect a positive relationship of shopping enjoyment with out-of-store promotion use, as well as with in-store promotion use. The in-store relationship may not be as strong, but in-store promotions also provide marketing information that shopping enthusiasts would enjoy processing. There is no evidence to suggest that using store brands is related to the quest for shopping enjoyment. For example, Bellizzi and colleagues (1981) find that store brand buyers are not more likely to enjoy shopping than other consumers.

Exploration. Exploration evokes characteristics such as innovation, variety seeking, and impulsiveness. Innovativeness and variety seeking should be positively associated with deal usage, because deals encourage product trial (e.g., Montgomery 1971). We cannot make a clear prediction for the relationship of innovativeness with store brand use. It will be positive if innovative consumers view store brands as new and untried (Granzin 1981) or negative if they view them as run-of-the-mill. Variety seekers should be less apt to use store brands, because regular use of store brands does not provide variety. Impulsiveness should be positively associated with in-store deal use but not with out-of-store deal use, because out-of-store deals require preparation before the shopping trip. We also find little reason to expect a relationship between impulsiveness and store brand usage. Store brands can be bought on impulse, but we do not expect store brands to be especially conducive to impulse behavior, as in-store promotions are.

Self-expression. Self-expression is salient to shopping mavens. Mavens are particularly attentive to media as a basis for their expertise (Higie, Feick, and Price 1987). They are more likely to read direct mail and local advertising (Higie, Feick, and Price 1987) and are heavier users of coupons (Price, Feick, and Guskey-Federouch 1988). We therefore expect mavens to be heavier users of out-of-store promotions. They should not be especially apt to use in-store promotions, which require less effort and therefore are less reflective of individual shopping expertise. Mavens attach extra importance to both quality and price (Williams and Slama 1995). Depending on which is stronger, there could be a positive or negative relationship between mavenism and store brand usage.

Self-expression is also related to consumers' motivation to conform to peer expectations. There is a strong theoretical and empirical basis for including motivation to conform. For example, Shimp and Kavas (1984) and Chandon, Wansink, and Laurent (2000) discuss the role of social recognition and conformity in deal usage, and Dick, Jain, and Richardson (1995) discuss the role of social approval in store brand usage. However, it is difficult to formulate directional hypotheses, because it is unclear what relevant others think of deal and store brand use. Both deal and store brand use have become common, and peers may consider them smart, so they may be positively related to motivation to conform. However, peers may look down on these behaviors as cheap, which would lead to a negative relationship.

Switching costs. Switching costs are high for brand-loyal or store-loyal consumers. We expect a negative relationship between in-store deal use and national brand loyalty, because in-store deals often require the consumer to switch brands (Bawa and Shoemaker 1987; Webster 1965). However, brand-loyal consumers can seek out coupons and specials for their favorite brands. Thus, out-of-store deal use may be less negatively, or even positively, related to national brand loyalty. Finally, national brand-loyal consumers by definition will be less likely to use store brands.[3]

Store loyalty should be negatively related with out-of-store deals, because these deals often require store switching (Bawa and Shoemaker 1987). There should also be a relationship between store loyalty and in-store promotions, but we are unable to specify the sign. Perceptions of retailer promotion activity have been found to correlate with store loyalty (Sirohi, McLaughlin, and Wittink 1998), which suggests a positive relationship. However, there is evidence that store-loyal people are less price sensitive (Kim, Srinivasan, and Wilcox 1999), which suggests a negative relationship. In contrast, store loyalty should be positively associated with store brand use, because store-loyal consumers trust their chosen store and become familiar with its store brands (Dick, Jain, and Richardson 1995; Richardson, Jain, and Dick 1996). The ability to buy a single brand across a wide range of product categories also facilitates shopping (Baltas and Doyle 1998; Steenkamp and Dekimpe 1997).

Search costs. Search costs are related to consumer planning and time pressure. Consumers who plan their shopping will be more apt to consider out-of-store promotions, because these promotions encourage planning. Indeed, there is evidence that consumers use out-of-store promotions to plan their shopping (Henderson 1985; NCH NuWorld 1999, p. 25; *Progressive Grocer* 1975). We therefore hypothesize a positive relationship between planning and out-of-store promotion use. We also hypothesize a positive relationship, though not as strong, between planning and in-store promotion. One way to take advantage of in-store promotions is for consumers to be highly conscious both of promotion schedules (Krishna, Currim, and Shoemaker 1991) and of their inventory levels so they know how much to buy to last until the next deal. Planners should be highly conscious of their inventory, and this should facilitate 'deal-to-deal' buying. Planning may also play a role in store brand use, but previous research does not point to a clear direction. Omar (1996) finds a positive association, but Cobb and Hoyer (1986) find an ambiguous relationship, in which more extensive planners have less favorable attitudes toward store brands than less extensive planners.

Consumers under time pressure should be deterred from using out-of-store promotions. Bawa and Shoemaker (1987) emphasize that coupons require high effort, and it is likely that scanning and making use of weekly flyers requires the same. But time-pressured consumers may use in-store promotions and store brands to save time, as both provide easily recognizable cues for simplifying the buying process. Store brands provide additional convenience and time saving by facilitating shopping across several categories (Baltas and Doyle 1998; Steenkamp and Dekimpe 1997). Therefore, we expect time pressure to be negatively related to out-of-store promotion use and positively related to in-store promotion use and store brand use.

Thinking costs. Thinking costs are related to need-for-cognition (NFC). High NFC has been found to be associated with more extensive information processing in a variety of contexts (Inman, McAlister, and Hoyer 1990; Mantel and Kardes 1999; Zhang 1996). We expect NFC to be positively associated with out-of-store promotion use, because such deals require significant cognitive effort, for example, in selecting, clipping, and organizing coupons. We expect a negative relationship between NFC and in-store deal use, because low-NFC people respond to both signal-only promotions, such as displays, and price-off promotions, such as store specials, whereas high-NFC people respond only to price-off promotions (Inman, McAlister, and Hoyer 1990). The relationship between NFC and store brand use is not clear. It would depend on whether low-NFC people use the store brand label as a cue for good value or as a cue for low quality.

Inventory holding costs. Inventory costs are related to the perceived availability of storage space. Having sufficient storage space makes it easier for consumers to use both in-store and out-of-store national brand deals, because they can stock up on the product (Blattberg et al. 1978). In contrast, consumers who perceive storage space constraints may buy store brands because they are always available at a low price and therefore need not be stockpiled. Thus, perceived storage space should have a positive association with the use of both types of national brand promotions and a negative association with store brand use.

In Table 1, we summarize our hypotheses about the relationship between psychographic characteristics and the three behaviors of interest. Viewed holistically, these individual hypotheses enable us to generate expectations about the fundamental question in our research; that is, Are these distinct behaviors or is there a lot of overlap between them? Table 1 suggests substantial overlap between users of in-store and out-of-store promotions. But even these two groups should be distinguishable on the basis of hedonic characteristics, such as impulsiveness and mavenism, and cost-related characteristics, such as time pressure and NFC. In contrast, Table 1 suggests much less overlap between store brand use and promotion use (in-store and out-of-store promotions taken collectively). Promotion users and store brand users should be clearly distinguishable on the basis of quality consciousness and several of the hedonic and cost-related characteristics.

The role of demographic characteristics

Identification of demographic characteristics. The benefits and costs of store brand and deal use suggest seven demographic characteristics: income, employment status, children in the household, type of residence, age, sex, and education. Income is linked to savings benefits, employment status and children in the household are related to search costs, and type of residence is related to inventory holding costs. The remaining three demographics link to multiple benefits and/or costs. Education links not only to thinking costs but also to product

Table 1 Summary of hypothesized relationships

	Dependent variable		
Psychographic characteristics	*Store brand usage*	*In-store promotion usage*	*Out-of-store promotion usage*
Related to Economic Benefits:			
Price consciousness	+	+	+
Financial constraints	+	+	+
Quality consciousness	–	0	0
Related to Hedonic Benefits:			
Shopping enjoyment	0	+	+
Innovativeness	?	+	+
Variety seeking	–	+	+
Impulsiveness	0	+	0
Mavenism	?	0	+
Motivation to conform	?	?	?
Related to Costs:			
Brand loyalty	–	–	?
Store loyalty	+	?	–
Planning	?	+	+
Time pressure	+	+	–
NFC	?	–	+
Perceived storage space	–	+	+

quality, exploration, and search costs (e.g., Narasimhan 1984; Raju 1980; Urbany, Dickson, and Kalapurakal 1996). Age links not only to entertainment but also to exploration, self-expression, and search costs (e.g., Raju 1980; Urbany, Dickson, and Kalapurakal 1996). Sex links not only to self-expression but also to exploration and search costs (e.g., Feick and Price 1987; Schindler 1989). Because the purpose of Figure 2 is simply to identify the relevant consumer characteristics, we keep it simple by showing only one major link.

Relationship with store brand and deal usage. Much research has hypothesized direct relationships between demographics and store brand or deal proneness. However, these hypotheses often rely on the association between demographics and psychographics for theoretical support. For example, income is expected to be negatively related to deal use, because higher-income households are less price conscious. Similarly, full-time employment is expected to be negatively associated with deal use, because people who work full time are more pressed for time (e.g., Blattberg et al. 1978). And dwelling in a home rather than an apartment is expected to be positively associated with deal use, because home-owners have more storage space for stockpiling products. As a result, it is unclear what the direct relationship of demographic variables is with store brand or deal usage when the indirect influence through psychographics has been accounted for. Therefore, we do not propose a priori hypotheses about the direct relationship between demographics and these behaviors.

Relationship with psychographics. We can propose hypotheses about the relationship of some demographic variables with specific psychographics. First, we expect income to have a negative relationship with price consciousness and financial constraints. Second, we expect full-time employment and the presence of children to have positive relationships with time pressure. Third, we expect living in a house rather than an apartment or townhouse to have a positive relationship with storage space.

The remaining three demographic variables – age, education, and sex – can be related to several of the psychographic characteristics in Figure 2. For example, older people may be more likely to enjoy shopping and be mavens (Urbany, Dickson, and Kalapurakal 1996), but they may be less likely to seek variety (Raju 1980) or be pressured for time. More educated people may be less likely to be mavens (Feick and Price 1987), more pressured for time (Narasimhan 1984), and more likely to seek variety (Raju 1980). Women may be more likely to be shopping mavens and planners (Feick and Price 1987). Relationships of these three demographic variables with other psychographics can be conceived of as well. For example, education may be related to quality consciousness or NFC; age may be related to the motivation to conform to the expectations of others or NFC; and sex may be related to shopping enjoyment, innovativeness, impulsiveness, or time pressure. Therefore, we examine the relationship of these three demographic variables with all fifteen psychographic variables.

Structural model

We first specify Model A, in which use of store brands (sbuse), use of in-store promotions on national brands (inuse), and use of out-of-store promotions on national brands (outuse) are each influenced by the fifteen psychographic characteristics. The error terms for the three equations are allowed to covary, because we expect that, like the included variables, some of the unobserved variables that influence one behavior may also influence the other behaviors:

(1) $\text{sbuse}_i = \gamma_{1,0} + \gamma_{1,1}\text{pricecon}_i + \gamma_{1,2}\text{finconst}_i + \ldots + \gamma_{1,15}\text{storage}_i + \varepsilon_{1i}$,
$\text{inuse}_i = \gamma_{2,0} + \gamma_{2,1}\text{pricecon}_i + \gamma_{2,2}\text{finconst}_i + \ldots + \gamma_{2,15}\text{storage}_i\ \varepsilon_{2i}$, and
$\text{outuse}_i = \gamma_{3,0} + \gamma_{3,1}\text{pricecon}_i + \gamma_{3,2}\text{finconst}_i + \ldots + \gamma_{3,15}\text{storage}_i + \varepsilon_{3i}$.

Next, we add the seven demographic characteristics identified in Figure 2 and obtain three additional model specifications depending on whether demographics have only a direct effect on the three behaviors, only an indirect effect through psychographics, or both a direct and an indirect effect. Model B, containing direct effects of demographics, is obtained by adding the demographic variables to each equation in Equation 1:[4]

(2) $\text{sbuse}_i = \gamma_{1,0} + \ldots + \gamma_{1,16}\text{age}_i + \gamma_{1,17}\text{income}_i + \ldots + \gamma_{1,22}\text{employ}_i + \mu_{1i}$,
$\text{inuse}_i = \gamma_{2,0} + \ldots + \gamma_{2,16}\text{age}_i + \gamma_{2,17}\text{income}_i + \ldots + \gamma_{2,22}\text{employ}_i + \mu_{2i}$, and
$\text{outuse}_i = \gamma_{3,0} + \ldots + \gamma_{3,16}\text{age}_i + \gamma_{3,17}\text{income}_i + \ldots + \gamma_{3,22}\text{employ}_i + \mu_{3i}$.

We incorporate the indirect effects of demographics by specifying equations for each of the psychographics as a function of demographics. As discussed previously, we model relationships of income, employment status, children in the family, and residence type with specific psychographics, but allow age, education, and sex to affect all fifteen psychographics. Thus, Model C, with indirect effects of demographics, is obtained by adding the following fifteen equations for psychographics to Equation 1 and allowing covariation between their error terms:

(3)
$$\begin{aligned}
\text{pricecon}_i &= \gamma_{4,0} + \gamma_{4,1}\text{age}_i + \gamma_{4,2}\text{educ}_i + \gamma_{4,3}\text{sex}_i + \gamma_{4,4}\text{income}_i + \varepsilon_{4i},\\
\text{finconst}_i &= \gamma_{5,0} + \gamma_{5,1}\text{age}_i + \gamma_{5,2}\text{educ}_i + \gamma_{5,3}\text{sex}_i + \gamma_{5,4}\text{income}_i + \varepsilon_{5i},\\
\text{timepres}_i &= \gamma_{14,0} + \gamma_{14,1}\text{age}_i + \gamma_{14,2}\text{educ}_i + \gamma_{14,3}\text{sex}_i\\
&\quad + \gamma_{14,4}\text{kids}_i + \gamma_{14,5}\text{employ}_i + \varepsilon_{14i},\\
\text{storage}_i &= \gamma_{15,0} + \gamma_{15,1}\text{age}_i + \gamma_{15,2}\text{educ}_i + \gamma_{15,3}\text{sex}_i + \gamma_{15,4}\text{home}_i + \varepsilon_{15i},\\
\text{qualcon}_i &= \gamma_{5,0} + \gamma_{5,1}\text{age}_i + \gamma_{5,2}\text{educ}_i + \gamma_{5,3}\text{sex}_i + \varepsilon_{5i} \ldots \text{ and}\\
\text{planning}_i &= \gamma_{18,0} + \gamma_{18,1}\text{age}_i + \gamma_{18,2}\text{educ}_i + \gamma_{18,3}\text{sex}_i + \varepsilon_{18i}.
\end{aligned}$$

Finally, Model D, with both direct and indirect effects of demographics, is obtained by combining Equations 2 and 3. Note that Models A and B are not nested within Model D even though Model D is the most general. This is because the psychographic variables are exogenous in Models A and B, whereas they are endogenous in Models C and D. Model A, however, is nested within Model B, and Model C is nested within Model D.

Data

We obtain data from a mall intercept consumer survey. The survey consisted of personal interviews with 319 adults who were intercepted at four shopping malls in Massachusetts at various times of day and on different days of the week. A professional market research firm conducted the interviews over a four-week period in the summer of 1998. Each interview lasted approximately thirty minutes, and respondents were given three scratch-and-win lottery tickets, each costing \$1.00, as an incentive for participation. The conditions for inclusion in the survey were that the respondent must be at least 18 years of age and must do at least some of the grocery shopping for the household. The demographic profile of the sample is summarized in Table 2.

At the beginning of each interview, the interviewer provided the respondent with definitions and examples of (1) store brands, (2) national brands, (3) in-store promotions on national brands, and (4) out-of-store promotions on national brands. The definitions and examples were printed in bold capital letters on a card, and the card was placed in front of the respondent during the entire length of the interview. The interviewers were instructed to clarify any questions about the definitions of these four terms before proceeding with the interview. This procedure ensured that there was no confusion among respondents about what was meant by these terms.

Table 2 Sample demographics

Demographic characteristic	*Percentage of sample*
Sex	
Female	66.5
Age (years)	
<25	12.2
25–34	25.7
35–44	27.6
45–59	23.2
60–74	8.2
>74	3.1
Education level	
High school or less	19.7
Some college	29.2
College	40.1
Advanced degree	11.0
Employment status	
Homemaker	10.7
Student	6.6
Retired	6.0
Employed full time or self-employed	61.7
Employed part time or other	15.0
Annual household income ($)	
<30,000	6.3
30,000–45,000	13.9
45,000–60,000	20.5
60,000–75,000	25.9
75,000–100,000	19.6
100,000–150,000	12.0
>150,000	1.9
Other characteristics	
Household has kids under 12 years of age	35.1
Live in a house (versus apartment)	67.7

The Appendix provides the items for all the constructs used in the study as well as all the demographic variables. All constructs except demographic variables are measured on five-point scales. The national brand promotion and store brand usage scales measure frequency of use and are anchored by 'never' and 'very often,' and all other scales are of the agree/disagree type and are anchored by 'strongly disagree' and 'strongly agree.'[5]

Note that we need to measure the usage of store brands and the usage of promotions on national brands, not the feelings associated with them. Thus, our scales are fundamentally different from those in the deal proneness studies of researchers such as Lichtenstein, Netemeyer, and Burton (1990). Also, our research calls for consumer-level measures of store brand usage and national brand deal usage. Therefore, our scales are designed to assess a general usage level across product categories, though we recognize that usage also varies by product category, especially for store brands (Sethuraman and Cole 1997).

Items for many of the scales are taken either in part or in their entirety from the literature. Because we created some new scales and did not use some of the other scales in their entirety, we pretested all the scales with forty respondents. The pretest led us to reword a few items and delete a few others that had low item-to-total correlations. We use EQS software (Bentler 1995) to estimate the structural equation model.

Structural Model Analysis

Measurement model

We evaluate the reliability and validity of our constructs using confirmatory factor analysis. In Table 3, we list the constructs and reliability statistics. The composite reliability index has been shown to have advantages over Cronbach's alpha when the measures are not tau-equivalent (Raykov 1997). The table shows that the reliabilities of all the constructs are quite high. Only one Cronbach's alpha (planning) falls below Nunnally's (1978) cutoff of 0.70 for such scales.

To assess the dimensionality and validity of our constructs, we specify two confirmatory factor analysis models, one for the eleven items related to the three behaviors (i.e., store brand use, in-store national brand promotion use, and out-of-store national brand promotion use) and another for the 40 items related to the fifteen psychographic constructs. For both models, we do not allow any cross-loadings, and we do not allow measurement errors to covary. Furthermore, all interfactor covariances are freely estimated. Even under the high standards of measurement quality imposed by these conditions and with fifteen constructs in the psychographics measurement model, the fit of both models is acceptable. The robust comparative fit index is 0.914 for the store brand and promotion use measurement model and 0.916 for the psychographics measurement model. Similarly, the standardized root mean square residual is 0.094 for the former model and 0.053 for the latter. The fit of the former model is significantly improved if measurement error covariances between the items related to store flyer use are allowed. We free up these covariances because doing so makes conceptual sense. As a result, the robust comparative fit index increases from 0.914 to 0.964, whereas the standardized root mean squared residual decreases from 0.094 to 0.074. Although model fit could be improved by freeing up some other measurement paths, no modification indices stand out as being substantially bigger than the others. Therefore, we do not make further model modifications simply to boost the fit of the models (see Baumgartner and Homburg 1996).

Table 3 Reliabilities of constructs

Construct	*Relevant literature for scale items*	*Number of items*	*Cronbach's alpha*	*Composite reliability*
Characteristics associated with economic/utilitarian benefits				
Price consciousness	Darden and Perreault (1976)	3	0.790	0.826
Financial constraints	Urbany, Dickson, and Kalapurakal (1996)	2	0.808	0.817
Quality consciousness		3	0.842	0.850
Characteristics associated with psychosocial/hedonic benefits				
Shopping enjoyment	Urbany, Dickson, and Kalapurakal (1996)	3	0.768	0.812
Shopping mavenism	Feick and Price (1987); Urbany, Dickson, and Kalapurakal (1996)	3	0.852	0.876
Innovativeness	Darden and Perreault (1976)	3	0.808	0.810
Impulsiveness	Narasimhan, Neslin, and Sen (1996)	2	0.854	0.856
Variety seeking		2	0.712	0.789
Motivation to conform	Bearden, Netemeyer, and Teel (1989)	3	0.803	0.824
Characteristics associated with costs				
Planner		2	0.610	0.616
Time pressure	Hawes and Lumpkin (1984)	3	0.861	0.870
Need for cognition	Cacioppo and Petty (1982)	3	0.878	0.882
Perceived storage space		2	0.921	0.933
Brand loyalty		3	0.864	0.865
Store loyalty		3	0.875	0.876
Dependent behaviors				
Store brand usage		3	0.905	0.906
In-store promotion usage		4	0.760	0.767
Out-of-store promotion usage		4	0.861	0.799

Loadings of all the items on their factors are strong. The magnitude of their t-statistics ranges from 6.07 to 29.26. On average, 63% of the variation in an item is explained by its factor. The magnitude of interfactor correlations ranges from 0.009 to 0.618, and none of the 90% confidence intervals around the correlations include 1 (or −1), thus supporting the discriminant validity of our constructs (Anderson and Gerbing 1988; Bagozzi 1980).

Comparison of competing models

In Table 4, we summarize the fit of Models A, B, C, and D. Although the comparative fit indices are not as impressive as those of some other structural equation models, we note that our models contain many more constructs than the typical model (see Baumgartner and Homburg 1996), and many of our hypotheses are new. Some of the structural paths are hypothesized to be insignificant, but we do not constrain them to zero because our purpose is to test the hypotheses, not to maximize model fit. We use the fit indices not so much to evaluate a particular model on an absolute level as to compare the four competing models. Note also that these measures assess covariance fit, whereas variance fit, the percentage of variance in the dependent behaviors explained by the independent constructs, and the meaningfulness of individual structural parameters are important for our study. Baumgartner and Homburg (1996) caution that emphasis on covariance fit can detract from a 'proper concern' for variance fit. As we show subsequently, the structural models perform well on the latter dimension.

As mentioned previously, the four models are not nested. Therefore, we provide four measures that can be used to compare and rank-order nonnested models, apart from the χ^2 statistic and the robust comparative fit index. These measures are root mean square error of approximation (RMSEA; Steiger 1990), Akaike information criterion (AIC; Akaike 1987; Jöreskog 1993), corrected Akaike information criterion (CAIC; Bozdogan 1987), and the expected cross-validation index (ECVI; Browne and Cudeck 1989). Definitions of these measures are available in recent books on structural equation models (e.g., Maruyama 1998).

A test for the difference in χ^2 statistics between Models A and B concludes that Model B is superior; that is, adding direct effects of demographics improves model fit. However, other measures of fit show that this improvement is not very

Table 4 Fit of four alternative model specifications

	Effect of demographics on store brand usage and promotion usage			
Fit measure	*None (Model A)*	*Direct only (Model B)*	*Indirect only (Model C)*	*Both (Model D)*
χ^2 (d.f.)	2809.64 (1427)	2758.76 (1397)	2974.41 (1523)	2921.708 (1493)
Robust comparative fit index	0.891	0.893	0.883	0.886
RMSEA [90% confidence interval]	0.055 [0.052, 0.058]	0.055 [0.052, 0.058]	0.055 [0.052, 0.058]	0.055 [0.052, 0.058]
AIC	−44.359	−35.241	−71.593	−64.292
CAIC	−6844.286	−6692.212	−7328.979	−7178.72
ECVI	11.754	11.782	11.668	11.691

strong. When we consider measures such as AIC and CAIC, which penalize models with a large number of parameters more strongly than the χ^2 test does (Hayduk 1996), we conclude that adding direct effects of demographics does not improve the model. However, when we compare Model C with either Model A or Model B, there is a vast improvement in these measures of fit. Thus, demographic variables improve model fit, but modeling indirect effects is much better than modeling direct effects.

To determine whether we should include both direct and indirect effects or only indirect effects, we compare Models C and D. The χ^2 test concludes that Model D is superior. However, the improvement is not much, because Model C has better AIC, CAIC, and ECVI. Also, we find that only five of thirty direct demographic effects estimated in Model D are statistically significant. Thus, we conclude that the more parsimonious Model C is a better representation of the effect of demographics. Therefore, we proceed with results from Model C.[6]

Role of demographic characteristics

In Table 5, we present the standardized parameters and model R^2 for the relationship of demographics with each of the fifteen psychographic characteristics.

Table 5 Effect of demographic variables on psychographic characteristics

Dependent variable	*Structural parameters (standardized)*	R^2
Price consciousness	0.094 age – 0.044 sex – 0.100 education – 0.172** pcincome	0.051
Financial constraints	–0.045 age + 0.052 sex –0.317*** education – 0.202*** pcincome	0.184
Quality consciousness	0.070 age + 0.032 sex + 0.206*** education + 0.081 pcincome	0.063
Shopping enjoyment	–0.075 age + 0.001 sex – 0.135*** education	0.022
Innovativeness	0.064 age + 0.106* sex + 0.288*** education	0.092
Variety seeking	0.093 age – 0.044 sex – 0.068 education	0.015
Impulsiveness	–0.009 age + 0.106*sex + 0.079 education	0.016
Mavenism	0.139** age + 0.192*** sex + 0.041 education	0.061
Motivation to conform	0.148** age + 0.073 sex – 0.002 education	0.030
Brand loyalty	0.37 age + 0.073 sex + 0.066 education	0.010
Store loyalty	0.080 age + 0.133*** sex – 0.024 education	0.027
Planning	0.035 age + 0.137** sex + 0.070 education	0.027
Time pressure	–0.212*** age + 0.073 sex + 0.065 education + 0.039 kids – 0.068 homemaker – 0.138** student – 0.219*** parttime – 0.103*retired	0.118
NFC	0.071 age – 0.105* sex + 0.192*** education	0.052
Perceived storage space	0.100* age + 0.017 sex + 0.227*** education + 0.170*** house	0.096

* $p < 0.10$, ** $p < 0.05$, *** $p < 0.01$.

Notes: pcincome = per capita income, kids = has kids under 12 years of age, house = lives in a house.

Although the R^2s are not high, at least one demographic variable has a significant relationship with each of the psychographic variables except brand loyalty. All five of our specific hypotheses about the effect of demographics on psychographics are supported. Consumers with higher incomes are less price conscious and less financially constrained. People who are employed full time and those with children in the household are more pressured for time. And people who live in a house perceive that they have more storage space.

As we expected, age, sex, and education are associated with many psychographic variables. Older consumers are more likely to be shopping mavens, have higher motivation to conform with the expectations of others, are less pressured for time, and have more storage space. Women are more likely than men to be innovative, impulsive, shopping mavens, and planners. They are also more store loyal and have lower NFC. Finally, more educated consumers are less financially constrained, more quality conscious, more innovative, and have higher NFC. They do not enjoy shopping and have more storage space.

Thus, the relationships between demographic and psychographic characteristics are both significant and intuitively appealing. Although the direct effect of demographic variables on store brand use and in-store and out-of-store promotion use is weak, these significant indirect effects show that demographics play a role in determining shopping behavior.

Role of psychographic characteristics

In Table 6, we present standardized parameters and model R^2 for store brand use, in-store promotion use, and out-of-store promotion use. The models explain approximately 40% of the variation in each behavior. This level of explanatory power compares favorably with other studies of deal proneness or store brand proneness.

In Table 6 we also present χ^2 statistics for each psychographic variable to test whether the coefficient of that psychographic variable is equal for each of the three behaviors. That eleven of the fifteen χ^2 statistics are significant shows that most of the psychographic variables have significantly different associations with the three behaviors. Indeed, many of the coefficients have opposite signs for one versus the other behavior.

The first column of coefficients in Table 6 shows that most of our hypotheses about the psychographic correlates of store brand use are supported. There is only one instance in which a coefficient is statistically significant and has the 'wrong' sign: Variety seeking is positively associated with store brand use. Perhaps variety seekers use store brands for a change of pace. Where we had directional hypotheses, the coefficient has the right sign and is significant except in one case (impulsiveness). Where we did not have directional hypotheses, the coefficients are insignificant except for NFC, which has a significantly positive coefficient. Overall, economic benefit and cost-related characteristics are the strongest correlates of store brand usage. Store brand users are financially constrained, highly price conscious, and not very quality conscious; they are variety seekers; they have storage and time constraints, high store loyalty, and high NFC.

Table 6 Effects of psychographic characteristics (standardized coefficient estimates)

Psychographic characteristic	*Dependent variable*			
	Store brand usage	*In-store promotion usage*	*Out-of-store promotion usage*	χ^2 *Statistic*[a] *(2 d.f.)*
Economic benefits				
Price consciousness	0.211***	0.057	−0.098	12.06***
	(3.01)	(0.68)	(−1.30)	
Financial constraints	0.121*	0.358***	0.115	11.87***
	(1.80)	(3.94)	(1.56)	
Quality consciousness	−0.288***	0.007	0.148	12.30***
	(−3.36)	(0.07)	(1.58)	
Hedonic benefits				
Shopping enjoyment	0.008	0.173*	0.252***	2.41
	(0.11)	(1.91)	(2.99)	
Innovativeness	0.007	0.060	−0.024	1.03
	(0.10)	(0.72)	(−0.33)	
Variety seeking	0.109*	−0.031	0.095	2.97
	(1.70)	(−0.39)	(1.36)	
Impulsiveness	−0.098	0.363***	0.090	15.14***
	(−1.23)	(3.47)	(1.02)	
Mavenism	0.074	−0.109	0.124*	7.89**
	(1.13)	(−1.31)	(1.67)	
Motivation to conform	0.070	−0.081	−0.169***	5.95*
	(1.19)	(−1.11)	(−2.51)	
Costs				
Brand loyalty	−0.093	0.015	0.159*	5.73*
	(−1.28)	(0.17)	(1.96)	
Store loyalty	0.148***	−0.123	−0.124*	10.02***
	(2.41)	(−1.62)	(−1.82)	
Planning	−0.083	0.492***	0.412***	14.99***
	(−0.96)	(3.86)	(3.58)	
Time pressure	0.108*	0.041	−0.020	3.66
	(1.94)	(0.60)	(−0.32)	
NFC	0.097*	−0.017	−0.208***	12.09***
	(1.65)	(−0.24)	(−3.04)	
Perceived storage space	−0.102*	0.192***	0.214***	11.41***
	(−1.84)	(2.74)	(3.30)	
R^2	0.402	0.397	0.448	–

[a] Statistic for testing equality of coefficients across the three equations.
* $p<0.10$. ** $p<0.05$. *** $p<0.01$.
Notes: t-statistics are in parentheses under coefficient estimates.

In-store promotion users have fewer distinguishing characteristics. This is not surprising. Because in-store deals require little effort, they attract a variety of people. All the significant coefficients have the hypothesized sign. However, the coefficients of many characteristics are not significant. Overall, in-store promotion users are financially constrained, are impulsive, enjoy and plan their shopping, and have plenty of storage space.

Several of our hypotheses about characteristics of out-of-store deal users are supported. All significant coefficients, except for NFC, are of the hypothesized sign. It appears that low-NFC people use out-of-store promotions as decision-simplifying cues (e.g., Henderson 1985). In both cases in which we could not advance a directional hypothesis, the coefficients are significant. Users of out-of-store promotions have low motivation to conform to others' expectations and are brand loyal. The latter supports our conjecture that users of this type of promotion seek out deals on their favorite brands. Overall, hedonic benefit and costrelated characteristics are the strongest correlates of out-of-store promotion use. Users of these promotions enjoy shopping, are shopping mavens, and do not consider it necessary to conform to the expectations of others; they are brand loyal but not store loyal; they plan their shopping; they have low NFC and plenty of storage space.

This analysis shows that there are distinct differences between the psychographic correlates of store brand use, in-store national brand promotion use, and out-of-store national brand promotion use. As we hypothesized, however, the correlates of in-store and out-of-store deal use are the most similar, whereas the correlates of store brand and out-of-store promotion use are the most dissimilar. Store brand users are the opposite of out-of-store promotion users on many fronts, for example, quality consciousness, store loyalty, NFC, and storage space. In line with these patterns, the correlation between in-store and out-of-store promotion coefficients is +0.64, that between store brand and in-store promotion coefficients is −0.30, and that between store brand and out-of-store promotion coefficients is −0.57.

Segmentation Analysis

Defining the segments

The previous analysis shows that store brand use, in-store promotion use, and out-of-store promotion use are driven by different psychographic characteristics. In this section, we determine how these differences produce different market segments. We cluster-analyze the sample using factor scores on store brand use, in-store promotion use, and out-of-store promotion use. We use K-means cluster analysis on the basis of Euclidean distances (Anderberg 1973). In Table 7, we summarize the key measures for evaluating the three-, four-, five-, and six-cluster solutions.

Table 7 shows that all measures improve substantially from the three- to the four-cluster solution. However, adding further clusters reduces the pseudo F-statistic (Calinski and Harabasz 1974), which has been shown to be one of the best ways to determine the number of clusters in a data set (Milligan and Cooper 1985). Also, the rate of increase in the other two measures is much lower. Furthermore, our examination of the cluster means shows that the four-cluster solution adds substantial insight over the three-cluster solution by identifying a very different cluster, whereas the fifth and sixth clusters separate out relatively minor gradations of store brand and promotion use. We therefore use the four-cluster solution.

Table 7 Cluster analysis summary

	Store brand usage		*In-store promotion usage*		*Out-of-store promotion usage*		*Overall*		
Number of clusters	R^2	*Between/ within variance*	R^2	*Between/ within variance*	R^2	*Between/ within variance*	R^2	*Between/ within variance*	*F-Statistic*
3	0.650	1.857	0.366	0.577	0.294	0.417	0.528	1.121	177.05
4	0.703	2.365	0.544	1.193	0.518	1.077	0.637	1.755	184.28
5	0.775	3.436	0.617	1.608	0.522	1.092	0.699	2.322	182.25
6	0.812	4.304	0.633	1.724	0.573	1.339	0.733	2.743	171.71

Before going further, we examine the stability of the four-cluster solution in two ways. First, we use several random starting cluster seeds and find that the substantive nature of the clusters is not sensitive to them. Second, we use McIntyre and Blashfield's (1980) cross-validation procedure, which has been recommended by Punj and Stewart (1983). Specifically, we split our data into two random halves, perform cluster analysis on the first split-half, and use the Euclidean distances from the resulting cluster centroids to assign respondents in the second split-half to clusters. We then examine the agreement between this assignment and a cluster analysis performed on the second split-half sample. We find that there is agreement between the assignments in 86% of the cases. These results provide evidence that our clusters are reliable.

We describe the four clusters in our sample in Table 8. The first and second clusters, comprising more than one-third of the sample, clearly represent separate deal-focused and store brand-focused market segments. The third cluster, consisting of a little less than one-third of the sample, represents a 'use all' market segment. Cluster 4, also almost one-third of the sample, represents a 'use none' market segment.

This segmentation is quite consistent with our structural model results. The specific psychographic associations and the correlation pattern among the coefficients in the structural model suggested a store brand-focused segment and indicated that in-store and out-of-store users could be combined into a deal-focused segment. There is also enough in common among all three

Table 8 Description of four clusters

	Mean factor score for			
Cluster number	*Store brand usage*	*In-store promotion usage*	*Out-of-store promotion usage*	*Number of observations*
1	−0.958	0.440	0.443	51
2	0.987	−0.340	−0.305	68
3	0.393	0.412	0.242	97
4	−0.547	−0.382	−0.246	103

behaviors to produce a segment that partakes in all of them, and, of course, there is a segment that partakes in none.

Predicting segment membership

To predict segment membership, we compute the normalized Euclidean distance of each respondent from each of the four cluster centroids and multiply by −1 to obtain proximity rather than distance. We then regress the four proximity measures on the psychographic variables. Normalization ensures that an observation cannot move closer to (or farther away from) all four clusters simultaneously. For logical consistency, we constrain the coefficients of each psychographic variable to add to zero across the four equations.[7] A significant coefficient shows that the variable is a good predictor of segment membership, and a positive sign increases the likelihood of its being in a given segment relative to the other segments.

Although the results of these segment regressions should be somewhat consistent with the structural model results in Table 6, we also expect some differences. First, the dealfocused and use-all segments in the segmentation analysis combine both in-store and out-of-store deal use. Second, the deal-focused and store brand-focused segments contain only hard-core users. Multiple users have been separated out into the use-all segment. Third, the use-all segment should be difficult to predict, because it involves behaviors that have been shown to relate with opposite signs to various psychographics.

In Table 9, we summarize the results. The table shows that the psychographics have significant overall discriminatory power for all four clusters; adjusted R^2s range from 0.14 to 0.31.

Membership in the deal-focused segment can be predicted by most of the characteristics that were significant in the structural equation model for predicting in-store or out-of-store promotion usage. These characteristics include impulsiveness, shopping enjoyment, planning, storage availability, motivation to conform, brand loyalty, store loyalty, and NFC. This is intuitively appealing because members of this segment use both in-store and out-of-store promotions and these behaviors are similar enough that the influences of most characteristics do not cancel one another. In addition, consumers who are highly price conscious do not focus exclusively on deals and instead gravitate toward the store brand or use-all segments. However, quality-conscious consumers avoid the store brand and use-all segments and shift their attention to deals. This reinforces the role of deals as a means to deliver a quality benefit (Chandon, Wansink, and Laurent 2000).

It makes sense that the signs of the coefficients for predicting membership in the store brand-focused segment are the same as they are in the structural equation model for thirteen of the fifteen psychographics. Many of the highly significant variables in the structural equation model – price consciousness, quality consciousness, store loyalty, and storage space – are also highly significant in the prediction equation. In addition, membership in this segment can be predicted on the basis of lower shopping enjoyment, less impulsiveness, more mavenism, more motivation to conform, less brand loyalty, and less planning.

Note that the lowest R^2 is for the use-all segment. This is to be expected

Table 9 Psychographic correlates of segments

Variable	*Standardized coefficient in regression for proximity to*			
	Cluster 1 Deal-focused	*Cluster 2 Store brand-focused*	*Cluster 3 Use all*	*Cluster 4 Use none*
Price consciousness	−0.119**	0.224***	0.028	−0.178***
Financial constraints	0.055	−0.101*	0.190***	−0.104*
Quality consciousness	0.270***	−0.229***	−0.148*	0.103
Shopping enjoyment	0.097**	−0.103*	0.123*	−0.095
Innovativeness	0.018	0.028	−0.069	0.001
Variety seeking	−0.084*	0.066	0.108**	−0.081
Impulsiveness	0.138**	−0.168***	0.166**	−0.096
Mavenism	−0.034	0.157***	0.007	−0.175***
Motivation to conform	−0.167***	0.135***	0.120**	−0.081
Brand loyalty	0.123**	−0.120**	−0.048	0.050
Store loyalty	−0.129***	0.150***	−0.004	−0.037
Planning	0.178***	−0.252***	0.233***	−0.096
Time pressure	−0.075*	0.049	0.152***	−0.109**
NFC	−0.109**	0.064	0.003	0.046
Perceived storage space	0.179***	−0.145***	0.062	−0.084
Adjusted R^2	0.309	0.291	0.140	0.168

* $p < 0.10$. ** $p < 0.05$. *** $p < 0.01$.

because this segment is an amalgam of behaviors that the structural model shows are generated by different psychographic factors. Membership in this segment is more likely if the consumer is financially constrained, is not quality conscious, enjoys shopping, is variety seeking and impulsive, is motivated to conform to peer pressure, plans shopping, and feels time pressure. In summary, people in this group want to save money, but they also want to save time and they value hedonic benefits, so they make the best of both store brands and deals.

Finally, the use-none segment is a diverse group and can be distinguished from the rest of the market in only a few ways. Not surprisingly, members of this group are neither price conscious nor financially constrained. They are not shopping mavens either, nor are they pressured for time. Therefore, they are not attracted to either the monetary or time savings promised by promotions and store brands. They are not drawn to these behaviors by the self-expressive desires that shopping mavens have.

Conclusion

Summary of findings

We have investigated the extent to which store brands and national brand promotions attract the same consumers. To do so, we have employed a structural model to study the characteristics of consumers who buy store brands, national brands on in-store promotions, or national brands on out-of-store promotions.

We then clustered consumers into segments on the basis of their use of store brand and national brand promotions and distinguished between the segments using the consumer characteristics from the structural model.

Our structural model analysis shows that the impact of demographics on these behaviors is funneled through psychographics instead of being direct. Furthermore, the psychographic drivers of store brand use, in-store promotion use, and out-of-store promotion use differ substantially. The biggest difference in psychographic drivers is between store-brand and promotion usage, especially out-of-store promotion usage. Store brand use is particularly associated with price consciousness, low quality consciousness, and store loyalty. Store brand users thus transfer their store loyalty into saving money, even at the expense of quality.

Out-of-store promotion use, in contrast, is associated with higher shopping enjoyment and mavenism and less pressure to conform to the expectations of others. Heavy users of these promotions plan their shopping, are willing to switch stores but not brands, have plenty of storage space, and have low NFC. Thus, the hedonic aspect of promotions is more salient to them than to store brand users, and their costs are low, so they are willing to incur the effort involved in using promotions.

In-store promotion use is driven by psychographics that are similar to those that drive out-of-store promotion use, especially shopping enjoyment, planning, and available storage space. However, in-store deal users differ in that they feel more financially constrained; are impulsive; and are not driven by mavenism, motivation to conform, and NFC. An interesting aspect of in-store promotion usage is that both impulsive and planning orientations lead to the same behavior. This is a sensible result. Consumers can make use of in-store promotions by either buying on impulse or planning to use these promotions.

Overall, our structural equation model shows that store brand usage is quite different from either in-store or out-of-store promotion usage, whereas in-store and out-of-store promotion usage share several similar drivers. It makes sense, then, that our cluster analysis reveals a store-brand focused segment and a general deal-focused segment. In addition, however, there is a well-defined segment that partakes in all three behaviors, as well as a segment that partakes in none. Membership in the store brand-focused segment can be predicted on the basis of many of the psychographics that drive store brand purchasing in general. Membership in the deal-focused segment can be predicted by a combination of the psychographics that predict these behaviors separately. The use-all segment is the least easy to predict, because it combines three behaviors that are driven in opposite directions by some psychographics.

Our analysis provides important insight on whether store-brand users and deal users are different market segments. These behaviors are driven by different psychographics, and there are market segments that focus exclusively on one behavior or the other. In that sense, they are different market segments. However, the delineation is not so sharp that it precludes a market segment that partakes in both store brands and national brand promotions. Indeed, we find that a significant portion of the market belongs to this segment.

Implications for researchers

There are several implications of our work for researchers. First, we have shown that not only deal buying but also store brand buying is driven by the economic/utilitarian returns, psychosocial/hedonic returns, and costs that have been conceptualized by researchers such as Shimp and Kavas (1984), Urbany, Dickson, and Kalapurakal (1996), and Chandon, Wansink, and Laurent (2000). Our findings support the use of this framework to study the behavior of consumers who seek better value in the marketplace.

Second, we have shown that though demographics may not be effective for directly predicting these three behaviors, they do have a significant association with psychographic characteristics and are therefore useful in segmentation, targeting, and communication. For example, our findings buttress prior work that shows that women value self-expression and exploration more than men do (e.g., Feick and Price 1987; Urbany, Dickson, and Kalapurakal 1996). As might be expected, education is positively related with quality consciousness and NFC, full-time employment and having young children are associated with time pressure, and higher income is associated with lower financial constraints and price consciousness.

A third implication relates to our conceptualization of store brand usage as a consumer-level rather than a category-level characteristic. There are certainly differences in the use and perceptions of store brands across categories and retailers (Sethuraman and Cole 1997). However, our success in characterizing store brand users and distinguishing them from deal users on the basis of psychographic characteristics shows that consumers have overarching perceptions about using store brands that generalize across product categories.

Fourth, our work demonstrates the value of jointly examining multiple related behaviors (for other work in this spirit, see Kahn and Raju 1991). Using a common set of variables and one method to study these clearly related behaviors has enabled us to make direct comparisons among their antecedents without being hindered by noncomparable measures or methods.

Finally, we reveal some important specific relationships between consumer psychographics and the use of store brands and/or deals. For example, we show that planning and impulsiveness can go together and that in-store promotion usage is consistent with both tendencies. This dual role warrants further investigation. We find that brand-loyal consumers are more likely to buy national brands using out-of-store promotions. This must be because they selectively seek out and use promotions on the brands they regularly buy. In general, the positive associations between brand loyalty and deal use and between storage availability and deal use suggest that a significant role of out-of-store promotions is to induce loyal users to stock up on the brand. This finding is somewhat at odds with the notion that the predominant effect of promotions is on brand switching (e.g., Gupta 1988). Consistent with our findings, however, recent research has found that stockpiling and stockpiling-related consumption play a more important role than was previously thought, though switching does account for the majority of the promotion's effect (see Ailawadi and Neslin 1998; Bell, Chiang, and Padmanabhan 1999; Bucklin, Gupta, and Siddarth 1998; Dillon and Gupta 1996).

Furthermore, the decomposition of the promotion's effect may differ by type of promotion. Our results suggest that displays and in-store specials may induce more brand switching, whereas coupons and other out-of-store promotions may be more likely to attract consumers who are loyal to the brand. In any event, further research is needed to reconcile our findings with the brand switching effect of promotions.

Implications for managers

The major implication for managers is that manufacturers and retailers have the opportunity either to avoid each other or to compete head to head. Manufacturers can target the deal-focused segment, and retailers can target the store brand-focused segment. These strategies could reduce the tug-of-war between manufacturers and retailers. However, if manufacturers and retailers both target the use-all segment, it can exacerbate competition within the channel. Our analysis should help both parties design their programs after they have decided which segments to target. For example, manufacturers can target the deal-focused segment by appealing to quality-conscious consumers who stock up on their favorite brands. This means that the promotion should include a strong advertising message to trigger the quality considerations. If the manufacturer wants to encourage stockpiling – for example, to preempt a competitor – it can do so with this segment by suggesting large purchase quantities (Wansink, Kent, and Hoch 1998). The promotion can be designed as an impulse purchase or a planned purchase. That this target group may already be loyal to the brand means that these promotions should be seen more as customer retention than acquisition tools. This explains why such promotions may not pay off in the short run. That this target group is not store loyal may mean that manufacturers can run cooperative promotions with retailers, the carrot for the retailer being that these promotions will increase store traffic.

The retailer's store brand-focused segment is quite distinct. It contains store-loyal, price-conscious customers who are not quality conscious and are neither shopping experts nor stockpilers. Retailers can access this group through their frequent shopper programs, which can be used to identify store-loyal customers, thus avoiding the deal-focused and use-all segments. For the store brand-focused group, it would be appropriate to stress the relatively consistently low store brand price, so consumers do not need to stock up. Retailers should stress the simplicity of buying store brands, because consumers in the store brand segment are not expert shoppers and do not plan their shopping or enjoy it.

Another set of implications for managers relates to the desirability of using HI–LO versus everyday low pricing.[8] Our results imply that the best strategy for store brands is to set an everyday low price that is close to the promoted price of national brands. Customers in the store brand-focused segment do not plan or enjoy shopping, so a HI–LO pricing strategy would dissuade them from using store brands. In contrast, national brands would benefit from a HI–LO strategy. Manufacturers can use this strategy to price discriminate and to compete with store brands for the use-all segment. The use-none segment will buy national brands at the regular price, whereas the deal price will enable national brand manufacturers to compete with other national brands for the deal-focused segment and with store brands for the use-all segment.

Therefore, our answer to the question whether manufacturers can combat the store brand threat effectively through promotions is a partial yes. If manufacturers want to battle store brands for market share, they can target the use-all segment. They can do so with price- and convenience-oriented messages and in-store displays designed to encourage impulsive purchases. However, this will work only partially. There is still a segment that exclusively buys store brands and has very different characteristics than promotion users do. These people are not impulsive, do not plan, and do not stockpile. This segment seems inaccessible to the types of promotions commonly used by manufacturers. Our conclusion here is consistent with the mixed view of whether manufacturer promotions reduce store brand share. For example, Blattberg and Wisniewski (1989) find that promotions are effective at combating store brands, whereas Hoch and Banerji (1993) find that they are not.

In conclusion, our results contribute to the study of store brand and promotion usage conceptually, substantively, and managerially. Conceptually, we reinforce the economic benefits/hedonic benefits/costs framework and support the role of demographics as an indirect rather than direct cause of these behaviors. Substantively, we find that store brands and national brand promotions attract consumers with distinctly different psychographic profiles; the national brand promotion user profile relates more to hedonic benefits and costs, whereas the store brand user profile relates more to economic benefits and costs. Store brand and national brand promotion usage are therefore different consumer behaviors. Managerially, we suggest that manufacturers and retailers can avoid or escalate conflict depending on which segments they target; that promotions are only a partial way for manufacturers to address the private label threat; and that the psychographic characteristics of store brand and promotion users make everyday low price a promising strategy for store brands, whereas HI–LO pricing might be better for national brands. There is still much to do in this area, as we pointed out previously. This work is important because the way manufacturers and retailers play out their dual roles as competitors and partners, which includes their promotion and store brand strategies, will define the twenty-first-century marketplace.

Appendix

Survey Items

1 Store brand usage scale

I buy store brands.
I look for store brands when I go shopping.
My shopping cart contains store brands for several products.

2 Out-of-store national brand promotion usage scale

I clip coupons for national brands from newspapers and magazines.
I take along coupons for national brands and use them when I go shopping.
I scan store flyers for sales on national brands before going shopping.
I use store flyers to decide what to buy and where to shop.

3 In-Store national brand promotion usage scale

I am influenced by special displays of national brands in the store.
I use a coupon if I see it on a package or in the store.
I pick up and use the store flyer when I am shopping in the store.
I take advantage of specials on national brands in the store.

4 Psychographic characteristics

Price consciousness

I compare prices of at least a few brands before I choose one.
I find myself checking the prices even for small items.
It is important to me to get the best price for the products I buy.

Financial constraints

My household budget is always tight.
My household often has problems making ends meet.

Quality consciousness

I will not give up high quality for a lower price.
I always buy the best.
It is important to me to buy high-quality products.

Shopping enjoyment

I think grocery shopping is a chore.
I like to finish my shopping as quickly as possible and get out of the store.
I enjoy grocery shopping.

Innovativeness

When I see a product somewhat different from the usual, I check it out.
I am often among the first people to try a new product.
I like to try new and different things.

Variety seeking

If I use the same brands over and over again, I get tired of them.
I buy different brands to get some variety.

Impulsiveness

I often find myself buying products on impulse in the grocery store.
I often make an unplanned purchase when the urge strikes me.

Mavenism

I am somewhat of an expert when it comes to shopping.
People think of me as a good source of shopping information.
I enjoy giving people tips on shopping.

Motivation to conform

It bothers me if other people disapprove of my choices.
It is important to me to fit in.
My behavior often depends on how I feel others wish me to behave.

Brand loyalty

I prefer one brand of most products I buy.
I am willing to make an effort to search for my favorite brand.
Usually, I care a lot about which particular brand I buy.

Store loyalty

I prefer to always shop at one grocery store.
I am willing to make an effort to shop at my favorite grocery store.
Usually, I care a lot about which particular grocery store I shop at.

Planning

I spend a lot of time planning my grocery shopping trips.
I make a shopping list before I go grocery shopping.

Time pressure

Most days, I have no time to relax.
I always seem to be in a hurry.
I never seem to have enough time for the things I want to do.

NFC

Thinking is not my idea of fun.
I like tasks that don't require much thinking once I have learned them.
I only think as hard as I have to.

Storage space

I have plenty of storage space at home.
I have a lot of room at home to stock extra grocery products.

5 Demographic variables

Age

1 = less than 25 years   4 = 45–59 years
2 = 25–34 years   5 = 60–74 years
3 = 35–44 years   6 = 75 years or older

Sex

0 = male   1 = female

Education

1 = high school or less   3 = college
2 = some college   4 = advanced degree

Employment (dummy variable coded from multicategory question)

0/1 = homemaker   0/1 = student   0/1 = part time/other
0/1 = full time/self-employed   0/1 = retired

Children Under Age 12 (dummy variable coded from multicategory question)

0 = no 1 = yes

Live in a House (dummy variable coded from multicategory question)

0 = no 1 = yes

Annual household income

1 = <$30,000   5 = $75,000 to <$100,000
2 = $30,000 to <$45,000   6 = $100,00 to <$150,000
3 = $45,000 to <$60,000   7 = >$150,000
4 = $60,000 to <$75,000

Per Capita Income (Computed)

Annual household income/number of members in household

Notes

1 In the remainder of the article, when we refer to promotion or deal usage, we mean promotions on national brands.

2 Chandon, Wansink, and Laurent (2000) do not examine costs and list convenience as an economic benefit. Our typology includes the specific aspects of convenience in search, switching, thinking, and inventory costs.

3 Although our hypotheses refer to national brand loyalty, a limitation of our data is that our measurement scale for brand loyalty does not refer specifically to national brands. However, we believe that consumers were thinking of national brands when they responded, because national brands are more salient. As a whole, they have higher market shares and higher loyalty as measured by share of requirements (Information Resources Inc. 1998).

4 Some of the demographic characteristics – for example, employment status – are operationalized as a set of dummy variables in the empirical analysis. For simplicity of exposition at this stage, we simply represent each demographic characteristic as a single variable.

5 The Appendix lists the psychographic scales in the order in which they were discussed in the previous section. Their order was random in the actual survey.

6 There are no substantive differences in the estimated psychographic coefficients for Model C and Model D. Complete results for Model D are available from the first author on request.

7 We also performed four logistic regressions using the dichotomous cluster membership variables, one for distinguishing each cluster from the other three. We did not find any substantive differences in conclusions, though there were fewer significant coefficients in the logistic regressions. We believe that using the continuous proximity variables is preferable, because they retain more information than the dichotomized cluster membership variables. However, results of the logistic regressions are available from the first author on request.

8 We thank an anonymous reviewer for suggesting the insights stated in this paragraph.

References

Ailawadi, Kusum L. and Scott A. Neslin (1998), 'The Effect of Promotion on Consumption: Buying More and Consuming It Faster,' *Journal of Marketing Research*, 35 (August), 390–98.

Akaike, Hirotugu (1987), 'Factor Analysis and AIC,' *Psychometrika*, 52 (September), 317–32.

Anderberg, M.R. (1973), *Cluster Analysis for Applications*. New York: Academic Press.

Anderson, James C. and David W. Gerbing (1988), 'Structural Equation Modeling in Practice: A Review and Recommended Two Step Approach.' *Psychological Bulletin*, 103 (3), 411–23.

Bagozzi, Richard P. (1980), *Causal Models in Marketing*. New York: John Wiley & Sons.

Baltas, George and Peter Doyle (1998), 'Exploring Private Brand Buying,' in *Proceedings of the 27th EMAC Conference*, Track 5: Marketing Research, Per Andersson, ed. Stockholm: European Marketing Association, 183–200.

Baumgartner, Hans and Christian Homburg (1996), 'Applications of Structural Equation Modeling in Marketing and Consumer Research: A Review,' *International Journal of Research in Marketing*, 13 (October), 139–61.

Bawa, Kapil and Robert W. Shoemaker (1987), 'The Coupon-Prone Consumer: Some Findings Based on Purchase Behavior Across Product Classes,' *Journal of Marketing*, 51 (October), 99–110.

Bearden, William, Richard G. Netemeyer, and Jesse E. Teel (1989), 'Measurement of Consumer Susceptibility to Interpersonal Influence,' *Journal of Consumer Research*, 15 (March), 473–81.

Bell, David R., Jeongwen Chiang, and V. Padmanabhan (1999), 'The Decomposition of Promotional Response: An Empirical Generalization,' *Marketing Science*, 18 (4), 504–26.

Bellizzi, Joseph A., John R. Hamilton, Harry F. Krueckeberg, and Warren S. Martin (1981), 'Consumer Perceptions of National, Private, and Generic Brands,' *Journal of Retailing*, 57 (Winter), 56–70.

Bentler, Peter M. (1995), *EQS Structural Equations Program Manual*. Los Angeles: BMDP Statistical Software.

Blattberg, Robert C., Thomas Buesing, Peter Peacock, and Subrata Sen (1978), 'Identifying the Deal Prone Segment,' *Journal of Marketing Research*, 15 (August), 369–77.

—— and Scott A. Neslin (1990), *Sales Promotion: Concepts, Methods, and Strategies*. Englewood Cliffs, NJ: Prentice Hall.

—— and Kenneth Wisniewski (1989), 'Price-Induced Patterns of Competition,' *Marketing Science*, 8 (Fall), 291–309.

Bozdogan, Hamparsum (1987), 'Model Selection and Akaike's Information Criteria (AIC): The General Theory and Its Analytical Extensions,' *Psychometrika*, 52 (September), 345–70.

Browne, Michael W. and Robert Cudeck (1989), 'Single Sample Cross-Validation Indices for Covariance Structures,' *Multivariate Behavioral Research*, 24 (October), 445–55.

Bucklin, Randolph E., Sunil Gupta, and S. Siddarth (1998), 'Determining Segmentation in Sales Response Across Consumer Purchase Behaviors,' *Journal of Marketing Research*, 35 (May), 189–97.

—— and James M. Lattin (1991) 'A Two-State Model of Purchase Incidence and Brand Choice,' *Marketing Science*, 19 (Winter), 24–39.

Cacioppo, John T. and Richard E. Petty (1982), 'The Need for Cognition,' *Journal of Personality and Social Psychology*, 42 (1), 116–31.

Calinski, R.B. and J. Harabasz (1974), 'A Dendrite Method for Cluster Analysis,' *Communications in Statistics*, 3, 1–27.

Chandon, Pierre, Brian Wansink, and Gilles Laurent (2000), 'A Benefit Congruency Framework of Sales Promotion Effectiveness,' *Journal of Marketing*, 64 (October), 65–81.

Cobb, Cathy J. and Wayne D. Hoyer (1986), 'Planned Versus Impulse Purchase Behavior,' *Journal of Retailing*, 62 (Winter), 384–409.

Cox Direct (1998), *20th Annual Survey of Promotional Practices*. Largo, FL: Cox Direct.

Cunningham, Isabelle C.M., Andrew P. Hardy, and Giovanna Imperia (1982), 'Generic Brands Versus National Brands and Store Brands,' *Journal of Advertising Research*, 22 (October/November), 25–32.

Darden, William R. and William D. Perreault (1976), 'Identifying Interurban Shoppers: Multiproduct Purchase Patterns and Segmentation Profiles,' *Journal of Marketing Research*, 13 (February), 51–60.

Dick, Alan, Arun Jain, and Paul Richardson (1995), 'Correlates of Store Brand Proneness: Some Empirical Observations,' *Journal of Product and Brand Management*, 4 (4), 15–22.

Dillon, William R. and Sunil Gupta (1996), 'A Segment-Level Model of Category Volume and Brand Choice,' *Marketing Science*, 15 (1), 38–59.

Donnelley Marketing Inc. (1995), *17th Annual Survey of Promotional Practices*. Oakbrook Terrace, IL: Donnelley Marketing Inc.

Dunne, David and Chakravarthi Narasimhan (1999), 'The New Appeal of Private Labels,' *Harvard Business Review*, 77 (May/June), 41–52.

Feick, Lawrence F. and Linda L. Price (1987), 'The Market Maven: A Diffuser of Marketplace Information,' *Journal of Marketing*, 51 (January), 83–97.

Granzin, Kent L. (1981), 'An Investigation of the Market for Generic Products,' *Journal of Retailing*, 57 (Winter), 39–55.

Gupta, Sunil (1988), 'Impact of Sales Promotions on When, What, and How Much to Buy,' *Journal of Marketing Research*, 25 (November), 342–55.

Hawes, Jon M. and James R. Lumpkin (1984), 'Understanding the Outshopper,' *Journal of the Academy of Marketing Science*, 12 (Fall), 200–18.

Hayduk, Leslie (1996), *LISREL Issues, Debates, and Strategies*. Baltimore: Johns Hopkins University Press.

Henderson, Caroline M. (1984), 'Sales Promotion Segmentation: Refining the Deal-Proneness Construct,' working paper, Amos Tuck School of Business Administration, Dartmouth College.

—— (1985), 'Modeling the Coupon Redemption Decision,' in *Advances in Consumer Research*, Vol. 12, Elizabeth C. Hirschman and Morris B. Holbrook, eds. Provo, UT: Association for Consumer Research, 138–43.

Higie, Robin A., Lawrence Feick, and Linda L. Price (1987), 'Types and Amount of Word-of-Mouth Communications About Retailers,' *Journal of Retailing*, 63 (Fall), 260–78.

Hoch, Stephen J. and Shumeet Banerji (1993), 'When Do Private Labels Succeed?' *Sloan Management Review*, 34 (Summer), 57–67.

Information Resources Inc. (1998), *IRI Marketing Fact Book*, Annual Report. Chicago: Information Resources Inc.

Inman, Jeffrey J., Leigh McAlister, and Wayne D. Hoyer (1990), 'Promotion Signal: Proxy for a Price Cut?' *Journal of Consumer Research*, 17 (June), 74–81.

Jöreskog, Karl G. (1993), 'Testing Structural Equation Models,' in *Testing Structural Equation Models*, K. Bollen and R. Stine, eds. Newbury Park, CA: Sage Publications, 294–316.

Kahn, Barbara E. and Jagmohan S. Raju (1991), 'Effects of Price Promotions on Variety-Seeking and Reinforcement Behavior,' *Marketing Science*, 10 (Fall), 316–37.

Kim, Byung-Do, Kannan Srinivasan, and Ronald T. Wilcox (1999), 'Identifying Price Sensitive Consumers: The Relative Merits of Demographic vs. Purchase Pattern Information,' *Journal of Retailing*, 75 (Summer), 173–93.

Kolodinsky, Jane (1990). 'Time as a Direct Source of Utility: The Case of Price Information Search for Groceries,' *Journal of Consumer Affairs*, 24 (Summer), 89–109.

Krishna, Aradhna, Imran S. Currim, and Robert W. Shoemaker (1991), 'Consumer Perceptions of Promotional Activity,' *Journal of Marketing*, 55 (April), 4–16.

Lal, Rajiv (1990), 'Manufacturer Trade Deals and Retail Price Promotions,' *Journal of Marketing Research*, 27 (November), 428–44.

Lichtenstein, Donald R., Richard G. Netemeyer, and Scot Burton (1990), 'Distinguishing Coupon Proneness from Value Consciousness: An Acquisition-Transaction Utility Theory Perspective,' *Journal of Marketing*, 54 (July), 54–67.

——, —— and —— (1995), 'Assessing the Domain Specificity of Deal Proneness: A Field Study,' *Journal of Consumer Research*, 22 (December), 314–26.

Mantel, Susan Powell and Frank R. Kardes (1999), 'The Role of Direction of Comparison, Attribute-Based Processing, and Attitude-Based Processing in Consumer Preference,' *Journal of Consumer Research*, 25 (March), 335–52.

Maruyama, Geoffrey M. (1998), *Basics of Structural Equation Modeling*. Thousand Oaks, CA: Sage Publications.

McIntyre, R.M. and R.K. Blashfield (1980), 'A Nearest-Centroid Technique for Evaluating the Minimum-Variance Clustering Procedure,' *Multivariate Behavioral Research*, 15(2), 225–38.

Milligan, G.W. and M.C. Cooper (1985), 'An Examination of Procedures for Determining the Number of Clusters in a Data Set,' *Psychometrika*, 50(2), 159–79.

Mittal, Banwari (1994), 'Bridging the Gap Between Our Knowledge of "Who" Uses Coupons and "Why" Coupons Are Used,' *Marketing Science Institute Working Paper No. 94–112*. Cambridge, MA: Marketing Science Institute.

Montgomery, David B. (1971), 'Consumer Characteristics Associated with Dealing: An Empirical Example,' *Journal of Marketing Research*, 8 (February), 118–20.

Moorthy, K. Sridhar (1988), 'Product and Price Competition in a Duopoly,' *Marketing Science*, 5 (3), 141–68.

Narasimhan, Chakravarthi (1984), 'A Price Discrimination Theory of Coupons,' *Marketing Science*, 3 (Spring), 128–47.

——, Scott A. Neslin, and Subrata Sen (1996), 'Promotional Elasticities and Category Characteristics,' *Journal of Marketing*, 60 (April), 17–30.

NCH NuWorld (1999), *Worldwide Coupon Distribution & Redemption Trends*. Lincolnshire, IL: NCH NuWorld Marketing Limited.

Nunnally, Jum C. (1978), *Psychometric Theory*, 2d ed. New York: McGraw-Hill Publishers.

Omar, Ogenyi Ejye (1996), 'Grocery Purchase Behaviour for National and Own-Label Brands,' *Service Industries Journal*, 16 (January), 58–67.

Price, Linda L., Lawrence F. Feick, and Audrey Guskey-Federouch (1988), 'Couponing Behaviors of the Market Maven: Profile of a Super-Couponer,' in *Advances in Consumer Research*, Vol. 15, Michael J. Houston, ed. Provo, UT: Association for Consumer Research, 354–59.

Progressive Grocer (1975), 'Consumer Behavior in the Supermarket,' (October), 37–46.

Punj, Girish and David W. Stewart (1983), 'Cluster Analysis in Marketing Research: Review and Suggestions for Applications,' *Journal of Marketing Research*, 20 (May), 134–48.

Quelch, John and David Harding (1996), 'Brands Versus Private Labels: Fighting to Win, *Harvard Business Review*, 74 (January/February), 99–109.

Raju, P.S. (1980), 'Optimal Stimulation Level: Its Relationship to Personality, Demographics and Exploratory Behavior,' *Journal of Consumer Research*, 7 (December), 795–809.

Raykov, Tenko (1997), 'Estimation of Composite Reliability for Congeneric Measures,' *Applied Psychological Measurement*, 21 (June), 173–84.

Richardson, P.S., A.S. Dick, and A.K. Jain (1994), 'Extrinsic and Intrinsic Cue Effects on Perceptions of Store Brand Quality,' *Journal of Marketing*, 58 (October), 28–36.

——, A.K. Jain, and A.S. Dick (1996), 'Household Store Brand Proneness: A Framework,' *Journal of Retailing*, 72 (2), 159–85.

Schindler, Robert M. (1989), 'The Excitement of Getting a Bargain: Some Hypotheses Concerning the Origin and Effects of Smart-Shopper Feelings,' in *Advances in Consumer Research*, Vol. 16, Thomas K. Srull, ed. Provo, UT: Association for Consumer Research, 447–53.

Schneider, Linda G. and Imran S. Currim (1991), 'Consumer Purchase Behaviors Associated with Active and Passive Deal-Proneness,' *International Journal of Research in Marketing*, 8 (3), 205–22.

Sethuraman, Raj (1992), 'Understanding Cross-Category Differences in Private Label Shares of Grocery Products,' *Marketing Science Institute Working Paper No.* 92–128. Cambridge, MA: Marketing Science Institute.

—— and Catherine Cole (1997), 'Why Do Consumers Pay More for National Brands Than for Store Brands?' *Marketing Science Institute Working Paper No. 97–126*. Cambridge, MA: Marketing Science Institute.

Shimp, Terence A. and Alican Kavas (1984), 'The Theory of Reasoned Action Applied to Coupon Usage,' *Journal of Consumer Research*, 11 (December), 795–809.

Sirohi, Niren, Edward W. McLaughlin, and Dick R. Wittink (1998), 'A Model of Consumer Perceptions and Store Loyalty Intentions for a Supermarket Retailer,' *Journal of Retailing*, 74 (2), 223–45.

Steenkamp, Jan-Benedict E.M. and Marnik G. Dekimpe (1997), 'The Increasing Power of Store Brands: Building Loyalty and Market Share,' *Long Range Planning*, 30 (6), 917–30.

Steiger, J.H. (1990), 'Structural Model Evaluation and Modification: An Interval Estimation Approach,' *Multivariate Behavioral Research*, 25 (April), 173–80.

Urbany, Joel E., Peter R. Dickson, and Rosemary Kalapurakal (1996), 'Price Search in the Retail Grocery Market,' *Journal of Marketing*, 60 (April), 91–104.

Wansink, Brian, R.J. Kent, and S.J. Hoch (1998), 'An Anchoring and Adjustment Model of Purchase Quantity Decisions,' *Journal of Marketing Research*, 35 (February), 71–81.

Webster, Frederick R., Jr. (1965), 'The Deal Prone Consumer,' *Journal of Marketing Research*, 2 (May), 186–9.

Williams, Terrell G. and Mark E. Slama (1995), 'Market Mavens' Purchase Decision Evaluative Criteria: Implications for Brand and Store Promotion Efforts,' *Journal of Consumer Marketing*, 12 (3), 4–21.

Zhang, Yong (1996), 'Responses to Humorous Advertising: The Moderating Effect of Need for Cognition,' *Journal of Advertising*, 25 (Spring), 15–32.

? Questions

1 What are the unique contributions and insights of this study?
2 Explain the assumed links between shopping motives and demographic and psychographic variables.
3 Explain the assumed link between the demographic and psychographic variables and the shopping behaviour variables.
4 Discuss the role of reference groups (peer expectations) in the model.
5 Discuss the role of brand and store loyalty in the model.
6 Discuss the role of Need for Cognition (NFC) in the model.
7 Discuss the assumed effects of demographics on psychographic variables in this model.
8 Describe the four clusters in terms of buying behaviour and psychographic characteristics.
9 On the basis of the results, is it correct to conclude that demographic variables are less important than psychographic variables in explaining store brand and promotional buying behaviour? Why or why not?
10 Is it correct to conclude that there is not much difference between in-store and out-of-store promotion buyers? Why or why not?
11 Describe the 'typical' store brand buyer and the 'typical' out-of-store promotion buyer.
12 The authors conclude that planning and impulsiveness can go together. Why? According to you, is that correct?
13 Are the results of this study consistent with the expectation that promotions mainly affect brand switching behaviour? Why or why not?
14 How can the results be used to target sales promotion efforts to customer acquisition or to customer retention?
15 Given the results, what should retailers do to promote their store brands?
16 Given the results, which competitive strategies should national brands adopt to promote their products?
17 The independent variables in this study are measured across product categories and, consequently, the results are generalized across product categories. Is this reasonable? What could be the moderating impact of different product categories in this study?
18 What are the limitations of this study?
19 Given the results of this study, in what respect would a marketing communications plan have to be different to appeal to store brand buyers versus promotion buyers?

Vignette

Kuwait and Delhaize team up for joint customer loyalty programmes

Kuwait (Q8) is the second largest car fuel seller on the Belgian market, with 467 fuel stations and a market share of 12.18 per cent in 2002. Fuel is a convenience product that cannot as such be differentiated. Furthermore, drivers become less and less loyal to one single station: only 54 per cent always stop at the same station, while 27 per cent stop at the same station fewer than seven times out of ten. The Belgian government decides upon maximum prices, and petroleum companies use price discounts to adapt to local competitive situations. Most companies use a system of saving cards to keep their customers loyal. They do not systematically support their images by means of above-the-line advertising campaigns. Delhaize is one of the largest Belgian food retailers, with a market share of about 16 per cent. The company also has extensive operations abroad (among others Food Lion in the US). For many years Delhaize had issued shopping cards to its customers (Delhaize Plus card). Card owners earn Plus points when they shop at Delhaize's, and can use the points to buy presents or get discounts. The retailer uses the Plus card as a loyalty sales promotion tool. From June 2000 onwards people buying fuel with Kuwait can also collect Plus points.

From June 2000 until December 2002 Kuwait launched a campaign to communicate this joint promotion programme. The core target groups of the campaign were the Delhaize and Kuwait customers. The objective was to issue at least 50 per cent of the Plus points on the cards of the 1.7 million Delhaize customers, to issue a card to at least 25 per cent of the 420,000 Kuwait customers and to issue Plus points for at least 40 per cent of the fuel volume sold, by the end of 2002. The campaign used above-the-line as well as below-the-line media. Gradually, the focus shifted from below the line to mass media (newspapers, magazines and radio). At launch, mainly Kuwait and Delhaize point-of-sale media were used: the Delhaize loyal customers newsletter, Delhaize caddies, on Delhaize tickets and by means of animation at the supermarket entries. Also Kuwait used POS media: posters, pump toppers, decoration, brochures and special 'extra Plus point' actions during launch and special periods (Easter, Christmas).

At the end of 2002 almost 20 per cent of Delhaize customers were regular buyers of Kuwait fuel (up 50 per cent), and more than 60 per cent of the Plus points were issued by Kuwait. 120,000 cards were issued to existing Kuwait customers, and the issue rate of Plus points was 45 per cent. Furthermore, as a result of this consumer promotion campaign Kuwait realized a substantial increase in fuel sales in a saturated market with fewer stations than in 2000.

Sources: Belgian Petroleum Federation; A. C. Nielsen Belgium; Belgian Effie Award, 2003; www.Delhaize.be; www.Q8.be.

Chapter 5

Don E. Schultz

FROM DIRECT MAIL TO DIRECT RESPONSE MARKETING

THIS CHAPTER, WHICH DESCRIBES and illustrates the transition of direct mail to direct response marketing to today's direct marketing is unique in this text book. It does not come from the academic literature, nor is it necessarily theory-based. Indeed, when the following two articles were written – actually excerpts from a book entitled *The Great Marketing Turnaround* (1990) there was little academic research and even less direct mail theory as an academic subject. Almost all existing knowledge was based on the in-market experiences of direct mail practitioners, since that was the primary delivery system being used. Most knowledge and almost all the writings were based on case histories and anecdotal evidence that resulted in rather gross generalizations, e.g. actual postal stamps on the envelope generate better response rates than printed indicia, long-form sales letters generate greater response than short letters, and so on. The problem with this knowledge base was, of course, there were few generalizable concepts or theories underlying the various marketplace experiences of the direct mailers. Practitioners learned by 'doing', that is, trial and error, correcting and adapting each future direct mail programme based on the results obtained from the last one. Thus there were few replicable models and even less theoretical underpinnings.

When Stan Rapp and Tom Collins, two of the leading US direct mail practitioners (they owned an agency of the same name, Rapp & Collins), began to use the emerging technologies brought about by digitalization, computerization, advanced statistics and financial investment and return approaches, they literally revolutionized direct mail practice. Initially, they quantified and built predictive models of direct mail marketing. Then they expanded their concept to include other forms of media delivery from which a response could be generated, the telephone, television and radio in particular. Thus they leveraged the concept of direct mail from a single media form to direct response in any one of many media forms.

Given the rapid development of technology at the time, it was only a short step from direct response to direct marketing. They illustrated these new concepts in two books, *The Great Marketing Turnaround*, cited in this chapter, and its predecessor, *MaxiMarketing* (discussed later). The focus of both texts was the marketing organization's increasing ability to create and implement marketing programmes against specific individuals based on customer data that had been captured, stored, managed and analysed on an on-going basis. Thus marketing was able to move from mass to individual and marketing by name, not by delivery medium. This transition of direct mail practices into direct marketing concepts and theories was one of the most revolutionary steps in the development of marketing communication in the twentieth century.

In the two articles that follow, Rapp and Collins describe the developments that had occurred since they published their first text in the field, *MaxiMarketing* (1986), four years earlier. In these two books, Rapp and Collins accurately predicted most of the opportunities, changes and challenges that have impacted all forms of marketing over the past twenty years. They raised a number of issues with which marketing communication professionals still struggle today, i.e., whether the communication should be mass or targeted, the continuing tension between image and short-term incremental sales as the measure of communication effects, the issues of the importance of brands in consumer response and a host of other relevant issues brought on by technological innovation. Indeed, these two visionaries even accurately predicted the challenges traditional advertising agencies face today as they try to come to grips with the rising number of media alternatives available to reach and influence customers and prospects.

Although the book from which these two articles were excerpted were based primarily on the experience and predictions of the two authors, they were amazingly accurate in their forecasts of the massive changes technology would have on marketing communications in the first decade of the twenty-first century. For example, they accurately predicted the rise of the individual as the primary focus for most marketing communication, thus moving the practice away from markets, geographies and the mass media, where the ability to deliver huge numbers of advertising and promotion messages and offers was important to a more sophisticated approach based on planning and executing marketing communication programmes using response rates, cost per order and lifetime customer value as the measurement yardstick. While there are few tested or testable theories in the two articles, the issues, concerns, practices and predictions of Rapp and Collins accurately identify what has happened and continues to occur not just in direct marketing but in almost all forms of marketing communication today.

It may be difficult for students and younger practitioners to realize that much of our knowledge of direct mail, direct response and direct marketing is less than thirty years old. Indeed, the World Wide Web and the commercial use of the Internet are only a few years beyond a decade old as well. In truth, direct mail, direct response and direct marketing, although direct mail has been practised for more than two centuries in the US, is still an emerging discipline and that the changes that have impacted the development were largely predicted by Rapp and Collins in their two books that were developed in the 1980s.

While direct mail continues to be one of the major forms of marketing communication around the world, the concepts that support the transition of direct mail to direct response and to today's database marketing all evolved from the concepts that Rapp and Collins accurately explained and predicted. It is for this reason that the excerpts from *The Great Marketing Turnaound* and its precursor *MaxiMarketing* have really set the pace for direct marketing as we know it today.

THE GREAT MARKETING TURNAROUND

Stan Rapp and Tom Collins

'When the light of a new day dawns on January 1, 1990, I believe that all service companies and many product manufacturers will be spending as much time and money maximizing their relationships with known customers as they now do on their brand-image advertising to the world at large.' This quote comes from Stan Rapp and the pages of *Direct Marketing* magazine (September 1986), when he and Tom Collins introduced their book MaxiMarketing just four years ago. Now the authors, who have a direct response and agency that bears their names, have opened another door in their latest book. *The Great Marketing Turnaround: The Age of the Individual – and How to Profit from It*. The following is an excerpt from the final chapter, in which they take a look at the past and, again, a look at the new future of direct response advertising.

[I]

WE FACE A PERIOD in which the familiar institutions of mass marketing must be rethought and reshaped to deal with the new reality, not only by marketers but by their supporting services as well. And because of the need for 'time out for mental digestion' on the part of the armies of people involved, the changeover simply can't all take place overnight. Before everyone gets in line behind the Early Adapters, here are some of the marketing institutions that we believe must change, will change and are changing:

The Coming Reinvention of the Art of Advertising

The brilliance of TV advertising has been developed about as far as it can go. It has evolved into an extraordinary new human language all its own. For advert-

---

Direct Marketing, October 1990, pp. 57–60; November 1990, pp. 49–52.

isers who have a product with a broad enough appeal and big enough budget, it can be unmatched for effectiveness in creating excitement and desire.

But as we have seen, even for these advertisers it is a frightening game of roulette in which your lucky number fails to come up more often than it succeeds. Even a multimillion dollar campaign on national television sometimes shows little effect on sales. In fact, sometimes sales decline.

And then there are all those other advertisers with more specialized niche products and smaller budgets who either know they can't afford national television or make the mistake of thinking that they can.

Yes, they can and do run awareness advertising in all the other traditional media – in the magazines, in the newspapers, on radio. Yet for these smaller-budget advertisers there is often the uneasy feeling that these other media simply can't compare with the glamour and power of television. And indeed it is a fairly uncommon event when awareness advertising in these other media produces a distinct, traceable, profitable effect on sales. Admittedly some new customers can be influenced and won with this increasingly inefficient shotgun advertising, but often at a prohibitive cost per incremental sale.

So, in recognition of this reality, an increasing number of marketers are taking their first hesitant steps toward increasing their odds of success by turning to a different view of how advertising can be made to work better.

But there is a danger here of what Mr. Gorbachev called trying to 'fill new forms with old content.' What is called for is not just a modification of the art of advertising to fit a new situation but a whole new way of thinking about advertising communication.

Today the path from the prospect's need to the purchase and repurchase of the product is often longer than the 30 seconds of mind-blowing images on the small screen or the passage from the headline at the top of the page to the phone number or reply coupon at the bottom. It is a journey from the first contact, established by the prospect's response to the advertising, to the step-by-step building of the confidence of the respondent in the advertised product or service, whether in one long communication or a series of communications.

And it calls at every step of the way for use of the cultivation skills developed over decades of trial and error, test-and-observe by direct order marketers who live or die by their ability to gain the confidence of faraway customers.

Two common errors are made by those who are 'filling new forms with old content'.

1. *The error of overreliance on image and awareness advertising creative techniques in advertising where maximized response and continuing contact is the objective.* So much general advertising employs a cleverness and indirection which may or may not be effective in getting the public to laugh and to retain a favorable impression, but are fatally ineffective when it comes to getting people to respond – and, even worse, when it comes to continued communication with people who do respond and want useful information and guidance.

If you are thinking that we are advocating a return to hard sell mail order advertising techniques of half a century ago, think again. Instead we are urging the application of the wonderful creative credo of Shirley Polykoff, the great advertising woman who first made Clairol hair coloring acceptable for millions of women with the theme, '*Does She Or Doesn't She? Only Her Hairdresser Knows for Sure*.' Shirley's whole advertising philosophy was distilled in just eight words, 'Think it out square, say it with flair.'

The turnaround from mass marketing to individualized marketing calls for a new creativity to meet a new set of standards. If the need now is for dialogue and the ability to know and respond to what the consumer is thinking almost before it is thought, then cleverness must give way to clarity and 'show biz' to the business of being understood.

2. *The error of focusing all of the talent and money and creativity 'up front.'* The same kind and amount of attention and loving care that is expended 'up front' must also be devoted to the 'back end,' to everything that happens after the prospect responds to the first advertising message or makes the first purchase. Yet again and again we have answered ads offering a free sample or a booklet or a membership and received a cheap looking package with either a curt businesslike form letter or, more often, no letter at all – a practice that makes a direct order merchant hoot with derision.

It is as if the advertisers had expended all of the creative talent in the act of reaching out to the consumer, and now that the consumer was interested, there was nothing more to do or say. It's the Casanova Syndrome in marketing. We see advertisers frantically moving on to the next 'conquest' while losing interest in yesterday's love.

In both of these common errors, we see signs of the fear that seems to be so ever-present in preparing awareness advertising. It is the fear of telling the prospect too much. And indeed this is a realistic fear if the additional words would be just so much boring puffery. Yet the annals of advertising are filled with legendary examples of ads which held the audience in their grip for an extended period.

Think about your personal relationships. Think of the friend or acquaintance whose conversation sparkles with interesting, enlightening, persuasive information. Could it all really have been condensed into one paragraph . . . or a fifteen-second 'sound bite'?

The creative challenge posed by individualized marketing is to find ways to recreate the same values of a good conversation in your advertising communications, and to find opportunities to do so. The Cheer-Free detergent mailing package containing the free sample sent in response to TV requests showed the same creativity and careful attention to the relationship with the recipient as was lavished on the advertising which prompted the response in the first place. This is a total reversal of the usual back-of-the-hand sales promotion fulfillment practice.

As another example of this, we pointed to the page after page of wonderful information about tea in the Stash Tea catalog. If this much information were fired at you broadside, in the form of a booklet about tea, it is unlikely you would ever get around to reading it. But in the easy-browsing format of a mail order catalog, you are exposed to an astonishing amount of selling information one delightful little bit at a time.

If you would like to hold in your hands and study a varitable textbook of relationship building, write to Garden Way Manufacturing Co., 102nd St. and

9th Ave., Troy, NY 12180, and ask them to send you a copy of the latest *Troy-Bilt Owner News*, their tabloid newspaper of articles and advertising about their lawn and garden equipment. Much of it is written by their customers, a poor way to win advertising awards but a great way to build a warm feeling of community and sell goods.

We're not saying that the Stash Tea way or the Garden Way approach necessarily is right for your own particular marketing challenge.

What we are urging is that you open your eyes to how different these communications are from typical brand advertising promotional fulfillment material and much of today's direct marketing communication, and then open your mind to daring new possibilities in your own situation.

And we are not only talking about the printed word. A new generation of marketers is communicating with a new generation of consumers with audio discs, videocassettes, computer disks and 'long-form' cable advertising shows. To say nothing of the new art of direct response commercials which manage to artfully build brand imagery and maximize response at the same time.

A hallmark of good direct response advertising and follow-up is simply clarity – quite different from what we have come to expect from advertising singled out for praise in the advertising trade press. A great deal of awareness advertising, both in print and on television, can get tangled up in a copywriter's joke so subtle or an art director's special effect so tricky that people just don't get it – and there is no reality check in the form of viewer responses to tip off the advertiser that a mistake in communication has been made.

Haven't you ever had the experience of turning to a TV viewing companion and saying, 'That was a really clever commercial. But what were they selling?'

Neither the 'up-front' advertising nor the 'back-end' contact in the new marketing copy can afford the luxury of this kind of cleverness and obscurity. Yes, it can be droll, it can be witty – but clarity comes first.

The reinvented art of advertising, as advertisers move toward individualized marketing, will 'take the reader (or viewer) by the hand' and lead him or her to the desired sales result.

It will avoid the mistake of using overly clever awareness advertising techniques to get a response.

It will employ the same caliber of topflight creative talent on all the 'back-end' communications leading to the sale as it does in the 'up-front' message.

It will build the confidence and trust of the consumer with a mosaic of interesting, enlightening, persuasive information.

And it will do this with a clarity which will never leave the prospect or customer in doubt about what meaning was intended.

The Client–Agency Model of the Future

In *MaxiMarketing*, we said that the time had come for all advertisers to choose and use the tools of direct marketing. In the years since, we have seen the mightiest of the mighty, including Procter & Gamble, IBM, Bristol-Myers and Ford Motor Company pick up these tools and begin to put them to good use.

If direct marketing techniques indeed play such a key role in the new marketing, then does it perhaps logically follow that a brand advertiser or other general advertiser should simply assign its account – or a piece of it – to a specialized direct response agency?

Many have done just that in recent years. And often the direct response ad agencies have responded with ingenious relationship marketing programs that many mainstream agencies might not have been capable of producing.

But in the broader landscape of individualized marketing as it is evolving, even the specialist direct response ad agency does not necessarily have all of the skills required to implement a multifaceted program involving targeted sales promotion, public relations, event marketing, field marketing to dealers and much more.

In some cases this will lead to the client being forced to shop for services among a variety of communications providers when the time comes to execute a multidiscipline MaxiMarketing program – choosing one specialist for direct response advertising, another for tie-in dealer promotions, another for cause-related marketing, another for publicity.

This can work, as Ron Fusile has demonstrated in the implementation of his Buick Open sweepstakes campaign, but it is not ideal. There is always the risk that it can lead to working with providers who do not really understand the importance of the broad strategy and who may execute their part of the program as just another project assignment.

So we believe you will see a new kind of advertising agency evolving, one that is capable of what we describe as fusion in marketing – first conceiving a new database-driven strategic direction for a client, then firing all of the elements together in the crucible of creative thinking to develop the marketing equivalent of what engineers call a 'composite,' a substance lighter, stronger and cheaper than steel. The substance of such an agency's creation will be the much-heralded but little understood 'New Advertising' referred to by John O'Toole in his farewell address as chairman of the American Association of Advertising Agencies.

With fusion of the marketing elements, nothing remains the same as it was. There is a new form of advertising, a new form of sales promotion, and a redefined role for direct marketing.

Advertising works to build image and awareness while at the same time promoting immediate sales and acquiring information for a marketing database.

Sales promotion, while ringing the cash register now, also finds ways to build brand equity and feed information into the relational database.

And direct relationship marketing, while reaching for long-term benefits, uses the tools of promotion to gain an immediate return on investment.

Often all three of these basic disciplines, plus public relations and event marketing, are fused in a single program in which no one element or its budget can be separated from the whole. The agency of the future will be a master at creating both the fused up-front advertising and back-end interactions to deliver a marketing force of unprecedented power and efficiency.

This agency of the future will not always evolve out of the mainstream agencies of the present.

In some cases it will. But in other cases it will be a direct marketing agency which acquires awareness advertising, sales promotion and public relations skills and a MaxiMarketing perspective.

Or sometimes it will be a sales promotion agency which sees that the market is moving inexorably from short-term promotions to long-term involvement that creates repeated opportunities for cultivation of the consumer, and which has the foresight to acquire the additional skills needed to meet this new need.

And sometimes this new kind of agency will emerge from a kind of provider you might not even know existed – the specialized companies that create and administer promotional programs, specialty advertising programs, customer assistance programs and frequent buyer programs, and who are ready and eager to expand their sphere of operations to include database building, advertising know-how and a complete repertoire of the 'New Advertising' skills.

But wherever it comes from, the MaxiMarketing agency of the future will not be hesitant to conceive and recommend a brilliant multifaceted individualized marketing program for fear of not fitting into the client's compartmentalized way of thinking.

Clients, on their part, will be looking for a truly wholistic approach, and some agencies will have developed the capability either to perform the entire job in-house – or to supervise the execution of parts of it by trusted agency suppliers, just as an agency today may contract for and supervise on behalf of its client such services as photography, TV production, printing and media buying.

The advertising shibboleth that will provide the most stubborn resistance to being cast aside is the old habit of thinking about image or awareness advertising as 'above the line' and direct mail, sales promotion and anything else that doesn't earn an agency commission as 'below the line.'

Christopher Woodward, the marketing director of 3i, the world's largest venture capital company and an important United Kingdom general advertiser, is one advertiser with absolutely no use for the divisions. He shared his views with us in a recent conversation in this way: 'The ridiculous concept of the line separating advertising from all the other marketing activities must be removed. It is all too common for general advertising agencies to deliver prepackaged, off-the-shelf solutions representing the cliché things they are good at doing. They always react with this bundle of creativity when what is needed is strategic and innovative thinking. They just aren't in a marketing mode at all.'

Looking to the future, Woodward continued, 'What is needed is an outside, totally dispassionate consultant in marketing communications, not a specialist in one area interested mainly in pushing its own specialty.'

There are many on the general agency side who would take exception to this view. And certainly there are mainstream agencies offering integrated marketing services in the United States and Europe that have removed the 'line' of separation. Such agencies are making great strides in developing harmonious working relationships among their various service components and providing successfully 'integrated' campaigns.

The ultimate choice as to which agency model fits an advertiser's needs will be determined in part by the client's situation and own capabilities. One thing is certain, however. The number and variety of operational and philosophical models to choose from will far exceed the options available a decade ago.

There will be the providers of a complete menu of services under one agency conglomerate roof. There will continue to be the agencies with special expertise from which the advertiser can order à la carte. And there will be a powerful new force – the agency striving to fuse the advertising and the relationship-building marketing disciplines into an entirely new form of unified agency service.

Advertisers in the 1990s will be making their selection of agencies in an environment of steadily rising media costs and advertising clutter. We can expect rising pressure to make every advertising dollar as accountable as possible.

As a result, there will be more double-duty, triple-duty and quadruple-duty expenditures. Advertisers will turn around their thinking and increasingly ask: Why settle for doing *only* a promotion project or *only* a public relations event or *only* an awareness ad or *only* adding names or information to a database, when so much more can be accomplished for the same amount of money with a truly multidimensional effort?

Whatever agency model is chosen, the pressure will be on all concerned, both on the agency side and the client side, to turn their thinking away from the compartmentalized marketing approach that leads to doing advertising by itself, sales promotion by itself, and direct marketing by itself.

On the client side, the turn away from compartmentalized thinking will require a management reappraisal of how marketing and advertising departments are organized.

Instead of the traditional approach of appointing one manager for advertising, another for promotion, and lately a third for direct marketing, it would be more in keeping with the new realities of marketing to break down the dividing line between these three functions. You would put one manager in charge of all of the marketing activities leading up to the acquisition of a new customer, including the awareness advertising, direct response advertising and sales promotion. A second manager would then be in charge of all of the marketing activities involved in keeping and cultivating that new customer, including database design and enhancement and all of the communications with – and promotions to – the people in the database.

With this organizational structure, both the front-end manager and the back-end manager would be equally at home with the disciplines of brand building and sales promotion. A natural consequence would be the development of multifaceted, wholistic programs that achieve both the short-term and long-term objectives of the advertiser.

Of course the 'customer acquisition manager' and the 'customer cultivation manager' would work in tandem to maximize sales and profits in this new era of fused marketing activity. And each of them would be in a position to get the best work from their new multidisciplined marketing agency.

[II]

Market research firms are paid more than $1 billion a year by advertisers who need to know what products to make and how to sell them. But the state of the art still suffers from certain significant drawbacks.

One problem is that in-depth research is expensive and often takes a long time to complete. Because of the expense, it may not be economic to update the findings frequently, and consequently the findings are soon out of date.

Another problem is that much advertising research is conducted in an artificial laboratory situation in which consumers speculate on how they might react to a new product, a new positioning, or a new campaign theme.

This has proven to be a special problem in copy research, where there is no completely satisfactory substitute for observing how consumers react to real advertising in a real world situation.

Individualized marketing, although it does not provide an answer to all of a company's research needs, does offer exciting opportunities for adding a new dimension to market research. As we have seen in such companies as Nintendo in the United States, Austin-Rover in the United Kingdom, and Sopad Nestlé in France, it can provide real-time real-world insights into the constantly changing likes, wants, complaints and needs of a company's customers.

As part of their ongoing communication (surveys, questionnaires, phone calls, customer correspondence, etc.) with many thousands, even millions, of customers, the best and the boldest MaxiMarketers can often sense with uncanny accuracy where the market is going. It's a turnaround from research that quickly grows stale to a continuous information exchange that is always fresh and meaningful.

Another research opportunity, as we have discussed, lies in split-run direct response advertising testing. It can zero in on the right headline, the right picture, the right product, the right offer, the right price, with a precision that other kinds of copy research are not capable of. And this A-B testing is not limited to magazine and newspaper advertising. It can be done in direct mail, take-ones, card programs, the way you handle incoming phone calls – anything involving direct communications with the consumer.

If you have a mail order catalog for customers not reached by your retail distributors or a company-sponsored magazine, it can become a living, breathing laboratory for product and copy development.

In weighing the possible effectiveness of promotions ideas being considered, offers can be pretested against the small segments of the database and rolled out only if cost-effective.

And these are only a few of the possibilities. Once you start communicating directly with your prospects and customers, you will constantly discover new ways to learn more about them, how to serve them better, how to activate them to buy your product, and what new products you can develop in answer to expressed needs and wants.

Rethinking Accountability

During the '80s, direct marketing as a concept spread from the direct order marketers [mail order] such as the book and record clubs, to the banks, the airlines, the hotels and other service companies, and finally to many manufacturers and retailers. In due course, what is commonly referred to as direct marketing became the new 'in' thing to add to the marketing mix.

The even more fashionable term to use was relationship marketing, and 'having a long-term relationship with prospects and customers' was now seen as a good thing to do. Only there was one catch. There was heavy emphasis on long-term relationships, and advocates of direct marketing would get very defensive when asked about the cost in the meanwhile of making all these good things happen.

Direct marketers preaching their gospel of LifeTime Customer Value were out of sync with the hard-nosed world of the product manager in the packaged goods field who waits with bated breath for the latest SAMI figures and worries about meeting this year's sales target. The same problem to a greater or lesser degree confronted direct marketers in all product and service categories which are not based on direct order marketing. We haven't met a product manager or marketing director yet who isn't fixated on this year's budget and projected sales figures.

Mass marketers distributing their products in thousands of retail outlets are mostly interested in measuring current share of mind and share of market, not in tracking the effect of this year's expenditure on sales in future years.

As the decade progressed, the realization began to sink in that not only direct marketing, but also awareness advertising itself was very often at best a long-term solution. It was needed to support the brand over the long haul, but very few awareness campaigns showed an immediate effect on sales. To get sales right now, management in the '80s increasingly turned to consumer promotions and dealer promotions. Such promotions might cheapen the brand image, but they could, when properly executed, get those vital short-term sales through the door.

So, by the end of the decade, the growth of mass advertising had come to a virtual halt while promotional spending boomed, and some marketers were tinkering with databases and various aspects of customer relationship building in a minor way, with limited objectives.

The New Direction: Short-term And Long-term Results

Actually, with turnaround thinking, it is not really a question of being forced to choose between short-term and long-term results. You can have it all. As we have shown throughout *The Great Marketing Turnaround*, the new approach to marketing in which advertising, sales promotion and direct marketing budgets are fused to implement a single unified strategy, is producing impressive short-term results while also establishing long-term relationships that tie the customer closely to the brand. And at less cost than tackling awareness advertising, sales promotion and direct marketing separately.

Many of the case histories that we have explored represent a new phenomenon. The new technology of marketing built on the increasingly powerful capabilities of the computer has opened up new vistas which could not be imagined a decade earlier. Being able to send a relevant, motivating advertising and promotional message to precisely those people who are most ready, willing and able to respond can be counted on to produce astonishing short term results while also setting the stage for a profitable long-term relationship. But how do you measure the effect of the new marketing when it is part advertising, part promotion and part database building?

We were recently involved in developing a customer's club employing targeted sales promotion for a mass marketer selling a $2.50 product through retail distribution. The product is purchased, on the average, only ten times a year. That adds up to $25 in total annual revenue, yielding a $5 or $6 contribution to profit.

By the yardstick of direct order marketing, the club was not very successful. Market research told the company that it took about twenty-four months for directly accountable sales to earn back the expenditures charged to membership acquisition and the activation mailings to members. But this was not a direct order marketer and the club was not a direct order marketing proposition. It was a database-driven program to get the consumer involved with the product and to impact sales in stores.

While the advertising was acquiring club members, it was also making millions of impressions on those in the target market who did not choose to sign up. These impressions, and the word-of-mouth advertising resulting from the various club events and activities, became a potent force for sales in the total market as well as among club members.

When share of market and annual sales growth was used as the measurement for the first year of the program, it showed an overall sales increase that was more than enough to offset the entire cost of acquiring and servicing club members.

The paradox was that what seemed to be a short-term drain on profits when measured in narrowly accountable terms, based on the number of customers enrolled in the program, was actually a net contributor to profit when measured on the basis of total impact on the company's sales that year.

As we rethink marketing in the '90s to become more focused on fusing the advertising, promotion and direct marketing elements in the marketing mix, we will also have to rethink how we are going to measure short-term and long-term success.

Methods used to measure awareness advertising effectiveness that do not take into account actual sales results are no longer acceptable.

Measurement criteria for sales from promotions that do not take into account negative impact on brand image are no longer acceptable.

And the focus on the long-term payout of direct relationship marketing without taking into account the immediate impact on sales and brand image of the direct response advertising that builds the database is no longer acceptable.

A new scorecard will be needed for the marketing games we will be playing in the '90s. The 'synergy effect' of combining all the elements in a

MaxiMarketing program has turned out to be far greater than we ever expected. The challenge now is to find out how to measure it fully and fairly.

When the two of us launched our own advertising agency, a generation ago, the advertising communications field was populated by 'advertising men,' mail order people, promoters and publicists.

Today the 'ad man' is just as likely to be a woman. The mail order people have been transformed into direct marketers. And publicists are public relations specialists.

There is the illusion of great change in the advertising communication disciplines. But the reality is that by and large, over the past twenty-five years, we have seen only evolutionary growth to higher sophistication and greater specialization. The fundamentals have changed very little.

A stumbling block that will trip up communications professionals in the '90s is the failure to realize that evolutionary change is no longer enough to gain the advantage. The propensity to see marketing merely as a series of separate but equal components, linked together in a chain of 'integrated' communications, will keep them from embracing the revolutionary principles of genuine individualized marketing discussed in *The Great Marketing Turnaround*.

As the '90s begin, we are seeing a rush to the banner of a new advertising – which is essentially the same old 'above and below the line' advertising disciplines rearranged to give added importance to what was formerly 'below the line.' It is a new advertising that fails to reconsider those aspects of the established advertising and promotion doctrines that no longer work very well in the age of the individual.

In this new decade, the likelihood of getting a dramatic breakthrough which increases market share is far greater if your new advertising uses new marketing technologies to contact and get involved with identified prospects and customers than if you merely rely on more creative application of traditional advertising and sales promotion alone. Think for a moment how different the Benadryl success story is from the conventional '80s wisdom of how to come up with a winning advertising campaign. For Benadryl, the agency took a relatively minor tactical move and turned it almost overnight into a brilliant individualized marketing strategy. By reacting quickly to how the marketplace responded to their pollen count 800-number telephone information service, they were able to establish a productive relationship with more than 1 million prospects and customers. Warner Lambert, on their part, was also quick to shift dollars from conventional marketing programs that were unlikely to produce a breakthrough and turn to this revolutionary new way of building awareness and boosting sales.

Think of the astonishing gain in market share by Miller Lite with their 'biggest party ever thrown in Texas' regional marketing extravaganza. They found a way to get directly and deeply involved with 2 million beer drinkers. They devised an extra value proposition that set them clearly apart from the competition. And they fused all the skills of awareness advertising, sales promotion and direct marketing to totally capture the attention and enthusiasm of the Texas beer-drinking crowd.

Think of Nintendo, Stash Tea, Austin-Rover, Toddler University and other companies large and small that we have observed. Note how they responded to the opportunities made possible by the 10 turn-arounds in marketing we have described and the big rewards they have enjoyed.

What these turnaround-thinking companies have shown is that what you do with your marketing communication, whether it is 'integrated' or not, is what makes the difference between standing still and moving ahead.

In the real new advertising of the '90s, individualized marketing will increasingly be seen as the right way to go. And, we believe, the MaxiMarketing model is the way to get there.

By the time you get to read *The Great Marketing Turnaround*, there will have been even more extraordinary developments in many fields than we talk about. And you may worry that you have already been left behind and it's too late to catch up.

The answer is that it is never too late.

Certainly there is an advantage to being first in your field – there always is.

But if it is too late for you and your company to be first, there is also a lot to be said for being second. You have a chance to study and learn from your competitor who went first, to learn from their mistakes and improve on their model.

And if it is too late for you to be either first or second, it is still not too late to get started with your own innovative individualized marketing program that builds on your company's unique strengths and opportunities. Innovation is never out of style. There is always a better way to do things waiting to be discovered by those who dare to reach beyond what has already been tried.

For inspiration, we will leave you with our five-point guiding star [Figure 1]:

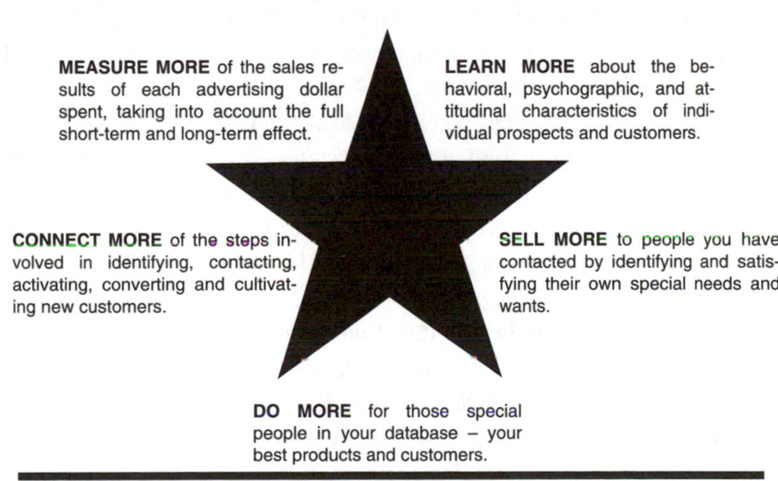

MEASURE MORE of the sales results of each advertising dollar spent, taking into account the full short-term and long-term effect.
LEARN MORE about the behavioral, psychographic, and attitudinal characteristics of individual prospects and customers.
CONNECT MORE of the steps involved in identifying, contacting, activating, converting and cultivating new customers.
SELL MORE to people you have contacted by identifying and satisfying their own special needs and wants.
DO MORE for those special people in your database – your best products and customers.

Figure 1

Whatever you do, you are part of marketing history. And if you act boldly, you can help write it.

By casting off the shackles of outmoded mass marketing thinking and entering the age of the individual, you can invent your own new ways to get closer to your customers and serve them better in a mutually rewarding relationship.

In the '80s, Nike proclaimed, 'Just do it!' and it became the rallying cry of a generation of fitness lovers. In the '90s, it is also a good slogan for marketers.

Certainly it makes sense to exercise proper business caution in moving into this new territory. But it is also important not to let undue caution keep you from acting at all. At some point, once you're ready, *just do it*. And do it even better than the marketers you can learn from in this book.

Be better at keeping a dialogue going with the consumer – at exceeding your prospect's and customer's expectations – at applying every step of the MaxiMarketing concept.

This is the challenge and the satisfaction of being part of the great marketing turnaround.

Stan Rapp and Tom Collins are notable experts in direct response advertising. Between the two, they have numerous years of experience, and are co-founders of an advertising agency that bears their names. They can be reached at CCR Consulting Group, 333 E. 30th St., New York, NY 10016–212/779–1575.

? Questions

1. What technological innovations enabled Land's End and Dell to transition from their initial focus on direct mail marketing to direct response and to today's direct marketing approaches?
2. Why has it been so difficult for traditional mass marketing organizations, such as consumer package goods manufacturers, to accept and transition to direct marketing approaches and methodologies?
3. Today's direct marketing relies heavily on capturing, organizing, managing and analysing customer information. There are clearly major consumer issues and concerns about the data being held on them in marketers' databases. What type of privacy policy do you believe will be needed to protect customers yet, at the same time, enable marketers to gain the efficiencies of direct marketing approaches?
4. One of the major issues in direct marketing is the importance and value of the brand. Direct mail and direct response marketers traditionally have focused on immediate response and incremental sales. How can today's direct marketing approaches be used to build brand value and create long-term relationships for the marketing organization and the customer?
5. Rapp and Collins argue for the demise of functional specializations, e.g., advertising managers, sales promotion directors, public relations practitioners and the like, suggesting that a holistic approach to marketing communication development is superior. Suggest how you might convince the management of a functionally based organization to move to this holistic view of marketing communications management.

Rapp and Collins argue for a radically different measurement system for returns on marketing communication, that is, moving from the distribution of messages to the measurement of returns. Today, marketing metrics and measurement continue to plague the entire marketing communication industry. How can marketing communication managers refocus their measurement approaches, using the concepts and ideas presented by the two authors, i.e., holistic planning, communication synergy, pre-testing, re-thinking accountability, and measuring short and long term results?

Vignette

Evolving with Technology and the Customer

A fairly large number of organizations have evolved from direct mail to direct response to direct marketing as forecast by Rapp and Collins. Dell Computer Corporation and L. L. Bean are two that took radically different paths in their evolution but ended up in the same place, as two of the premier US-based direct marketing firms.

L. L. Bean started as a one-man operation in Freeport, ME, in 1912, dedicated to making and providing quality apparel and reliable outdoor equipment. Leon Longwood Bean, the founder, started the business by inventing and testing the Maine Hunting Shoe ('Bean Boot') which he sold from a basement store in Freeport. Bean quickly moved from the single retail location into direct mail marketing. In the second year of operation, Bean expanded the scope of his market from the single retail location when he started sending out a four-page mailer to out-of-state sportsmen. He thus launched L. L. Bean into the direct mail business.

By the 1920s Bean had evolved their customer mailings to a full-size catalogue as additional apparel and sporting goods were added to the product line. Over the next forty years, Bean continued to expand and extend its reach across the US, primarily by using increasingly sophisticated direct mail techniques. By the 1960s L. L. Bean was one of the most well established and recognized direct mail selling companies in the country. In 1969, in line with emerging computer technologies, the Bean mailing list was converted from hand-typed to computerized addresses, thus launching Bean into the direct response category.

By 1992 L. L. Bean had evolved into a global organization as a retail store was opened in Tokyo. In 1995 llbean.com launched the traditional direct mail and direct response into the interactive arena. Today L. L. Bean continues to maintain its strong direct approaches. It is active in Web-based and on-line marketing, operates retail stores and continues to evolve its direct mail expertise based on its nearly hundred year history of gathering information on customers and prospects and creating the type of marketing programmes customers want. All this is supported by outstanding service, used to support and build relationships with customers on an on-going basis.

Dell Computer Corporation started differently from L. L. Bean but has evolved in much the same way. In 1984 Michel Dell founded Dell on a simple concept: he would assemble and sell computer systems to customers by direct delivery. Dell reasoned that he could best understand and fulfill customers' needs if he dealt directly with them rather than going through some type of second-level distribution system. By 'building' a computer specifically for each customer, Dell came to know his customers and their needs individually. Thus Dell had data on each customer that only the customer and Dell shared. A true relationship approach.

Clearly, the Dell model has worked. And it has evolved over time. Starting with a direct response approach, generally mailing brochures, catalogues and flyers to lists of potential customers and prospects, Dell grew rapidly. In 1994, the first year the World Wide Web was commercially viable, Dell added the Internet to its marketing arsenal. E-commerce capability was added in 1996. Today, Dell operates one of the highest-volume Internet commerce sites in the world. The company's Web site receives more than one billion page requests per quarter in eighty-four country sites in twenty-eight languages and deals in twenty-nine currencies.

While Dell started as a direct mailer, the current focus on providing products and services in any way the customer wants to buy or acquire illustrates the evolution Dell has made from direct mailer to direct response marketer to its present position as one of today's most sophisticated direct marketers.

Clearly, Rapp and Collins described the concepts that L. L. Bean and Dell used as they evolved their processes, i.e. the two books that accurately predicted the evolution of direct mail to direct response to direct marketing to relationship marketing. The evolution of technology and the ability of organizations to use that technology has moved relationship marketing much further and much faster than even Grönroos and Gummeson imagined in their original articles on the subject. We are left to wonder what will come next.

Chapter 6

Philip J. Kitchen

MARKETING PUBLIC RELATIONS

FOR A SUBJECT AS wide in scope and scale as the application of public relations for marketing purposes, there is a remarkable paucity of academic papers on the topic. A wide search for papers on the topic reveals its popularity in terms of application, but very little in the way of conceptual or empirical research. It is for this reason that the paper chosen is by one of the four editors. Before critiquing the paper it seems evident that:

- The emergence of MPR was a major and significant development in marketing communications and public relations in the early to mid-1980s.
- Its emergence can be viewed from either a PR or a marketing communications angle.
- Evidently, marketing practitioners and theorists have views regarding MPR's emergence, so do PR practitioners and theorists; these views are often divergent and can be hostile.
- Public relations has a far wider application in terms of communications than just as an adjunct to the promotional mix. However, here we are merely exploring MPR from a marketing communications context.
- Integrated marketing communication and Integrated communication can provide an individual or corporate umbrella under which MPR can play a strategic role.

The paper by Kitchen and Papasolomou explores five related concepts: (1) the emergence of MPR as a conceptual discipline, (2) the location of MPR, (3) whether MPR was likely to become a separate marketing management discipline, or whether it will be anchored to PR in general, (4) ascertain the influence of the protracted debate concerning boundaries (i.e. marketing and PR), (5) explore the relationship between MPR and CPR. Let us explore their findings.

Emergence. Marketing PR was not perceived to be a new discipline in 1997, but a new label for PR activities in support of marketing objectives. Many PR consultancies in 1997 had been practising the concept for years, albeit in its wider dimensionality. Marketing PR did not amount to the emergence of a new marketing-related discipline. In 2005 MPR has rightly taken its position alongside advertising, sales promotion and the like, in other words as a complementary tool alongside other promotional mix variables. With the accelerating trend away from advertising, MPR has much to offer as a key element of integrated approaches to marketing communications.

Location. Neither the marketing or PR disciplines can lay full claim or ownership in terms of MPR's conceptual location. Instead, it belongs or can be drawn upon as needed by both disciplines. Given MPR's emergence and the empirical evidence to date, MPR did not have the legitimacy to be termed a new discipline from either camp. Since the paper was published, the location of MPR has not changed. PR tools, techniques, systems, processes and procedures can be drawn upon by either PR or marketing, as needed, in support of marketing or corporate communication objectives.

Disciplinary Separatism. Based on the previous two paragraphs, MPR was unlikely in 1997 to become a separate discipline. By 2005 this position is unchanged. However, more and more marketing campaigns incorporate the use of PR. What seems to matter is *effective integrated communication* and whatever tools need to be drawn upon to achieve this, *can be and will be used*.

Boundaries debate. The debate is well rehearsed by the authors. Undoubtedly, this was the cause of controversy in 1997 and the recommendation was made as to the need for further research. By 2005, however, circumstances in the highly competitive world of the twenty-first century meant that the need for such research has been overtaken by the need for effective communications of either a marketing or a corporate nature. Certainly, it would seem important to establish boundaries. Today, however, communication is about breaking boundaries down and effectively integrating communications in a cross-disciplinary way.

Relationship between MPR and CPR was important in 1997, according to the authors. Today, communication is absolutely vital with stakeholders, customers and consumers.

MPR extended beyond window dressing in 1997. It was then seen as more than a label. By 2005 MPR was an integral part of promotional campaigns. It can effectively reach and persuade audiences. There is still a need for more research.

MARKETING PUBLIC RELATIONS: CONCEPTUAL LEGITIMACY OR WINDOW DRESSING?

Philip J. Kitchen and Ioanna C. Papasolomou

Explores the development of the marketing public relations (MPR) concept examining the arguments advanced concerning MPR's emergence and legitimacy to be a separate marketing or PR discipline. Some marketing academics suggest that MPR should be incorporated into the marketing discipline whereas the majority of PR academics argue that MPR represents a further attempt by marketeers to 'hijack' PR, incorporating it into the promotional mix. Indeed, certain academics claim that MPR may evolve into a new marketing or PR discipline separate from corporate public relations. The research is compared with the findings from a review of pertinent literature. Exploratory findings indicate that what MPR represents is merely a new term for PR applied to marketing promotion. However, the fact that a new label has been applied does not amount to the emergence of a new marketing discipline. MPR would appear to enjoy a growing importance in the expensive world of marketing communication activities.

Introduction

THIS PAPER IS CONCERNED with exploring the legitimacy of 'marketing public relations' (MPR) and the claim by Harris (1993) that it is either a new marketing management discipline or new public relations (PR) discipline distinct from the better known subject of corporate public relations (CPR). Harris suggests that the explosive growth in MPR in the 1980s was initiated by: the recognition of its intrinsic value by business executives; and the ability of PR professionals to devise programmes to support marketing strategies. The major issue this paper addresses is whether MPR has a legitimate claim to be either a new PR or marketing discipline, or whether in fact MPR is simply 'window dressing', that is the dressing up of an old discipline in the clothing of modern forms deemed appropriate to business organizations in the 1990s. This paper has the following objectives:

1 to examine MPR in terms of its perceived emergence as a conceptual discipline;
2 to determine, if such an emergence has taken place, where MPR should be located;
3 to identify whether MPR is likely to become a separate marketing management discipline, or whether it will be anchored to PR in general;

Marketing Intelligence and Planning, Vol. 15, No. 2 (1997), pp. 71–84. © MCB University Press [ISSN 0263–4503]. Reprinted by kind permission of Emerald and of Market Intelligence and Planning.
Philip J. Kitchen, Department of Marketing, University of Strathclyde, Glasgow. Ionna C. Papasolomou, University of Keele, Staffordshire.

4 to establish the influence of the protracted debate concerning boundaries between PR and marketing, on MPR;
5 to explore the relationship between MPR and CPR.

These objectives are preceded by a broad literature review concerning the emergence and legitimacy of the MPR concept. This will serve to provide a conceptual foundation for the issues under consideration as well as enabling greater understanding of the subject. Details of the exploratory research design involving interviewing executives from leading UK PR agencies are given. Research findings indicate that MPR cannot legitimately at this time be termed a new discipline, irrespective of its conceptual closeness to marketing or PR. Rather, the findings indicate that at best MPR may be simply a new label for well-established usage and traditions and procedures in support of marketing communications.

Literature Review

The marketing literature indicates that many businesses have elevated marketing activities to a dominant organizational position and, thus, marketing is treated as the most important commitment within an organization (Kotler, 1993; Cohen, 1991). While not denying the perceived need for the trend, this has meant that the PR discipline has often been subsumed under the marketing function (Kitchen and Moss, 1995; Kotler and Mindak, 1978) and thus is often awarded a lower priority within organizations. PR as an adjunct to marketing is evident in the literature (e.g. Bernstein, 1988; Gage, 1981; Kreitzman, 1986). However, present evidence also tends to show that there is some confusion concerning the distinction between PR and marketing in the literature. This is supported by an increasing number of articles in which PR and marketing communications practices are recognized as increasingly integrated and converging concepts (Goldman, 1988; Merims, 1972; Novelli, 1988). Despite the fact that these articles were initially developed to give emphasis to the emergence of the concept of PR in the marketing support context, they reflect a growing tendency for PR and marketing to be seen as converging disciplines in both professional and academic circles. This trend is supported by the emergence of the concept of marketing public relations – a term which appeared in both the marketing and PR vocabularies in the 1980s. Kotler (1991a) described MPR as:

> a healthy offspring of two parents: marketing and PR. MPR represents an opportunity for companies to regain a share of voice in a message-satiated society. MPR not only delivers a strong share of voice to win share of mind and heart; it also delivers a better, more effective voice in many cases.

The growth of PR and its acceptance as a valuable or even essential marketing tool seems widespread. Companies assign PR specialists to their product marketing teams and engage PR firms to help them get mileage from product introductions, keep brands prominent throughout product life cycles, and defend products at risk (Harris, 1993).

Harris (1993) argues that the 1980s witnessed MPR emerging as a distinctive new promotional discipline which comprises specialized application techniques that support marketing activities. He suggests that MPR is a separate practice from corporate PR, and that it will move closer to marketing. According to Harris, corporate PR will remain a management function concerned with company relationships with all publics. However, in his view, MPR and CPR will maintain a necessary strategic alliance.

Various surveys have been carried out in order to identify the degree of awareness of the business sector regarding MPR and the general attitude towards this concept. One of these surveys which documents the increasing awareness and use of MPR questioned a sample of 286 *Advertising Age* subscribers who held marketing and advertising positions with client organizations (Duncan, 1985). Among the key findings were the following:

1 MPR was perceived as being effective in a variety of areas that were traditionally the responsibility of advertising.
2 MPR was thought to be especially effective in building brand awareness and brand knowledge.
3 There were no areas in which the majority of clients said MPR would not be effective.
4 The importance of MPR had increased in the previous five years and was expected to continue to increase. The main reasons given were that marketers are becoming more sophisticated and that MPR:
   - is made cost-effective by increases in media advertising costs;
   - breaks through clutter;
   - complements advertising (increases the credibility of messages);
   - is proving itself (Harris, 1993).

Gage (1981), indicated that MPR has become one of the fastest growing segments of the PR field, a finding supported by Kitchen and Proctor (1991) and Kitchen (1991). Indeed, there are many signs that PR has become a big and profitable business. During 1980 an article in *PR Week* stated:

> The proven power of PR and its cost effectiveness in contrast to advertising motivated the advertising industry to add PR departments to their operations in order to help alleviate its financial woes.

MPR has been described as the largest and fastest growing segment of a fast growing industry. A study of the world market for PR services, conducted by the Shandwick Consultancy (1989), estimated that 20 per cent of the fee income of PR firms throughout the world is generated by PR for consumer products. In fact, 70 per cent of the business handled by PR firms is marketing-related, with the remaining 30 per cent distributed among corporate, governmental, environmental (issues related), and financial billing Cantor Concern (Harris, 1993).

According to a leading recruiting firm in the US PR field, companies have recognized the growing importance of MPR with larger budgets and greater renumerations for PR specialisms. MPR now 'leads all PR disciplines with its rapidly increasing importance, and, PR marketing skills are in greater demand than ever before,' Also, Dilenschneider (1988), president and CEO of one of the largest worldwide PR agencies stated that: 'the million-dollar worldwide program, almost unheard of ten years ago, is now experienced with increasing regularity'.

PR is also getting increasing interest in the marketing and business media. On 13 March 1989, *Advertising Age* ran a forum titled 'PR on the offensive'. In the same year, a cover story in *Adweek's* 'Marketing week' section declared that 'the new PR is used virtually everywhere,' and gave advice to its readers to 'stir some PR into their communications mix'.

Finally the academic community is showing greater interest in PR (Kitchen, 1993). A number of American (Harris, 1993) and British (Kitchen, 1993) universities are responding to the growing demand for business leaders trained in PR and for PR practitioners trained in business.

But despite the growing acceptance of public relations in a general sense the question still needs to be tackled: What is MPR? Definitions and interpretations would appear to vary widely. While PR experts cannot agree what MPR is, they all agree it is not free advertising. 'We work very hard to eliminate that misconception' according to a senior figure in a major American PR firm. (Gage, 1981). According to Harris (1993), the designation (MPR) arose in the 1980s because of the need to distinguish the specialized application of PR techniques that support marketing from the general practice of PR. He contends that MPR has grown rapidly and pragmatically to meet the opportunities of a changing marketplace. In the process, it has borrowed and amalgamated thinking from traditional PR, marketing, advertising, and research. The issue of defining MPR is complicated by the fact that there are many definitions of both marketing and PR. Harris believes that MPR can be defined more precisely than the larger concept of PR because of its relevance to marketing, especially in helping an organization meet its marketing objectives. He suggests the following definition:

> MPR is the process of planning, executing and evaluating programmes that encourage purchase and consumer satisfaction through credible communication of information and impressions that identify companies and their products with the needs, wants, concerns, and interests of consumers.

According to Kotler (1988), MPR can contribute to the following tasks:

- assist in the launch of new products (e.g. Cabbage Patch Kids);
- assist in repositioning a mature product (e.g. New York City);
- build up interest in a product category (e.g. milk, egg, cheese consumption);

- influence specific target groups (e.g. sponsorship of local community activities);
- defend products that have encountered public problems (e.g. Johnson & Johnson and Tylenol);
- build the corporate image in a way that projects favourably on its products (e.g. Lee Iaccoca and the image of Chrysler Corporation).

Obviously, there is evidence which would appear to indicate the emergence of a new concept. However, the existing disagreement (Kitchen and Moss, 1995) between marketing and PR practitioners and academics regarding a universal definition for both the marketing and PR disciplines has impacted on defining marketing public relations in an acceptable manner. Despite this, it seems that the contribution of a potentially new concept may be significant. Its benefits could act as a basis on which a single definition could be developed and established.

In most cases, MPR is launched in conjunction with an advertising and marketing campaign. It complements other marketing efforts, but serves a distinct and unique purpose, often giving a product, service or marketer added credibility, exposure and newsworthiness. In some MPR efforts, for example, one objective may be to enhance product credibility and also position the company in a favourable light, as a company that has a genuine concern for people – one that uses its resources and know-how to make life better for them (Gage, 1981). This could be no more than social responsibility ethos or the societal marketing orientation coming to the fore.

However, in a marketing sense, Gumm (1978), suggests that: 'MPR can be proven to be a valuable addition to the marketing mix'. Similarly, Kitchen (1993), says:

> Latterly, advertising, sales promotion, and personal selling have undergone difficulties in relation to achievement of cost-effective communication objectives . . . the emergence and application of MPR in the communications mix may be playing a more significant complementary role in business organizations facing a more turbulent competitive environment.

Seemingly, as the power of advertising weakens as a result of cost, clutter, and audience receptivity; as criticism is levelled at sales promotions in terms of sales effects and profits; and as sales forces diminish in size due to retail concentration and key account selling, firms could practically consider MPR alongside the other promotional tools (Kitchen, 1993).

Several UK case histories, for example the relaunch of Beechams Brylcreem, the PR effort supporting the 'garden city' concepts, and the repositioning of Glasgow as a city of culture, illustrate that MPR has been used alongside traditional marketing communications tools or alone to achieve marketing and/or corporate goals (Kitchen and Proctor, 1991).

The above examples are given to illustrate that MPR can be used either alone or in conjunction with other communication mix tools to achieve marketing objectives. Some firms have utilized PR in a marketing sense usually by working with and alongside experienced PR agencies. The key point to be derived from this is that MPR in some firms appears to be working alongside or in a complementary manner to other elements in the communications mix. It is also noticeable that there may be some interaction with its more important relation: corporate public relations (CPR). Throughout the literature reviewed, it seems evident that the new concept is either considered part of CPR or as an independent approach to the broader area of PR, specifically one in support of marketing activities. Diversity of opinion and thought suggest that it may be difficult to provide a definite answer to the issue of MPR's legitimacy.

Harris (1993), claims that the term MPR is used to distinguish this field from the broader one of PR. However, this opinion seems to suggest division sometime in the future, that is, the split-off of marketing-support PR from those other PR activities that define the corporation's relationships with its non-customer publics. The corporate public relations function may, however, well remain a corporate management function, whereas MPR may become a marketing management function. Under this scheme, the mission of CPR would be to support corporate objectives, and the mission of MPR would be to support marketing objectives. MPR practitioners would become marketing associates, and their career paths would be directed towards marketing management. CPR practitioners will continue to report to top management (Harris, 1993).

The need for co-operation between CPR and MPR seems vital now and may be increasingly so in the future. Some give and take will inevitably be required from both. PR may have to abandon its intellectual pretensions and its disdain of the marketing function, and marketers will have to become increasingly aware of how the social, political, and economic environment affects consumers and the opinion makers who influence attitudes towards companies and their products. This synergy cannot be achieved if marketing and PR are seen as rivals rather than allies, according to Harris (1993). He states that it seems strange that many PR professionals and academics reject this view and see it as an attempt by marketers to 'hijack' an important part of the PR function and place it under marketing's control.

While there is evidence of a move towards closer integration of corporate and marketing messages, and hence the need for closer cooperation between marketing and PR practitioners, this trend alone does not support the argument for a further subdivision of the PR function in the way advocated by Harris. Such a division of responsibilities would seem to create potential for confusion and possible conflict between the messages communicated to an organization's various shareholder audiences without necessarily bringing any recognizable communications benefits.

However, even if the value of MPR as a set of PR techniques and tools has been acknowledged by the business sector globally and it has been assigned to many uses, its value as a concept and its place in either the marketing or PR literature is still debated. Kotler (1989), recognizes the role of PR as an essential communication function, which serves as a tool of marketing. On the contrary, PR academics such as Grunig (1992) say that PR activities can be distinguished from those of marketing and that both are essential functions for a modern organization. From these two views, which represent the marketing and PR practitioners' and academics' views concerning the two disciplines respectively, it is obvious that a debate exists in both the marketing and PR literatures.

Perhaps, the above debate circumscribes the disagreement among the marketing and PR circles concerning the emergence of the MPR concept. Specifically, Harris (1993), although acknowledging and accepting the role of PR as a distinct discipline separate from the marketing discipline, also states that MPR and CPR should be recognized as separate, self-sufficient disciplines. However, this opinion is contradictory to the opinion held by PR practitioners according to which the concept of MPR is seen as an attempt by marketeers to 'hijack' PR, incorporating it as an extra element within the promotional mix in order to inform, persuade or remind existing and prospective customers of product or company benefits. From both the PR and marketing literatures it seems that a particular application of PR publicity techniques exists. But on the basis of this evidence it is not justified whether a separate specialist area of PR or marketing practice has been or will be established. Such debate can be explored in relation to empirical research with firms dealing with both PR and MPR – i.e. public relations agencies.

Research Method

The major objective with which this paper is concerned is to explore the conceptual legitimacy of MPR as a new marketing-related discipline, or alternately to explore whether the title MPR is no more than window dressing. The paper also explores the objectives presented in the introductory section. The survey method was chosen for the empirical work required in the exploration. This method draws most of its data from the present, and will be carried out in order to establish people's views of what they think, believe, value, or feel in an attempt to explore the major issues involved (Jankowicz, 1994).

According to Weiers (1988), depth interviews accessing those with expertise in the area are an acceptable method for initial exploratory research. Typically, executives were selected because they were representative of the subject and population of interest. Eight major British PR consultancies from among the top twenty; by fee income (*PR Week*, 1994) were interviewed. Firms were chosen based on the 1994 rank analysis of top British PR agencies (*PR Week*, 1994). Depth interviews followed a written interview guide which provided item sequence detailed steering instructions, and alternatives. The purpose of the guide was to ensure that the researcher handled each interview in essentially the same way. The interviews were carried out with either CEOs or managing directors of eight PR consultancies. These individuals were chosen because their views were relevant to the project's main issues and because their opinions were worth obtaining due to their expertise on marketing and PR issues. All the individuals interviewed were directors in their organizations having a length of time in the PR field ranging from seven to twenty-five years. The majority of them had a Master's degree either in PR or marketing. Their age ranged between thirty and fifty-two years. It should be noted that in the survey work, the individual interview was used as a means by which the researchers conducted initial, relatively unstructured studies in order to identify the questions to ask, the answer categories to provide, and the sequence to be followed in a later more structured main study (Jankowicz, 1994). Figure 1 illustrates the theoretical framework in which the empirical research is located (Coombs et al., 1954; Wiseman, 1974).

The theory underlying the descriptive model in Figure 1 is that the communication overlap between the marketing and PR disciplines represent the perceived and emergent MPR concept. A company's marketing activities involve a communications process aiming at achieving desired exchange outcomes with target markets. However, in order to achieve this, the company needs to have trust and understanding with the various publics that constitute the various markets. PR is the organizational practice responsible for fostering goodwill between a company and its various publics through continuous communication. In essence, the marketing and PR disciplines are interdependent (Kotler's view). The communication overlap, which results from the interaction of marketing and PR communication activities led to the emergence of the MPR concept. However, the emergence of this concept and its subsequent benefits and value to the organization may serve to revitalize the somewhat sterile debate between the marketing and PR disciplines. The literature review indicated that PR and marketing practitioners and academics disagree as to whether MPR is likely to become a new PR discipline or a marketing management discipline distinct from the broader area of corporate PR.

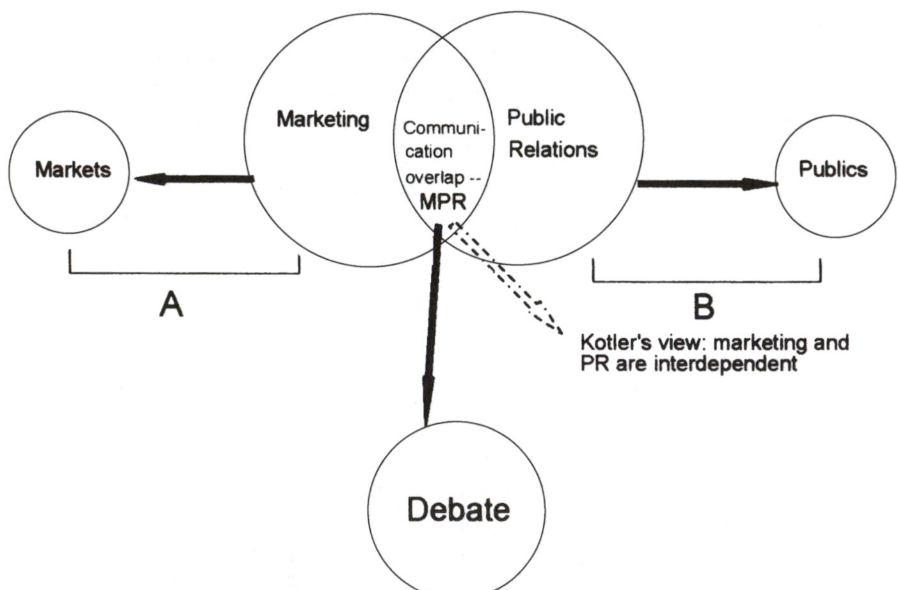

Figure 1 The descriptive model of this research

Research Findings

General overview

In relation to the literature review MPR was portrayed as a newly emerged concept. However, the findings indicate that MPR has always existed as part of the marketing and PR disciplines. Executives indicated that MPR is simply a new name – a new label, for a particular PR activity that the UK PR consultancies have been practising for years. A new name, however, does not amount to emergence of a new marketing-related discipline.

Similarly, throughout the literature reviewed, it was indicated that MPR is either considered as part of CPR or as an independent approach to the broader area of PR. Executives indicated that PR activities in support of marketing activities are still under the domain of general public relations and therefore should be incorporated into CPR. Opinions were expressed suggesting that MPR is part of both the marketing and PR disciplines mainly because the two share a set of common activities which perhaps represent what MPR is all about. Some respondents indicated that MPR is simply fundamental PR and is intrinsic to effective PR practice. Others, following a similar tack, argued that MPR is a derivative of PR and as such is not viewed as a separate marketing management discipline. Overview findings seem to illustrate that MPR does not yet have the legitimacy and potentiality to be either a new PR or marketing management discipline in its own right. It may well remain a concept or communication vehicle shared by both disciplines.

Exploration of objectives

Emergence of MPR as a conceptual discipline

From the literature reviewed, it seemed that MPR had emerged as a distinct new promotional discipline which comprises specialized application techniques that support marketing activities. According to Harris (1993), MPR arose in the 1980s because of the need to distinguish the specialized application of PR techniques that support marketing from the general practice of PR. Furthermore, Gage (1981), claimed that there are many signs that MPR has come of age. By examining the opinions received from the interviewees presented in Figure 2, it was indicated that MPR is simply a new label for PR activities in support of marketing objectives. It is something that PR consultancies have been practising for years.

The overall conclusion regarding the emergence of the MPR concept, as indicated from the research findings and the findings from the literature reviewed, is that MPR is not a newly emerged concept. It has always existed as part of the marketing and PR disciplines. It was pointed out that MPR is a new name – a new label, for a particular PR activity. A new name, however, does not amount to emergence of a new marketing-related discipline.

"MPR is not so much a new discipline as a new approach and new attitude"

"It is a new label for PR activity in support of marketing objectives; something PR agencies have been practising for years"

Four executives agreed with the following:

"It is not something particularly new. Again and again authors come out with lots of new buzz words which do not actually say anything new; it is just a different format and different name"

Other executives suggested that:

"MPR has always existed as part of both the PR and marketing disciplines; people may not have labelled it, but it is not new"

"It is not a new discipline, it is a new label; if MPR equals people are more concerned, more focused, more targeted about how they achieve their marketing, then fair enough. But MPR has always been like that and a new label does not imply a new discipline"

Figure 2 The emergence of MPR

The location of MPR

Throughout the literature reviewed, it was indicated that MPR is either considered as part of CPR or as an independent approach to the broader area of PR. Some public relations professionals and academics, such as Grunig (1992), reject the view that MPR should be treated as part of the marketing communications mix and thus treated as a distinct function from the broader area of CPR. According to them, the term MPR is considered to be a further attempt by marketeers to 'hijack' public relations. In other words the opinion suggested above implies that the concept of MPR is and must always be incorporated into CPR. The majority of PR professionals proclaim that no matter what they are called, PR activities in support of marketing or MPR activities, are part of general public relations and therefore incorporated into CPR. The issue of whether or not MPR should be part of the marketing or PR disciplines is crucial to the research as it this will provide some response to the issue MPR's legitimacy. Figure 3 presents the findings received from interviewees.

"PR is part of marketing and marketing includes PR; so MPR is by definition part of both"

"It is not there as a management function, it is there as part of the marketing department – part of marketing communications. In the PR agency world, many PR consultants work with primary responsibility to marketing directors within organizations; so MPR is part of the marketing function"

"Marketing is the central core; whereas PR is part of that core. MPR is part of both PR and marketing as the label suggests"

"It is part of both because the two share a set of common activities; it is a combination of marketing, PR, business, communication psychology and how to get messages across effectively"

Figure 3 MPR's inclusion as part of the marketing or PR disciplines

Many of the opinions expressed concerning the above issue by the interviewees, suggest that MPR is part of both the marketing and PR disciplines mainly because the two share a set of common activities which perhaps represent what the MPR concept is all about. Some individuals said that MPR is fundamental PR, it is derivative of PR and as such it must not become subsumed as a new marketing discipline or as a separate marketing management discipline. It was also indicated that MPR does not have the legitimacy as yet to be either a new PR or marketing discipline because it has always existed as part of both disciplines.

The legitimacy of MPR to be a new PR or marketing discipline

Regarding the objective of determining whether MPR is likely to become a separate marketing management discipline distinct from CPR the literature review revealed that MPR is likely to become a separate marketing management discipline distinct from CPR. Specifically, Harris (1993) claims that the term MPR is used to distinguish the marketing support PR from those other PR activities that define the corporation's relationships with its non-customer publics. According to Harris's view, the CPR function may remain a corporate management function, whereas MPR may become a marketing management function. Similarly, the mission of CPR would be to support marketing objectives. When the above issue was put forward for consideration by the interviewees, it was indicated that MPR is not there as a management function but as part of the marketing department – part of marketing communications. Also, it was strongly suggested that MPR does not have the legitimacy to be either a new PR discipline or a new marketing management discipline separate from CPR but is part of the marketing domain. Figure 4 presents the feedback received from the interviewees regarding the legitimacy of MPR to be a new PR or marketing discipline.

There is a certain degree of controversy concerning the issue of whether MPR has the legitimate claim to be a new PR or marketing discipline. Some PR practitioners agree that it does not. The reason given is that it always existed as part of both disciplines and that PR consultancies have been doing it for years. On the other hand, another opinion expressed was that it is perhaps more likely

"No, It has always existed"

"It depends on how the concept is defined and the underlying rationale. However, given time, it may become a distinct discipline combining elements from both parents"

"No; it has always existed as part of both the marketing and PR disciplines. People may not have labelled it, but it is not new"

"In-house marketing departments are increasingly moving toward more integrated marketing approaches, including using PR specialists. An increasing number of PR agencies' key focus is MPR"

Figure 4 MPR's legitimacy as a new PR or marketing discipline

> "It will not become such. However, MPR holds that the marketing manager and director have to be well aware of what goes on in MPR and make sure that marketing has the best PR ideas in relation to strategic goals"
>
> "It is just a way of marketing communication"
>
> "Both marketing and PR try to get themselves on the boardroom table with varying degrees of success. MPR is an emergence from the PR and marketing disciplines so it draws on compositive skills ... it may become an independent third discipline"

Figure 5 The likelihood of MPR becoming a marketing management discipline in its own right

that MPR will be used as a distinct discipline combining elements of both marketing and PR. Similarly, managing directors were asked to consider the likelihood that MPR would become a marketing management discipline in its own right. Figure 5 presents the feedback received from the interviewees regarding this issue.

The general outcome from the above opinions is that MPR is not likely to become a marketing management discipline in its own right. The reasons given are that MPR is a form of marketing communications and thus, part of the marketing discipline. However, it was suggested that perhaps it will become an independent discipline in its own right having elements from the marketing and PR disciplines. The research revealed that the majority of those who practise public relations believe that MPR does not have the legitimacy to be a new marketing management discipline separate from CPR, but that it is part of the marketing domain.

The influence of the debate between PR and marketing on MPR

One of the main objectives of this research was to find out whether the legitimacy of MPR is affected by the debate between marketing and PR disciplines. From the literature reviewed, it was found that the relationship between the marketing and PR disciplines seems controversial. The main controversy is that of delineating between the respective roles of the two functions. On the one hand, the majority of marketing professionals say that PR is or should be part of marketing and be managed as a marketing activity. This view represents the marketing perspective of PR which also holds that MPR is a new approach to the practice of PR which is closely related to marketing. On the other hand, the majority of PR professionals suggest that PR activities can be distinguished from those of marketing. This view is known as the PR perspective of public relations, according to which marketing and PR serve different functions. Also from a PR perspective, MPR is an attempt by marketeers to 'hijack' PR incorporating it as an extra element within the promotional mix. The field research showed that such a debate does not exist pointing at the possibility that the debate may be a question of definition or even an academic invention. However, some research participants stipulated that if a debate existed then it would strengthen the legitimacy of MPR since the integration of the two disciplines will not be possible and thus, MPR will be the only concept combining benefits from using both disciplines. Figure 6 presents quotations taken from the interviews in relation to this issue.

The above issue produced a wealth of controversy. Some of the interviewees suggested that there has never been a debate between the two disciplines. One practitioner claimed that it is the Chartered Institute of Marketing which has actually created this 'assumed' debate with its attempt to become the federal body of all communications disciplines. Others pointed at the fact that marketing and PR are basically one discipline, with PR being a sub-function of marketing. Some others suggested that MPR will be strengthened by the debate since it is the concept that integrates elements from both disciplines. Finally, another advanced the opinion that the benefits resulting from the use of MPR will decrease because of the debate since the lack of integration between the two disciplines will affect all other organizational functions. Figure 7 presents the opinions expressed by executives in relation to the nature of the debate.

Again, there is controversy regarding this issue. Certain PR practitioners argue that there is no debate between PR and marketing since in the majority of cases the two disciplines are integrated in order to achieve maximum benefit. On the other hand, others suggest that the debate is a question of definition and in other words, 'a war of words'. Others identify that there is a 'war' between PR and marketing practitioners about ownership of MPR in relation to the two

"There is no debate. What there is, is that the Chartered Institute of Marketing wishes to become the federal body of all communications disciplines. CIM may claim invention of MPR and they may succeed in getting academic support in order to claim parenthood. In reality, they do not own it – they can use it, but did not invent it"

"The legitimacy of MPR will probably be strengthened by the debate, as will proposed integration between all communication disciplines in relation to business activities"

"No! The marketing and PR functions are basically one – one discipline, with PR as part of marketing"

Figure 6 Impact of the debate between the marketing and PR disciplines on MPR

"There is no debate, as PR is a subset of the marketing discipline"
"The debate is really over definition – i.e. a war of words. However in the real world marketing and PR people are fighting for the likelihood of one being superior to the other"

"It is about territory, power, and in essence, budget control"

"It is academic. In the PR agencies industry there is continuous integration between the two disciplines in the majority of cases. There is wide recognition and appreciation of the benefits each can bring to the overall company effort"

Figure 7 The nature of the debate

disciplines; which of the two is superior and higher up a perceived hierarchy of important functions. Finally, some others claimed that the debate is about territory, power and budget control. From the above, it could be said that the debate is controversial in the sense that it needs to be investigated and discussed in both professional and academic circles.

The relationship between MPR and CPR

Concerning the fifth objective which refers to the exploration of the relationship between MPR and CPR, the literature review indicated that certain authors, notably Harris (1993), advance the opinion that even though PR is a distinct discipline separate from the marketing discipline, MPR and CPR should be recognized as separate and self-sufficient disciplines. However, this opinion is contradictory to the opinion held by PR academics such as Grunig (1992) according to whom a separation of the two implies the subordination of PR into a promotional tool. Figure 8 presents quotations taken from interview transcripts in order to illustrate the points being made when the interviewees were asked to state whether there is interaction between MPR and CPR.

It seems evident that even though some PR practitioners believed that CPR and MPR are maintained as separate and distinct, it is essential that there be some integration between the two. Marketing activities should be carried out within the parameters set at a corporate level, as should all other organizational activities. On the other hand, the corporate strategy and specifically the CPR should be extremely sensitive to the marketing issues, as well as to other issues (e.g. financial).

Another important issue put to interviewees for consideration concerned the gap between CPR and MPR. Figure 9 presents the overall benefits as perceived by interviewees which illustrate the points being made. The exploration of this issue is crucial to the subject matter of this paper since it aims to explore the legitimacy of MPR to become a separate marketing management discipline distinct from the broader area of corporate public relations. The overall opinion

"They are maintained as separate and distinct in FMCG companies because they are driven by two separate parts of the company. It is important there be conflict between the two. MPR campaigns should operate with the same value, style, and image as CPR"

"There should be considerable interaction between MPR and CPR ... all stakeholders should have a consistent and coherent view of the company – otherwise you're either lying or just incompetent"

"When you are doing a job for a corporate entity, the goal is to protect and promote the reputation of that corporate entity. Therefore requirements of what work has been done in marketing support is to ensure that it is operating within parameters of the overall company or brand. There is no need, generally, for much interaction, providing the rules have been set at corporate level"

"It is important that MPR activities as well as other organizational activities are carried out within parameters set at corporate level"

Figure 8 The existence of interaction between MPR and CPR

all agreed the "gap" was closing

Need to be seen as efficient and effective

Squeeze maximum value from all communications

Evidence of direct relationship between CPR and MPR (re-impact)

Both link to overall strategy

Figure 9 The gap between CPR and MPR

concerning this issue is that it is essential that all the company's activities are integrated effectively. Failure to achieve long-lasting integration, may lead to less effective communication.

Finally, interviewees were asked to consider whether MPR and CPR require integration in an overall communications programme (see Figure 10).

The majority of PR practitioners acknowledge the fact that, if there is not any considerable interaction between CPR and MPR, then obviously the company will be unable to survive and compete with its rivals. The main reason is that if the various organizational activities do not operate within the 'route' set at corporate level then the company will have no scope, no direction, and no mission. The direct adverse impact of such a situation will not only affect the company, it will also affect its publics with which it interacts.

The discussion of the research objectives provides ground for the exploration of the core objective which is to explore whether the concept of MPR has a legitimate claim to be a new public relations discipline *or* whether it is likely to become a separate marketing management discipline. Agency executives recognize that MPR is not a recently emerged concept. It has been utilized on a regular and consistent basis for decades but was practised under perhaps a different name by the majority of PR consultancies. However, some practitioners argued that MPR is synonymous with product publicity mainly because of the cases in which it is used, such as the launch of a new product. A similar opinion is shared by the majority of marketing academics who contend that the MPR concept is distinct from mainstream public relations. That is, since it is performing a marketing function, it is serving as a tool of marketing.

In other words, what marketeers define as MPR may be simply what has been repeatedly described as a marketing stepchild, i.e. product publicity. On

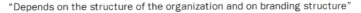

"Depends on the structure of the organization and on branding structure"

"Must be so, as both corporate and marketing audiences are interrelated"

"Effectiveness of an overall communications programme depends on whether or not considerable integration between CPR and MPR exists"

Figure 10 The integration between CPR and MPR in communications programmes

the other hand, the majority of PR academics suggest that the concept of MPR can be perceived as an attempt by marketeers to dominate the PR function and subsume it into a promotional tool. The research has revealed that the majority of PR practitioners share the opinion that MPR is a part of both the marketing and PR disciplines since the two share a common set of activities which are included in the MPR concept. However, it was argued that MPR is fundamental PR and it should therefore be incorporated into CPR. Others suggested that marketing is the central core of the organization, and PR is the manifestation of that. MPR is equally a part of that central core and of that manifestation since it includes elements of both.

Summary and Conclusions

The literature review and field research provide a basis for exploring the MPR concept, and specifically, in investigating whether MPR has the legitimate claim to be either a new public relations discipline or a separate marketing management discipline. Although the core conclusion of this research is that MPR does not yet have the legitimate claim to be either a distinct public relations or marketing management discipline, it is indicated on the basis of current evidence that MPR emerged from the interaction of the PR and marketing disciplines and is therefore a concept shared by both. In real terms, those who practise PR and have the knowledge and expertise to contribute to the achievement of marketing and corporate goals deny the 'birth' of a new discipline. Specifically, the main conclusions are:

- MPR is what UK PR consultancies have been doing for years under perhaps a different name. MPR is not a newly emerged concept but has existed for a significant amount of time.
- MPR is a term used to describe the use of PR techniques and approaches in support of marketing objectives. But there is nothing new about MPR in its marketing context except perhaps the title.
- MPR does not have a legitimate claim to be a new public relations discipline or a separate marketing management discipline distinct from the broader area of corporate public relations.
- MPR is an essential component of promotional activity, but by definition part of the marketing and PR disciplines drawing on required skills from both managerial disciplines.
- The debate between the marketing and PR disciplines is characterized as academic.
- MPR and CPR are maintained as separate and distinct but they may require integration in an overall communications programme.
- MPR's importance has been appreciated and recognized by companies over the past five years and should continue to increase as a result of recognition and application.
- The average annual budget spent on MPR activities by the customers of UK PR consultancies is expected to increase in the next five years.

The findings from this small-scale study indicate that PR consultancies have been using MPR for and on behalf of marketing clients for many years. For example, the research revealed that it has been extremely effective in the past fifty years in support of marketing for industrial products. It is not therefore a newly emerged concept, but it is certainly a new label or name used to define a set of activities under the parenthood of marketing and PR. The research revealed that MPR is about 60 per cent of what PR consultancies do – continuous pursuance of marketing objectives and in support of marketing functions.

MPR is important in a company's promotional activities because, no matter how one defines PR, whether it is PR that uses the media as a way to reach a target audience or whether it does it directly through some form of local activity, it is a key component of the company's overall promotional activity. Essentially, it has been stated by research participants that MPR should be part of the promotional mix since it can be used to strengthen the promotional activities of a company. It should be used alongside other promotional tools as part of an integrated communications programme in order to increase the effectiveness of the overall promotional effort targeted at a particular objective.

Essentially, MPR is a communications tool used to help change attitudes and beliefs or assist in creating sales. It can be effective wherever it is used as long as it is used intelligently and be integrated with the other promotional tools as part of an integrated marketing communications programme. Likewise, despite the fact that MPR and corporate communications are maintained as separate and distinct, they often require integration and synergy in order to contribute substantially to the success of an overall communication programme. The gap between the two forms of PR activity seems to be narrowing.

In the academic literature, reference has been made to the debate between public relations and marketing academics over respective positions and spheres of influence of the two disciplines. However, evidence received from the field research indicates that such a debate does not exist in reality. In many cases, in the UK PR consultancy industry, marketing and PR people work closely together for the achievement of common client marketing-related objectives. What has been identified is a tendency among marketing and PR practitioners to compete over power, territory, and in essence, budget control. In fact, practitioners suggest that the debate between the two disciplines is a question of definition or, in other words, academic.

Clearly, the MPR concept has been used for years and its importance and effectiveness is widely appreciated by marketing and PR academics and practitioners. Despite the evidence of controversy between marketing academics who suggest that MPR represents a new discipline, and PR academics who proclaim that the concept does not represent either a new PR discipline or a marketing management discipline, MPR is a concept that may lead all PR disciplines with its perceived importance in the promotional sphere. Companies appreciate the benefits and contribution of PR, and subsequently of MPR, with bigger budgets and a larger share of the overall promotional budget.

Essentially, despite the fact that the MPR concept does not as yet represent a new management discipline, its contribution to organizational success and effectiveness is recognized and widely appreciated by those who either have been using it or have carried out research as to its value and validity in the promotional sphere. It is an offspring of both the PR and marketing disciplines and should, therefore, be shared by both. Academic and empirical evidence indicate that the future of the MPR concept seems to be bright and that, eventually, it may evolve into a separate new management discipline sharing elements from its two parents, the marketing and public relations disciplines, but having a wider scope: that of managing and controlling those PR and marketing activities which are under its jurisdiction with the aim of achieving well-defined marketing communication objectives.

This paper has explored the legitimacy of MPR in relation to the marketing or public relations disciplines by an exploratory study in UK PR consultancy industry. Owing to the fact that MPR is a relatively new area, there has not been any empirical research carried out by authors that have written and published articles and books about marketing public relations, such as Gumm (1978), Shimp (1993) and Harris (1993). Thus, the literature related to MPR is limited and may have constrained operationalization of the exploratory research in this paper. An important problem encountered during the exploration was the reluctance of the respondents to mention their names as providers of information.

Given the small scale of the study, further research needs to be undertaken in order to expand the sample, perhaps via a more deductive hypothesis testing study. Given a substantial increase in financial and time resources then perhaps the sample size may include PR consultancies that have headquarters in other European countries in order to explore the emergence and legitimacy of MPR in Europe in general. Also, the research can be expanded to include organizations that have their own PR department and as a result, do not use the services of PR consultancies. In addition, empirical research can also be carried out into the interaction between public relations, marketing communications, and promotional practices in order to provide a more general picture of the implications involved in exploring the emergence of various concepts or disciplines.

Despite the limitations of the research which have been described, the exploration revealed some interesting facts concerning the MPR concept. MPR does not have as yet the legitimate claim to be either a new public relations or marketing management discipline. It was suggested however from both the academic literature and the field research, that MPR's importance and effectiveness in the company's promotional activity is well recognized and appreciated. As a distinct concept, MPR requires close integration with other promotional tools in an integrated marketing communications programme. In terms of integration with CPR, its multi-usage has proven valuable in many situations faced by organizations, such as crisis management or community relations. Despite the fact that the research participants failed to recognize the existence of a debate between the PR and marketing disciplines, whereas the academics suggested that such a debate exists, it is stipulated that the impact of the debate on MPR will be positive. For many years, PR practitioners have been using MPR effectively together with the traditional promotional tools. Its cost effectiveness and credibility has made it popular with both clients and consultancies. As a result, its budgets are rapidly rising and it is a fast growing segment in the promotional area. In the future, MPR may evolve into a distinct new management discipline separate from PR and marketing, but combining elements from both. Certainly MPR extends beyond mere window dressing, or labelling of an old aspect of marketing communications under a new label. But its legitimacy as a new conceptual discipline requires further research and debate.

References

Aucamp, J. (1971), *The Effective Use of Market Research*, Staples Press, London, pp. 49–51, 62.

Bernstein, J. (1988), 'PR in top communication role', *Advertising Age*, Vol. 59, November, p. 28.

Black, G. (1952), *Planned Industrial Publicity*, Putnam, Chicago, IL, p. 3.

Burgess, R.G. (1982), 'Elements of sampling in field research', in Burgess, R.G. (Ed.), *Field Research: A Sourcebook and Field Manual*, George Allen and Unwin, London.

Business Week (1987), 'Nothing sells like sports', 30 August.

Cassell, C. and Symon, G. (1994), *Qualitative Methods in Organizational Research*, Sage Publications, Newbury Park, CA, pp. 14–35, 210–11.

Charles, E. (1994), 'Is the future bright?' *The Rise of PR Consultancy*, Haymarket Business Publications Ltd, London, p. 13.

Chisnall, P.M. (1981), *Marketing Research: Analysis and Measurement*, McGraw-Hill, New York, NY, pp. 140–52, 155–60.

Chisnall, P.M. (1986), *Marketing Research*, McGraw-Hill, New York, NY, pp. 36–7, 62–83.

Chisnall, P.M. (1992), *Marketing Research*, McGraw-Hill, New York, NY, pp.109–35, 139–52.

Churchill, G.A. (1983), *Marketing Research: Methodological Foundations*, The Dryden Press, Chicago, IL, pp. 140–5, 345–6.

Cohen, W. (1991), *The Practice of Marketing Management*, Maxwell Macmillan, London.

Coombs, C.H., Raiffa, H. and Thrall, R.M. (1954), 'Some views on mathematical models and measurement theory', in Thrall, R.M., Coombs, C.H. and Davis, R.L. (Eds), *Decision Processes*, John Wiley and Sons, New York, NY, pp. 20–1.

Crimp, M. (1981), *The Marketing Research Process*, Prentice-Hall, Englewood Cliffs, NJ, pp. 17–22.

Crimp, M. (1990), *The Marketing Research Process*, Prentice-Hall, Englewood Cliffs, NJ, pp. 78–82.

Cutlip, S.M., Center, A.H. and Broom, G.M. (1985), *Effective Public Relations*, Prentice-Hall, Englewood Cliffs, NJ, p. 89.

Dark, S., Hall, A. and Farish, S. (1993), 'Darkness before the dawn', *PR Week – UK Top 150 PR Consultancies*, Haymarket Publications, London, 29 April, p. 31.

De Vans, D.A. (1991), *Surveys in Social Research*, UCL press, London, pp. 25–6.

Dilenschneider, R. (1988), 'PR on the offensive: bigger part of marketing mix', *Advertising Age*, Vol. 60, 13 March, p. 20.

Duncan, T. (1985), 'A study of how manufacturers and service companies perceive and use MPR', Ball State University, Muncie, IN (unpublished).

Friend, C. (1994), 'Pielle case studies', (unpublished), pp. 1–14.

Gage, T.J. (1981), 'Public relations ripens role in marketing', *Advertising Age*, 5 January, pp. 10–11.

Gardner, G. (1978), *Social Surveys for Social Planners*, The Open University Press, pp. 19–21, 35–6, 77–85.

Goldman, T. (1988), 'Big spenders develop newspaper communications', *Marketing Communications*, Vol. 13, No. 1, p. 24.

Grunig, J.E. (1992), *Excellence in PR and Communication Management*, Lawrence Erlbaum Associates, Hillsdale, NJ, p. 357.

Gumm, J. (1978), 'Public relations is a primary element in Beech-Nut food's marketing program', *Advertising Age*, 6 February, p. 39.

Hague, P. (1992), *The Industrial Market Research*, Kogan Page, London, pp. 205–30.

Hague, P.N. and Jackson, P. (1990), *Do Your own Market Research*, Kogan Page, London, pp. 95–6.

Harris, T. (1993), *The Marketer's Guide to PR: How Today's Companies Are Using the New Public Relations to Gain a Competitive Edge*, John Wiley and Sons, New York, NY.

Jankowicz, A.D. (1994), *Business Research Projects for Students*, Chapman and Hall, London, pp. 9, 19–21, 61, 166–7, 142–3, 205, 178–9, 188.

Johnson & Johnson Special Reports, *The Tylenol Comeback*, undated, p. 8.

Kalton, G. and Moser, C.A. (1971), *Survey Methods in Social Investigation*, Heinemann Educational Books, Oxford, p. 256.

Kitchen, P.J. (1991), 'The developing use of PR in a fragmented, demassified market', *Marketing Intelligence Planning*, Vol. 19 No. 2, pp. 29–33.

Kitchen, P.J. (1993), 'Public relations: a rationale for its development and usage within UK fast-moving consumer goods firms', *European Journal of Marketing*, Vol. 27 No. 7, pp. 367, 379–84.

Kitchen, P.J. and Proctor, R.A. (1991), 'The increasing importance of public relations in FMCG firms', *Journal of Marketing Management*, Vol. 7 No. 2, pp. 360, 366–7.

Kitchen, P.J. and Moss, D. (1995), 'Marketing and public relations: the relationship revisited', *Journal of Marketing Communications*, Vol. 1 No. 2, pp. 8–11.

Kleiner, A. (1989), 'The public relations coup', *Adweek's Marketing Week*, 16 January.

Kotler, P. (1988), *Marketing Management*, Prentice-Hall, Englewood Cliffs, NJ, pp. 655–8.

Kotler, P. (1989), 'Public relations versus marketing: dividing the conceptual domain and operational turf', a position paper prepared for the Public Relations Colloquium, San Diego, CA, 24 January, p. 4.

Kotler, P. (1991a), *Marketing Management*, Prentice-Hall, Englewood Cliffs, NJ, pp. 29, 642.

Kotler, P. (1991), *Marketing Management*, 9th edition, Prentice-Hall, Englewood Cliffs, NJ, pp. 621–48.

Kotler, P. and Mindak, W. (1978), 'Marketing and public relations', *Journal of Marketing*, 14 October, p. 15.

Kreitzman, L. (1986), 'Balancing brand building blocks', *Marketing*, 13 November, pp. 43–6.

Layder, D. (1993), *New Strategies in Social Research*, Polity Press, Cambridge, pp. 115–6.

Lazer, W. (1962), 'The role of models in marketing', *Journal of Marketing*, April, pp. 9–14.

Lightcap, K. (1984), 'Marketing support', in Cantor, B. (Ed.), *Experts in Action: Inside Public Relations*, Longman, New York, NY, Ch. 8.

Love, J.F. (1986), *McDonald's: behind the Arches*, Bantam Books, New York, NY, p. 212.

Merims, A.M. (1972), 'Marketing's stepchild: product publicity', *Harvard Business Review*, Vol. 36 No. 5, November/December, pp. 107–13.

Nachimias, C. and Nachimias, D. (1976), *Research Methods in the Social Sciences*, Edward Arnold, New York, NY, pp.116–7, 260.

Novelli, W.D. (1988), 'Stir some PR into your communications mix', *Marketing News*, Vol. 22, 5 December, p. 19.

Philadelphia Inquirer, (1984), 'McDonald's deserves praise', editorial, July.

PR Week (1981), 'The going gets tougher', 23 May, p. 7.

PR Week – UK Top 150 PR Consultancies (1994), 'Mixed fortunes for the top ten', Haymarket Publication, 28 April p. 37.

PR Week – UK Top 150 PR Consultancies (1992), 'Tougher all round for the top ten', Haymarket publication, 30 April, p. 27.

Shandwick plc, *The Public Relations Consultancy Market Worldwide*, Autumn, study published by Shandwick plc, London.

Shimp, T.A. (1990), *Promotion Management and Marketing Communications, The* Dryden Press, Chicago, IL, p. 486.

Shimp, T.A. (1993), *Promotion Management and Marketing Communications*, Harcourt Brace and Co., San Diego, CA, pp. 590–3.

Weiers, R.M. (1988), *Marketing Research*, Prentice-Hall, Englewood Cliffs, NJ, pp. 65–7, 103–6.

Wiseman, J.P. (1974), 'The research web', *Urban Life and Culture*, Vol. 3 No. 1, pp. 317–28.

Yin, R.K. (1981), 'The case study crisis: some answers', *Administrative Science Quarterly*, Vol. 26, pp. 58–65.

Zaltman, G. and Burger, P.C. (1975), *Marketing Research: Fundamentals and Dynamics*, The Dryden Press, Chicago, IL, pp. 283–6, 293–4.

? Questions

1 Where should MPR fit – marketing or PR? Does it need to 'fit' in any specific discipline?

2 Using a brand of your choice, illustrate how MPR has helped the brand to succeed. (Information from *PR Week, Campaign* or Tom Harris may help in illustrating this area. See Tom Harris's chapter in *Raising the Corporate Umbrella* by Kitchen, P.J. and Schultz, D.E. eds (2001) Palgrave-Macmillan, Basingstoke).

3 Is the debate raised by the authors in terms of boundaries still relevant today? Why or why not?

4 Should all businesses have an MPR programme? Discuss.

5 Justify the view taken by some PR academics that PR is not about marketing.

6 Does MPR have the legitimacy to be regarded as a separate marketing management discipline?

7 Is MPR a contradiction in terms?

Vignette

Kodak sharpens its Focus on China through Ogilvy & Mather PR

In 1997 Kodak appointed Ogilvy & Mather PR to run its consumer marketing programme in China. Notably, Ogilvy & Mather had worked with Kodak for eighteen months on the corporate brief. However, Ogilvy & Mather's contract had been extended to include support for consumer branding, new product launches, sponsorship and events.

In 1997 Scott Konrick, MD for Ogilvy & Mather in Beijing, commented, 'most people who are buying PR services . . . are multinationals who want to deepen their roots in China'.

The trend away from project-based work, toward more comprehensive campaigns was signalled in another O&M win, with computer giant IBM. Ogilvy & Mather won the brand building and corporate account after a three-way pitch (Kitchen and Papasolomou 1997, reprinted here).

By 2005, although multinational corporations made up the majority of clients for China-based PR firms, Chinese corporations were catching on. They are starting to take advantage of PR firms' marketing and communication expertise in an effort to compete with multinationals (see Dora Chen, *http://www.prcanada.ca/CHINA-WATCH/HEATT.HTM*, accessed 3 January 2005).

From these early beginnings Ogilvy Public Relations Worldwide (Ogilvy PR) has emerged as the leading public relations group in China with the acquisition of H-Line Public Relations, one of China's top domestic public relations firms. Ogilvy PR now holds a majority stake in a new venture called H-Line Ogilvy Communications Company Ltd (H-Line Ogilvy), which will continue to operate separately and replace the former H-Line Public Relations organization. H-Line's founders and key executives of the company hold a significant portion of the equity in the new venture.

Demand for public relations and public affairs services has grown rapidly in China, where Ogilvy PR has been among the fastest-growing firms. Ogilvy PR, which will continue to operate as a separate network, has tripled its fee income since 1997. Together, Ogilvy PR and H-Line Ogilvy have more than 130 employees working from six offices in three cities (Beijing, 10 June 2002) (source: *http://www.ogilvypr.com/pressroom/h-line-acquired.cfm,* accessed 3 January 2005).

Source: P.J. Kitchen, *Marketing Communications: Principles and Practice*, London: International Thomson (1999), p. 358. Used by permission of the author and as cited in the text above.

Chapter 7

Lynne Eagle

SPONSORSHIP

THIS PAPER ILLUSTRATES THE growing importance of sponsorship as a strategic marketing communications tool. It also highlights a problem common to other marketing communications areas – how to evaluate return on investment. The cases used to illustrate the complexity of effective and efficient sponsorship management relate to high-profile sports that are increasingly global in profile. Thus investment in sport sponsorship in one country may result in exposure in many other markets.

The problems addressed in the paper regarding the lack of 'standard units of measurement and evaluation' must extend beyond the markets of immediate sponsorship interest. Global marketers must consider the impact of sponsorship spill-over in multiple markets and how it is perceived within the context of overall, often localized, marketing communication activity. A key problem that is not addressed in the paper is that of accidental or deliberate 'ambush marketing' – competitive activity in one or more markets that may dilute or negate the effects of the original sponsors' communication activity. For example, event signage and logos negotiated as part of a multinational sponsorship package may be countered by competitors' local advertising within the sports broadcast – or even sponsorship of the sports programme broadcast itself.

Verity notes that support for sponsorships such as Formula 1 motor racing may vary widely by country. Global brands may thus be particularly vulnerable when local managers do not support the sponsorship objectives or see it as taking resources from what they deem to be more appropriate localized activity. She does not address strategies for agreeing on levels of support, or for dealing with situations when local opposition may be sufficiently strong for local managers to actively attempt to hamper activity they may see as unfairly and inappropriately imposed by managers who lack depth of understanding of the dynamics of their local market.

Verity discusses the distinction between active and passive communication and the need to identify accurately the impact of the communication on customer groups who may have little declared interest in the sponsored event itself but who may see benefit in associated activity such as merchandising. Thus there is a need to identify the impact of, and opportunities presented by, the inclusion of sponsorship activity within an integrated marketing communications programme, globally and in individual markets. While the establishment of clear objectives is important, so is gaining the support and 'buy-in' across markets. In addition, rather than imposing support and risking resentment and thus minimal co-operation, ways of customizing local activity to best suit the unique market conditions should be investigated.

Another area not addressed by Verity is provision for contingency planning – determining what action should be taken in the event of short or long-term problems. This may include serious accidents or prolonged performance decline. Marketers must consider the impact on the brands for which they are stewards between being associated with a 'winner' versus a poor performer and be prepared to adapt their communications accordingly. These considerations should, of course, be built into the sponsorship agreement itself.

MAXIMISING THE MARKETING POTENTIAL OF SPONSORSHIP FOR GLOBAL BRANDS

Julie Verity

Sponsorship is not a new marketing communication tool, but has become much more popular over the last two decades. During the 1990s global deals were estimated to have nearly quadrupled in value, a trend that was forecast to continue during the first five years of the new millennium. Traditionally, companies investing in sponsorship relationships as part of the corporate communication mix learnt from experience, over time, how to manage their sponsorship properties. But, as the size of sponsorship deals has grown and their strategic importance for marketing communications increased, it has become more urgent for marketers to deliver value from these investments. Speeding the learning process is important, therefore, especially in an area where literature is scarce and, expert practitioners and the media report a relatively low level of capability.

This paper aims to explore some of the issues companies commonly encounter when engaging in a sponsorship relationship. Following a summary of

---

European Business Journal, Vol. 14, No. 4 (2002), pp. 161–73. Reproduced by kind permission of Whurr Publishers Ltd.
Dr Julie Verity, Lecturer in Strategic Management, Cranfield School of Management, Cranfield University.
The case study in this article was used in a shorter version as a submission to the Marketing Society Awards 2001, when Shell won in the 'Customer Insight' category.

the main problem areas and theories of best practice, the paper describes how one organisation (the Anglo-Dutch oil group Shell) improved the use made of its Formula 1 sponsorship relationship with the Italian motor racing company Ferrari.

Conclusions will be drawn that should improve practice in this marketing growth area.

Sponsorship is a major Global Industry

SPONSORSHIP HAS BEEN A steadily growing proportion of companies' marketing budgets over the past twenty years, a trend which shows no sign of slowing. In 1990 global expenditure was estimated at $7.7 bn by FT Sport Marketing Survey (1999). Another survey conducted by Sponsorclick in 2001 put worldwide spend in the same year at $29.3 bn and estimated that growth over the next four years would result in expenditure of $45.2 bn by 2005. Even at these figures, sponsorship still only accounted for 4 per cent of the total, global advertising spend in 2000 but, the report argued, as advertising budgets were curtailed in the economic downturn early in the millennium, sponsorship had become a more significant part of brands' promotional budgets. This was partly due to the length of sponsorship contracts and the difficulty of relinquishing them at short notice, but also because of their growing popularity as a marketing communication tool.

Of the sponsorship areas, sport dominates marketers' choice. In 2001 in the UK, 63 per cent of all sponsorship expenditure went to sports teams and events, the majority of this being spent on motor sport and football. Vodafone, the UK mobile phone group, provides the perfect example, spending $46 mn to place its name on the shirts of Manchester United players and $41 mn to place its name on world motor racing champion Michael Schumacher's Formula 1 Ferrari. Apart from the sponsorship fee (which as demand grows, will become more sizeable), companies typically double or triple the expenditure made to the project surrounding the sponsorship contract so that, increasingly, the sponsorship is seen as driving the overall marketing communication programme.

Commentators explain the growth in sponsorship as due to:

- restrictive government policies on tobacco and alcohol advertising
- escalating costs of media advertising
- increased leisure activities and sporting events and interest in them
- greater media coverage of sponsored events
- reduced efficiencies of traditional media advertising (e.g. clutter and zapping between television programmes, but also consumers' increasing sophistication and cynicism when seeing traditional advertising).

The globalisation of sporting events, teams and personalities, and sport's centrality to an emerging global culture generally, are cited as reasons why this area of sponsorship specifically is a valuable communication tool for international and global brands. Indeed, some writers have argued that sports sponsorship will become the optimal positioning tool for international marketers seeking to communicate global messages.

Sponsorship outside sport, in the arts, society and community areas, is still relatively small, but is also growing and this is explained by the increasing popularity of corporate social responsibility programmes.

Finding different ways to communicate brand and corporate credentials to target audiences, apart from traditional advertising, is therefore a significant trend. Sponsorship is a major part of that trend.

Issues arising from Sponsorship as a Marketing Communication Tool

Setting objectives and evaluation of effectiveness As the proportion of the total marketing budget allotted to sponsorship has increased, management attention to its worth has also risen. However, disciplined processes of research, evaluation and 'business case justification' have been slow to emerge because there has been no standard unit of measurement and evaluation. Specific research conducted by Research International, a specialist market research agency (August 1999), on behalf of Shell, for example, amongst companies using sports sponsorship on an international scale concluded that:

> Evaluation of sponsorship activity was seen as a complex area for which no rigorous method currently exists.

Whilst textbooks quote the need for sponsorship deals to be evaluated in terms of meeting objectives and delivering for the brand, in reality the sophistication of monitoring has been relatively crude. At best, this has involved measurement of media coverage and name mentions/sightings (commonly recorded by a specialist monitoring agency), and converting this to a money figure of worth. For example, Volvo's £2 mn sponsorship of tennis resulted in 1.4 bn impressions (number of mentions or sightings times audience size), which was calculated to be worth £12 mn in media advertising (Jobber, 2001).

Another issue slowing the development of standard methodologies for evaluation has been the wide range of objectives companies have for their sponsorship investments, as noted by the Research International report:

> The relative value of sponsorship activity in the overall marketing mix was seen to depend upon the specific brand and business objectives: some companies valued image-building activity and exposure, whilst others valued opportunities for PR activity and providing hospitality to key clients.

Both corporate-related objectives and product/brand-related objectives are within the potential of sponsorship communication programmes. These might include the following:

Corporate

- Increase public awareness of the organisation.
- Enhance company image.
- Alter public perception.
- Increase community involvement.
- Build business/trade relations and goodwill.
- Enhance staff/employees' relations and motivation.

Product/Brand

- Increase target market awareness.
- Build positive image dimensions.
- Brand preference and increased sales.
- Block the competition.

Defining objectives for sponsorship deals has not always been a well-executed first step inside organisations. Even where this has been thought through in marketing departments, the message can get lost within large organisations. This was the situation Shell found when they reviewed their sponsorship deal with Ferrari in 2000. Worldwide, many managers held the view that Formula 1 sponsorship only provided an opportunity for corporate hospitality. Others saw the sport as irrelevant and often quoted their local customer base as being as uninterested in Formula 1 as they were themselves. Some found it difficult to believe that the relationship could deliver tangible business results such as improved sales. These differing opinions reflected the different use of the sponsorship by Shell's local marketing companies around the world. It was acknowledged that no formal attempt was made to measure the value of the relationship to Shell's businesses.

Understanding how sponsorship marketing activity works

There is often a lack of clarity in organisations about how sponsorship works as a marketing support activity. The basic 'model' for any sponsorship effect is, essentially, the same as that for all brand marketing support activities:

1. Build awareness, *which leads to . . .*
2. top of mind, positive brand image dimensions, *which leads to . . .*
3. brand preference, *which leads to . . .*
4. repeat purchase and loyalty.

The use of sponsorship to drive this model involves two main differences from other forms of marketing support. Firstly, the brand seeks to gain *additional* attention, via association with a 'property' which already enjoys a high level of interest, involvement and credibility for the brand's key target groups. In Shell's case the property was two-fold, Formula 1 itself and the Ferrari brand. The emphasis is given to 'additional', since the sponsorship cannot be a substitute for a customer value proposition that already offers desirable benefits to target customers.

Secondly, 'communication' with the brand's target groups comes in two forms, active and passive. Although these two forms of communication are related, they are fundamentally different in the way that they contribute to the brand's objectives:

- *Passive*. General media coverage in the form of TV broadcasts (and related press and PR coverage) creates the opportunity for brand exposure and the building of basic awareness of the association. In Formula 1, the skill lies in sponsoring a successful and popular team and in ensuring that the brand identity is placed in visible, on-camera positions. The audiences reached by this kind of coverage are those people who are interested enough in Formula 1 to watch Grand Prix.
- *Active*. Marketing exploitation programmes do not suffer from the constraints of general media coverage. They can be targeted and carry specific brand and product messages with incentives to purchase. Crucial for Shell was the understanding that active communication programmes need not be limited by the variable 'interested in Formula 1'. For example, a mother repeatedly buying Shell fuel because her son wishes to collect a highly desirable range of model Ferrari 'classic cars' need have no interest whatsoever in Formula 1 (and will register amongst those 'not interested' in Formula 1 research).

Failure to appreciate the difference between these two forms of sponsorship 'communication' was, Shell learned from their own research, one of the most common problems in sports sponsorship generally. Simply attaching a name to an event or a logo on a shirt does not result in the target consumer being any more aware of the sponsorship or the value statement the sponsoring brand is attempting to make. The FT report (1999) confirmed this finding by reporting that:

> McDonald's spend $50m currently on NBA Sponsor in the USA alone and comment: 'the important element is that McDonald's placed its sports identity directly on its products both to sell the products to customers and to reinforce the promotional connection.

And, in the same report, M. Reynolds, the CEO of the Institute of Sports Sponsorship, was quoted:

> Buying the rights to be a sponsor is only the start. Brands need to exploit this. They spend anything between a further 100–200 per cent of the budget supporting it.

The weakness of many sponsorship associations is the tenuous link between the sponsoring company and the property it supports. Where consumers cannot make sense of the link, they believe that sponsors are simply 'buying' endorsements. For example, there were a record 15 major sponsorship deals agreed for the 2002 Football World Cup, each one costing somewhere between $20 mn and $28 mn. When asked if these would return value for money to the sponsoring companies, the chairman of the advertising agency TBWA responded negatively: 'Sponsorship can work if you are a sports brand, or a brand with close associations with a particular sport, but most of the time that is not the case' (reported in the *Financial Times*, 30 April 2002). An example of this lack of close association is the UK-based telecommunications company Vodafone and its football sponsorship, where no genuine connection exists. By contrast Nike, the US sportswear manufacturer, does have genuine connectedness to sport to underpin its sponsorship associations. So too does Shell, as a producer of automotive-related products, in its relationship to motor sports.

An integrated approach to marketing communications

Optimal communication effectiveness is gained when sponsorship associations are used as part of the corporate communications mix, and the sponsorship is used actively alongside and integrated with other promotional initiatives. This means marketing communications that share common themes and visual properties and, where these also appear in promotions and sales activities, will have greater consumer impact. When fully exploited in this way, theoretically the sum of all communications is greater than its individual parts. Studies have proven empirically that a sponsorship is more effective when supported by other communication mix elements, reinforcing the fact that sponsorship alone is less effective as a communication tool (Tripodi, 2001). However, there are few published examples proving that an integrated approach can deliver such synergistic effects.

The next section describes in detail the sponsorship relationship between Shell and Ferrari. It is presented here to demonstrate how improved sponsorship management, alongside an initiative to take tighter control globally, can deliver measurable business value.

An evolving Sponsorship Relationship

Shell and Formula 1

In 2000, the global brand management team at Shell set themselves the task of reviewing their Formula 1 sponsorship contract with Ferrari. The sponsorship relationship had been in place since 1995 (although Shell had a long history of association with the sport) and was due for extension, renegotiation or termination early in the millennium. Renewal of the contract with Ferrari provided an opportunity for Shell to challenge what the organisation gained from the relationship and, if valuable, to search for ways to optimise its value. The self-imposed brief for the global brand team was to make a dispassionate, quantitative and qualitative data-based evaluation of the case for continuing, or not, with the sponsorship.

Shell and Ferrari have a long history of working together. The relationship reached back as far as 1947 to the very beginnings of the, by now, legendary Ferrari team. During the 1950s and 1960s the bright red cars of Ferrari dominated motor racing. During this period, the reputation of Shell and Ferrari for technical excellence, innovation and success were closely knit. The team's founder Enzo Ferrari, in his trademark purple ink, wrote: 'Shell . . . worked closely with us to help us resolve the numerous problems related to our use of fuel and lubricants. Shell has always acknowledged the paramount importance of racing experience and this has enabled it to achieve remarkable results.'

Enzo's words reflect the essence of the relationship at that time, one of technical collaboration, striving for engine, lubricant and fuel performance perfection. During the 1980s and early 1990s, Shell collaborated with and sponsored the McLaren Formula 1 team. In 1995, the historic partnership between the Pecten (the Latin name of the shell that is used as the model for the red and yellow brand logo of Shell and how the organisation commonly refer to their brand) and the Prancing Horse (the famous Ferrari badge) was renewed. Again the motivation was to reap the potential technical synergy between the two dedicated innovators, but it was also about building positive brand associations. At the time of the reunion, Shell's management recognized the prize that the Ferrari brand could bring. The benefits of aligning Shell with the Ferrari values of dynamism, success and passion were compelling. As the then, global brand manager said: 'We share professionalism and expertise, but there are a lot of emotional values associated with Ferrari that we would like to have linked with Shell. Ferrari is about Passion and Romance. The name is a dream for most people.'

When the reunion was made, Shell set the objectives:

- to sustain Shell's position as the technology and quality leader in performance fuels and lubricants;
- to enhance relationships with key stakeholders;
- to create awareness and image for Shell premium products;
- to encourage purchase and loyalty through media activity and retail promotions.

It was against these objectives that the 2000 review was made.

Technology Leadership, Stakeholder Relationships

Many sponsorship associations are ineffective because consumers believe sponsors are simply 'buying' endorsements, but this was not the case with Shell and Formula 1. By working exclusively with a Formula 1 team, Shell was perceived to be sponsoring an activity in which its credentials and expertise were directly relevant (internal market research). Documented customer information proved the organisation's long established reputation for technical excellence. Shell also gained technical benefits from exposing its products to the pressure of the Formula 1 track. Working at the extremes of performance with Ferrari had challenged some classical technology theories which gave Shell Research a number of valuable technical insights that could not have been found easily another way. Against the first objective, therefore, the brand team could argue positively for the sponsorship, but could not place a value on it.

Also, significant but unquantifiable value was gained from corporate hospitality and Ferrari factory visits. When surveyed, many of Shell's local companies acknowledged the positive value they gained from the association in these areas.

Assessing Awareness, Purchase Behaviour and resultant Value

As no standard methodology existed in the industry for measuring sponsorship effectiveness against the objectives of raising awareness and encouraging purchase loyalty, the brand team devised their own. Since 1996 they had been collecting data about their customers in major markets around the world. A range of consistent brand image marketing metrics were tested annually, providing trend data about customer perceptions of the products and services offered (the database is called the Global Brand Tracker – GBT). In 1999, customer opinion in more than fifty markets, accounting for about 96 per cent of the Group's retail business, had been collected for four years. This database included customer responses to a series of questions directly related to Shell's Formula 1/Ferrari sponsorship activities.

Method 1 – awareness and preference

Detailed analysis of the data in the GBT showed that the association with Ferrari affected both customer attitudes and behaviour. Customers who were aware of the Shell–Ferrari relationship also had a higher preference for Shell (Figure 1). Here, *preference* is defined as customers' emotional predisposition toward the brand, i.e. all other things being equal, customers would choose Shell above competitor products and services. This did not necessarily mean that customers who preferred Shell purchased from Shell; the data did not allow this conclusion to be drawn unequivocally at the time. However, the theoretical implication was that a preference for Shell was likely to lead to trial and be followed by positive changes in purchase behaviour. The preference measure was used, therefore, as an indicator of brand health and possible future market share gains.

Reviewing the GBT database revealed that 17 per cent of motorists were aware of the Shell–Ferrari relationship and that this 17 per cent had a 3.3 percentage point higher preference for Shell, which was equivalent to a 0.5 percentage point increase in global preference. The financial benefit likely to accrue from this preference was quantifiable, which the team found to be of major significance to Shell's financial performance.

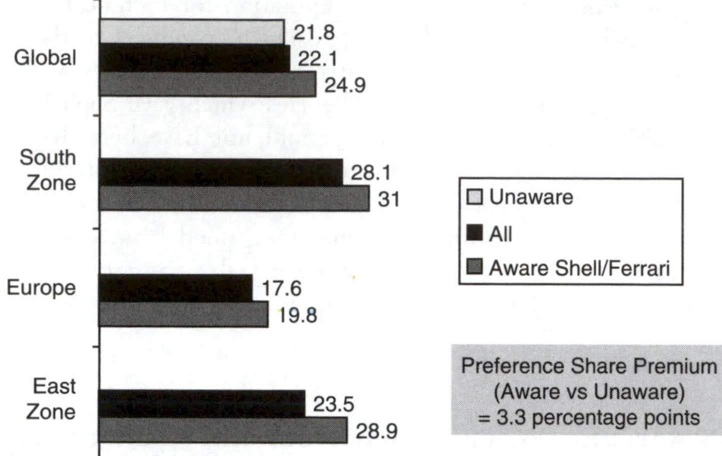

Figure 1 Preference for Shell and awareness of sponsorship: those aware of Shell's Ferrari sponsorship have a higher preference for the Shell brand.
Source: Retail Global Brand tracker 1998

This significant finding led to further investigations into the linkages between awareness of the relationship and a higher preference for Shell. Research International looked at the variables that were likely to influence this relationship and concluded that regardless of high or low usage of Shell, and high or low interest in Formula 1, awareness of Shell's sponsorship of Ferrari had a significant positive impact on preference for Shell.

From this work, the team drew the conclusion that where awareness of the Shell–Ferrari relationship was created effectively, there was a significant impact on Shell brand preference (and thus on Shell's business performance).

Method 2 – awareness and purchase behaviour

A second conclusion could be drawn from looking at the GBT data in a different direction: that consumers who were aware of the Shell–Ferrari relationship also had a higher propensity to purchase from Shell.

The 17 per cent of motorists who were aware had a 3.9 percentage point higher purchase share than those not aware, which was equivalent to a 0.6 percentage point higher global market share. This was also translated into an estimated financial return.

Method 3 – independent assessment

Not wanting to rely on internal analysis alone, the global brand team commissioned Brand Finance, an established consultancy in the field of brand valuation which advises on values of brands for balance sheet or royalty purposes, to evaluate the benefits of the Shell–Ferrari relationship. The conclusions from this analysis were also positive.

The three methodologies provided different perspectives of value. All were positive. Overall, it was concluded that the benefit of the sponsorship was in the range of one and three times the cost of the sponsorship.

Exploiting the Value Worldwide

The next step was to find out more about how well the organisation had exploited the relationship and what could be learnt from best practice around Shell's many local marketing companies.

Shell had a long history of working with a decentralized organisation. Marketing companies made local decisions about using the Shell–Ferrari relationship in their brand communications. Despite the central endorsement of the relationship, plus the advertising and promotional ideas generated centrally (at a higher quality and lower cost than could be made in individual markets), local managers varied hugely in their opinion about the value of presenting this to their customers. As a result, the property was used extensively in some countries, not at all in others and sporadically elsewhere. Many marketing companies exploited the relationship but produced their own communications materials, which they argued were tailored specifically for their markets.

However, GBT data showed that high exploitation resulted in a higher preference for Shell even among customers who claimed to have no interest in Formula 1. On this basis there was little customer rationale for the low exploitation by some local marketing managers. Data also showed consistently high levels of customer interest in Formula 1 across countries, irrespective of whether a race was hosted locally – a commonly expressed reason for marketing managers not to use the relationship in their local communications. Centrally produced advertising, when tested across countries, also proved to be equally effective and often recorded comparatively greater consumer impact against locally produced executions.

Being able to prove that customers across the world were consistently interested in Formula 1, and that building awareness of Shell's association with Ferrari could deliver better business results, was a major step forward (Figure 2). This customer insight was, as one of the global brand team said, 'a major contradiction and challenge to the internal assumption that sponsorship is only about corporate hospitality or corporate imagery. This work linked the relationship with business performance. Later, when we talked to non-exploiters we could talk objectively and take out the personal bias that was in the decision-making in the past. Our findings have been genuinely surprising to some people, we are changing mindsets.'

The loss to Shell from this under-exploitation was estimated to be in the region of twice the cost of the sponsorship.

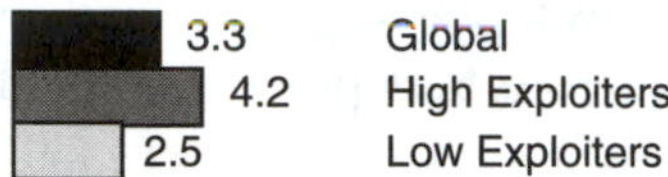

Figure 2 Benefits of higher exploitation of sponsorship: higher exploiters of the Ferrari association have on average higher preference share premiums.
Source: Retail Global brand tracker 1997 and 1998

Learning and Changes

The conclusion of the 2000 review was that the sponsorship of Ferrari had delivered significant, quantified value, but that it had been under-exploited. A positive decision to renew the Ferrari contract was made, but under new terms which focused on a more explicit connection between the Ferrari brand and Shell's main fuel and lubricant products. This resulted in:

- a changed emphasis of centrally-produced advertising from statements about the two organisations simply working together, to more active marketing exploitation promoting the association in terms of benefits to motorists;
- direct endorsements on product packs and pumps of differentiated fuels.

Internally, the learning from the review led to significant changes in the way the sponsorship was managed. These included:

- restatement and clarity of the sponsorship objectives across the organisation;
- greater internal belief about the benefit of and consequently, greater use of global advertising executions and turnkey promotion packages worldwide. This resulted in:
  - global advertising production cost savings in 2000 estimated at $11.6 mn;
  - consistent and high quality advertising around the world;
  - substantial savings on turnkey promotion packages;
- specific recommendations about (and first examples of) using the relationship as a fully integrated part of the marketing mix, plus active monitoring of exploitation;
- new research initiatives aimed at improving on-going evaluation and understanding of consumer response to sponsorship initiatives.

Communicating Differently

Advertising in support of the association up to 2000 was typically passive in its message or reinforced technical aspects of Shell. Images of the Prancing Horse and the Pecten were shown with sounds of Ferrari cars on the soundtrack. An advertisement called 'Refuelling' showed a beautiful Ferrari in the desert and a refuelling plane flying in to refill it. The plane and the car linked through a refuelling pipe while the car was travelling and the plane still in the air. When the refuelling was complete, the Ferrari pulled away into the desert and the plane climbed away showing a Shell logo on its tail fin. The communication message was about two world-class names with huge amounts of technical ability doing the impossible in the middle of a desert.

Advertisements like 'Refuelling' were known to result in consistent improvements in consumer attitudes to Shell and its products in a wide range of countries (including Argentina, Australia, Brazil, Czech Republic, France, Germany, Hong Kong, Japan, Portugal, Saudi Arabia, Singapore, Spain, Thailand and the UK) (Figure 3). However, the key components to these increased scores derived primarily from improved perceptions of Shell's relatively high-level attributes such as technological leadership, overall quality (because Shell's products are used by experts) and professionalism. It became obvious that more marketing value could be gained by shifting the focus to more explicit communication of the Shell–Ferrari relationship in the context of consumer-relevant benefits. New creative ideas were designed by J. W. Thompson to make target segments of motorists more aware of the benefits in Shell's products derived from the Group's close relationship with Ferrari – actively using the relationship.

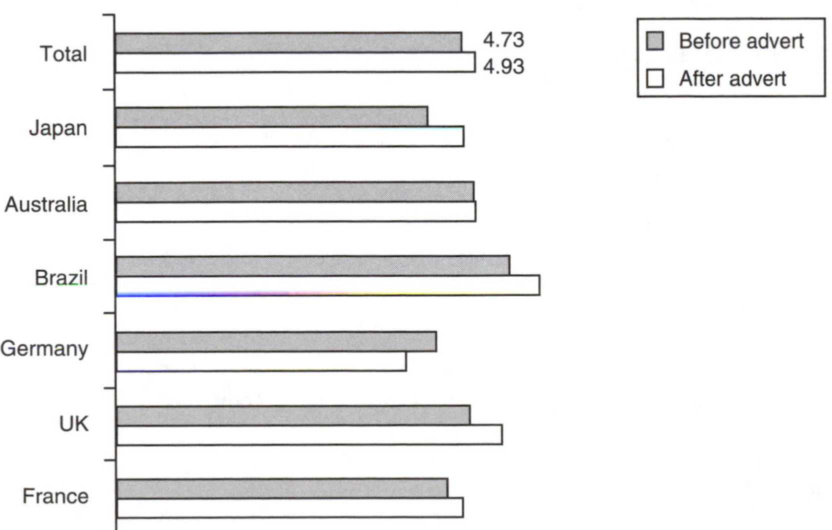

Figure 3 'Refuelling', all countries: overall opinion of Shell products (mean ratings).
Sources: Shell/Ferrari Ad Survey August 1997; Broadbent Associates

The earliest of the new advertisements – 'Desert Wave' – showed a Ferrari driving across a sun-baked landscape, trailing a huge wave behind. The caption read 'And you thought all petrols were the same' (an example of a print execution is shown in Figure 4). Research in Spain and Portugal following a campaign using the 'Desert Wave' advertisement recorded impressive customer impact and influence. As a result, Shell Portugal recorded increased sales of its unleaded gasoline products as well as a significant improvement in the product mix with more customers buying its higher octane, higher margin product (Table 1).

Figure 4 'Desert waves' advertisement

Table 1 'Waves' tracking research: Spain and Portugal, 'Waves' impact

Shell top of mind	5% → 19% (+4)
Currently using Shell	17% → 22% (+5)
Preference	16% → 18% (+2)
Preference reasons:	
product performance	8% → 23%
product attributes	45% → 68%
total product-related reasons for preference	53% → 91%
Advertisement appeal was 20% higher than competitors (BP, Mobil, Galp)	
Impressions from advertisement	
cares about clients	43% → 54%
advanced technology	41% → 57%
quality products/services	36% → 52%

Source: Quaestio Research, Portugal.

Later, 'Traffic' was developed to support Shell's new premium high performance fuel, Shell V-power/Optimax, a product targeted at 'responsible performance seekers for whom their car is a prized possession'. The advertisement (a computer-graphic style of film) was used as the launch commercial in Argentina in 2000 and as follow-up advertising where the fuel was already in the market. The advertisement tells the story of our hero fish facing the cut and thrust of today's traffic with the help of Shell's new performance fuel. The voice-over asks us: 'What difference do you think a petrol developed with Ferrari would make?', as we watch our hero dodge and weave through the long vehicles and marlins on his journey to reach his destination – safely (an example of a print execution is shown in Figure 5).

When tested in six markets around the world, results proved the positive impact of the Ferrari link. Qualitative feedback was summarized: 'The mention of Ferrari adds veracity to performance product claims in all markets. It appears to be part of the "magic" in the potion.' Quantitative testing in Argentina also showed significant changes in consumers' views about Shell after watching 'Traffic' (Table 2).

A significant shift in use of centrally produced Ferrari-based advertising occurred with the change in emphasis to more product-centred messages. Use around Shell was not tracked consistently before 'Desert Wave', but in the memory of those in the global brand team, only a handful of marketing units had incorporated these early global advertisements into their communication strategies. In comparison, since 'Desert Wave', sixty-four countries had used the

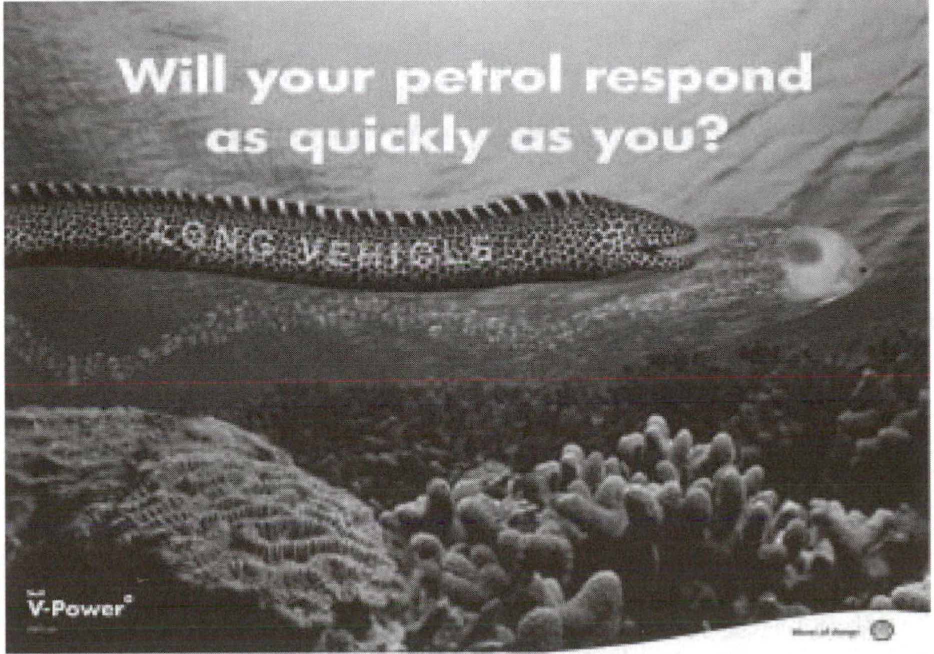

Figure 5 'Traffic' advertisement

Table 2 Shell 'Traffic' advertising survey: Argentina – before and after Significant improvement post viewing

Company attributes
– Produces the best petrol
– Produces petrol which improves the performance of my car
– Takes the lead in producing new fuels
– Has new ideas relevant to me
– A dynamic company
– A company whose products I like to buy

Source: Broadbent Associates.

Table 3 Global advertising production costs savings

	Cost ($ mn)	*No. of countries used*
Wave (fuels + Helix)	2.20	39
Traffic (fuels)	0.75	9
Seascope (Helix)	1.40	16
Total	4.35	64
Cost per country = $68 000		
Normal local cost per country = $250 000		
Saving = $182 000 per country		
Total saving = $11.6 mn		

advertising, a change which Shell estimated had resulted in production savings of $11.6 mn (Table 3).

Maximising Value through an Integrated Campaign

Shell Brazil used another advertisement from the global portfolio – 'Seascope' – in conjunction with a Ferrari-linked promotion at the service station as part of their Shell Helix (lubricant) revitalisation campaign – an example of integrated marketing.

The TV campaign ran during October and November 2000. Seascope is rich with images of Ferrari sports cars scorching around test tracks and through sea waves. Ferrari and Shell engineers monitor the car's performance with sophisticated equipment and the soundtrack tells how, with Shell Helix, the engine stays calm. The voice poses the question, 'If Shell can protect a Ferrari, who better to protect your car?'

Understanding that although powerful, this advertising would not motivate Brazilian customers to have their oil levels checked by attendants at service stations and, knowing from market research that 25 per cent of these customers actually did need oil, Shell Brazil ran a point-of-sale promotion simultaneously with the TV campaign. Customers agreeing to have their oil checked and topped-up where necessary, were given a 'dipstick' which could turn a winning pink, or a losing white, when exposed. The prize for a pink dipstick was an official Ferrari polo shirt. The promotion had a planned duration of one month (5 October to 1 November), which had to be cut short at some sites due to its popularity; 750 service stations supported the promotion and 1.6 million dipsticks were 'dipped', of which 1 per cent were winners.

In the context of a highly competitive market with at least seven high-profile competitor lubricant brands, the results were dramatic. Shell Helix sales at promotional sites rose on average by 17 per cent and fuel sales through the core network increased by 1.17 per cent. Market research highlighted other significant gains; for example, preference for Shell Helix increased from 3 per cent to 9 per cent, awareness increased from 23 per cent to 30 per cent, and consumer knowledge and awareness about the association between Shell and Ferrari also improved dramatically (Figures 6 and 7).

Conclusion

Sponsorship accounts for a growing proportion of companies' marketing budgets and is increasingly a strategic part of the communication programme for brands. Therefore, it is more important to maximize the value in sponsorship relationships and to do so faster than has been the case in the past. This paper illustrates the basis for best practice in managing sponsorship programmes.

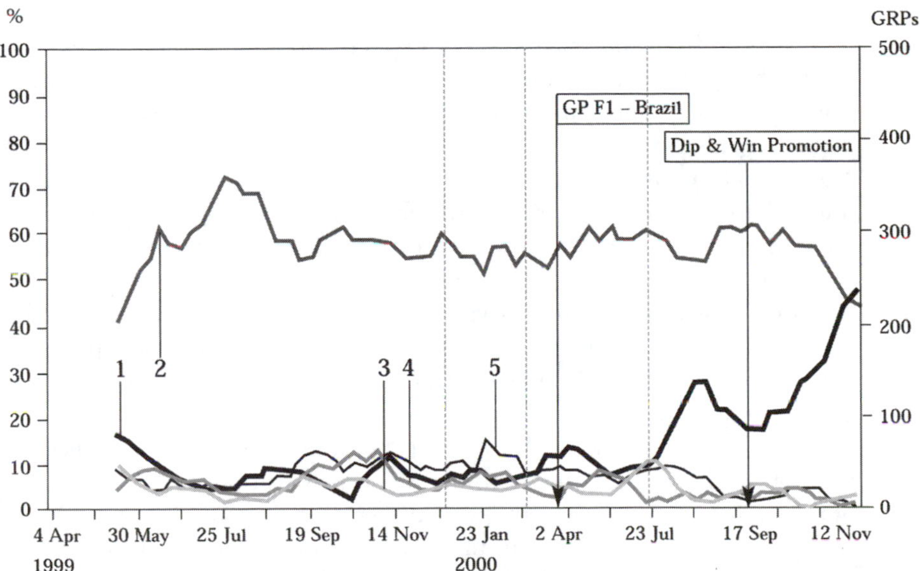

Figure 6 Consumer awareness: brand used by Ferrari (figures are four weekly moving averages). 1 Helix (Shell); 2 'Don't know'; 3 Havoline (Texaco); 4 F1 Master (Ipiranga); 5 Lubrax (BR).

Source: MarketMind™ Continuous Interactive Intelligence ©

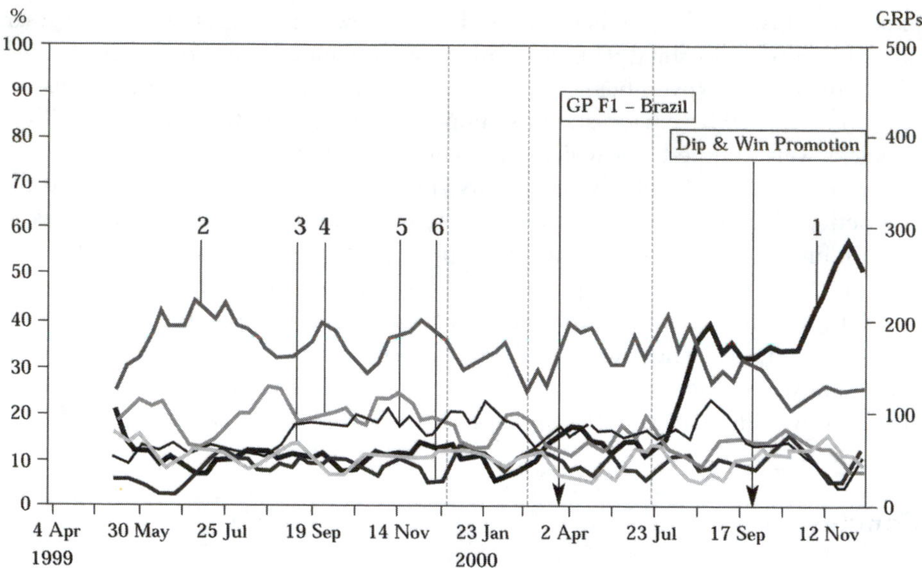

Figure 7 Consumer awareness: brand more associated with F1 (figures are four weekly moving averages). 1 Helix (Shell); 2 'Don't know'; 3 Havoline (Texaco); 4 F1 Master (Ipiranga); 5 Lubrax (BR); 6 GTX (Castrol). (GRPs, gross rating points).
Source: MarketMind™ Continuous Interactive Intelligence ©

Recommendations include:

- Setting objectives and making them explicit throughout the organisation. Without objectives it is impossible to monitor performance of the sponsorship relationship and harder to discipline its use in an international or global organisation.
- Making clear what constitutes 'performance' for each objective and finding methodologies for researching how effective sponsorship communications are with target audiences – essential for proving the worth of the relationship and finding ways to extract more value from the investment.
- In global organisations that have sponsorship properties with potential worldwide value, managing exploitation of the sponsorship across country markets can deliver significant cost savings and raise the quality of advertisements and promotion packages.
- Creating communications that *actively* use the sponsorship property to promote and reinforce the customer value proposition of the sponsoring brand or improve the perception of the corporate brand. Simply putting the sponsoring brand's logo on the track-side of a sporting event will not influence consumers to feel differently about the sponsoring brand.
- Understanding that the positive attributes of a sponsorship property will not automatically transfer to a product or service brand that, to consumers, have no apparent overlap. Such relationships will appear to consumers as ones where sponsoring companies are 'buying endorsements'. There is a

logic therefore in the global sport shoe company Nike spending $155 mn in 2002, 40 per cent of its global marketing expenditure, on football endorsements. Plus, £300 mn to provide Manchester United with its kit for the next thirteen years, a deal which out-sized any made to date. But, it is harder to make sense of a Vodafone logo on the Nike branded shirts of the Manchester United team.

- Integrating sponsorship communications into the marketing mix to produce promotion packages will ensure optimum value is returned to the investment. Getting this right is shown in the Shell Brazil example to deliver not only consumer impact and awareness, but also significant improvements in sales at promotional sites for the target product, plus pull-through sales of other products at the same sites.

Whilst it is evident that sponsorship is more and more popular among marketers as a communication tool, there are some who predict it has reached its peak of success. As more companies try to ride the popular tide, both the cost and clutter grow, making it harder for brands to stand out. For example, as many as sixty brands sought 'official sponsor' status for the 2002 football World Cup, all proposing to build campaigns in the UK. It is difficult to believe that consumers were not bemused and confused by the sheer number and variety of brands that tried to claim a share of the goodwill, excitement, hype and spirit of the event.

However, sponsorship has a very different future in the mind of the chief executive of MC Saatchi Sponsorship who was quoted in *The Guardian* in January 2002: 'The trend against above-the-line advertising means that both brands and TV companies need to replace advertising with something'. The article suggested that in the near future marketers would take an even bolder step by creating their own media content, so creating their own vehicle for advertising rather than having to sponsor other properties. The Saatchi executive continued: 'Broadcasters are becoming more flexible and taking sponsorship more seriously. It is no longer thought of in the traditional way – ghettoised into sports or arts sponsorships. They are beginning to embrace the idea of advertiser-funded programming. Instead of broadcasters creating their formats to drive ratings, companies can do it to drive their marketing. And broadcasters will grasp it with open arms.' The changeover to digital TV, he suggested, would make this shift in content ownership even more inevitable. This would allow marketing companies to own entertainment and time around the programmes far beyond two-minute breaks or sponsorship bumpers.

Given either scenario, the need for marketers to grow their competence in managing sponsorship investments is clear. The guidelines suggested here will help them to do this more effectively.

References

FT Report (1999) *Maximising the Value of Sports Sponsorship*.

Jobber D (2001) *Principles and Practice of Marketing*. Maidenhead, Berks: McGraw-Hill.

Tripodi JA (2001) Sponsorship – a confirmed weapon in the promotional armoury. *International Journal of Sports Marketing & Sponsorship* March/April: 95–115.

Questions

1 Explain how global sponsorship activity such as the Shell Formula 1 programme discussed by Verity could be 'localized' in individual countries within each of the following regions: Europe, North America and the Asia-Pacific rim.
2 Discuss how the potential of a sponsorship proposal for a rising young star (such as Mark Todd) could be evaluated and what performance indicators might be appropriate as part of the contract.
3 Under what circumstances would termination of a sponsorship programme be appropriate? Discuss the positives and negatives of such action for the sponsoring organization.
4 Assume you have a global sports sponsorship programme in place which will provide international television coverage of your signage at all events, logos on competitors' uniforms, etc. A marketing manager in another country has advised that this activity is irrelevant in that market and that there will be no local support. What action do you recommend?
5 You have been advised that, while you have high-profile sponsorship of a top-rated team in an event that will achieve international media coverage, your main competitor has negotiated sponsorship of the telecasts of the competition in many key markets around the world. What action do you recommend?
6 Your organization, a sportswear company with a primarily domestic market, but a growing export sector, has been approached to sponsor a multi-country tour by young (teenage) athletes. (a) Discuss the positives and negatives of a sponsorship agreement. (b) What objectives would be appropriate? (c) How would you measure whether these objectives had been achieved? (d) What contingency provisions would you put in place?
7 You sponsor a high-profile sports person. There have recently been a number of allegations about misconduct in their private life. This has no impact on their performance in their sport. Discuss any implications for your on-going sponsorship activity.

Vignette

Olympic Watches

In New Zealand in the early 1980s, Olympic Watches provided sponsorship of a young equestrian. This was in the form of funding to assist with the costs of travelling to competitions, offset by the use of the personable young man (wearing Olympic watches) in a series of magazine advertisements.

The sponsorship was terminated as a result of a decision that equestrian activity did not constitute a high-profile sport. Some six months later, the equestrian (Mark Todd) won the prestigious Badminton Three Day Event and went on to win gold medals at two consecutive Olympic Games, among numerous other high-profile global achievements. The global fit between Olympic watches and a (potential) future Olympic champion was obvious, but local management failed to identify the wider opportunities or to evaluate the risk versus potential benefits of on-going involvement. Mark Todd's highly successful international career spanned two decades and was sustained by a range of other sponsorships.

Chapter 8

Lynne Eagle

PERSONAL SELLING

THIS PAPER PROVIDES A number of valuable insights. First, it stresses that the modern sales force is an integral part of the marketing function. Second, the authors stress that new electronic technology, including database management and the Internet, is radically changing the organization–customer interface. They note, therefore, that traditional order-taking sales forces, often primarily paid by commission, are under threat.

Piercy and Lane suggest that the onus is on companies to determine what combinations of sales channels are effective and efficient for their current and future operations. They imply, but do not make explicit, the fundamental challenge facing sales forces – to remain as part of a company's overall distribution channel, they must add value to the various exchanges between the organization and its customers. The authors do not discuss the interface of the sales force with the wider marketing function and make little reference to the way that marketing overall is being forced to re-examine its role in a dynamic and turbulent, increasingly global, market place. An area that should have been incorporated into the discussion is the role of the sales force in contributing to brand profitability, not just sales volume.

The discussion of electronic technology as a tool to significantly reduce the costs of order taking in contrast to the substantial role for sales personnel in generating new sales leads and creating new orders provides useful insights. The danger of sales force demotivation if technology-based purchasing systems are perceived as a direct competitor also provides some salutary warnings for modern managers. These issues, together with the need for sales personnel to understand the need to reconfigure their role into customer relationship management functions is well illustrated by a range of short vignettes, both positive and negative.

Further cautions for upper management are provided via the discussion of key account management (KAM) and its perceived role in taking attractive customers away from the traditional sales force. The issues raised regarding the potential to force a particular relationship on customers and the considerable difference between the rhetoric offered by KAM and relationship marketing versus the reality offered by different categories of purchasers are valuable, but deserve more detailed discussion than the overview provided.

Also missing is a discussion of the increasing power of large retail chains such as supermarkets in dictating the role required of the sales force and the terms of trade expected by these substantial organizations, often across national borders. As purchasing becomes increasingly regionalized, the sales force structure must evolve to meet the challenges presented, not only market by market but on a regional, if not global, basis. By creating competitive advantage, customer relationships may avoid being determined solely by price. However, the large retail chains are primarily price-focused in their dealings with suppliers, both for branded product and often also for the production of house brands or unbranded product. The management of the relationships in this sector offers a unique set of challenges that merit more detailed discussion.

In spite of the challenges that are outlined, the authors do not, however, predict the demise of the traditional sales force. They do stress the range and complexity of the challenges that they face and emphasize the considerable opportunities for proactive forces to evolve into effective strategic customer management operations, with the flexibility to manage relationships as they evolve.

TRANSFORMATION OF THE TRADITIONAL SALESFORCE: IMPERATIVES FOR INTELLIGENCE, INTERFACE AND INTEGRATION

Nigel F. Piercy and Nikala Lane

Many conventional sales organizations are under intense pressure from escalating customer demands for superior value, accompanied by the emergence of new business models that replace some traditional sales functions and processes (e.g., Internet-based direct channels, Customer Relationship Management technology), and new organizational strategies to partner with major customers (e.g., key account management and global account management). While this scenario suggests continued down-sizing and closure of conventional sales operations, particularly those with primarily order taking roles, it also identifies

---

Journal of Marketing Management, Vol. 19, No. 3 (2003), pp. 563–82.

Professor Nigel F. Piercy is Professor of Marketing at Warwick Business School. He was previously Professor and Head of the Marketing Group at Cranfield School of Management. Dr Nikala Lane is Lecturer in Marketing and Strategic Management at Warwick Business School. She was previously a Senior Research Associate at Cardiff Business School.

a major opportunity for the evolution of the conventional sales organization towards a strategic customer management role. Underpinning this role are three major issues: new ways of leveraging of *intelligence* to provide added-value for major customers, better management of the *interfaces* between sales and other parts of the organization to identify new value-creating opportunities; and, the *integration* of all processes and activities that impact on a company's ability to deliver seamless and superior value to customers. We identify the major challenges for marketing and sales executives to address in transforming the sales organization towards strategic customer management.

Declining Status for the Sales Organization

MANY IMPORTANT QUESTIONS CAN be raised about the future role and prospects for the traditional salesforce, most particularly in the business-to-business marketplace. Indeed, probably the most vexed question for the sales manager is simply whether the sales organization will survive – at current levels of employment, in current forms, or indeed at all. In particular, some prominent indicators suggest that sales is in effect a profession under siege, and that many of the new business models emerging in leading organizations provide alternative, and possibly more economical, ways of achieving the functions that were conventionally located in the sales organization.

For example, we suggest in Figure 1 a scenario which may be perceived by many sales organizations, where the market space left to the salesforce is becoming progressively smaller as a result of two major changes in the management of buyer–seller relationships.

On one side, consider the development of business models that integrate Internet-based and other direct marketing channels to the traditional process used by the company to go to market. To the company, the 'bricks and clicks' model offers many substantial economies and information-based advantages in reaching at least part of the market. However, from the salesperson's perspective – the company has now become a competitor, quite possibly the most significant competitor, likely taking off into its direct channel many of the routinised sales transactions with relatively low service requirements, that previously provided a solid base of sales volume in the salesperson's territory (and quite possibly a significant amount of sales commission as well). In addition, many of the traditional customer relationship responsibilities are likely to be subsumed within the basic 'off-the-shelf' Customer Relationship Management systems that many companies are acquiring and implementing to enhance customer transaction management.

On the other side, the development of key account management and global account management structures by companies to focus resources on their most profitable and highest potential customers also represents a source of competition for the conventional sales organization – the largest and most productive customers are likely handled by account teams backed by more sophisticated Customer Relationship Management technology linking buyer and seller systems and processes.

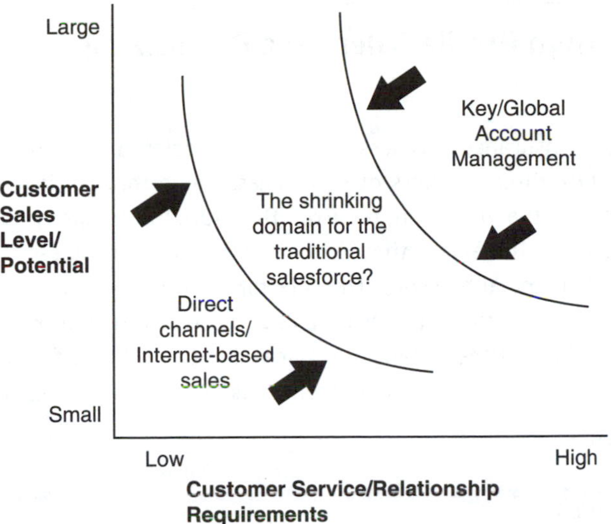

Figure 1 What's left for Sales?

The market space remaining to the traditional salesforce may be restricted to:

- accounts with good sales prospects but low service/relationship requirements, where the sales role is little more than order-taking, e.g., selling basic materials or components to units of large customers within the confines of supply contracts determined centrally; and
- customers with limited sales prospects, but who are highly demanding in terms of service and relationship requirements, e.g., selling IT equipment to budget-restricted educational institutions, or sophisticated machinery and services to small businesses.

Neither of these areas looks like a potential stronghold for traditional sales organizations. Larger accounts with low service requirements are likely highly susceptible to being subsumed within expanding key account management structures because of their attractive sales prospects, or handled more economically through direct channels, while smaller accounts with high service requirements are extremely vulnerable to pruning as CRM technology seeks out expensive and less profitable customers as candidates for deletion. If these sectors in the market disappear, there appears little role left for the conventional sales organization in the new marketplace.

While possibly unduly pessimistic, this scenario appears worryingly plausible to many sales managers. Indeed, several high-profile down-sizing and restructuring activities in the sales area have reinforced this fear – see Exhibit 1.

Exhibit 1: High Profile Salesforce Downsizing

Prudential

The Prudential insurance business was long associated with direct selling of policies. In 1995, three-quarters of its business came through its 6000 door-to-door salespeople – the 'man from the Pru'. By 2000, the company had reduced its direct salesforce to the extent that three-quarters of its business was generated by independent financial advisors. The salesforce of 2000 was one-third the size of the 1995 branch. Direct Internet-based sales promise further reductions in the size of the salesforce. Other financial services companies have followed the Pru's lead in closing or drastically pruning their consumer sales organizations in 2001 and 2002.

Avon Cosmetics

Long time icon of door-to-door selling by part-time salespeople and catalogues, Avon in the USA is withdrawing from direct sales to establish itself in shopping malls. Door-to-door selling simply is not an effective way to reach modern cosmetics consumers.

Encyclopaedia Britannica

Encyclopaedia Britannica was first published in Edinburgh more than 200 years ago. By 1990, Encyclopaedia's Britannica's sales in the US had reached $650 million with profits of $40 million. However, during the early 1990s, CD-ROM technology gained acceptance in the consumer market for encyclopaedias, especially in the key US market. The management of Encyclopaedia Britannica did not respond to this threat because management did not believe that CD-ROM technology could undermine their traditional market. The company's marketing advantage in the US was a 2,300 person direct salesforce, each earning a commission of $300 on the sale of a $1500 encyclopaedia. In fact, by the early 1990s, the competitors' CD-ROM packages were available to 7 million US households, with computers with CD drives, at prices ranging from $99 to $395. By 1994, Encyclopaedia Britannica's US sales had declined so far that the salesforce was halved in size, and the company was in serious financial trouble. To compete against CD-ROM competition would have required the company to change both its product and its direct selling strategy. By 1997, the US and European direct salesforces had been disbanded. By 1999, the content of the thirty-two-volume tome was available free on the Internet as a portal, with income generated by advertising and hot links.

The Web Changes Everything for Sales

It is impossible to conceive a world where the Internet ceased to be part of the business model. It is simply too powerful not to be. But we are still early enough in the real adoption of Web-based initiatives that predicting its full impact remains uncertain. However, an interesting point can be made about the impact of the Web and Internet-based business models on intermediaries, if we identify both external intermediaries (distributors, retailers) but also internal intermediaries (sales, customer service, distribution, some aspects of marketing management).

Figure 2 makes these comparisons. In the external marketplace, the early Internet business models were associated with many claims that they would lead to widespread disintermediation – Amazon.com spelled the end for the bookstore; direct holiday sales would destroy the travel agency; online banking would lead to the closure of the traditional retail bank network, and so on. In fact, what we saw was reintermediation in two senses: (1) many of the new Internet business models quickly transformed into quite different types of business – Amazon.com is much more than a bookseller, online travel merchants like lastminute.com have a very different value proposition to those of traditional suppliers; and (2) traditional intermediaries responded by changing the basis of their added-value to compete against the new business models – Waterstones and Borders offer an enhanced and different book-buying experience; banks have integrated online services into their traditional operations to add value for their customers.

The interesting parallel is that disintermediation and reintermediation may also be seen in a similar way inside organizations and the results may be just as surprising. We have seen that Internet-initiatives have led directly or indirectly

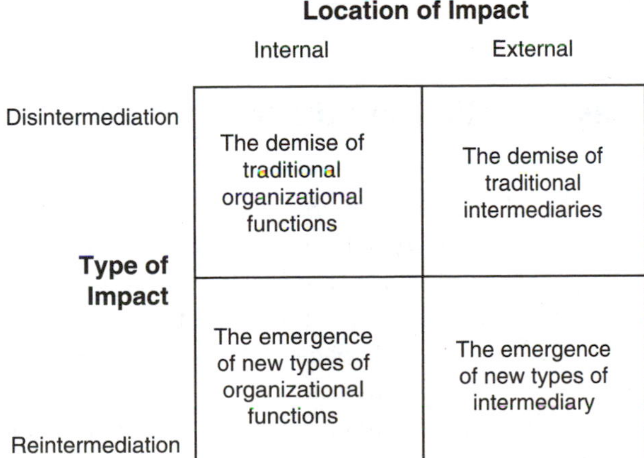

Location of Impact
Internal
External
Disintermediation
The demise of traditional organizational functions
The demise of traditional intermediaries
Type of Impact
The emergence of new types of organizational functions
The emergence of new types of intermediary
Reintermediation

Figure 2 The impact of the Internet

to the closure or down-sizing of some sales organizations (Exhibit 1), in a form of disintermediation. However, what we are likely to see is the transformation of traditional sales operations into something different, in a form of reintermediation inside the company. In this sense the challenge for sales management is to identify these processes of structural adjustment and to design the sales organization of the future as a new type of organizational intermediary. As we will see, a start is in examining the Internet and the salesforce as complementary parts of a multiple channel strategy.

Consider, for example that in 1999 Neil Rackham predicted that 'I have no doubt that the direct effect of e-commerce is make more than half of sales jobs go away' (Rackham 1999). Yet, in 2000, US pharmaceuticals group Merck, announced the expansion of its salesforce by 30 per cent to build sales of existing and new products (Michaels 2000). The same year saw Allied Dunbar, part of the Zurich Financial group, growing its direct salesforce to 5,000 and driving premiums written up 10 per cent, in spite of the predictions that direct insurance salesforces could not survive in the face of the low costs of telephone and Internet selling (English 2000). The challenge is to match salesforce investment to competitive strategy, not to blindly down-size (Olson et al. 2001).

The Fat Lady on the Web May Have Yet to Sing

In fact, there are signs in even the most advanced Internet-based business-to the obituary for the salesforce may have been written somewhat prematurely. For example, while Dell Computers has taken leadership in the world-wide market for PCs, based on its direct marketing and focus on major business accounts, when asked about maintaining relationships with major customers like Boeing (with an installed base of more than 100,000 Dell computers), CEO Michael Dell conceded 'Boeing, you go see . . .' (Magretta 1998). Dell maintains a substantial salesforce in addition to its Internet-driven direct model and Exhibit 2 suggests no move towards salesforce downsizing at Dell.

Exhibit 2: Dell's Sales Operation and the Internet

Dell Computers has become global PC market leader through its direct business model, boosted by the impact of the Internet. Suppliers are linked to Dell (valuechain.dell.com), and own the inventory until it is scanned at Dell's factory doors. Dell runs its operation on four days stock. The Dell operation is integrated around inside.dell.com, and end-user customers use www.dell.com to order products, or their own PremierDell.com Web pages and support.dell.com for after-sales service. By 2002, more than 50 percent of Dell's sales were made online, with Web sales running at around $50 million sales a day, in addition to 40,000 Premier Pages providing customized ordering sites for major Dell customers. The bulk of Dell's business (some 80 to 90 per cent) is sales to organizations ranging from Government to major corporates. Dell's operation is extremely lean and relies on a cost advantage to maintain competitive position.

For major public sector customers in the US, Dell employs Field Account Executives (FAE) in the field and Sales Representatives (internal), covering the same customer base and sharing credit for sales. The FAEs get around 40 per cent of their income in incentive pay, while the Sales Representatives typically get around 30 percent of their remuneration in incentives. The Sales Representatives may earn anything from $50,000 to $100,000 a year.

Dell's management has approached the integration of Internet sales with personal selling as a multiple channels issue, not simply salesforce automation. It is central to the company's business model that routine ordering should be Web-based to hold order processing costs low. Salespeople are actually targeted with converting customers to the Internet channel. The goal is to free expensive salesperson time from transactional selling (which the Website does better, faster and cheaper), in order to devote selling efforts to hunting for bigger deals. For example, in selling to a university, the FAE focuses on the point of the organization controlling multiple purchases, not the individual user (e.g., the Dean, not the individual teacher). Nonetheless, the salesperson retains control of the account and gets credit for all sales made to an account, whichever channel the customer uses. This is particularly the case with the largest customers and Premier Pages (which define the ordering opportunities for computer users inside the organization). It is in the salesperson's self-interest to get more customers making small repeat orders via the Web, or risk missing quota (and the dramatically higher than average rewards that come with beating quota).

The Dell strategy for integrating the Internet channel with the sales operation is to develop the latter into the order making role, while putting as much order taking as possible onto the Web. The goal is to reduce the headcount and costs of order taking in the sales operation, while freeing order making capabilities.

(Based on a presentation by Aldor Lanctot, Divisional Director, Dell Computers at the American Marketing Association Winter Educators' Conference, February 2002.)

Our contention is that it is increasingly likely that the pressure for superior service from vendors by major corporate customers (H. R. Challey Group 1997) will actively define a role for personal selling that cannot easily be replaced by key account management, direct business models, or CRM technology. Indeed, there are already some signs that notwithstanding the promises, the implementation of CRM systems is commonly an approach to better managing customer *transactions*, not impacting more strategically on *relationships* with major customers.

Now the initial hyperbole has subsided, there are some major holes in the argument that the Web will replace traditional sales efforts in all situations. Home Depot, for example, has asked many of its suppliers, including Black & Decker, to pull back from their more extreme Internet strategies, or risk losing the HD business (Friedman 2002). Consider, for example the disaster scenario for one company described in Exhibit 3.

Exhibit 3: The Less Attractive Internet Scenario

Sales Strategy Institute consultant Lawrence Friedman describes his experiences with a $210 million manufacturer of speciality industrial lubricants, based in Atlanta. Anticipating that the 400 person salesforce was increasingly irrelevant in an Internet-enabled world, the company had spent $16 million on Web sites, e-portals, call centres, and an integrated CRM system. The new sales model went live on June 1 1999. By August 2000, the anticipated 35 per cent increase in sales had turned out to be an 18 per cent decrease, with margins falling (mainly to pay for the new Internet infrastructure). Nearly, a third of the salesforce had resigned in just over a year (including seventeen of the top twenty salespeople). The general feeling was there was no future in staying to compete with their own company's Website, after devoting years to building personal relationships with their customers.

Friedman's investigations of the company's situation quickly revealed that there had been no customer involvement in developing the new sales model – the company had not bothered to ask its customers how they wanted to do business. Worse, when asked, customers identified this company's only competitive advantage as the expertise of the salesforce and their ability to design solutions to solve technical problems for customers.

The company is retrieving its position by providing salesperson expertise to customers in specification and design phases, and in negotiating prices and terms, using the Web for routine repeat purchases and order-tracking.

(Based on: Lawrence G. Friedman, Go To Market Strategy, Woburn, MA: Butterworth-Heinemann Business Books 2002.)

Indeed, there is long-standing opinion that ideas about the traditional 'order-taking' role of the salesforce have long been superseded by the evidence that the most effective sales organizations have been those that play a strategic role in designing and implementing superior customer relationships (Cravens 1995; Weitz and Bradford 1999). In this sense, the pressures we have described in Figure 1 are actually no more than the most recent manifestations of a long-established trend which is changing the role of the salesforce from order-taking to managing and coordinating customer relationships. However, this conclusion in no way undermines the urgent need for sales management to manage the continuing process of redefining the role of their sales operations and working towards the total integration of how customer relationships are designed, established, managed and sustained. For example, companies like Cisco have already established sales strategies that use personal selling when the purchase is significant, complicated and the decision uncertain – typically the first sale to a customer or the new application – leaving subsequent purchases to be made over the Internet (Royal 1999).

The Threat from Key Account Management

Recall from Figure 1 that we saw one of the other 'threats' to the traditional salesforce was the emergence of key account management systems, effectively taking the largest and most attractive customers away from the sales organization. There is plenty of evidence that key account management (KAM) and global account management (GAM) structures have emerged as an important new way of developing close relationships with the most important customers and meeting their needs in ways which the traditional salesforce did not (Homburg et al. 2002). Indeed, there can be few KAM executives who have not flourished models like that in Figure 3 in front of top management and told them that only full-blown integration of systems and processes with major accounts will secure the long-term relationship that will retain the account and build profitability. Indeed, there is some justice in the claim – it is some time now since companies like Boeing and Motorola warned all suppliers that those who could not make the transition to Web-based supply models, would simply be locked out of their businesses (Royal 1999). However, what we are starting to learn, in several cases through hard experience, is that there several reasons why the logic for KAM may be exaggerated, flawed and considerably less attractive to sellers than might at first appear to be the case.

It is too easy for advocates of KAM and relationship marketing to assume that all major customers want to have close, partnered relationships with suppliers. In fact, some companies do not do business on this basis at all – their purchasing professionals reduce all supply decisions to transactions based on trading-off quality with price, and flexing market power to obtain the best result. Suppliers to some of our major retailers, for example, rarely use the term 'partnership' without grimacing, and some substitute words like 'partner-shaft' to describe the reality of relationships with these key accounts. Different customers have different value requirements, and it is this reality that leads Rackham and De Vincentis (1999) to distinguish between: intrinsic value buyers, who require transactional selling; extrinsic value buyers, who require consultative selling, and strategic value buyers, who require enterprise selling. Some advocates of the implementation of relationship marketing strategies through key account management appear to take little heed of this reality.

Consider, for example, how one purchasing professional categorizes suppliers in the way shown in Figure 4. This purchaser's view is that based on market risk (e.g. the ability to source a product elsewhere) and value or impact on the purchaser's business (e.g. reducing costs, increasing competitiveness), then suppliers may be divided into:

> *Show-stoppers* – the supplier is low in impact on the purchaser's business, but high in market risk (for example, this supplier is the only source for the product). The purchaser's goal is to reduce market risk, for example by dual sourcing, in-house production, or demanding contracts for guaranteed supplies. Show-stoppers are an irritation to the purchaser, not prospective partners in alliance.

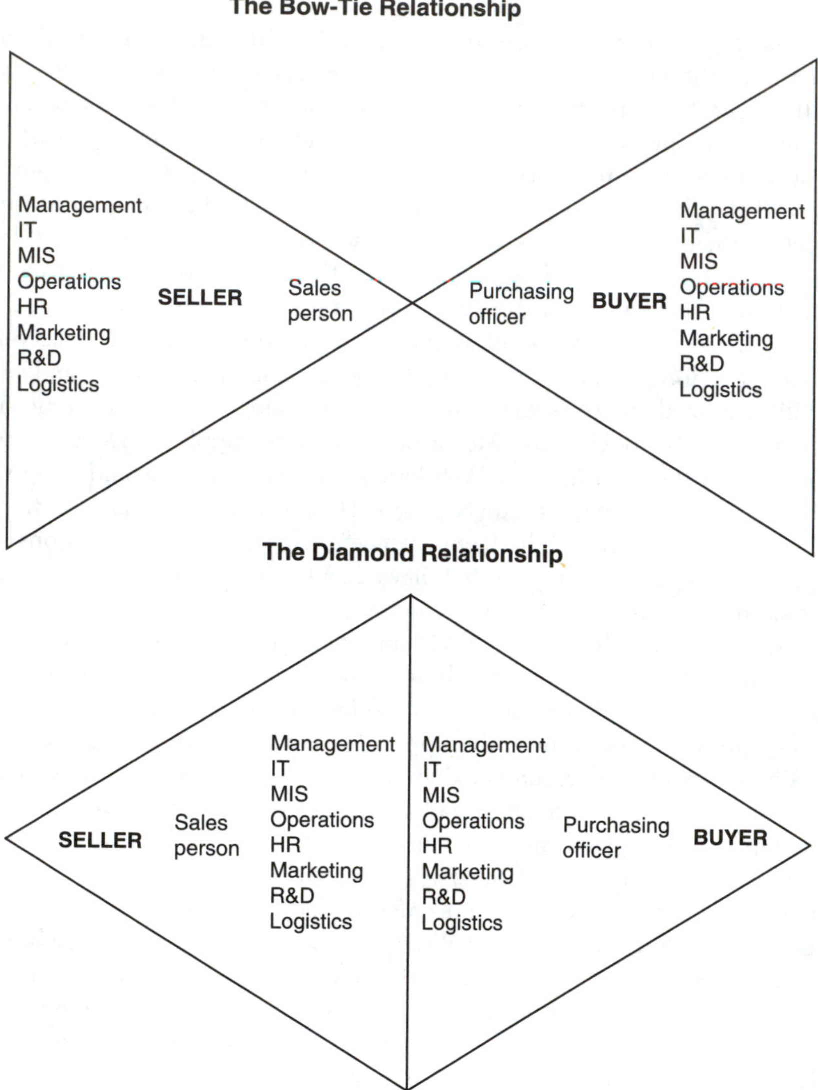

Figure 3 Changing buyer–seller relationships

Recurring – the supplier is low both in market risk and impact on the purchaser's business, the goal with these suppliers is transactional efficiency – there is no advantage for the purchaser in anything else. The purchaser regards these suppliers as commodities not partners, and may well look to enhance efficiency through supplier base reduction. Commodity suppliers make money through transactional and supply chain efficiency not close partnering with customers.

Leverage – these suppliers have a major impact on the purchaser's business, but market risk is low. The overwhelming pressure here is to reduce prices through negotiation and the exploitation of the

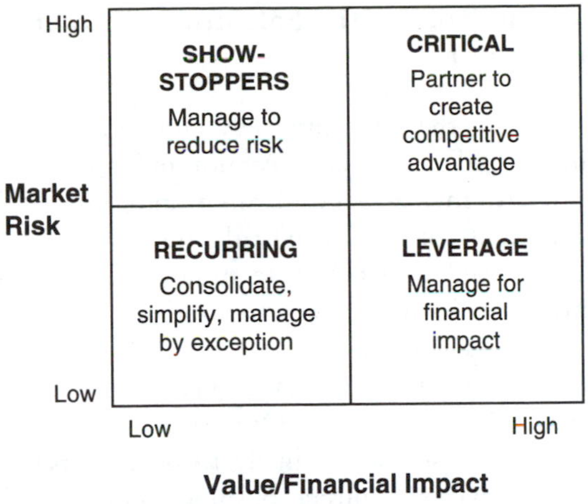

Market Risk	Low	High
High	**SHOW-STOPPERS** Manage to reduce risk	**CRITICAL** Partner to create competitive advantage
Low	**RECURRING** Consolidate, simplify, manage by exception	**LEVERAGE** Manage for financial impact

Value/Financial Impact

Figure 4 How corporate customers see suppliers.

Source: Purchasing Director of a major British brewery group

customer's market power. These suppliers may regard the customer as a key account, but the purchaser is unlikely to see them as a strategic supplier.

Critical – finally, there may be a small number of suppliers who have a major impact on the purchaser's business and market risk is high. If there is potential for added-value from the supplier to enhance the purchaser's competitive advantage, then there may be opportunities for a key account/strategic supplier relationship. Typically, this will be a very small group of suppliers, and there is no guarantee that any supplier will remain in this category beyond the duration of a single project.

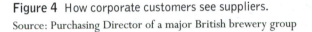

The implications of this model are two-fold. First, corporate purchasers do not seek close partnerships with show-stoppers, recurring or leverage suppliers – almost by definition most suppliers are not strategic suppliers as far as the customer is concerned. Providing key account support for customers interested only in lower prices, transactional efficiency or dual sourcing is likely to be expensive and unproductive. Second, also by definition, the majority of most selling companies' accounts – some smaller and some major – will remain the domain of the salesforce, not key account management. The Purchasing Director whose approach is contained in Figure 4 emphasizes that in dealing with 2,600 suppliers, with a staff of fourteen buyers, it is likely that, spookily enough, the number of strategic suppliers will never exceed fourteen.

It is also worth considering what we have learned from other forms of strategic alliance model – that the majority fail. When buyer–seller partnerships dissolve, it is likely by default that it will fall to the traditional salesforce to rebuild the residual business in the account. Research suggests the need for defining a strategic role for the salesforce that reflects different stages in the customer relationship life cycle (Jap 2001).

The Evolution of the Role of the Salesforce into Strategic Customer Management

In fact, we argue that it is the same intensely competitive environment out of which direct business models and key account management approaches have grown in response to customer demands for new and greater value, which is also the stimulus for significant changes in the role and operation of the traditional sales organization. For want of a better terminology, we describe this as the transition from conventional sales strategy to strategic customer management.

Our earlier commentary is underlined by the Figure 5 model. Where customer demands are mainly transactional and remain so, then the critical need is for effective order taking approaches. Our earlier examples suggest that the order taking role of the salesperson is likely to decline, particularly in simple consumer goods and services – direct business models and other channels offer better ways to take orders, if this is the only interaction with the customer that is needed. It is also quite conventional to argue that as the sales task becomes more complex, customers demand more interaction when they buy and investigate more alternatives, then the order making role becomes more important, and this provides the obvious role for the salesperson. However, we argue that as customer demands for superior relationships continue to evolve (typically in ways which suit customers not suppliers), then a new role becomes important – the strategic management of the relationship with the customer. We see this as the role of the transformed sales organization. There may be surprises of many kinds in this transition – for example, Oracle recently stopped allowing its salespeople to place orders, they have to leave customers after a software demonstration to place their own orders on the Web site (Clark and Callahan 2000).

Our ideas regarding the imperatives driving the traditional sales organization towards a strategic customer management approach are organized around three key issues:

> *Intelligence* – concerned with leveraging and enhancing customer knowledge to add value to customer relationships
>
> *Interfaces* – refocusing salesforce efforts onto the management and exploitation of critical interfaces that impact on customer value (e.g., with CRM and KAM, as discussed above), and
>
> *Integration* – the responsibility for welding all the company activities and processes that impact on customer value into a single, seamless and sustained point of value delivery to customers.

We will examine each of these issues in turn, as a foundation for a broader consideration of the competitive necessity of evolving the role of the salesforce.

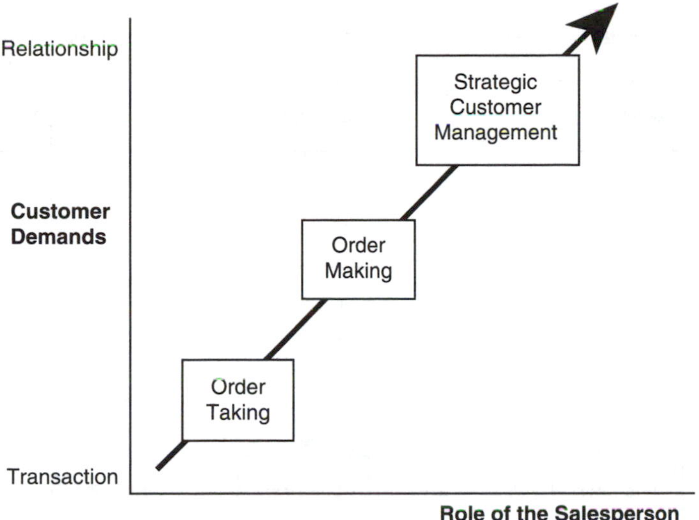

Figure 5 Substitution and evolution of the sales role

Intelligence

One of the clearest findings in the H. R. Challey investigation of corporate purchasers' views of the determining characteristics of world class sales organizations is that their salespeople demonstrate deep knowledge of the customer's business, such that they can identify needs and opportunities ahead of the customer (H. R. Challey 1997). The logic is simple – if the seller cannot bring added-value by identifying new opportunities for gaining competitive advantage in the end-use marketplace, then the seller is no more than a commodity supplier.

This represents a distinct change in focus in the way sellers must deploy their efforts at the customer interface, in the way suggested in Figure 6. The argument is that traditionally selling focussed on the seller's needs – essentially to convert product and service into cash flow. By contrast, conventional marketing changed the focus to the customer's needs and adapting the offering to match customer needs, priorities and preferences. What we suggest now is that the focus must change again from simple knowledge of the customer's organization to understanding the customer's end-use markets. The new salesforce role is to leverage knowledge to build competitive position with customers.

There are a growing number of examples of how end-user market knowledge is becoming the critical resource for a supplier to leverage in order to add value for customers. For instance, Dell does not sell computers to Boeing. Dell manages Boeing's IT strategy as an 'outsource of preference'. Dell's knowledge base centres on the air transport industry – for how else can they predict and plan Boeing's IT needs? When Johnson Controls in the US won the business for the seats and electronic controls in Ford's F-Series trucks, it was not by talking to Ford about seats and switches. Johnson's critical competitive edge was

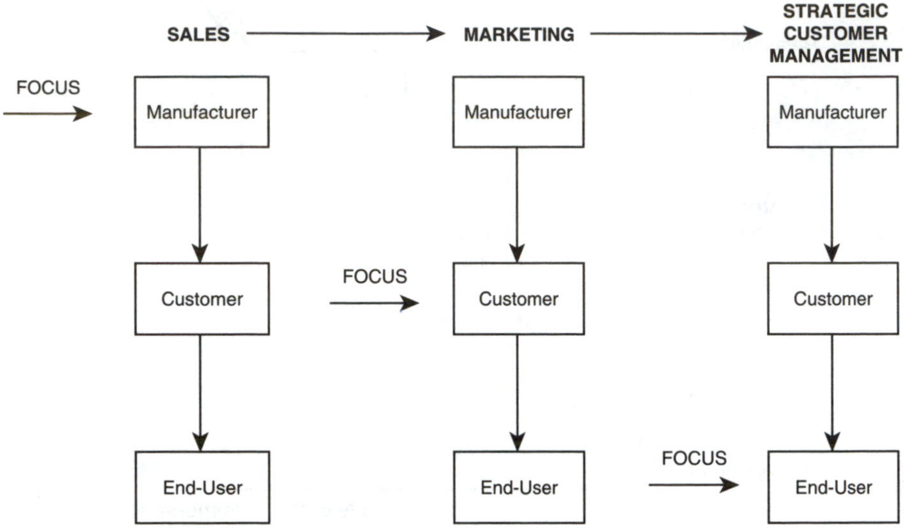

Figure 6 Changing the focus from selling to strategic customer management

knowing more about the truck driver's seating and control preferences than did Ford. Suppliers of equipment to companies like Coca-Cola and McDonalds already face a quarterly supplier rating system that demands an answer to the question: 'what did you do to enhance my competitive advantage with my consumers this quarter?'.

Suppliers who cannot provide added-value through offering purchasers enhanced competitive advantage in their end-use markets are simply selling commodities, and should expect to be treated as such by their customers. Many suppliers do not yet realize this, most corporate purchasers probably do. The challenge to suppliers is to understand the customer's business and the customer's markets, to leverage that knowledge to create competitive advantage, or stand back and watch the customer negotiate prices to ever lower levels. The change in perspective for those who manage customer relationships is as challenging as it is unavoidable for companies who do not wish to be commodity suppliers. This challenge is central to making the transition from conventional selling to strategic customer management.

Interfaces

We referred earlier to the need to identify the role of a salesforce as part of a multiple channel strategy. Consider again our Figure 1 model. The new salesforce role should include working closely with CRM resources to manage the process of customer channel choice. There are likely to be growing opportunities in the future to negotiate purchasing patterns with major customers to mutual advantage, that will be lost if there is no process for negotiating channel choice with customers. Similarly, the interface with KAM is likely to be critical in retaining residual business when key account partnerships fail, as well as in prospecting for the key accounts of the future. In both these examples, the challenge for the new salesforce is the effective management of these critical interfaces within the company.

Indeed, it is remarkable how many of the management approaches which have emerged over recent years and which are embedded in many organizations, share an espoused focus on customer value and customer satisfaction, though admittedly the lean supply chain places a wholly different meaning on these terms compared to the marketing or sales discipline. The issue has become one of paradigms competing for priority in delivering superior customer value (Piercy 1998). Our Figure 7 model for example lists a dozen business approaches and areas of activity common to many organizations, all claiming to enhance value and satisfaction with customers, and all construing these terms differently.

We suggest that the second major challenge facing managers and sales organizations in the transition to strategic customer management is to actively manage the company processes that impact on customer value. This new skills in managing the interfaces and relationships between those processes and activities inside the selling organization and its partners.

Integration

Related to the last issue of effectively managing interfaces between those processes impacting on the customer relationship, but broader in scope is the challenge of cross-functional, cross-level and cross-border integration. It has long been apparent that functional specialization, divisionalization, and multi-leveled bureaucracies are frequently poor at delivering consistent and superior

Figure 7 A new point of strategic focus in buyer–seller relationships

value to customers (Hulbert et al. 2003). Examples of the impact of integration failures on customer relationships are numerous, and some examples are given in Exhibit 4.

Exhibit 4: The Penalties of Poor Integration

Sales and Supply Chain Management

In one company, the Sales Director found that his major customer was ordering a product sporadically, as and when stock control indicated the need for more supplies. He realized that if the customer could be persuaded to adopt continuous replenishment, he could substantially reduce the stock cover he needed to keep to cover the sporadic orders. This was successfully negotiated with the customer. Two days into the new system, the very unhappy customer phoned to say he was almost out-of-stock and on the point of taking his business elsewhere. The Sales Director raced to the distribution depot to find out what had happened. The answer was simple, the distribution system prioritized large orders. The smallest orders were lowest priority and often not fulfilled by the end of the day. By definition, continuous replenishment gives small orders . . .

Sales and Operations

In a leading clothing company, the sales manager was told to increase sales targets and not to worry about production capacity. Urged on by his manager, a salesperson pulled off a major deal with a national retailer. The factory cannot deliver, the customer is furious, the salesperson is demotivated, and the sales manager is tearing his hair out . . .

Customer Relationships and the Accounts Department

Many salespeople report that one of the most negative impacts on customer relationships can come from the Accounts Department. The internal employees who operate credit control, invoicing, and handle account queries can inadvertently undo large investments of salesforce resource in building a customer relationship, simply because no-one has ever provided them with information about sales strategy and customer preferences.

Sales and Human Resource Management

The quality and skills of the people who deliver service and manage relationships with customers directly reflects HR strategy. If HR managers are not party to marketing and sales strategy, how can they recruit and train people appropriately to implement the strategy? Yet, in many companies this appears to be what HR specialists are expected to do. It is hardly surprising that they work to out-of-date person profiles and skills requirements.

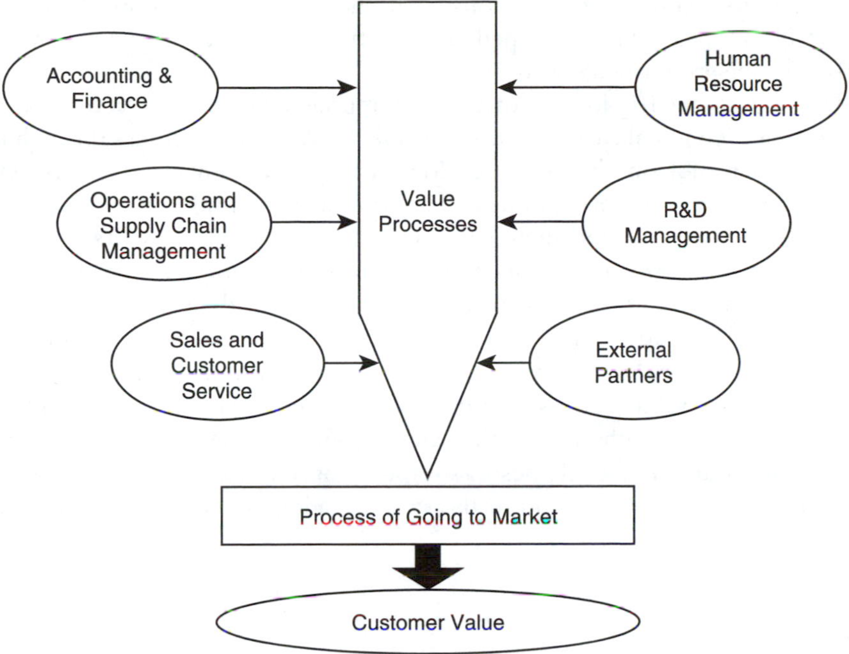

Figure 8 The pressure for total integrated marketing

Our Figure 8 model is a framework for managers to track the different functions and external partner organizations impacting on the delivery of value to customers as a basis for addressing the issue of integration. The imperative is clear – customers will no longer solve the seller's organizational problems (H. R. Challey 1997). The new customer demand is that the seller sorts out the seller's own problems – the days when the buyer would tolerate the need to phone to argue with Accounts about billing arrangements and credit, contact the factory about delivery and service, deal separately with maintenance about issues like installation and repair, and so on, have largely gone. The demand is seamless value delivery – nothing else will win status as the 'outsource of preference' and retain the business.

The third challenge in moving towards strategic customer management is to address the need for integration in all the functions and organizations that are involved in creating and delivering value to the customer.

Strategic Customer Management

Even this brief discussion of the potential gains from the evolution of conventional sales operations into strategic customer management underlines the case for a strategic perspective on the sales function, which does not simply examine the tactical management of sales transactions but focuses on the relationships formed in different ways with different types of customers as the basis for long-term strategic business development (Olson et al. 2001). One commentator suggests: 'sales functions are in the early stages of a transformation comparable to that which reshaped manufacturing twenty years ago' (Mazur 2000). The biggest challenge is to manage that transformation.

The urgent need is for evaluation and appraisal of the new activities and processes needed to enhance and sustain value delivery to customers through the sales operation, not simply the search for economies by downsizing. It is likely that this appraisal will cover domains far beyond those traditionally associated with selling activities (Ogbuchi and Sharma 1999). Our case suggests that these are issues for the board room, which involve important strategic choices in how a company addresses its markets. Some may suggest that the challenges we have identified – competitive advantage through knowledge-leverage, the management of diverse interfaces between sales and other customer-facing activities; the integration of value processes across functions and organizational boundaries – are too important to be left to the sales organization, new or reconstituted. Our responses are simple: if these issues are not addressed by the salesforce, then who will address them; and, if they are not addressed now, when will they be addressed?

References

Cravens, David W. (1995), 'The Changing Role of the Salesforce', *Marketing Management*, Summer, pp. 49–57

Clark, Philip B. and Callahan, Sean (2000), 'Sales Staffs: Adapt Or Die', *B to B*, April 10, p. 55

English, Simon (2000), 'Dunbar Drives Up Sales On The Road', *Daily Telegraph*, April 16

Friedman, Lawrence G. (2002), *Go To Market Strategy*, Woburn, MA, Butterworth-Heinemann Business Books

H. R. Challey Report (1997), *The Customer Selected World Class Sales Executive Report*, Ohio, The H. R. Challey Group

Homburg, Christian, Workman, John P. and Ove, Jensen (2002), 'A Configurational Perspective on Key Account Management', *Journal of Marketing*, April, pp. 38–60

Hulbert, James M., Capon, Noel and Piercy, Nigel F. (2003), *Total Integrated Marketing: Breaking the Bounds of the Function*, New York, Free Press

Jap, Sandy (2001), 'The Strategic Role of the Salesforce in Developing Customer Satisfaction across the Relationship Lifecycle', *Journal of Personal Selling and sales Management*, **XXI**, (2), pp. 95–108

Magretta, Joan, 'The Power of Virtual Integration: An Interview with Dell Computer's Michael Dell', *Harvard Business Review*, March-April 1998

Mazur, Laura (2000), 'The Changing Face of Sales', *Marketing Business*, May, p.31

Michaels, Adrian (2000), 'Merck Shifts Focus From Science to Its Salesforce', *Financial Times*, December 13

Ogbuchi, Alphonso O. and Varinder M. Sharma (1999), 'Redefining Industrial Salesforce Roles in a Changing Environment', *Journal of Marketing Theory and Practice*, **7**, (1), pp.64–71

Olson, Eric M., Cravens, David, W. and Slater, Stanley F. (2001), 'Competitiveness and Sales Management: A Marriage of Strategies', *Business Horizons*, March-April, pp.25–30

Piercy, Nigel F. (1998), 'Marketing Implementation: The Implications of Marketing Paradigm Weakness for the Strategy Execution Process', *Journal of the Academy of Marketing Science*, **26**, (3), pp.222–236

Rackham, Neil and De Vincentis, John (1999), *Rethinking the Salesforce: Redefining Selling To Create and Capture Customer Value*, New York, McGraw-Hill

Royal, Weld (1999), 'Death of Salesmen', *wwwindustryweek.com*, May 17, pp.59–60

Weitz, Barton A. and Bradford, Kevin (1999), 'Personal Selling and Sales Management: A Relationship Marketing Perspective', *Journal of Personal Selling and Sales Management*, **27**, (2), pp.241–254

? Questions

1 Piercy and Lane discuss the changing role of the sales force in isolation from the overall marketing function. Discuss how various types of sales forces, from the traditional through key account management to the newer forms of organization proposed by the authors can most effectively interface with the marketing functions within an organization.

2 Assume that you have recently joined an organization in which marketing and sales continue to be operated as totally separate functions. Frustrations are high between the two operations, with frequent claims that neither understands the specific challenges facing them. Write a memo outlining the advantages of closer integration between the two areas.

3 Your marketing department has recently developed a major consumer sales promotion. Outline the reasons for getting 'buy-in' from the sales force and discuss how the sales force may gather market intelligence for brand managers.

4 Your longest-serving sales representative is resisting moves towards an integrated electronic sales management system that will allow him to place orders from the customer premises, check stock availability and track despatch of orders already placed. This system has been proved by other members of the sales force to be considerably faster and more accurate than the previous paper-based order system. What should you do?

5 A large client is demanding a considerable discount for the next order. Your data indicate that you will make a loss if you provide the stock at the price requested. Discuss the positives and negatives of the request and make a recommendation as to the next action to be taken.

6 A recent marketing graduate without previous work experience is hoping for a career in marketing management but is disappointed to be offered a sales position. Discuss whether they should consider the offer seriously before making a decision.

7 You find that one of your sales staff has significantly improved their sales and profitability levels. Further investigation, however, shows that this has been achieved by giving away other products from the firm's range as a 'bonus buy'

coupled with the sale of the products for which the representative is responsible. This action has been taken without authorization. Discuss the implications of this action.

Vignette

Richard joined a large multi-brand fast-moving consumer goods company which had a history of high sales but low individual brand profitability. The company acted as marketing agent for a number of brands which did not have full marketing and distribution resources in each country in which their products were sold. He negotiated the somewhat unusual position of both marketing and sales manager rather than just marketing manager as the firm had intended.

Richard set up a simple spreadsheet for each of his sales representatives to use prior to negotiating major sales deals. The spreadsheet enabled fixed and variable costs, sales price per unit and contribution margins to be identified, along with profitability at various unit price levels. Initially the sales force members found the spreadsheet disturbing, suggesting that there was something wrong as price-based sales deals that had been negotiated several times in the past showed negative returns (i.e. losses). It took several months before all sales staff fully appreciated that simply moving volume without considering both short and long-term profitability was not in the organization's best interest.

Once these linkages were fully understood and alternatives to price deals explored, there was a substantial increase in brand profitability, together with an improvement in the morale of the sales force, who were then rewarded for their part in these achievements.

Chapter 9

Patrick de Pelsmacker

THE INTERNET AND THE WORLD WIDE WEB

ALTHOUGH INTERNET ADVERTISING CONSTITUTES only a minor part (slightly over 1 per cent) of all advertising investment in Europe, it is growing at a far more rapid pace than traditional advertising, and will probably keep on doing so, due to the increasing penetration and use of the Internet. And although there is a huge empirical literature on the factors influencing the effectiveness of advertisements in traditional advertising media, relatively few academic studies have concentrated on Web advertising. This form of advertising has characteristics that, on the one hand, do not make it very different from traditional advertising, but, on the other hand, are fundamentally new in terms of format and content. Indeed, similar to ads in traditional media, Web ads can be rational argument-based or emotion-oriented, can use endorsers or not, or can have a direct response-appeal or not.

On the other hand, Web advertisements have specific formats, such as banners, buttons, pop-ups, pop-unders, superstitials and interstitials, etc., that are not found in traditional media. Moreover, they allow a degree of flexibility and interactivity that cannot easily be reached in other, more traditional, advertising media. This direct interactivity allows a relatively simple and direct measurement of advertising effectiveness, for instance via the number of click-throughs (CTR, click-through rate) on Web ads. Finally, unlike most traditional advertising media, the Internet is frequently used as a business-to-business marketing communications instrument.

This study's unique contribution is that it is one of the first systematic and large-scale (almost 9,000 banner ads) empirical investigations into the determinants of click-through rates of real-life banner advertisements on Web sites. As such it tries to establish the link between banner characteristics and a behavioural advertising effect measure (CTR). Furthermore, it is one of the few studies in which the differences between responses of business and consumer target groups are measured, thereby acknowledging the great importance of the Internet for business-to-business (B-to-B) marketing, and exploring the differences in ideal characteristics of marketing communications in B-to-B and business-to-consumer (B-to-C) situations. On the one hand, the article replicates the effect of 'traditional advertising' characteristics, such as the use of emotions and colour, incentives and expert endorsements. On the other hand, it also focuses upon the specific and unique features of the Internet and Web advertising by studying interactivity and animation in banner ads.

The core objective of the study was to explore the difference between the effectiveness (measured as CTR) of a number of cognitive and affective content and design elements between B-to-B and B-to-C ads. It builds upon partial insights from industry research, and tries to integrate these insights into a comprehensive and testable framework. Thereby the authors provide links to concepts and research in 'traditional advertising' studies, such as the impact of emotions in advertising, the role of involvement, behavioural incentives (sales promotion) and the dual-processing (central and peripheral route) model of persuasion. The authors' basic conclusion is that there is a significant moderating effect of all the content and design elements studied on the responses to B-to-B versus B-to-C banner ads. In other words, in order to be effective, B-to-B ads on Web sites should be different from B-to-C ads. On the other hand, individuals in a B-to-B versus a B-to-C situation are not fundamentally different in all respects. The effects of colour, interactivity and incentives, for instance, are to a certain degree similar in both situations. One of the surprising and counter-intuitive results is that, in both situations, interactivity and incentives lower click-through rates.

Although the study is based on a large sample of advertisements, it is limited in scope: only one (though important) effect measure is studied (CTR), and a limited (though, again, very relevant) set of banner characteristics is investigated. Furthermore, these characteristics are measured in relatively few categories (for example, 'emotional or not'). Consequently, the article explores a very rich research direction, and can be used as a starting point of more in-depth investigations.

THE IMPACT OF CONTENT AND DESIGN ELEMENTS ON BANNER ADVERTISING CLICK-THROUGH RATES

Ritu Lohtia, Naveen Donthu and Edmund K. Hershberger

This study investigates the impact of content and design elements on the click-through rates of banner advertisements using data from 8,725 real banner advertisements. It is one of the first empirical studies to examine banner advertising effectiveness (measured by click-through rates) and also one of the first to examine the differences between business-to-business (B2B) and business-to-consumer (B2C) banner advertisements.

Content elements examined include the use of incentives and emotional appeals. Design elements examined include the use of interactivity, color, and animation. Results suggest that content and design elements do not work the same way for B2B and B2C banner advertisements.

In 1994, the now ubiquitous banner advertisement was first introduced. In the eight years since, the Internet advertising industry has exploded. According to the Interactive Advertising Bureau (IAB: www.iab.net). Internet advertising in 2001 was approximately a $7.2 billion industry in the United States alone. About 35 percent of that was accounted for by banner advertisements (interactive Advertising Bureau, 2002).

Evidence about the effectiveness of this advertising medium has come mainly from industry reports. Five recent reports conclude that internet advertisements build brands (i.e., increase advertisement awareness, brand awareness, brand image, or intent to purchase). These studies suggest that size, use of interactive elements (such as flash or DHTML), and advertisement position (such as Interstitial) increase branding (Interactive Advertising Bureau, 2002).

Industry beliefs also suggest that creative execution impacts branding. Advertisements that perform best reveal the brand early on. Similarly, lighter backgrounds, high contrast, and dynamic messages improve branding. Another study concludes that limiting clutter, using larger brand logos, and depicting human faces improves branding. Keeping the message simple and straightforward helps advertising performance (Briggs, 200lb).

This study, based on a large sample of real data from an online advertising company, comprehensively explores the effectiveness of Internet banner advertising. The objectives of this research are twofold: to define what constitutes an effective banner advertisement and to analyze if there are differences in

---

Journal of Advertising Research, Vol. 43, No. 4 (December 2003), pp. 410–18. ISSN 0021–8499. Database: Business Source Premier.

Ritu Lohtia (Ph.D., University of Maryland) is associate professor of marketing at Georgia State University. Naveen Donthu (Ph.D., University of Texas at Austin) is the Katherine S. Bernhardt Research Professor of Marketing at Georgia State University. Edmund K. Hershberger (Ph.D., Georgia State University) is an assistant professor of marketing at Southern Illinois University at Edwardsville.

what constitutes effectiveness across business-to-business (B2B) versus business-to-consumer (B2C) banner advertisements.

While a lot of resources are being spent on Internet banner advertising, there has been little formal empirical research that provides guidelines for effective banner advertising. Most industry reports are based on market polls or experiments and have examined the effectiveness of banner advertisements on branding. Market polls ask respondents for their opinions about banner advertising effectiveness and are qualitative in nature. In experiments, groups of consumers are shown an advertisement and their branding scores (or other dependent measures) are examined before and after the advertisement is shown. Any changes in branding scores compared to a control group are attributed to the banner advertisement (Interactive Advertising Bureau, 2002). Most of this research, however, has examined the effectiveness of only a few advertisements (ranging from 1 to 45), and often advertisements of well-established brands (Li and Bukovac, 1999). Thus the results may not be generalizable. Further, subjective inferences are made to determine what makes certain advertisements more effective (Briggs, 200lb; Briggs, Sullivan, and Webster, 2001a, 2001b, 2001c). Consumers need to agree to participate in these research studies, and this can bias the results. In addition, while branding is important, click-through is the most commonly used measure of success in the advertising industry. Market polls and experiments often do not measure click-through rates (CTRs).

This study overcomes some of the limitations of previous research. It uses a large sample of real banner advertisements to examine what constitutes the effectiveness of banner advertisements. We used 10,000 actual advertisements placed by an Internet advertising company on different websites for its customers over a period of time. The click rate used in the analysis is the actual click rate recorded by the advertising company for each of the advertisements. Further, the consumers were not aware that they were involved in an advertising effectiveness study. Using judges to code the advertisements with respect to their characteristics, we empirically examine what banner advertising characteristics impact the effectiveness of B2B versus B2C advertisements.

This research makes several contributions to both practice and theory. First, it is one of the first empirical studies to examine what constitutes banner advertising effectiveness (measured by CTRs). Second, it is based on an extremely large sample of real banner advertisements, making the results extremely reliable. Third, it is one of the first to examine the differences between B2B and B2C banner advertisements. Very few studies have focused on comparing B2B and B2C advertising (Lambert, Morris, and Pitt, 1995). This research will help B2B and B2C media planners use their online dollars more effectively.

Dependent Variable: Click-through Rate (CTR)

WHILE THERE IS NO industry standard for measuring the effectiveness of a banner advertisement, one specific metric that has been used extensively is CTR. According to a recent online advertisement measurement study (PriceWaterHouseCoopers, 2001), a click is a 'user-initiated action of clicking on an ad element, causing a redirect to another web location' (p. 17). Clicks and advertisement impressions, i.e., number of times an advertisement is served to a user's browser, are the top two metrics used for advertisement delivery reporting and audience measurement. CTR is the ratio of number of times an advertisement is clicked to the number of advertisement impressions.

The role of advertising context in banner advertising effectiveness

It is well established in the literature that, depending on certain environmental, personal, or contextual characteristics, people utilize different information processing approaches (Meyers-Levy and Malaviya, 1999; Petty and Cacioppo, 1986). The primary driver of information processing strategy is involvement, resulting in what is known as the dual-process model of information processing. The basic tenet to this model, also known as the Elaboration Likelihood Model, is that people tend to process information differently depending on their level of involvement with the message. For a high-involvement situation, people tend to use 'central route' processing, meaning that they make a cognitive effort to evaluate statements or attend to claims or other message stimuli. It has been shown that during central route processing, non-essential stimuli, such as colors or sound, are not processed very heavily. Because these 'secondary' elements do not convey any specific information, they merely exist as a background to the content that is most important, namely the more cognitive elements of the advertisement, such as incentives. On the other hand, in situations of low involvement, people tend to use 'peripheral route' processing, meaning that they are engaged in more subconscious processing where they simply do not make an effort to attend to any specific message elements. Affective components take the lead in this situation, and attitude change is effected through the use of peripheral cues, such as color, animation, or music.

To apply this model to this research, we utilized the context of the banner advertisements (B2B versus B2C) as a moderating variable. It is a common belief that business purchase decisions are more likely to be high involvement compared to consumer purchase decisions. Products purchased are often customized, are seldom impulse purchases, and are usually the result of group decision making. The purchase cycles are also longer, and purchase scales are considerably larger. Because involvement drives the information processing task, we suggest that viewers will process banner advertisements differently based upon the advertisement context. B2B advertisements should be more cognitive in nature, because in high-involvement situations, people tend to use central route processing where cognitions are used heavily. B2C advertisements should be more affective in nature, because low-involvement situations are more conducive to peripheral route information processing.

Independent Variables: Message Content and Advertisement Design

To determine the advertisement characteristics that may have an Impact on CTR in these two contexts, we examined advertising research in traditional media such as print, broadcast, and billboards (Bhargava, Donthu, and Caron, 1994; Henssens and Weitz, 1980; Lohtia, Johnston, and Aab, 1995; Stewart and Furse, 1986; Wells, Bumett, and Moriarty, 2000). This research suggests that both the content and design of banner advertisements should impact click-through. Within each of these types of variables, we selected variables to represent both cognitive and affective components. Thus, we identified banner advertisement characteristics for each of four groups: cognitive content, affective content, affective content, cognitive design, and affective design (see Table 1).

Content elements

Content elements include message, appeal type, and offers made and can involve the viewer at a cognitive or affective level. Message content is often used to deliver a message making some claim and utilizing some appeal type. We look at two message content characteristics, one cognitive and one affective. We chose the use of incentives to measure cognitive message elements. It is thought that while banner advertisements are typically more useful for improving brand attitude or recognition, action can be generated if the advertisement offers an incentive for action (Krishnamurthy, 2000). For example, a banner advertisement could offer a dollars-off coupon in return for clicking on a banner advertisement. According to a survey conducted by Greenfield Online Inc. (Mullaney, 1999), most web surfers are looking for incentives to read an advertisement before they click to another page. For example, 66 percent look for an advertisement containing a free offer.

For the affective message element, we measured the use of emotional appeals. A popular method of gaining attention and generating action from any type of advertising is through the use of an emotional appeal (Holbrook and Batra, 1987). Emotional appeals can take the form of fear, love, happiness, etc. By eliciting an emotional response from an advertisement, we expect greater CTR through increased involvement with the advertisement. Research suggests that, in general, consumer advertisements are less factual and more emotional in appeal (Lambert, Morris, and Pitt, 1995).

Table 1 Cognitive and affective content and design variables

Variables	*Cognitive*	*Affective*
Message content	Incentives	Emotional appeal
Advertisement design	Interactivity	Color, Animation

Design elements

To assess the design characteristics of a banner advertisement, we selected three criteria: interactivity, color, and animation. While there may be other design elements that could be considered, these three seem to be emerging in the industry as key factors to banner advertising success (Krishnamurthy, 2000).

As with the content elements, design elements can be used to elicit either a cognitive or affective response. Interactive elements of a banner advertisement attempt to elicit a cognitive response by allowing the viewer to submit searches, enter forms, or simply click to visit the advertiser's website. By allowing interactivity, the advertiser is attempting to increase viewer involvement by creating two-way communication, instead of the usual one-way communication that most traditional types of advertising accomplish. There is evidence that interactivity of banner advertisements has a substantial impact on CTR (Mand, 1998). However, superfluous interactivity can be distracting and should be avoided (Interactive Advertising Bureau, 2001).

Affective components are intended to elicit some type of emotional or feeling response, usually invisible to the viewer. Typical ways that advertisements can be used to elicit affective response are through the use of color and animation. The amount of color used in advertising has been shown to impact advertising effectiveness in traditional media (Gronhaug, Kvitastein, and Gronmo, 1991). Past research suggests that there may not be a direct positive relation between color and effectiveness. Gronhaug, Kvitastein, and Gronmo (1991) found that low levels of color increased effect, while adding more colors beyond that had no effect at all. This suggests that there may be an optimum level of color in an advertisement. Perhaps too much color detracts from the message. According to a survey done by Greenfield Online Inc. (Mullaney, 1999), bright colors in web advertising were of interest to few respondents. However, DoubleClick, an Internet advertising agency, recommends the use of bright colors in banner advertisements (http://www.doubleclick.com:-1920/learning%5f center/research%5ffindings/effectiveness.htm).

The final independent variable is animation. The first banner advertisements were simply static images containing advertising content, much akin to print advertisements. However, new technologies such as plug-ins, java script, and streaming media have transformed banners in remarkable ways (Wells, Burnett, and Moriarty, 2000, p. 277). Many advertisers have begun to implement loop-animated banners to deliver a progressive and sequential image. It is well known that television is one of the most intrusive, involving media forms because of its ability to use moving images. When banners use animation, they also take on the character of television advertisements, and this may suggest that animated banner advertisements will attract more attention and hence be clicked more (Wegert, 2002). Studies of side-by-side performance of advertisements for different companies conducted by ACNielsen suggest that animation increases click rate (Briggs, 2001b).

Based on an experiment, Li and Bukovac (1999) illustrate that animation increases response times and recall of banner advertisements. They use distinctiveness theory to suggest that animated banner advertisements are distinctive from static ones and are more likely to attract attention. Li and Bukovac state that banner advertisements are likely to '. . . create unique memory traces' (p. 342) and result in better recall.

Looking at our five independent variables (Table 1), incentives and interactivity deal more directly with central route processing, i.e., both of these variables deal with active, cognitive thought processes. We suggest that B2B advertisements are viewed more often in high-involvement situations and hence are processed through more central route processing. The other three independent variables (emotional appeal, color, and animation) are usually not actively processed and can be considered peripheral cues. Therefore, emotional appeals, color, and animation are likely to be used more in low-involvement situations. We have suggested that B2C advertisements are more likely to be viewed in low-involvement situations. Based on the above discussion, we present the following hypotheses:

H1a: When the banner advertising context is B2B, the relation between incentives and CTR is stronger than when the banner advertising context is B2C.

H1b: When the banner advertising context is B2B, the relation between interactivity and CTR is stronger than when the banner advertising context is B2C.

H2a: When the banner advertising context is B2B, the relation between use of emotional appeals and CTR is weaker than when the advertising context is B2C.

H2b: When the banner advertising context is B2B, the relation between color level and CTR is weaker than when the advertising context is B2C.

H2c: When the banner advertising context is B2B, the relation between animation and CTR is weaker than when the advertising context is B2C.

Methodology

The empirical study was conducted at the individual banner advertisement level. A large online advertising company provided us with 10,000 banner advertisements that were randomly selected out of an inventory of real world banner advertisements that were online in the previous months. Five independent judges remotely coded these advertisements. The judges were marketing doctoral candidates that completed a joint training session where they were familiarized with the coding scheme. An online coding tool was developed, and each coder had a unique password to the website where the banners could be viewed and coded.

We measured incentives by evaluating the banner advertisements for the presence or absence of incentives to click. The literature has conceptualized emotion in different ways (Batra and Ray, 1986; Chandy, Tellis, Macinnis, and Thaivanich, 2001), either treating each emotion as a construct itself or treating all emotions as a scale from negative through neutral to positive (Bagozzi and Moore, 1994). In this research, we followed the latter route. We assessed banner advertisings' use of emotional appeals by capturing a range of positive and negative emotions. Some advertisements used no emotional appeal at all. Because less than one percent of the advertisements used negative emotions, we defined emotion as a binary variable to capture the use of emotions or the lack thereof.

We measured interactivity by evaluating the banner advertisements for the presence or absence of interactive elements. To assess the impact of color on the level of banner advertising effectiveness, we evaluated the impact of the number of colors present. Then we collapsed that scale to low, medium, and high color. We conceptualized animation to be either present or not, and we measured it on a two-point scale.

The judges were instructed to check boxes for the banner advertisement's appeal, number of colors, inclusion of interactive elements, animation, and direct incentives to click. They also were instructed to code the advertisements' context as either B2B or B2C. To ascertain interjudge reliability, all judges coded a subsample of 100 randomly selected advertisements. For all independent variables, we estimated the interjudge reliability coefficient using Rust and Cooil's (1994) proportional reduction in loss (PRL) reliability measure, which can be evaluated using the same criteria as evaluating Cronbach's alpha-i.e., 0.70 is acceptable, 0.90 is desirable. All reliabilities were high and in the desirable range (mean = 0.94).

The actual CTR for each banner advertisement was provided by the online advertising firm; however, not all advertisements had click data. Those advertisements without click data were eliminated from the data, leaving a total of 7,421 B2C advertisements and 1,304 B2B advertisements, for a total of 8,725 advertisements. The banner advertisements included in the sample represented a wide variety of products and services.

Analysis of variance (ANOVA) was used to test the moderating effect of advertisement context. The results of this analysis are discussed in the following section.

Results

Table 2 shows the usage of the various elements in B2B and B2C banner advertisements. It appears that both kinds of advertisements use all the elements. No specific content or design strategy seems to be dominating in either type of advertisements. The ANOVA (results in Table 3) confirms that for all the relationships the moderating effect of advertisement context is significant at the 0.01 level.

To support our hypotheses that advertisement context moderates these relationships, we need to see a significant difference in CTR between the interaction term measures. Consistent with Hypothesis Hla, the results show that for B2B banner advertisements, the relationship between incentives and CTR was stronger than for B2C advertisements. Figure 1 (A) demonstrates the dramatic impact of advertisement context on this relationship. It also shows that, while the presence of incentives does not influence the CTR of B2C banner advertisements, the presence of incentives hurts B2B banner advertisement CTR.

Table 2 Mean usage of content and design elements in banner advertisements (%)

	Incen-tives	*Inter-activity*	*Emotional appeals*	*Low color*	*Moderate color*	*High color*	*Anima-tion*
B2B advertisements	35	36	55	4	42	53	29
B2C advertisements	32	37	54	5	37	58	27

Table 3 ANOVA for testing moderating effect of advertisement context on the impact of content and design elements on CTR

Source	*F*
Incentives × advertisement context	11.196*
Interactivity × advertisement context	33.286*
Emotional appeal × advertisement context	19.689*
Color level × advertisement context	24.642*
Animation × advertisement context	7.524*

Significant at the 0.01 level.

Hypothesis H1b suggests that for B2B advertisements, the relationship between interactivity and CTR is stronger than for B2C advertisements. This moderating role of advertisement context as illustrated in Figure 1 (B) is supported by ANOVA. It appears that interactivity actually lowers CTR; however, in B2C banner advertisements, the losses are far less than those for B2B banner advertisements.

The second set of hypotheses dealt with design elements, namely the use of emotional appeals, color, and animation. Hypothesis H2a suggested that the relationship between the use of emotional appeals and CTR is stronger for B2C advertisements than B2B advertisements. Figure 1 (C) shows that advertisement context plays a substantial role in the effect of emotional appeal use. For B2B banner advertisements, emotional appeals decrease CTR; however, for B2C banner advertisements, there is an increase in CTR when emotional appeals are used. According to Hypothesis H2b, color would have a greater impact on CTR for B2C advertisements than for B2B advertisements. The results, however, show (see Figure 1 (D) and Table 3 results) that color has a strong impact for both B2B and B2C banner advertisements. For both B2B and B2C banner advertisements, a medium level of color produces the highest CTR. As hypothesized in H2c, the interaction effect between context and animation is significant and is illustrated in Figure 1 (E). We see that animation lowers CTR in B2B advertisements, but increases CTR in B2C advertisements.

Discussion

After analyzing the CTRs of a large sample of banner advertisements, the main conclusions are:

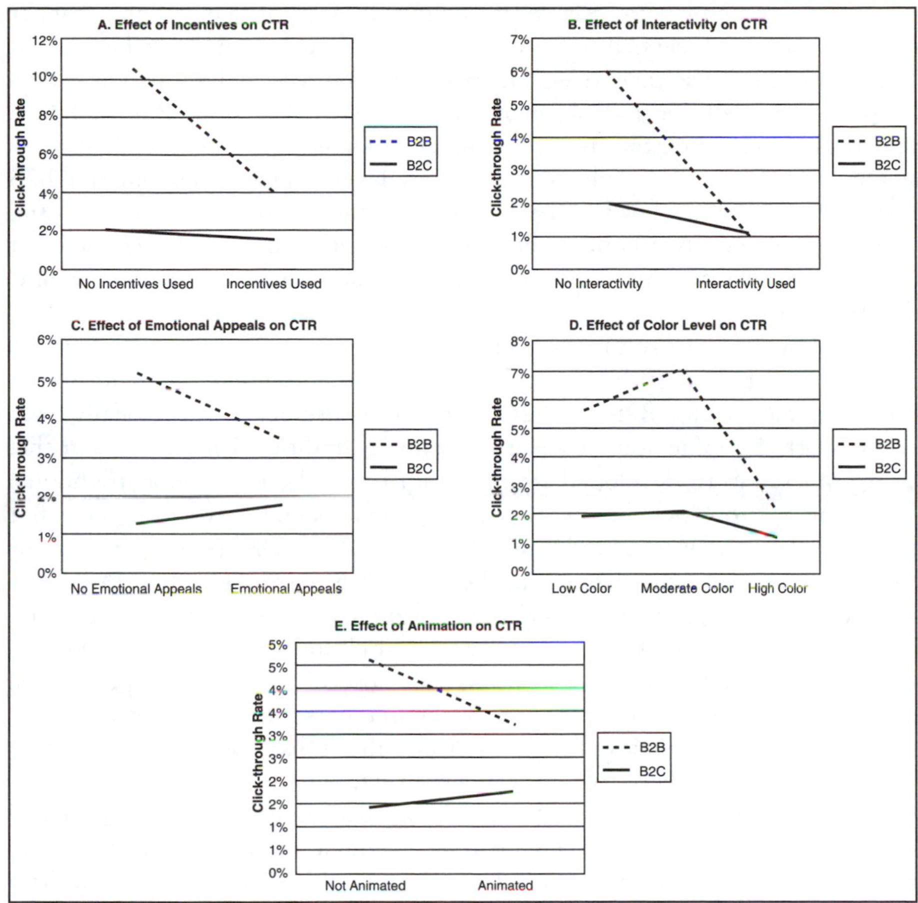

Figure 1 Interaction effects

1 Contrary to our expectation, the presence of incentives and interactivity lowered the CTR of banner advertisements. This was especially true for B2B banner advertisements than B2C banner advertisements.
2 As expected, the presence of emotion and animation increased the CTR for B2C banner advertisements and decreased the CTR for B2B banner advertisements.
3 Medium level of color was better than low or high levels of color for B2B and B2C banner advertisements.
4 B2B banner advertisements had higher CTR than B2C banner advertisements.

It is possible that the presence of incentives and interactivity detracts from the content of B2B advertisements because their presence lowered CTR considerably. Given that B2B purchases are often customized and high in dollar value, incentives that are tailored to specific customers and their needs may be more appropriate. Future research should examine if offering tailored incentives for B2B customers increases click rate.

The above information is very useful for web designers and banner advertisement producers. If a B2B banner advertisement aims for high CTR, then it should not use incentives, interactivity, emotion, and animation. These things are best left for B2C banner advertisements. For both B2B and B2C banner advertisements, the use of too much color is not recommended, but a medium level of color is preferred over a low level of color, especially for B2B banner advertisements. For B2C banner advertisements, the use of emotions and animation is especially recommended. It will be interesting to determine what types of emotional appeals and animation techniques are more effective for B2C advertisements.

The above findings and recommendations are not obvious and that is where the main contribution of this research lies. Content and design elements do not work the same way for B2B and B2C banner advertisements. Additionally, they do not work the same way as advertisements in traditional media. Given that the hypotheses were developed from literature based largely upon traditional advertising, it is obvious that in many cases, online banner advertising does not operate in the same way as traditional advertising does. One possible reason for this is the lack of media planning in the online advertising industry. A certain level of sophistication in traditional media planning has been achieved to date. That is to say it is likely that advertisements in traditional media have the benefit of proper placement and timing through the use of highly developed media planning models. By and large, banner advertisements are still placed randomly on websites. Characteristics of the viewer and the website should be incorporated in determining where to place banner advertisements.

Our research was based on the reasoning that in general.; B2B purchase decisions are more likely to be high involvement compared to B2C purchase decisions. How ever, we need to recognize that not all B2B purchase decisions are high involvement and not all B2C purchase decisions are low involvement. In future research, it may be useful to categorize the advertisement context into four categories: B2B high involvement, B2B low involvement, B2C high involvement, and B2C low involvement, and then examine the impact of advertisement content and design variables on CTR in these four contexts.

Future empirical studies should look at other measures of banner advertising effectiveness such as branding. Industry reports have shown that banner advertisements can impact these metrics favorably and that click-through may not always be an appropriate measure of the effectiveness of Internet advertisements (Briggs, 2001a). However, given that CTR was higher for B2B banner advertisements, it is possible that CTR is a more appropriate measure of effectiveness for B2B advertisements than B2C advertisements. In this study, we only looked at five independent variables. Other content and design elements need to be investigated. It will be interesting to see how the message content and advertisement design variables influence other dependent variables. While this study is based on an extremely large sample of banner advertisements and should be generalizable, the impact of content and design elements on different types of Internet advertisements should be examined.

Future studies may investigate the effectiveness of banner advertisements using experiments. Unlike experiments, our methodology did not allow us to control for all elements. Future research should investigate the relationship between banner advertising effectiveness and the websites where they are placed. Such efforts will have implications for banner advertising media planning.

The authors acknowledge the financial and data support of Michael Moore and Marianna Dizik in the conduct of this study.

References

Bagozzi, Richard P., and David J. Moore. Public Service Advertisements: Emotions and Empathy Guide Prosocial Behavior. Journal of Marketing 58, 1 (1994): 56–70.

Batra, Rajeev, and Michael L Ray. 'Affective Responses Mediating Acceptance of Advertising.' Journal of Consumer Research 13, 2 (1986): 234–48.

Bhargava, Mukesh, Naveen Donthu, and Rosannc Caron. 'Improving the Effectiveness of Outdoor Advertising: Lessons from a Study of 282 Campaigns.' *Journal of Advertising Research 34, 2 (1994): 46–55.*

Briggs, Rex. 'Measuring Advertising Success: The Value of Interactive Branding.' [URL: http://www.iab.net/measuringsuccess/img/ success.pdf], February 2001a.

——. 'The Role of Creative Execution in Online Advertising Success.' [URL: http://www.iab.net/measuringsuccess/img/ Creative.pdf], October 2001b.

——, Jessica Sullivan, and Ian Webster. 'Australian Online Advertising Effectiveness Study 2001.' [URL: http://www.consult.com.au/ pdf/AUSummary.pdf], 2001a.

——, ——, and ——. 'Hong Kong Online Advertising Effectiveness Study 2001.' [URL: http://www.consult.com.au/pdf/ HKSummary.pdf], 2001b.

——, ——, and ——. 'New Zealand Online Advertising Effectiveness Study 2001.' [URL: http://www.consult.com.au/pdf/ NZSummary.pdf]. 2001c.

Chandy, Rajesh K., Gerard J. Tellis, Deborah J. Macinnis, and Pattana Thaivanich. 'What to Say When: Advertising Appeals in Evolving Markets.' Journal of Marketing Research 38, 4 (2001): 399–414.

Gronhaug, Kjell, Olav Kvitastein, and Sigmund Gronmo. 'Factors Moderating Advertising Effectiveness as Reflected in 333 Tested Advertisements.' *Journal of Advertising Research, 34, 3 (1991): 42–50.*

Henssens, Dominique M., and Barton A. Weitz. 'The Effectiveness of Industrial Print Advertisements Across Product Categories.' Journal of Marketing Research 14, 3 (1980): 294–306.

Holbrook, Morris B., and Rajeev Batra. 'Assessing the Role of Emotions as Mediators of Consumer Responses to Advertising.' Journal of Consumer Research 14, 3 (1987): 404–20.

Interactive Advertising Bureau (IAB). 'Five Principles That Online Can Learn from Offline Marketing.' [URL: http://www.iab.net/ measuringsuccess/img/ measuringsuccess.pdf], June 2001.

—— 'InternetAdvertisingRevenueTotaled$1.7BillionforQ42001.'[URL:www.iab.net/ news/pr-2002–0523.asp], 2002.

Krishnamurthy, Sandeep. 'Deciphering the Internet Advertising Puzzle.' Marketing Management 9, 3 (2000): 35–39.

Lambert, David R., Michael H. Morris, and Leyland F. Pitt. 'Has Industrial Advertising Become Consumerized? A Longitudinal Perspective from the USA.' International Journal of Advertising 14, 4 (1995): 349–54.

Li, Hairong, and Janice L. Bukovac. 'Cognitive Impact of Banner Ad Characteristics: An Experimental Study.' Journalism & Mass Communication Quarterly 76, 2 (1999): 341–53.

Lohtia, Ritu, Wesley J. Johnston, and Linda Aab. 'Business-to-Business Advertising: What Are the Dimensions of an Effective Print Ad?' Industrial Marketing Management 24, 5 (1995): 369–78.

Mand, Adrienne. 'There's Gold in Them Banners!' Adweek 39, 17 (1998): 28–29.

Meyers-Levy, Joan, and Prashant Malaviya. 'Consumers' Processing of Persuasive Advertisements: An Integrative Framework of Persuasion Theories.' Journal of Marketing 63, Special Issue (1999): 45–60.

Mullaney, Timothy J. 'Online Marketing is Clicking.' Business Week, September 6, 1999.

Petty, Richard E., and John T. Cacioppo. Communication and Persuesion: Central and Peripheral Routes to Attitude Chenge. New York: Springer, 1986.

Pricewaterhousecoopers. 'IAB Online Ad Measurement Study.' [URL: http://www.iab.net/ standerds/pwc_report.pdf], December, 2001.

Rust, Roland T., and Bruce Cooil. 'Reliability Measures for Qualitative Data: Theory and Implications.' Journal of Marketing Research 31, 1 (1994): 1–14.

Stewart, David, and D. H. Furse. Effective Television Advertising: A Study of 1000 Commercials. Lexington, MA: Lexington Books, 1986.

Wegert, Tessa. 'Pop-Up Ads, Part 2: Usage Guidelinese for Legitimate Marketers.' [URL: http://www.clickz.com/media/media%5fbuy/ article.php/995311], March 21, 2002.

Wells, William, John Burnett, and Sandra Moriarty. Advertising: Principles and Practice. Upper Saddle River, NJ: Prentice Hall, 2000.

? Questions

1 What are the unique contributions and insights of this study?
2 What are the advantages and shortcomings of industrial versus academic research into the effectiveness of Web sites?
3 In what way do the authors link their study to the Elaboration Likelihood Model?
4 The authors refer to business-to-business contexts as to high-involvement situations, and to business-to-consumer contexts as low-involvement situations. Is this correct? Why or why not?
5 The definition of 'emotional banners' includes all types of emotional appeal. (The authors define the 'emotions' variable as binary.) What could be the effect of this on the validity of the study and its results?
6 The authors define interactivity and incentives as cognitive appeals. Is that correct? Why or why not?

7 Did the authors measure the possible effect of the 'optimal colour level' correctly? Why or why not?
8 The authors assume that interactivity and incentives will influence the viewers of banner ads via the central route of persuasion, while colour and emotions will primarily affect them via the peripheral route? Is this correct? Why or why not?
9 Use Figure 1 to describe the main results of the study.
10 Take a closer look at Figure 1D. Is the hypothesis that medium colour levels are the most effective fully supported? Is there a difference between B-to-B and B-to-C and, if so, is it in the expected direction? Do you agree with the conclusion of the authors that colour levels have an impact on the effectiveness of both B-to-B and B-to-C banner ads?
11 According to the authors, why do interactivity and incentives lower CTRs? Do you agree? Why or why not?
12 What are the managerial implications suggested by the authors? Do you agree? Can you think of other implications?
13 Given the results of this study, what do the ideal B-to-B and B-to-C banner ads look like?
14 Do you have suggestions for further research?

Vignette

Rabobank goes virtual: the Internet as part of an integrated communications campaign

Rabobank is a Dutch co-operative bank that was established in 1972 as a result of a merger between several co-operative banks. It is one of the few banks in the world that has a Moody's and Standard & Poor's AAA rating. Rabobank is a pioneer in Internet banking. At the end of 2002 the bank had 1.4 million Internet banking customers in the Netherlands. With 150,000 hits per day, the Rabobank site was the second largest financial portal in Europe. In 2001 the bank decided to offer its services to the Belgian public, and in November 2002 Rabobank.be was launched. The bank offers its products only via the Internet. Except for a 1 per cent starting cost fee (maximum €100), transactions are free of charge.

Belgians are not very highly involved with their banking problems: habits and convenience are important criteria to choose (and stay with) a bank. And, although 35 per cent of Belgian Internet users make use of on-line banking, the Internet is very much a secondary channel, and for most customers the office remains the primary point of contact with their bank. Rabobank was a new challenger on the Belgian bank market and could not benefit from the high awareness and visibility of most other banks that have a vast network of offices. Its strategy was therefore to offer high interest rates and to spend a considerable budget on a launching campaign.

Rabobank.be was launched by means of two waves of an integrated communications campaign: November 2002 to February 2003 and March 2003 to February

2004. During the first wave the share of voice of Rabobank was 7.6 per cent, and 1.6 per cent during the second wave. The commercial objective of the campaign was to attract 20,000 customers with a total invested amount of €200 million by the end of 2003. During the first wave, the main objective was to raise awareness with the online and financially involved part of the general public (the so-called 'on-line and mass affluent'), to position the bank as an aggressive challenger, and to generate traffic and trial on the site. The second wave was targeted at 'new financial freaks': people who actively seek the best solution for their banking problems and consider traditional banks as largely redundant and too expensive, and that trust new technology such as on-line banking.

The launch wave largely focused upon off-line media to build awareness of the bank and its Internet portal. Billboards were used to compensate for the lack of physical presence of the bank on the street. Selected newspaper advertising allowed the bank to appeal to the financially involved and to explain the Rabobank product range. These core media were supplemented by means of radio spots that enabled the bank to quickly build awareness with broad target groups. But also the Internet was actively used as a launch medium, to raise awareness and to generate traffic and trial. Banners, pop-ups, overlays and skyscrapers were put on a number of important portal sites and financial sites. An advergame was developed, that was also advertised off-line and on-line. The main purpose of the latter was to build a database of prospects and customers. During the second wave of the campaign newspapers were used again, but also magazines that selectively reached the 'new financial freaks'. In this second wave the Internet played a much more important role, since this channel is an important information source for the target group. A series of on-line video testimonials was created, and long-term deals with important portal sites and news sites were established to provide a link that guided the potential customer to a specifically designed mini-site on which the visitor could leave his/her e-mail address to receive concrete information. Also 'content deals' were used: specific banking offers were developed for the financial pages of specific portal sites. These 'advertorials' create a more credible environment than the standard webvertising formats.

The results of the campaign were impressive. After five months almost 90 per cent of Belgians knew the name of the bank, and more than 40 per cent were aware of the Internet site. Furthermore, 50 per cent of those who were aware of the Rabobank.be brand learned to know it via the Internet part of the campaign. Throughout the campaign, site visits increased to 60,000–70,000 by the end of 2003. Although at the end of 2003 Rabobank had only 13,700 customers (lower than expected), the combined investment of those customers was 45 per cent above target. Evidently a bank with a relatively low customer base, but high average investments, is not complaining . . .

Sources: Belgian Effie Award, 2004; www.rabobank.be; www.rabobank.nl.

Chapter 10

Don E. Schultz

THE ROOTS OF RELATIONSHIP MARKETING

THE ARTICLE SELECTED FOR relationship marketing came somewhat late in the development of the overall concept. Relationship marketing has its roots in the field of services marketing. Leonard Berry, a professor at Texas A&M University, and other colleagues in the US correctly identified the dramatic differences between physical product marketing and the marketing of various services and service-based products. That work began in the early 1970s and has evolved into a whole stream of service and service-based marketing concepts, theories and applications.

Although services marketing was well established by the late 1970s, Grönroos and others challenged and changed the approaches developed by Berry and others. Berry and his colleagues had developed services marketing along the lines of the traditional Four Ps of marketing, i.e., product, price, place and promotion, all functions under the control of the marketing organization. Grönroos, a professor at the Swedish School of Economics in Helsinki (Hanken), along with Evart Gummeson, School of Business, Stockholm University, and others developed what they called the 'Nordic school of services marketing'. In their approach, the focus was not on generating short-term, often one-time transactions with customers. Rather they focused on building long-term, on-going relationships with specific customers over time. They posited that customer value would develop and blossom if the seller treated the buyer in a service-oriented fashion. The concept of 'reciprocity' or shared value was the basis for their approach. They posited that both parties, that is, the buyer and seller, had to receive benefit if any relationship was to be built or could continue.

In the article that follows, 'Quo Vadis, Marketing? Toward a Relationship Marketing Paradigm', Grönroos became one of the pioneer academics to challenge the basic structural form of how marketing theory and practice had developed in the last half of the twentieth century. Arguing that the Four Ps of marketing were not theory at all, but simply a list of marketing variables, Grönroos developed a different theory of marketing, one based on customer relationships, not on customer transactions.

In the following article Grönroos challenged what he called the 'toolbox' approach to marketing, that is, marketing practitioners selecting various 'marketing tools' to be used against a set of commonly unidentified mass markets of customers or prospects. His argument that customers are people, not simply markets, has essentially been proven out over the past twenty or so years.

Clearly, the relationship approach developed by Grönroos and his colleagues gained added impetus as a result of the technological revolution that was occurring in the 1980s and 1990s. As marketers were able to gather more extensive and detailed knowledge and information about customers and prospects through on-going interactions and dialogues, the concept of developing on-going, long-term relationships with customers became more and more practical. Thus, in this article, we see the framework for the numerous forms of on-going, often loyalty-based, marketing programmes that have become the hallmark of sophisticated marketing firms around the world.

Perhaps the most valuable portions of the following article are the challenges Grönroos raises against traditional, and still widely accepted, marketing concepts, articulated as the Four Ps of marketing, popularized by Jerome McCarthy in the late 1950s. That argument is still raging in both the academic and the professional fields. The Grönroos's article provides a clear and solid background and argument for the student who must make the decision about what really is or should be 'marketing theory'. If nothing else, Grönroos's review of the questions about the Four Ps are justified and the bibliography provides a rich source of additional reading.

Clearly, the concept of relationship marketing is one of immense importance in today's complex and evolving marketing world. One must recognize, however, that the development and widely voiced view that customer relationship management (CRM) is a failed construct has raised serious questions about the overall value of relationship marketing. When one reads Grönroos's description of what he and the others in the 'Nordic school' define as relationship marketing, and compare it with what has developed in much of Europe and North America as CRM or techno-marketing, it becomes clear that the software-driven technologies and contact management approaches that have taken on the mantle of relationship marketing are not even closely related to what Grönroos and his associates describe in their view of creating real customer relationships.

There is an interesting link between the Grönroos article on relationship marketing in this chapter and the articles by Rapp and Collins in Chapter 5 on direct marketing. Both focus on the individual as the key element in successful marketing. Both rely extensively on new technologies. Although Grönroos does not mention technology as such, technological capabilities underlie most of his approaches to relationship marketing. The interesting intersection is that direct marketing as conceived by Rapp and Collins is focused almost entirely on physical products while Grönroos's approach is rooted in the delivery of services. Both, however, benefit from the individual approaches that are the foundation of what will likely be the marketing paradigms of the twenty-first century.

QUO VADIS, MARKETING?

Toward a Relationship Marketing Paradigm[1]

Christian Grönroos

The marketing mix and its Four Ps have remained the marketing paradigm for decades. In the article it is argued that the foundation for this paradigm is weak and that it has had negative effects on marketing research and practice. Contemporary research into services marketing and industrial marketing demonstrates that a new approach to marketing is required. This new approach is based on building and management of relationships. A paradigm shift in marketing is under way. The thoughts and actions of marketing academics and practitioners should not be constrained by a paradigm from the 1950s and 1960s.

Introduction

THE FIRST TRUE ANALYTICAL contribution to marketing was probably made by Joel Dean (e.g. 1951), an economist. However, marketing the way most textbooks treat it today was introduced around 1960. The concept of the *marketing mix* and the four P's of marketing – product, price, place and promotion – entered the marketing textbooks at that time (McCarthy 1960). Quickly they also became the unchallenged basic *theory of marketing* so totally overpowering previous models and approaches, such as, for example, the organic *functionalist* approach advocated by Wroe Alderson (1950 and 1957) as well as other systems-oriented approaches (e.g. Fisk 1967 and Fisk and Dixon 1969) and the *institutional approach* (e.g. Duddy and Revzan 1947) that these are hardly remembered even with a footnote in most textbooks of today. American Marketing Association, in its most recent definition states that 'marketing is the process of planning and executing the *conception, pricing, promotion* and *distribution* of ideas, goods and services to create exchange and satisfy individual and organizational objectives' (emphasis added) AMA Board 1985).

For decades the four P's of the marketing mix became an indisputable paradigm in academic research, the validity of which was taken for granted (Kent 1986; Grönroos 1989 and 1990a). For most marketing researchers in large parts

---

Journal of Marketing Management, Vol. 3, No. 5 (1993), pp. 347–60, reprinted, with a critical commentary by Michael Baker, *Marketing Review*, Vol. 3 (2002), pp. 129–46. With grateful acknowledgement of permission to cite this paper and the permission granted by Westburn Publishers Ltd.
Christian Grönroos, Swedish School of Economics and Business Administration. Michael J. Baker, University of Strathclyde.

of the academic world it seems to remain the marketing truth even today. Kent (1986) refers to the four P's of the marketing mix as 'the holy quadruple . . . of the marketing faith . . . written in tablets of stone' (p. 146). As he argues, 'the mnemonic of the four P's, by offering a seductive sense of simplicity to students, teachers and practitioners of marketing, has become an article of faith' (p. 145). For an academic researcher looking for tenure and promotion, to question it has been to stick out his or her neck too far. And prospective authors of textbooks, who suggest another organisation than the four P solution for their books, are quickly corrected by most publishers. As a result, empirical studies of what the key marketing variable are, and how they are perceived and used by marketing managers have been neglected. Moreover, structure has been vastly favoured over process considerations (Kent 1986).

In marketing education, teaching students how to use a toolbox has become the totally dominating task instead of discussing the meaning and consequences of the marketing concept and the process nature of market relationships. Marketing in practice has to a large extent been turned into managing this toolbox instead of truly exploring the nature of the firm's market relationships and genuinely taking care of the real needs and desires of customers.

What is the History of the Marketing Mix?

A paradigm like this has to be well founded by theoretical deduction and empirical research; otherwise much of marketing research is based on a loose foundation and the results of it questionable. Let us look at the history of the marketing mix paradigm and the four P's.

The marketing mix developed from a notion of the marketer as a 'mixer of ingredients', which was an expression originally used by James Culliton (1948) in a study of marketing costs in 1947 and 1948. The marketer plans various means of competition and blends them into a 'marketing mix' so that a profit function is optimized, or rather satisfied. The 'marketing mix' concept was introduced by Neil Borden in the 1950s (Borden 1964), and the mix of different means of competition was soon labelled the four P's (McCarthy 1960).[2]

The marketing mix is actually a list of categories of marketing variables, and to begin with this way of defining or describing a phenomenon can never be considered a very valid one. A list never includes all relevant elements, it does not fit every situation, and it becomes obsolete. And indeed, marketing academics every now and then offer additional P's to the list, once they have found the standard 'tablet of faith' too limited. Kotler (1986) has in the context of *megamarking*, added *public relations* and *politics*, thus expanding the list to six P's. In service marketing, Booms and Bitner (1982) have suggested three additional P's, *people, physical evidence* and *process*. Judd (1987) among others, has argued for just one new P, *people*.[3] Advocators of the marketing mix paradigm sometimes have suggested that *service* should be added to the list of P's (e.g. Lambert and Harrington 1989 and Collier 1991).[4] It is, by the way, interesting to notice that after the four P's were definitely canonized sometime in the early 1970s new items to the list are almost exclusively put in the form of P's.[5]

It is also noteworthy that Borden's original marketing mix included twelve elements, and that this list was not intended to be a definition at all. Borden considered it guidelines only which the marketer probably would have to reconsider in any given situation. In line with the 'mixer of ingredients' metaphor he also implied that the marketer would blend the various ingredients or variables of the mix into an integrated marketing program. This is a fact that advocators of the four P's (or five, six, seven or more P's) and of today's marketing mix approach seem to have totally forgotten.

In fact, the four P's represent a significant oversimplification of Borden's original concept. McCarthy either misunderstood the meaning of Borden's marketing mix when he reformulated the original list in the shape of the rigid mnemonic of the four P's where no blending of the P's is explicitly included; or his followers misinterpreted McCarthy's intentions. In many marketing textbooks organized around the marketing mix, such as Philip Kotler's well-known Marketing Management (e.g. 1991), the blending aspect and the need for integration of the four P's are discussed, even in depth, but such discussions are always limited due to the fact that the model does not explicitly include an integrative dimension.

The original idea of a list of a large number of marketing mix ingredients that have to be reconsidered in every given situation was probably shortened for pedagogical reasons and because a more limited number of marketing variables seemed to fit typical situations observed by the initiators of the short list of four standardized P's. These typical situations can be described as involving consumer packaged goods in a North American environment with huge mass media. However, in other markets the infrastructure is to varying degrees different and the products are only partly consumer packaged goods. Nevertheless the four P's of the marketing mix have become the *universal marketing theory* and an almost totally dominating *paradigm* for most academics, and they have had a tremendous impact on the practice of marketing as well. Is there any justification for this? Let us first look at the paradigm itself.

The Nature of the Marketing Mix

As has previously been said, the marketing mix is a list of variables, and we have already pointed out the shortcomings of such a way of defining a phenomenon. Moreover, any marketing paradigm should be well set to fulfil the *marketing concept*, i.e. the notion that the firm is best off by designing and directing its activities according to the needs and desires of customers in chosen target markets. How well is the marketing mix fit to do that?

One can easily argue that the four P's of the marketing mix are badly fit to fulfil the requirements of the marketing concept. As Dixon and Blois (1983) put it, '. . . indeed it would not be unfair to suggest that far from being concerned with a customer's interests (i.e. somebody *for whom* something is done) the views implicit in the four P approach is that the customer is somebody *to whom* something is done!' (emphasis added) (p. 4). To use a marketing metaphor, the marketing mix and its 4 P's constitute a *production-oriented* definition of marketing, and not a market-oriented or customer-oriented one (see Grönroos 1989 and 1990a). Moreover, although McCarthy (1960) recognizes the interactive nature of the P's, the model itself does not explicitly include any interactive elements. Furthermore, it does not indicate the nature and scope of such interactions.

The marketing mix makes marketing seem so easy to handle and organize. Marketing is separated from other activities of the firm and delegated to specialists who take care of the analysis, planning and implementation of various marketing tasks, such as market analysis, marketing planning, advertising, sales promotion, sales, pricing, distribution and product packaging. Marketing departments are created to take responsibility for the marketing function of the firm, sometimes together with outside specialists on, for example, market analysis and advertising. Both in the marketing literature and in everyday marketing vocabulary the expression *marketing department*, and organisational unit, is used as a synonym for *marketing function*, which is the process of taking care of the fulfilment of customer needs and desires. As a consequence, the rest of the organization is alienated from marketing, and the marketers are isolated from design, production, deliveries, technical service, complaints handling, and other activities of the firm.

In conclusion, the problems with the marketing mix paradigm are not the number or conceptualization of the decision variables, the P's, as the American Marketing Association as well as the authors of most publications criticising the marketing mix paradigm argue. Rather, the problem is of theoretical nature. The four P's and the whole marketing mix paradigm are, theoretically, based on a loose foundation, which in a recent *Journal of Marketing* article was demonstrated by van Watershoot and Van den Bulte (1992; see also Van den Bulte 1991 and Kent 1986). Many marketing-related phenomena are not included (Moller 1992), and as John Arndt (1980 and 1985) has concluded, marketing research remains narrow in scope and even myopic, and methodological issues become more important than substance matters. 'Research in marketing gives the impression of being based on a conceptually sterile and unimaginative positivism. . . . The consequence . . . is that most of the resources are directed toward less significant issues, overexplaining what we already know, and toward supporting and legitimizing the status quo.' (Arndt 1980, p. 399). Unfortunately, far too little has changed in mainstream marketing research since this was written over a decade ago.

The usefulness of the four P's as a general marketing theory for practical purposes is, to say the least, highly questionable. Originally, although they were largely based on empirical induction, they were probably developed under the influence of microeconomic theory and especially the theory of monopolistic competition of the 1930s (e.g. Chamberlin 1933), in order to add more realism to that theory. However, very soon the connection to microeconomic theory was cut off and subsequently totally forgotten. Theoretically, the marketing mix became just a list of P's without roots.

Marketing Variables in Economic Theory and in Parameter Theory

A closer analysis of the nature of the marketing mix shows that it is not a remarkable leap forward from microeconomic theory as developed 60 years ago. As Dixon and Blois (1983) observe, when discussing the work of Chamberlin (1933) and Joan Robinson (1933), '. . . thus Joan Robinson's . . . writing discusses the subdivision of market and the firm's response through the use of the price elements of the four P's. At the same time Chamberlin . . . recognizes that all aspects of the product, location, communication, as well as price may be altered with subsequent effects on demand' (p. 5). Chamberlin's basic decision variables were price, product and promotion, although in his theory of monopolistic competition, price was treated as the main variable. In this same tradition, for example, researchers such as Brems (1951) and Abbott (1955) added new decision variables to the traditional price variables of economic price theory. However, as Mickwitz (1959) observes, instead of price they '. . . have put quality in the centre of their systems' (p. 9). This is an interesting fact to observe today when quality again has become a key issue in business practice and research. For example, Abbott, who uses the term 'quality competition', has an astonishingly modern view of quality: 'The term "quality" will be used . . . in its broadest sense, to include all the qualitative elements in the competitive exchange process – *materials, design, services provided, location* and so forth' (Abbott 1955, p. 4) (emphasis added). The two other decision variables in his system were price and advertising (including sales promotion).

Later, but well before the four P's were formulated as the ultimate marketing wisdom for decades, Gosta Mickwitz (1959) and others (e.g. Kjaer-Hansen 1945 and Rasmussen 1955), representing a research approach for which Mickwitz (1966) coined the label 'Copenhagen School', discussed an expanded view along the same lines, which they labelled *parameter theory*. This theoretical approach, especially as it is presented by Gosta Mickwitz was, in fact, theoretically more developed and more realistic than the four P's of today's mainstream marketing literature. As Mickwitz (1959) observes, 'when empirically based works on marketing mechanisms show that the enterprise uses a number of different parameters markedly distinct from each other, a theory of the behaviour of the enterprise in the market will be very unrealistic if it is content to deal only with . . . [a few] . . . of them. We have therefore tried throughout to pay attention to the presence of a number of different methods which firms employ in order to increase their sales' (p. 237). The interactive nature of the marketing variables was explicitly recognized and accounted for in parameter theory by means of varying markets elasticities of the parameters over the product life cycle.

The concept 'parameter theory' further developed by Mickwitz was originally suggested by Arne Rasmussen (1955). However, the foundation for it was laid much earlier by Frisch (1933), who in 1933 introduced the idea of *action parameters*, although he did not in detail discuss more parameters than price and quality. In 1939, von Stackelberg expanded the number of parameters into a larger system (von Stackelberg 1939). He did not, however, go into any details in his analysis. Although it had its shortcomings, parameter theory was a step forward towards managerial realism, and it also had a theoretical base due to its background in microeconomic theory.

In conclusion, when analysing the firm's use of marketing variables, it is not unfair to say that as the parameter theory of the 1950s was a definite leap forward from the expanded price theory in the form of, for example, Chamberlin's theory of monopolistic competition of the 1930s, the introduction of the for P's of the marketing mix with their simplistic view of reality can be characterized as a step back to the level of, in a sense equally simplistic, microeconomic theory of the 1930s.

Contemporary Theories of Marketing

In most marketing textbooks the marketing mix paradigm and its four P's are still considered *the* theory of marketing. And indeed, this is the case in much of the academic research into marketing, especially in North America but also to a considerable extent in other parts of the world as well. However, since the 1960s, alternative theories of marketing have been developed. As Möller (1992) observes in a recent overview of research traditions in marketing, 'from the functional view of marketing "mix" management our focus has been extended to the strategic role of marketing, aspects of service marketing, political dimensions of channel management, interactions in industrial networks; to mention just a few evolving trends' (p. 197). Some of these theories have been based on studies of the market relationships of firms in specific types of industries. In this section the emerging theories and models of the *interaction/network approach to industrial marketing* and the *marketing of services* will be discussed. In the final section the *relationship marketing* concept will be described.

The *interaction/network* approach to industrial marketing originated in Sweden at Uppsala University during the 1960s (see, for example, Blankenburg and Holm 1990) and has since spread to a large number of European countries. Between the parties in a network various interactions take place, where exchanges and adaptations to each other occur. A flow of goods and information as well as financial and social exchanges takes place in the network. (See, for example, Håkansson 1982, Johanson and Mattsson 1985 and Kock 1991.) In such a network the role and forms of marketing are not very clear. All exchanges, all sorts of interactions have an impact on the position of the parties in the network. The interactions are not necessarily initiated by the seller – the marketer according to the marketing mix paradigm – and they may continue over a long period of time, for example, for several years.

The seller, who at the same time may be the buyer in a reciprocal setting, may of course employ marketing specialists, such as sales representatives, market communication people and market analysts but in addition to them a large number of persons in functions which according to the marketing mix paradigm are non-marketing, such as research and development, design, deliveries, customer training, invoicing and credit management, have a decisive impact on the marketing success of the 'seller' in the network. Gummesson (1987) has coined the term *part-time marketers* for such employees of a firm. He observes that in industrial markets and in service businesses, the part-time marketers typically outnumber several time the fulltime marketers, i.e. the marketing specialists of the marketing and sales departments. Furthermore, he concludes that 'marketing and sales departments (the full-time marketers) are not able to handle more than a limited portion of the marketing *as it staff cannot be at the right place at the right time with the right customer contacts*' (Gummesson 1990, p. 13). Hence, the part-time marketers do not only outnumber the full-time marketers, the specialists, often they are the only marketers around.

In the early 1970s the marketing of services started to emerge as a separate area of marketing with concepts and models of its own geared to typical characteristics of services. In Scandinavia and Finland the *Nordic School of Services* more than research into this field elsewhere looked at the marketing of services as something that cannot be separated from overall management (see Grönroos and Gummesson 1985). In North American research into service marketing has to a much greater extent remained within the boundaries of the marketing mix paradigm, although it had produced some creative results (e.g. Berry 1983, Berry and Parasuraman 1991). Grönroos brought quality back into a marketing context by introducing the *perceived service quality* concept in 1982 (Grönroos 1982), and he introduced the concept of the *interactive marketing function* (Grönroos 1979 and 1982) to cover the marketing impact on the customer during the consumption process, where the consumer of a service typically interacts with systems, physical resources and employees of the service provider. In France, Langeard and Eiglier (e.g. 1987) developed the *servuction* concept for this system of interactions. These interactions occur between the customer and employees who normally are not considered marketing people, neither by themselves nor by their managers, and who do not belong to a marketing or sales department. Nevertheless, they are part-time marketers. In many situations long-lasting relationships between service providers and their customers may develop. Again, the marketing success of a firm is only partly determined by the 'full-time marketers'. In fact, the 'part-time marketers' of a service provider may often have a much more important impact on the future purchasing decisions of a customer than for example, professional sales people or advertising campaigns (e.g. Gummesson 1987 and Grönroos 1990a).

The New Approaches and the Marketing Mix

The interaction and network approach of industrial marketing and modern service marketing approaches, especially the one by the Nordic School, clearly views marketing as an interactive process in a social context where *relationship building* and *management* is a vital cornerstone. They are in some respects clearly related to the systems-based approaches to marketing of the 1950s (compare, for example, Alderson 1957). The marketing mix paradigm and its four P's, on the other hand, is a much more clinical approach, which makes the seller the active part and the buyer and consumer passive. No personalized relationship with the producer and marketer of a product is supposed to exist, other that with professional sales representatives in some case.

Obviously, this later view of marketing does not fit the reality of industrial marketing and the marketing of services very well. Moreover, the organisational approach inherent in the marketing mix paradigm that puts marketing in the hands of marketing specialists in a marketing department is not very useful either (see, for example, Piercy 1985, and Grönroos 1982 and 1990a). The psychological effect on the rest of the organisation of a separate marketing department is, in the long run, often devastating to the development of a customer orientation or market orientation in a firm. A *marketing orientation* with, for example, high-budget advertising campaigns may be developed, but this does not necessarily have much to do with true *market orientation* and a real appreciation for the needs and desires of the customers. The existence or introduction of such a department may be a trigger that makes everybody else lose whatever little interest in the customers they may have had (Grönroos 1982). The marketing department approach to organising the marketing function has isolated marketing from other business functions and vice versa. Therefore, it has made it difficult, often even impossible, to turn marketing into the 'integrative function' that would provide other departments with the market-related input needed in order to make the organization truly market-oriented and reach a stage of 'coordinated marketing' (compare Kotler 1991, pp. 19–24).

The development of innovative theories, models and concepts of industrial marketing (interaction/network approach) and service marketing has clearly demonstrated that the marketing mix paradigm and its four P's finally have reached the end of the road as *the universal* marketing theory. Marketing research can, again, make a similar leap forward as the development of parameter theory out of the price-dominated microeconomic theory was in the 1950s. Parameter theory with its theoretical analysis of market elasticities was at least to a considerable degree market oriented, whereas from a theoretical point of view the marketing mix paradigm and the four P's turned the clock back.

From a management point of view the four P's, undoubtedly, may have been helpful. The use of various means of competition became more organized. However, the four P's were never applicable to all markets and to all types of marketing situations. The development of alternative marketing theories discussed above demonstrate that even from a management perspective, the marketing mix and its four P's became a problem. The pedagogic elegance and deceiving sense of simplicity made practical marketing management look all too clinical and straightforward even for actors in the consumer packaged goods field where they were originally intended to be used.

Consumer goods amounts to a considerable business, and there the four P's could still fulfil a function. However, many of the customer relationships of manufacturers of consumer goods are industrial-type relationships with wholesalers and retailers, and the retailers of consumer goods more and more consider themselves service providers. In such situations the four P's have less to offer even in the consumer goods field. Moreover, as far as the marketing of consumer goods from the manufacturer to the ultimate consumers is concerned, there is a growing debate whether one can continue to apply marketing in the traditional mass marketing way. Regis McKenna (1991), a respected marketing consultant and writer, concludes in a discussion about the decline in North America of advertising, the flagship of traditional marketing, that 'the underlying reasons behind . . . [this decline] . . . is advertising's dirty little secret: it serves no useful purpose. In today's market, advertising simply misses the fundamental point of marketing – adaptability, flexibility, and responsiveness' (p. 13). Undoubtedly, this is to take it a little bit to the extreme, but the point is well taken. An interest in turning anonymous masses of potential and existing customers into interactive relationships with well-defined customers is becoming increasingly important. However, the grip of the marketing mix paradigm as the 'marketing faith' is in many parts of the world so strong among academics working in the field of consumer goods marketing that this discussion seems to go on mostly between marketing practitioners (see, for example, Rapp and Collins 1990, McKenna 1991 and Clancy and Shulman 1991). In some standard marketing textbooks, though, one can already see some signs of these new concepts and approaches (e.g. Kotler 1991).

The Future: The Relationship Marketing Concept

The concept *relationship marketing* has emerged within the fields of service marketing and industrial marketing (e.g. Berry 1982, Jackson 1985a, Grönroos 1989 and 1990b, Grönroos 1991, and Gummesson 1987 and 1990). To a considerable extent both these approaches to marketing are based on establishing and maintaining relationships between sellers and buyers and other parties in the marketplace. Grönroos (1990a) defines relationship marketing in the following way: 'Marketing is to establish, maintain and enhance . . . relationships with customers and other partners, at a profit, so that the objectives of the parties involved are met. This is achieved by a mutual exchange and fulfilment of promises' (p. 138). Such relationships are usually but not necessarily always long term.

An integral element of the relationship marketing approach is the *promise concept*, which had been strongly emphasized by Henrik Calonius (e.g. 1988). According to him the responsibilities of marketing do not only, or predominantly, including giving promises and thus persuading customers as passive counterparts on the marketplace to act in a given way. Fulfilling promises that have been given is equally important as means of achieving customer satisfaction, retention of the customer base, and long-term profitability (compare also Reichheld and Sasser 1990). He also stresses the fact that promises are mutually given and fulfilled.

Relationship marketing is still in its infancy as a marketing concept. Its importance is recognized to a growing extent, however. Philip Kotler (1992) concludes in a recent article that 'companies must move from a short-term *transaction-oriented* goal to a long term *relationship-building* goal' (p. 1). So far, there seems to be only two books for textbook purpose that are based on this emerging paradigm (Christopher et al., 1992 in English and Blomqvist et al., 1993 in Swedish). However, relationship marketing is clearly the underlying approach in several books on service marketing (e.g. Grönroos 1990a and Berry and Parasuraman 1991) and industrial marketing (e.g. Håkansson 1982, Jackson 1985b and Vavara 1992). In a growing number of articles relationship issues are addressed (e.g. Jackson 1985a, Gummesson 1987, Sonnenberg 1988, Grönroos 1987 and 1990b, Copulinsky and Wolf 1990 and Czepiel 1990) and conferences on relationship marketing are being arranged. The importance of relationship building is advancing even into books from the world of consumer goods marketing (see, for example, Rapp and Collins 1990). In the future, this marketing approach most certainly will be the focal point of marketing research, thus positioning itself as a leading marketing paradigm. However, remembering the damaging long-term effects of the marketing mix, hopefully it will not establish itself as the only one.

Some Final Observations

Why has the marketing mix paradigm and the four P model become such a straightjacket for markets? The main reason for this is probably the pedagogical virtues of the four P's that makes teaching marketing so easy and straightforward. The simplicity of the model seduces teachers to toolbox thinking instead of constantly reminding them of the fact that marketing is a social process with far more facets than that. As a consequence of this researchers and marketing managers are also constrained by the simplistic nature of the four P's. The victims are marketing theory and customers.

The marketing mix paradigm served a function at one time in the development of marketing theory. However, when it established itself as the universal truth in marketing, it started to cause more harm than good. Most damaging is the fact that marketing and the marketers have become so isolated in the organization. Both from an organizational point of view and from a psychological standpoint the marketing department is off side. Relationship marketing requires the support of people in other departments and business functions to be effective and successful. Today, this is very difficult to achieve.

Furthermore, the marketing specialists organized in a marketing department may get alienated from the customers. Managing the marketing mix means relying on mass marketing. Customers become numbers for the marketing specialists, whose actions, therefore, are typically based on surface information obtained from market research reports and market share statistics. Frequently such 'full-time marketers' act without ever really having encountered a real customer.

The marketing department concept is obsolete and has to be replaced by some other way of organizing the marketing function, so that the organization shall have a chance to become market oriented. A traditional marketing department will always, in the final analysis, stay in the way of spreading market orientation and an interest in the customer throughout the organization (compare Piercy 1985, and Grönroos 1982 and 1990a).

Finally, the marketing mix paradigm and the four P's have alienated people in the rest of an organization from marketing and from the 'full-time markets', and vice versa. The term marketing has become a burden for the marketing function. Managers as well as their subordinates in other departments and functions do not want to take part in the marketing function. But according to the relationship marketing approach and contemporary models of industrial marketing and service marketing they do undoubtedly belong to this function. The use of the marketing mix paradigm and the four P's has made it very difficult for the marketing function to earn credibility. Some firms have solved this problem not only by downscalling or altogether terminating their marketing departments but also by banning the use of the term marketing for the marketing function (compare Grönroos 1982). Perhaps we even need this kind of semantics.

In the final analysis, what we are experiencing today with the growing awareness of the relationship marketing approach is a return to the 'natural' systems-oriented way of managing customer relationships that existed before marketing became a far too clinical decision making discipline, and an over-organized and isolated function. But even if the marketing mix is dying as a dominating marketing paradigm and the four P model needs to be replaced, this does not mean that the P's themselves would be less valuable than before as marketing variables. For example, advertising, pricing and product branding will still be needed, but along with a host of other activities and resources. However, what marketing deserves is new approaches, new paradigms, which are more market oriented and where the customer indeed is the focal point as suggested by the marketing concept. After all, we experience the enormous change and complexity of the 1990s. Our thoughts and actions should not be constrained by a paradigm from the 1950s and 1960s.

Notes

1 This paper was first published in the *Journal of Marketing Management* (1994), Volume 10, Issue 5, pp. 347–360

2 McCarthy was not, however, the first person to organize marketing variables in a four P-like structure. The first marketing textbook organized in this way was published by Harry Hansen (1956), where he used the following six categories product policy, distribution channel, advertising, personal selling, pricing and sales programs.

3 As a matter of fact, even in the homeland of the marketing mix there has been at least some debate about this paradigm. However, the basic way of handling the problem has always been to use the same clinical approach, i.e. to simplify the market relationship by developing a list of decision making variables. No real innovativeness and challenge of the foundation of the paradigm have been presented. In the 1960s and early 1970s, categories which did not begin with the letter P were suggested, e.g. Staudt and Taylor 1965, Lipson and Darling 1971 and Kelly and Lazer 1973 (three categories each), whereas the letter P almost always has been present in lists of categories put forward in the 1980s and 1990s, e.g. Traynor 1985 (five categories), Johnson 1986 (twelve), Keely 1987 (four C's), Berry 1990 1990, Mason and Mayer 1990 (six), Collier 1991 (seven) and LeDodoux 1991 (five)

4 This would be disastrous, because it would isolate customer service as a marketing variable from the rest of the organization, just as has happened with the four P marketing mix variable. It would effectively counteract all attempts to make customer service a responsibility of everyone and not of a separate department only

5 In spite of all the additional categories of marketing variables that have been offered by various authors, there is only one textbook that is thoroughly based on anything else than the four P's. Donald Cowell's (1984) book on the marketing of services which is organized around the seven P framework.

References

Abbott, L. (1955), *Quality and Competition*, New York, NY, Columbia University Press

Alderson (1950), 'Survival and Adjustment in Organized Behavior Systems', In: Cox, R. and Alderson, W. (Eds), *Theory of Marketing*, (Homewood, IL), Irwin, pp.65–88

Alderson, W. (1957), *Marketing Behavior and Executive Action*, Homewood, IL, Irwin

AMA Board Approves New Marketing Definition, *Marketing News*, 1 March 1985

Arndt, J. (1985), 'On Making Marketing Science More Scientific: Role of Orientations, Paradigms, Metaphors, and Puzzle Solving', *Journal of Marketing*, Vol. **49**, Summer, pp. 11–23

Berry, D. (1990), 'Marketing Mix for the 90's Adds an S and 2 C's to the 4 P's', *Marketing News*, 24 December p. 10

Berry, L.L. (1983), 'Relationship Marketing', In: Berry, L.L., Shostack, G.L. and Upah, G.D. (Eds), *Emerging Perspectives of Services Marketing*, Chicago, IL, American Marketing Association, pp.25–28

Berry, L.L. and Parasuraman, A. (1991), *Marketing Services. Competing Through Quality*, Lexington, MA, Free Press/Lexington Books

Blankenburg, D. and Holm, U. (1990), 'Centrala steg I utvecklingen av natverks-synsattet inom Uppsalaskolan', In: Gunnarsson, E. and Wallerstedt, E. (Eds), *Uppsalaskolan och dess rotter (The Uppsala School and its Roots)*, Uppsala University, Sweden

Blomqvist, R., Dahl, J. and Haeger, T. (1993), *Relationsmarknadsforing Strategi och metod fōr servicekonkurren, (Relationship marketing. Strategy and Methods for Service Competition)*, Goteborg, Sweden, IHM Forlag

Booms, B.H. and Bitner, M.J. (1982), 'Marketing Strategies and Organization Structures for Service Firms', In: Donnelly, J.H. and George, W.R. (Eds), *Marketing of Services*, (Chicago, IL), American Marketing Association, pp.47–51

Borden, N.H. (1964), 'The Concept of the Marketing Mix', *Journal of Advertising Research*, Vol. **4**, June, pp.2–7

Brems, H. (1951), *Product Equilibrium under Monopolistic Competition*, Cambridge, MA, Harvard University Press

Bruner, II, G.C. (1980), The Marketing Mix: Time for Reconceptualization', *Journal of Marketing Education*, Vol. **11**, summer, pp.72–77

Calonius, H. (1988), 'A Buying Process Model', In: *Innovative Marketing – A European Perspective*, (Eds), Blois, K. and Parkinson, S., *Proceedings from the XVIIth Annual Conference of the European Marketing Academy*, University of Bradford, England, pp.86–103

Chamberlin, E.H. (1933), *The Theory of Monopolistic Competition*, Cambridge, MA, Harvard University Press

Christopher, M., Payne, A. and Ballantyne, D. (1992), *Relationship Marketing Bringing Quality, Customer Service and Marketing Together*, London, Butterworth

Clancy, K.J. and Shulman, R.S. (1991), *The Marketing Revolution. A Radical Manifesto for Dominating the Marketplace*, New York, NY, Harper Business

Collier, D.A. (1991), 'New Marketing Mix Stresses Services', *The Journal of Business Strategy*, Vol. **12**, March-April, pp.42–45

Copulinksly, J.R. and Wold, M.J. (1990), 'Relationship Marketing: Positioning for the Future', *Journal of Business Strategy*, Vol. **11**, July/August, pp.116–120

Cowell, D. (1984), *The Marketing of Services*, London, Heinemann

Culliton, J.W. (1948), *The Management of Marketing Costs*, Boston, MA, Harvard University

Czepiel, J.A. (1990), 'Managing Relationships with Customers: A Differentiating Philosophy of Marketing', In: Bowen, D.E. and Chase, R.D. (Eds), *Service Management Effectiveness*, (San Francisco, CA), Jossey-Bass, pp.299–323

Dean, J. (1951), *Managerial Economics*, New York, NY, Prentice-Hall

Dixon, D.F. and Blois, K.J. (1983), *Some Limitations of the 4P's as a Paradigm for Marketing*, Marketing Education Group Annual Conference, Cranfield Institute of Technology, UK, July

Duddy, E.A. and Revzan, D.A. (1947), *Marketing. An Institutional Approach*, New York, NY, McGraw-Hill

Fisk, G (1967), *Marketing Systems*, New York, Harper and Row

Fisk, G. and Dixon, D.F. (1967), *Theories of Marketing Systems*, New York, Harper and Row

Frisch, R. (1933), 'Monopole – Polypole – la notion de la force dans l'economie', *Nationalokonomisk Tidsskrift*, Denmark, pp.241–259

Grönroos, C. (1979), *Marknadsforing av tjanster. En Studie av marknadsforingsfunktionen / tjansteforetag* (Marketing of Services. A study of the marketing function of service firms), With an English summary (diss, Swedish School of Economics and Business Administration Finland), Stockholm, Akademilittertur/Marketing Technique Center

Grönroos, C. (1982), *Strategic Management and Marketing in the Service Sector*, Helsingfors, Finland: Swedish School of Economics and Business Administration (published in 1983 in the US by Marketing Science Institute and in the UK by Studentlittertur/ Chartwell-Bratt)

Grönroos, C. (1989), 'Defining Marketing: A Market-Oriented Approach', *European Journal of Marketing*, Vol.**23**, No.1, pp.52–60

Grönroos, C. (1990a), *Service Management and Marketing. Managing the Moments of Truth in Service Competition*, Lexington, MA, Free Press/Lexington Books

Grönroos, C. (1990b), 'Relationship Approach to the Marketing Function in Service Contexts: The Marketing and Organizational Behavior Interface', *Journal of Business Research*, Vol.**20**, No.1, pp.3–12

Grönroos, C. (1991), 'The Marketing Strategy Continuum. A Marketing Concept for the 1990's', *Management Decision*, Vol.**29**, No.1, pp.7–13

Grönroos, C. and Gummesson, E. (1985), 'The Nordic School of Service Marketing', In: Grönroos, C. and Gummesson, E. (Eds), *Service Marketing – Nordic School Perspectives*, Stockholm University, Sweden, pp.6–11

Gummesson, E. (1987), 'The New Marketing – Developing Long-Term Interactive Relationships', *Long Range Planning*, Vol.**20**, No.4, pp.10–20

Gummesson, E. (1990), *The Part-Time Marketer*, Karlstad, Sweden, Center for Service Research

Hansen, H.L. (1956), *Marketing: Text, Cases and Readings*, Homewood, IL, Irwin

Håkansson, H. (Ed) (1982), *International Marketing and Purchasing of Industrial Goods*, New York, NY, Wiley

Jackson, B.B. (1985a), 'Build Customer Relationships That Last', *Harvard Business Review*, Vol.**63**, November/December, pp.120–128

Jackson, B.B. (1985b), *Winning and Keeping Industrial Customers. The Dynamics of Customer Relationships*, Lexington, MA, Lexington Books

Johanson, J. and Mattsson, L-G. (1985), 'Marketing Investments and Market Investments in Industrial Networks', *International Journal of Research in Marketing*, No.4, pp.185–195

Johnson, A.A. (1986), 'Adding more P's to the Pod or – 12 Essential Elements of Marketing', *Marketing News*, 11 April, p.2

Judd, V.C. (1987), 'Differentiate with the 5th P: People', *Industrial Marketing Management*, Vol.**16**, November, pp.241–7

Kelly, E.J. and Lazer, W. (1971), *Managerial Marketing*, Homewood, IL, Irwin

Kent, R.A. (1986), 'Faith in four P's: An Alternative', *Journal of Marketing Management*, Vol. **2**, No.2, pp.145–154

Keeley, A. (1987), 'The "New Marketing" Has Its Own Set of P's', *Marketing News*, Vol.**21**, 6 November, pp.10–11

Kjaer-Hansen, M. (1945), *Afsaetningsokonomi* (Marketing), Copenhagen, Denmark, Erhvervsokonomisk Forlag

Kock, S. (1991), *A Strategic Process for Gaining External Resources through Long-Lasting Relationships*, Helsingfors/Vasa, Finland, Swedish School of Economics and Business Administration

Kotler, p. (1986), 'Megamarketing', *Harvard Business Review*, Vol.**64**, March/April, pp.117–124

Kotler, p. (1991), *Marketing Management. Analysis, Planning and Control*, 7th ed., Englewood Cliffs, NJ, Prentice-Hall

Kotler, p. (1992), 'It's Time for Total Marketing', *Business Week ADVANCE Executive Brief*, Vol. **2**

Lambert, D.D. and Harrington, T.C. (1989), 'Establishing Customer Service Strategies within the Marketing Mix: More Empirical Evidence', *Journal of Business Logistics*, Vol. **10**, No. 2, pp.**44**–60

Langeard, E. and Eiglier, p. (1987), *Servuction. Le marketing des Services*, Paris, Wiley

LeDoux, L. (1991), 'Is Preservation the Fifth "P" or Just Another Microenvironmental Factor?', In: McKinnon, G.F. and Kelley, C.A. (Eds), *Challenges of New Decade in Marketing Education*, Western Marketing Educators' Association, pp.82–86

Lipson, H.A. and Darling, J.R. (1971), *Introduction to Marketing: An Administration Approach*, New York, NY, Wiley

Mason, B. and Mayer, M.L. (1990), *Modern Retailing Theory and Practice*, Homewood, IL, Irwin

McCarthy, E.J. (1960), *Basic Marketing*, Homewood, IL, Irwin

McKenna, R. (1991), *Relationship Marketing. Successful Strategies for the Age of the Customer*, Reading, MA, Addison-Wesley

Mickwitz, G. (1959), *Marketing and Competition*, Helsingfors, Finland, Societas Scientarium Fennica (available from University Microfilms, Ann Arbor, MI)

Mickwitz, G. (1966), 'The Copenhagen School and Scandinavian Theory of Competition and Marketing', In: Kjaer-Hansen, M. (Ed.), *Readings in Danish Theory of Marketing*, Copenhagen, Denmark, Erhvervsokonomisk Forlag (originally published in Det Danske Marked, May 1964)

Mickwitz, G. (1982), 'Non-linearities in the Marketing Mix of International Trade', *Discussion and working papers, No. 168*, University of Helsinki, Finland

Möller, K. (1992), 'Research Traditions in Marketing: Theoretical Notes', In: Blomqvist, H.C., Grönroos, C. and Lindqvist, L.J. (Eds), *Economics and Marketing. Essays in Honour of Gosta Mickwitz*, Economy and Society, No. 48, Helsingfors, Finland, Swedish School of Economics and Business Administration

Piercy, N. (1985), *Marketing Organisation An Analysis of Information Processing, Power and Politics*, London, George Allen and Unwin

Reichheld, F.E. and Sasser, Jr, W.E. (1990), 'Zero Defections. Quality Comes to Service', *Harvard Business Review*, Vol.**68**, September/October, pp.105–111

Rapp, S. and Collins, T. (1990), *The Great Marketing Turnaround*, Englewood Cliffs, NJ, Prentice-Hall

Rasmussen, A. (1955), *Pristeori eller parameterteori – studier omkring virksomhedens afsetning* (Price theory or parameter theory – studies of the sales of the firm), Copenhagan, Denmark, Erhvervsokonomisk Forlag

Robinson, J. (1933), *The Economics of Imperfect Competition*, London, Macmillan

Shugan, S. (forthcoming), *Marketing and Managing Services. A Context Specific Approach*, Homewood, IL, Dow-Jones-Irwin

Sonnenberg, H. von (1939), 'Theorie der Vertriebspolitik und der Qualitatsvariation', *Schmollers Jahrbuch*, 63/1

Staudt, T.A. and Taylor, D.A. (1965), *Marketing: A Managerial Approach*, Homewood, IL, Irwin

Traynor, K. (1985), 'Research Deserves Status as marketing's Fifth "P" ', *Marketing News* (special marketing manager's issue), 8 November

Van den Bulte, C. (1991), 'The Concept of Marketing Mix Revisited: A Case Analysis of Metaphor in Marketing Theory and Management', *Working Paper*, State University of Ghent, Belgium

Vavara, T.G. (1992), *Aftermarketing. How to Keep Customers for Life Through Relationship Marketing*, Homewood, IL, Business One Irwin

Waterschoot, W. van and Vanden Bulte, C. (1992), 'The 4P Classification of the Marketing Mix Revisited', *Journal of Marketing*, Vol. **56**, October, pp. 83–93

QUO VADIS? RETROSPECTIVE COMMENT

Michael J. Baker

TO BE INVITED BY the author to write a retrospective comment on a piece of work that has been chosen for republication as a 'Marketing Classic' is very flattering. So much so that one tends not to consider the implications. First, if this paper is considered a 'classic' then it has already found favour with one's peers so you need to be doubly careful about any criticism you make of it. Second, this is not a blind review and your identity will be known to all. Third, do you really have the expertise to comment in the first place? On the assumption that you have read the original, you will have to decide this for yourself.

As Grönroos acknowledges he was not the first to criticize the dominance of the marketing mix as the theoretical foundation of modern marketing practice. For example, in 1986 the *Journal of Marketing Management* had carried an article by R. A. Kent in which he deprecated the 'seductive simplicity' of the 4Ps and the way in which they had come to monopolize textbook writing and teaching – a point of view that was widely supported by a number of other European scholars at the time.

Nor was Grönroos the first to propose Relationship Marketing as an alternative paradigm that better reflected the marketing concept, the nature of the marketing process and the real needs of customers. As he points out, alternative theories concerned with the interaction/network approach to industrial marketing had begun to emerge in the 1960s. Similarly, the Nordic School evolved an original approach to the marketing of services in the 1970s while the Americans were seeing this as an application of mix principles to a distinctive sub-field of marketing. He observes 'The Nordic School clearly views marketing as an interactive process in a social context where *relationship building* and *management* is a vital cornerstone.'

Surprisingly, though, Grönroos makes no mention of a seminal paper that appeared in the *Journal of Marketing* in 1992 that had a radical effect on both research and practice in the USA – Fred Webster's 'The Changing Role of Marketing in the Corporation' – in which he advocated what many would regard as the blueprint for relationship marketing. This despite the fact that Webster was blissfully unaware of earlier and parallel developments in Europe.

So why should this paper be considered a classic? Well, it was timely, it is well written, it summarizes the main arguments against the production-oriented, oversimplified framework and toolbox methodology predicated by the 4Ps, and it points to alternative models that capture better the interactive and processual nature of marketing. Further, despite overlooking Webster, he identified Relationship Marketing as an important development when it was still in its infancy. In sum, he provided a powerful critique of a mechanistic and increasingly inappropriate way to practice marketing while offering credible alternative procedures.

And in retrospect? Perhaps Grönroos' main contribution is that he cautioned against the wholesale adoption of relationship marketing as a complete substitute for the old mix paradigm. Rather, he advocates a variety of theoretical explanations each suited to a given context but all representing the application of the marketing concept.

In making this recommendation Grönroos anticipated many of the criticisms that have emerged of relationship marketing as a universal solution to all marketing issues. Clearly, most consumers of mass produced, mass distributed convenience goods are not looking for a relationship with the seller and a mix management approach may well satisfy them better. Similarly, many regard the very idea of 'Customer Relationship Management' as oxymoronic and antithetical to the true nature of a relationship. If we are not careful the rhetoric of relationship marketing is liable to displace the reality.

One should also consider the fact that the last issue of *The Marketing Review* contained a 'classic' and a retrospective comment by its authors, namely 'Vanishing Point: The Mix Management Paradigm Re-Viewed'. This paper first appeared in 1998 four years after 'Quo Vadis' and the retrospective written in 2002 makes it clear that the marketing mix model is still with us.

Our own view is summarized in Chapter 1 of *The Marketing Book* (2003). The true marketing concept is concerned with mutually satisfying exchange relationship in which both parties get what they want – a win-win outcome that reflects the Golden Rule – 'Do unto others as you would be done by'. Implementation of this concept/orientation demands the existence of a marketing function and the management of the extended marketing mix. But, given the variety and complexity of possible exchange relationships, no single solution exists and multiple explanations are to be encouraged.

References

Baker, Michael J. (2003), 'One more time – what is marketing?', Chapter 1 *The Marketing Book*, 5th Edition, edited by Michael J Baker, Oxford: Butterworth-Heinemann

Kent, R. A. (1986) 'Faith in the 4Ps: An Alternative', *Journal of Marketing Management*, **2**(2), pp. 145–154

Webster, F.E. (1992) 'The Changing Role of Marketing in the Corporation', *Journal of Marketing*, **56** (October), pp. 1–17

? Questions

1 The basic concept of the 'marketing mix' is still favoured by a large number of marketing organizations. Why do you believe this concept is still so prevalent today in spite of the availability of marketing information that allows the marketing manager to focus increasingly on individual customers?

2 If the Four Ps of marketing are not truly a marketing theory but simply a list of marketing variables, how and in what way can a true theory of marketing be developed?

3 From the bibliography in the Grönroos article select two or three readings describing different marketing concepts or methodologies, i.e. the 'interaction/network' approach, 'parameter theory', the 'functionalist' approach or other. Compare and contrast those with the traditional four Ps of marketing and the Grönroos relationship approach. Which better supports the basic view of marketing as being an organizational initiative designed to gain and serve customers profitably?

4 Develop a methodology by which you would attempt to move a traditional marketing organization, that is, one focused on the four Ps of marketing, to one that could focus on on-going customer relationships. What would be the basic changes that would have to occur in the organization to make that change?

5 Grönroos suggests that most marketing in the organization is conducted by 'part-time marketers', that is, employees who have other tasks and duties in the organization and are generally untrained for marketing activities. Suggest a way the organization might go about training and developing the skills and abilities of these 'part-time marketers' to make them more proficient and focused on long-term relationships with customers and prospects.

6 Why do you believe customer relationship management (CRM) has often failed in organizations? Identify some examples where it has been successful.

Vignette

Creating Myriad Relationships: Federal Express

Anecdotal stories about the extra services Federal Express couriers have provided to customers, above and beyond the pick-up and delivery of parcels and overnight letters, are almost legend. For example, on their Web site (http://www.fedex.com/us/about/overview/people/?link) FedEx has a listing of specific examples of the unusual 'above-and-beyond' activities of employees. A site search showed stories such as the courier who stopped by a store to pick up three cans of beans for a snowbound customer, another courier who helped assemble stems in a set of wheels so the customer's shipment could go out on time and several other stories of couriers who helped accident victims when they happened across them on their route deliveries.

It is this type of what FedEx calls the 'absolutely, positively' service tradition that has become a key element in the FedEx organization. And it is what has enabled them to build long-term and on-going relationships with their customers. Indeed, FedEx typifies the focus the organization has developed that personifies Grönroos's view that marketing is done, for the most part, by 'part-time' marketers, that is, everyone and anyone within the organization who touches or interacts with customers and prospects is a 'marketer'. This focus on customer relationships is one of the reasons FedEx has grown sales to almost $25 billion based on the premier service/quality levels provided by the more than 240,000 employees and contractors all over the world. In addition, FedEx has consistently been named one of the 'World's Most Admired Companies' by *Fortune* magazine and is regularly listed as one of the '100 Best Companies to Work for in America' and, one of the 'fifty Best Companies for Minorities'.

The focus on relationships permeates the entire FedEx organization. That starts with the firm's three-pronged corporate philosophy of 'people–service–profits'. These three elements drive how the firm is organized, managed and how it measures its success.

People are still the key element at FedEx even though the organization has developed one of the most sophisticated logistical distribution systems in the world. The company truly believes it is the FedEx people who make the difference, whether they be the customer-facing courier, the customer service representatives or the manager focused on retaining and expanding the relationship with each individual customer. The company focuses on customer relationships and bases them on such factors as internal training, vertical and horizontal communication all the way to the 'Service Quality Indicator' (SQI) system that tells every employee how well the company did on customer service the day before.

FedEx builds customer relationships by being organized around customers and customer groups, not around products and services. As a result of its generally daily contacts with customers through their package shipments and receipts, the firm collects massive amounts of data and information on each of them. This customer information is used to provide internal analyses ranging from the proper level of service to provide to the resolution of service problems to the identification of likely future customer needs. FedEx has taken the concept of customer relationships and interaction to the point where it has provided computer software to customers that allows them to track the progress of their shipments themselves through the vast and complex FedEx distribution and logistic system. Customers can actually see, on their own computer screens, where each and every one of their shipments is at any given point in time. This is what FedEx calls 'transparency', that is, helping their customers understand what FedEx is doing at all times to help them and build the on-going relationships that are so important.

All these efforts are summarized in the emphasis FedEx puts on customer satisfaction. If there is no customer satisfaction, there can be no customer relationship. Thus each FedEx employee is trained and is constantly reminded of the value of customer service and satisfaction. And these concepts are not just empty phrases, FedEx tracks and measures on-going customer satisfaction through formal studies, through strategic communication audits all the way to face-to-face visits by managers with customers and prospects in the field. These efforts are co-ordinated by a dozen or so 'quality action teams' headed by a vice-president who is responsible for the improvement of one portion of the SQI customer satisfaction measurement tool.

Relationship marketing, as outlined by Grönroos in the article, is a practical and likely profitable approach for many organizations to take. But it does require a commitment on the part of management and employees to move marketing from something like a department or group of people do to something the organization does. If FedEx is any indicator, organizations which practise relationship marketing will likely be the ones that will succeed in the twenty-first-century market place.

Chapter 11

Don E. Schultz

MARKETING METRICS: FROM TACTICAL TO STRATEGIC MEASURES

MEASUREMENT OF MARKETING EFFECTS has always been difficult, for a number of reasons.

Historical marketing management has focused on 'outputs', i.e. creating deliverable marketing programmes, not on 'outcomes' or measurable results. This comes from the four Ps marketing management approach that encourages managers to combine organizational resources to create external programmes. Unfortunately, no 'feedback loop' to organizational returns is commonly included in the process (McCarthy 1975; Kotler 2003).

Marketing research measures have been based on attitudinal, not behavioural change. Historically, marketing research has used psychological measures such as consumer awareness, recognition, intent to purchase and the like to determine impact. While these measures have been helpful in understanding consumer 'take away' of marketing activities, they have been most difficult to connect to financial returns (Aaker 1991; Kotler 2002).

Marketing effects almost always occur in the future, but most marketing metrics are based on historical results. Since the market place is dynamic, historical measures are often not very relevant in terms of their predictive ability (Haigh 2003).

Organizations tend to be assemblages of functional specializations, i.e. marketing, finance, human resources, information technology, etc. Functional managers generally dedicate themselves to measuring the impact of their specialized discipline, ignoring the impact and effect of other organizational factors. Since consumers commonly respond to a bundle of product or service benefits, price, availability, on-going service and the like, it has been difficult to parse out the specific effects of marketing elements alone (McDonald et al. 2000).

In most traditional accounting and finance approaches, marketing is treated as an expense, not an investment. Since marketing expenditures are viewed as current period costs, there has been little incentive to develop investment and return methodologies (Ambler 2003).

Because of these inherent activities and beliefs, marketing practitioners, researchers and academics have devoted little attention to finding ways to measure marketing effects or returns. And, since senior management has often been content to treat marketing as an optional expense, the marketing spend being primarily determined by the short-term success of the firm, there has been little pressure to change the measurement tools.

While there have been some efforts to develop metrics for specific functional activities such as advertising, sales promotion, direct marketing and the like, general marketing metrics, certainly at the firm level, were, until the middle 1990s, more smoke than fire.

With the rise of quantitative management systems such as Six Sigma, EVA, Balanced Scorecards and the like, emphasis on marketing metrics has increased at the senior management level. These activities, generally ones that started in the middle 1980s, focused more attention on the management of the firm's intangible assets. It has developed much more rapidly from the 1990s (Ambler 2003).

The article featured in this chapter, 'Market-based Assets and Shareholder Value: a Framework for Analysis', by Srivastava, Shervani and Fahey (1998), has provided the impetus for moving marketing measurement from the analysis of short-term sales events to the more strategic view of marketing as a corporate resource to be invested in and valued over the longer term.

Prior to the development of the 'market-based assets' view developed and used in this article, senior management often viewed marketing measurement as 'soft and squishy' and an 'inexact science' at best, since the focus was on attitudinal change. And, as above, attitudinal change has proved most difficult to relate back to financial investments and returns. Therefore, most marketing measures were not considered terribly relevant or very reliable.

Day and Fahey (1998) were two of the first to suggest that marketing measurement could be raised to a more sophisticated and strategic level. In their article 'Valuing Marketing Strategies' they argued that measurable financial effects could and did occur as a result of management's choice and implementation of specific marketing strategies. Thus the marketing strategy the firm employed had much to do with the overall financial success it achieved in the market place. And, most important, that value could be tied directly to increases in shareholder value.

While the Day and Fahey concept was interesting, few senior managers, and even fewer marketing managers, appeared to accept the approach as a significant management tool. Financial measurement of marketing effects simply wasn't within the realm of what marketing managers did or how they perceived their role and responsibilities. Indeed, it took a decade, until 1998, for Srivastava et al. to create the intellectual underpinnings and develop the relevant concepts to move marketing metrics to the next level. Their approach has influenced a spate of new marketing measurement and metrics, as described in the Vignette that follows.

The approach Srivastava and his colleagues proposed provided an entirely new view of the value of marketing to the firm. Rather than marketing being an assemblage of tactical activities, the 'market-based assets' approach allowed managers to consider marketing as a strategic resource, one that could be planned, developed, managed, measured and compared with other alternative uses of finite corporate resources. This article articulated the basic concepts that underlie a number of new marketing measurement techniques that have been developed over the past few years (Ambler 2003; Doyle 2000; Blattberg et al. 2001).

As can be seen in the article, Srivastava and his associates have related basic accounting and financial approaches, already well accepted in organizational management, to the field of marketing. They have developed the view that marketing strategy can be used by managers to influence the overall value of the firm. They accomplished this by creating an effective internal interface between marketing and finance within the company.

Where these two groups have always been considered as oil and water – finance deals with tangible assets and economic returns while marketing is more focused on intangible assets and intellectual property – the model Srivastava et al. created brought the two together, logically and effectively.

The key ingredient in the approach is the idea of market-based assets, assets that are created by the co-mingling of the firm and its activities and engagements with various external entities. The basic premise they proposed was that various marketing activities could increase the value of the firm's market-based assets. By the proper management of those assets, the company could increase shareholder value over both the short and long-terms.

The process Srivastava and his colleagues developed is fairly simple. They first identify the customer and partner relationships that marketing activities generate for the firm. These relationships are then related to various market performance improvements that can occur, things such as price and share premiums, faster market penetration and the like. These activities create differential cash flows for the firm. Then they relate the changes in cash flows, such as cash-flow acceleration, cash-flow increases, stabilization of cash flow and the like, to increases in shareholder value. It is the use of cash flows and the management of those cash flows over time that provides the base for the concept.

Cash-flow analysis, which is central to every accounting and financial calculation, thus becomes the central focus for the development of marketing metrics. Clearly, the principles Srivastava et al. lay out in this seminal article have created a whole new type, form and level of marketing measurement. For that reason we consider it one of the most important articles in the entire field of marketing management. Understanding the concepts contained in the article will do much to equip the marketing student or practitioner to move to the next level of marketing management.

MARKET-BASED ASSETS AND SHAREHOLDER VALUE: A FRAMEWORK FOR ANALYSIS

Rajendra K. Srivastava, Tasadduq A. Shervani and Liam Fahey

The authors develop a conceptual framework of the marketing – finance interface and discuss its implications for the theory and practice of marketing. The framework proposes that marketing is concerned with the task of developing and managing market-based assets, or assets that arise from the commingling of the firm with entities in its external environment. Examples of market-based assets include customer relationships, channel relationships, and partner relationships. Market-based assets, in turn, increase shareholder value by accelerating and enhancing cash flows, lowering the volatility and vulnerability of cash flows, and increasing the residual value of cash flows.

> Too often marketing tends to focus on sales growth and market share, and it fails to recognize the impact of marketing decisions on such variables as inventory levels, working capital needs, financing costs, debt-to-equity ratios, and stock prices. To assume such factors are *purely* the responsibility of finance is to be guilty of a kind of marketing myopia not less damaging than that originally envisioned by Levitt (1960).
>
> (Paul Anderson, 'The Marketing Management/ Finance Interface')

THERE IS A QUIET revolution in the positive way that marketing activities are being viewed by some marketing professionals, enlightened senior managers, and innovative managers in other functions, particularly finance. Old inviolable assumptions about the purpose, content, and execution of marketing slowly are giving way to assumptions that more accurately reflect how it is practiced in leading organizations. In this article, we identify the new assumptions pertaining to the marketing – finance interface and discuss their consequences for the theory and practice of marketing.

Although they often are unstated, assumptions underlie. shape, and constrain both theory and practice (Hunt 1983; Senge 1990). Therefore, it is imperative that marketers continually identify and articulate changes in the underlying assumptions regarding the field of marketing. In particular, as the movement to adopt shareholder value-based measures of firm performance continues, marketing's traditional assumptions must be extended to address the marketing – finance interface. These new assumptions about the relationship between marketing and finance do not replace the traditional assumptions: rather, they add to and incorporate them. Marketing's traditional assumptions and the additional assumptions regarding the marketing – finance interface are summarized in Table 1.

Journal of Marketing, Vol. 62 (January 1998), pp. 2–18.

Rajendra K. Srivastava is Senior Associate Dean and Jack R. Crosby Hegent's Chair in Business, Graduate School of Business; and Tasadduq A. Shervani is an assistant professor. Department of Marketing, University of Texas at Austin. Liam Fahey is an adjunct professor, Babson College and Cranfield University (UK). The authors are grateful to three anonymous reviewers for their helpful comments.

Table 1 Assumptions about the marketing–finance interface

	Traditional assumptions	*Emerging assumptions*
Purpose of marketing	Create value for customers; win in the product marketplace	Create and manage market-based assets to deliver shareholder value
Relationship between marketing and finance	Positive product–market results translate into positive financial results	Marketing–finance interface must be managed systematically
Perspective on customers and channels	The object of marketing's actions	A relational asset that must be cultivated and leveraged
Input to marketing analysis	Understanding of the marketplace and organization	Financial consequences of marketing decisions
Conception of assets	Primarily specific to the organization	Result from the commingling of the organization and the environment
Marketing decision-making participants: internal	Principally marketing professionals; others if deemed necessary	All relevant managers irrespective of function or position
Marketing stakeholders: external	Customers, competitors, channels, regulators	Shareholders, potential investors
What is measured	Product–market results; assessments of customers, channels, and competitors	Financial results; configuration of market-based assets
Operational measures	Sales volume, market share, customer satisfaction, return on sales, assets, and equity	Net present value of cash flow; shareholder value

Traditionally, marketing activities focus on success in the product marketplace. Increasingly, however, top management requires that marketing view its ultimate purpose as contributing to the enhancement of shareholder returns (Day and Fahey 1988). This change has led to the recognition that the relationship between marketing and finance must be managed systematically; no longer can marketers afford to rely on the traditional assumption that positive product-market results will translate automatically into the best financial results. As a result, marketers are adopting the perspective that customers and channels are not simply the objects of marketing's actions; they are assets that must be cultivated and leveraged (cf. Hunt and Morgan 1995). These assets can be conceptualized as *market-based assets*, or assets that arise from the commingling of the firm with entities in its external environment. Lever-aging such assets requires marketers to go beyond the traditional inputs to marketing analysis, such as marketplace and organizational knowledge, and to include an understanding of the financial consequences of marketing decisions. Indeed, it also expands the external stakeholders of marketing to include explicitly the shareholders and potential shareholders of the firm and requires broader input into marketing decision making by other functional managers.

Another shift in the mind-set of marketers is occurring in the direction of expanding the set of measures of the success or failure of marketing activities. Marketers are moving beyond traditional financial measures – such as sales volume, market share, and gross margin – to include additional financial measures, such as the net present value of cash flows and hence shareholder value (Anderson 1979; Day and Fahey 1988; Pessemier and Root 1973). Indeed, it is interesting to note that as marketers are moving to assess the impact of marketing activities on shareholder value, accountants and finance professionals are broadening their thinking to include nonfinancial measures of firm performance as a means to develop a more 'balanced scorecard' (cf. Kaplan and Norton 1992, 1993).

As the new marketing assumptions emerge, the question is not whether marketing activities are useful and valuable but why marketing has played such a limited role in the process of strategy formulation (cf. Anderson 1981, 1982; Day 1992; Webster 1981, 1992). In our view, an important reason is that the marketing community historically has found it difficult, if not nearly impossible, to identify, measure, and communicate to other disciplines and top management the financial value created by marketing activities. Almost a decade ago, Day and Fahey (1988, p. 45) highlighted the increasing importance of new measures of firm performance that are linked closely to shareholder value: 'Managers of diversified companies are rapidly replacing their usual yardsticks of performance, such as market share, growth in sales, or return on investment, with approaches that judge market strategies by their abilities to enhance shareholder value.'

Although Day and Fahey (1988) and Day (1992) hoped that increasing acceptance of shareholder value as a yardstick for judging market strategies would encourage a close integration of marketing and financial perspectives, this has happened only to a limited extent. Despite the growing importance of shareholder value creation as a criterion for evaluation of strategic initiatives, attention to the role of marketing strategies in the creation of shareholder value has been relatively sparse in the marketing literature. Among the notable exceptions are event studies that link 'events,' such as new product announcements, brand extension announcements, celebrity endorsement announcements, and so on, to abnormal changes in the stock prices of firms (cf. Aaker and Jacobsen 1994; Agrawal and Kamakura 1995; Chaney, Devinney, and Winer 1991; Horsky and Swyngedouw 1987; Lane and Jacobsen 1995; Simon and Sullivan 1993).[1] At the same time, the finance literature has all but ignored the contribution of marketing activities to the creation of shareholder value. Consequently, financial appraisals of marketing strategy seldom involve trying to value long-term marketing strategies with uncertain outcomes (Barwise, Marsh, and Wensley 1989).

The purpose of this article is to develop a conceptual framework that makes explicit the contribution of marketing to shareholder value. To do so, we advance the notion of market-based assets as a principal bridge between marketing and shareholder value. Although internal processes, such as superior product development or customer intelligence, also can be leveraged to enhance shareholder value, our focus here is exclusively on external, market-based assets. As Constantin and Lusch (1994) point out, marketing activities are primarily external in their focus and are largely off the balance sheet.

The absence of a comprehensive conceptual framework that identifies and integrates the many linkages between marketing and finance has grave implications for the funding of marketing activities and the financial well-being of the firm. Aaker and Jacobsen (1994) note that assets that are harder to measure are more likely to be underfunded. In the absence of a strong understanding of the marketing – finance interface, marketing professionals cannot but have great difficulty in assessing the value of marketing activities. This, in turn, limits investment in marketing activities, which can restrict the ability of the firm to create shareholder value. Indeed, there is a growing recognition that a significant proportion of the market value of firms today lies in intangible, off-balance sheet assets, rather than in tangible book assets. 'Market-to-book' ratios for the *Fortune* 500 are approximately 3.5, which suggests that more than 70 percent of the market value of the *Fortune* 500 lies in intangible assets (Capraro and Srivastava 1997). As Lusch and Harvey (1994, p. 101) note, 'Organizational performance is increasingly tied to intangible assets such as corporate culture, customer relationships and brand equity. Yet controllers, who monitor and track firm performance, traditionally concentrate on tangible, balance-sheet assets such as cash, plants and equipment, and inventory.' Furthermore, as Lusch and Harvey (1994) observe, little has been done in the past 20 years to project more accurately the 'true' asset base of the corporation in the global marketplace. Thus, a failure to understand the contribution of marketing activities to shareholder value continues to diminish the role of marketing thought in corporate strategy.

We expect the framework developed in this article to advance both the conceptual understanding of the marketing – finance interface and the assessment and measurement of the value created by marketing activities. Following the example of Day and Fahey (1988), we discuss this framework partially in the language of finance, so that the communication of the value of marketing activities to other functions and top management is facilitated. To the best of our knowledge, this is the first attempt to develop a comprehensive framework of the impact of marketing activities on shareholder value.[2]

The rest of the article is organized as follows: We first define and describe what we mean by market-based assets. Next, in the context of discussing financial valuation approaches, we briefly discuss methods of asset valuation and identify the key drivers of shareholder value. Following this, we draw the linkages between market-based assets and the drivers of shareholder value and discuss how market-based assets can be leveraged to drive shareholder value. We conclude with a deliberation of the implications and potential applications of the framework.

Market-based Assets

To define, categorize, and leverage market-based assets (Sharp 1995), it is essential first to clarify the meaning, importance, and principal characteristics of the base construct – assets. Although there is much debate in the management, marketing, finance, and economics literature as to what constitutes an asset or a resource (Mahoney and Pandian 1992), an *asset* can be defined broadly as any physical, organizational, or human attribute that enables the firm to generate and implement strategies that improve its efficiency and effectiveness in the marketplace (Barney 1991). Thus, assets can be tangible or intangible, on or off the balance sheet, and internal or external to the firm (cf. Constantin and Lusch 1994). However, regardless of the type of asset, the definition clearly emphasizes that the value of any asset ultimately is realized, directly or indirectly, in the external product marketplace.

But which assets contribute to winning strategies or real advantage in prolonged marketplace rivalry? Which assets create and sustain value for customers and shareholders? And how can those assets that contribute more to value generation be distinguished from others? Or, stated differently, what makes an asset valuable? These questions constitute fundamental theoretical and practical issues at the heart of research in finance (Fama and Miller 1972: Stein 1989), strategy (Grant 1991), organizational economics (Barney and Ouchi 1986), industrial organization (Conner 1991), and marketing (Glazer 1991).

The resource-based perspective on what accounts for competitive success (Amit and Schoemaker 1993; Hunt and Morgan 1995; Itami 1987; Peteraf 1993) suggests that an asset is more likely to contribute to value generation when it satisfies the following four tests:

1 It is convertible: If the firm can use the asset to exploit an opportunity and/or neutralize a threat in the external environment, then the potential to create and sustain value is enhanced.
2 It is rare: If the asset is possessed by multiple rivals, its potential to be a source of sustained value is diminished.
3 It is imperfectly imitable: If it is difficult for rivals to imitate the asset, the potential to sustain value is enhanced.
4 It does not have perfect substitutes: If rivals do not possess strategically equivalent convertible assets and it is difficult to develop them, then the potential to sustain value is enhanced.

Therefore, if market-based assets are to contribute to customer and financial value, they must satisfy these four tests to some extent. However, before considering whether they do, we must retine the notion of market-based assets.

Types of market-based assets

Market-based assets are principally of two related types: relational and intellectual. Such assets are primarily external to the firm, generally do not appear on the balance sheet, and are largely intangible. Yet stocks of these assets can be developed, augmented, leveraged, and valued. And, as we discuss subsequently, because of their characteristics, they are suited particularly to meeting the resource value tests noted previously.

Relational market-based assets are outcomes of the relationship between a firm and key external stakeholders, including distributors, retailers, end customers, other strategic partners, community groups, and even governmental agencies. The bonds constituting these relationships and the sources of them can vary from one stakeholder type to another. For example, brand and channel equity reflect bonds between the firm and its customers and channels. Brand equity may be the result of extensive advertising and superior product functionality. Channel equity may be in part a result of long-standing and successful business relationships between the firm and key channel members.

Intellectual market-based assets are the types of knowledge a firm possesses about the environment, such as the emerging and potential state of market conditions and the entities in it, including competitors, customers, channels, suppliers, and social and political interest groups (cf. Nonaka and Takeuchi 1995). The content or elements of knowledge include facts, perceptions, beliefs, assumptions, and projections. The content of each type and its sources vary greatly from one to another. Thus, a firm may develop projections of the way its industry will evolve so that it knows how it will react when total industry sales decline by a particular percentage or when a substitute product might emerge. Or a firm may develop over time unique facts, beliefs, and assumptions about its customers' tastes, manufacturing processes, or proclivities to respond in certain ways to promotion, sales, and pricing moves (cf. Glazer 1991).

The development and evolution of relational and intellectual market-based assets intertwine in many ways. Both evolve in part out of the firm's unavoidable interaction with entities in its environment. Intimacy of relationships enables knowledge to be developed, tested, and refined. Knowledge of the environment guides the firm in choosing which entities to align with, how to do so, and when. Relationships with and knowledge of specific entities often are developed by the same set of individuals. Customer service personnel, because of the relationships they develop with multiple distinct sets of customers, often generate unique insight into customers' backgrounds, behaviors, and propensities. Relational and intellectual market-based assets also share several common characteristics. Both assets are intangible; they cannot be inventoried or divided physically into specific portions. Yet both can be assessed in terms of their stock and flow. *Stock* refers to a specific amount or extent of brand equity or knowledge of customers' purchasing criteria possessed by a firm. *Flow* refers to the extent to which a stock of a particular asset is augmenting or decaying. Thus, a firm can strive to augment its knowledge of a corporate customer's buying processes, the persons involved in it, and the organizational systems supporting them.

Market-based assets: three propositions

There are several interrelated research streams in the marketing literature that contribute to the concept of market-based assets: brand equity (cf. Aaker 1991; Keller 1993; Shocker, Srivastava, and Ruekert 1994), customer satisfaction (cf. Anderson and Sullivan 1993; Yi 1990), and the management of strategic relationships (cf. Anderson and Narus 1996; Bucklin and Sengupta 1993). These research streams collectively demonstrate that stronger customer relationships are created when the firm uses knowledge about buyer needs and preferences to build long-term relational bonds between external entities and the firm. Our purpose is not to provide an extensive review of this literature but to summarize their implications in an integrative framework.

Three central propositions for market-based assets now can be stated. First, the greater the value that can be generated from market-based assets for external entities, the greater their satisfaction and willingness to be involved with the firm and, as a consequence, the greater the potential value of these marketplace entities to the firm. Second, the more market-based assets satisfy the asset tests noted previously, the greater the value they generate and sustain for external entities. Third, shareholder value is created to the extent that the firm taps or leverages these market-based assets to improve its cash flows.

Market-based assets: generating customer value

The concept of market-based assets, as delineated previously, can be refined and extended through comparison with the more familiar notion of tangible, balance-sheet assets. Perhaps the distinguishing characteristic of internal, tangible, balance-sheet assets, such as plant and equipment, raw materials, supplies, inventory, and finished products, is that there is a market for them – they can be bought and sold (see Table 2). However, the value of such assets to any organization ultimately is not only their market or trade value, but also their value in use. Unless assets possess some value in use, they fail the critical initial test of potential contribution to competitive success noted previously; they are not convertible. In a nutshell, tangible assets can be leveraged by an organization to

1. Lower costs by enhancing productivity;
2. Enhance revenues through higher prices if, for example, the raw materials and equipment lead to superior product functionality, features, and durability;
3. Serve as a barrier to entry or mobility barrier because others must make similar investments:
4. Provide a competitive edge to the extent that they make other assets (e.g., employees) more valuable; and
5. Provide managers with options, for example, if the plant or equipment can be shared across products.

For these reasons, the value of many tangible assets, such as plant and equipment, raw materials, and finished products, historically has been measured and presented on balance sheets. Some tangible assets, such as plant and equipment, are capitalized and amortized over time. Unfortunately, compared with tangible assets, the value of market-based assets is harder to measure, does not appear on balance sheets, and therefore is less likely to be recognized. Furthermore, marketing expenditures to acquire and retain customers, develop brands,

Table 2 Attributes of balance sheet and off-balance sheet assets

Property	*Balance sheet assets*	*Off-balance sheet assets*
Type of asset	Largely tangible	Largely intangible
Examples	Plant and equipment	Market-based assets such as customer/brand and channel relationships
Can they be bought and sold?	Yes. Tangible property has salvage value	Yes. For example, AT&T's acquisition of McCaw Cellular
Can they be leveraged to lower costs?	Yes, by enhancing productivity	Yes. They can result in lower sales and service costs due to superior knowledge of customers and channels
Can they be leveraged to command higher prices or share?	Yes. Superior product quality or functionality can be used to justify higher prices	Yes. Brand and channel equity lead to higher perceived value that may be tapped through price or share premiums
Can they generate entry barriers?	Yes. Others must make similar investments to be competitive	Yes. Customer switching costs and loyalty reduce competitive vulnerability
Can they provide a competitive edge?	Yes. They can make other assets, such as employees, more productive	Yes, by making other resources more productive (e.g., satisfied buyers are more responsive to marketing efforts)
Can they create options for managers?	Yes, if plant and equipment can be shared across products	Yes. Satisfied customers are more likely to try brand and category extensions
Are asset acquisition costs capitalized?	Yes. Plant and equipment can be paid for over several years	No. Marketing costs are 'expensed' and must be justified in the short run

and create channel and other partnerships most often are 'expensed' – that is, they cannot be depreciated over time. Therefore, as less visible assets that must be paid for immediately, it is not surprising that market-based assets often are not valued and nurtured in the same way as assets that are important for, by way of example, supply-chain effectiveness and efficiencies. However, it is important to recognize that market-based assets can be utilized in the same manner as tangible, balance-sheet assets. They also can be leveraged by the firm to

1. Lower costs; superior relationships with and knowledge of channels and customers lead to lower sales and service costs;
2. Attain price premiums; brand and channel equity lead to higher perceived value;

3 Generate competitive barriers; customer loyalty and switching costs render channels and customers less inclined to purchase from rivals;
4 Provide a competitive edge by making other resources more productive (e.g., satisfied buyers are more responsive to marketing efforts); and
5 Provide managers with options – for example, by creating trial for brand and category extensions.

Not only can market-based assets be used for much the same purposes as tangible, balance-sheet assets, but they also are more likely to serve as a basis of long-term, sustained customer value for three specific though related reasons. First, market-based assets are more likely to satisfy the four resource-based tests noted previously. Second, they add to the value-generating capability of physical assets. Third, they are suited ideally to exploit the benefits of organizational networks. We discuss each separately.

Satisfy resource-based tests. Unless relational and intellectual assets are convertible into customer value, the remaining resource-based tests are irrelevant (Barney 1991). Knowledge is perhaps the ultimate source of opportunity (Drucker 1993; Leonard-Barton 1995): It is embedded in research and development; it guides product innovation; it energizes marketing and sales. Relationships now are so widely viewed as essential to opportunity creation that they are encapsulated in what has become known as 'relationship marketing' (Sheth and Parvatiyar 1995). Furthermore, relationships with end users can be exploited in building relationships with other entities (e.g., distributors).

Knowledge and relationships are often rare and in some cases may be unique. For example, some firms ability to project the future evolution of market sectors using scenarios and related tools provides a unique insight into emerging opportunities, how best to exploit these opportunities, what contingent strategies should be developed, and how to monitor which 'future' is emerging (Van der Hijden 1996). Such knowledge enables firms to exploit first-mover advantages, respond appropriately to the moves of competitors, and avoid the penalties associated with brash market moves (Kerin, Varadarajan, and Peterson 1992).

The intangible nature of market-based assets renders relational and intellectual assets extremely difficult to imitate (Hall 1992, 1993). Knowledge and relationships are socially complex and tacit phenomena. The intimacy of relationships with channels and customers attained by such firms as Home Depot, Nordstrom, and Johnson Controls has proved almost impenetrable by many rivals (Treacy and Wiersema 1995). Moreover, efforts to replicate these assets often necessitate extensive investments in marketing, sales, service, and human resources development with little, if any, guarantee of success.

Finally, knowledge and relationships present profound difficulties to rivals seeking to develop direct substitutes, that is, assets that enable them to pursue similar strategies. If a firm possesses truly unique knowledge of its customers, then a competitor must develop either another form of knowledge (such as technology knowledge) or another type of asset (perhaps a one-of-a-kind manufacturing process) that will enable it to achieve the same marketing outcomes. If, for example, the firm is using its distinct customer knowledge to customize its solutions (Pine 1993), it might be extremely difficult for rivals to develop substitute equivalent assets that will enable them to customize their solutions.

Add value to tangible assets. The role and importance of market-based assets is augmented further when the frequency with which they add to the value-generating capability of physical assets is recognized (Lane and Jacobsen 1995). For example, knowledge of customers' changing tastes and buying criteria enables a firm to adapt its manufacturing and engineering processes to produce products with the functionality and features demanded by customers. Strong customer relationships, manifested in channel and brand equity, enable a firm to commit human resources to entrepreneurial activity such as developing new products, extending existing product lines (Leonard-Barton 1995), and customizing existing solutions (Pine 1993). A firm's market-based assets can create value by exploiting not only the firm's own tangible assets, but also the tangible assets of partner firms. Thus, a manufacturing firm's relationship with a retailer (a market-based asset) can be used to leverage the retailer's physical asset (e.g., shelf space) to create value for the manufacturing firm.

Indeed, a strong argument can be made that relational and intellectual assets are necessary to invigorate and unleash the customer value-generating potential embedded in tangible assets such as plant and machinery and products. Without knowledge of and relationships with external entities, such as customers, channels, suppliers, and other strategic partners, marketing capabilities inherent in organizational processes, such as new product development, order fulfillment, and speed to market (Day 1994), can be neither created nor leveraged. Knowledge and relationships are essential sources of these capabilities and, in turn, are extended and augmented by the successful execution of these capabilities. Recent research (e.g., Badaracco 1991; Quinn 1992) has provided evidence of conceptual quagmires and managerial conundrums that ensue when researchers and managers fail to recognize that knowledge and relationships not only undergird every form of distinctive customer advantage but also are the essential building blocks of every form of competence or capability.

Exploit the benefits of networks. Finally, market-based assets underlie benefits that can be derived from 'networks' or product ecosystems. As individual firms increasingly become the nodes in an interconnected web of formal and informal relationships with external entities (Quinn 1992), including suppliers, channels, end customers, industry and trade associations, technology sources, advertising agencies, universities, and in many instances even competitors, their capacity to generate, integrate, and leverage knowledge and relationships extends considerably beyond the resources they own and control. For example, Intel's Pentium microprocessor's successful defense against both Digital Equipment Corporation's Alpha and the IBM/Motorola/Apple PowerPC chips is in part related to its network of users, original equipment manufacturers, and software vendors. Each network link enables customer value generation beyond what could be created by the nodal firm alone or any other network entity operating on its own. Therefore, a network can be viewed as a coordinated set of knowledge sources and cooperative relationships.

Illustrations of the role and importance of networked market-based assets are widely evident. A firm's offerings to customers become stronger when bolstered with superior service by members of the network. A car manufacturer can provide superior products that become even more valuable when accompanied by outstanding service provided by its dealers. A software publisher is likely to be more attentive to a hardware manufacturer with a dominant buyer installed base. Collectively, networked producers of complementary products are more valuable to buyers. Consequently, networked market-based assets help a firm create value over and above that created by market-based assets individually. Thus, the value of a network of market-based assets can be greater than the sum of its individual components.

Impact of market-based assets

To assess the value of market-based assets, we present a conceptual framework that links the contribution of these assets to the financial performance of the firm and begins to suggest ways in which the value of marketing activities can be identified, measured, and communicated. Figure 1 depicts the proposed framework.

In the first column in Figure 1, we present the two types of market-based assets – customer and partner relationships – that we focus on in this article. These relationships are formed on the basis of value delivered to customers through enhanced product functionality, such as superior performance, greater reliability and durability, unique features, better product and service quality, wider availability, greater ease of use, lower levels of perceived risks, higher levels of trust and confidence, and better reputation and image. This value is the

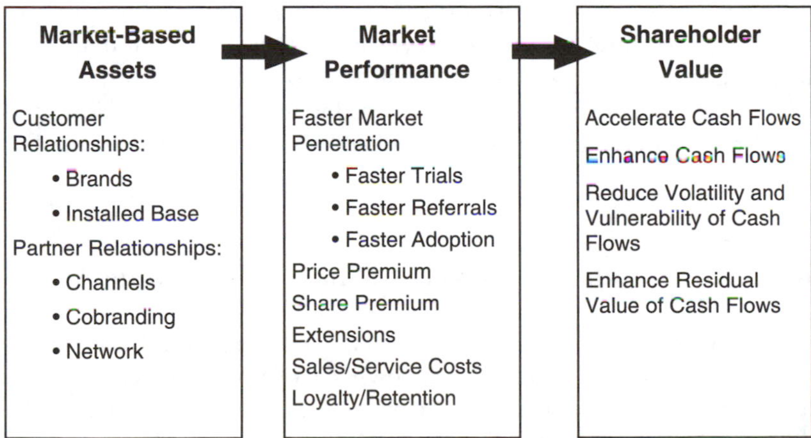

Figure 1 Linking market-based assets to shareholder value

basis for customer satisfaction and its surrogates. If customers are end consumers, customer satisfaction is linked directly to brand equity. For each brand, there are those who like and buy that brand and those who do not. Hence, it is important to note that brand equity is linked to the installed base of users. If customers are channel members, the same concepts apply, but the specific attributes might be different. For example, whereas automobile buyers might focus on manufacturer-provided leasing programs, dealers might be responsive to inventory financing programs.

The entries in the first column of Figure 1 represent outcomes of activities designed to deliver value to customers, and those in the second column summarize the consequences of customer behavior that are considered desirable by firms. That is, the second column deals with outcomes of customer satisfaction or brand equity and represents various measures of market performance. For example, research over the past decade shows that marketing activities such as advertising can lead to more differentiated and therefore more monopolistic products characterized by lower own-price elasticity (Boulding, Lee, and Staelin 1994). Brand equity can be tapped in a variety of ways. It enables firms to charge higher prices (Farquhar 1989), attain greater market shares (Boulding, Lee, and Staelin 1994), develop more efficient communications programs because well-differentiated brands are more responsive to advertising and promotions (Keller 1993: Smith and Park 1992), command greater buyer loyalty and distribution clout in the marketplace (Kamakura and Russell 1994), deflect competitive initiatives (Srivastava and Shocker 1991), stimulate earlier trial and referrals of products (Zandan 1992), and develop and extend product lines (Keller 1993; Keller and Aaker 1992). These conclusions are similar to findings from research on the effects of customer satisfaction and relationship marketing. The consequences of customer satisfaction include payoffs, such as buyer willingness to pay a price premium, use more of the product, and provide referrals, as well as lower sales and service costs and greater customer retention and loyalty (Reichheld 1996; Reichheld and Sasser 1990).

Although market-based assets can be expected to boost market performance and lower risks, little is known about how the stock market values the capability of market-based assets to enhance current and potential market performance. In the next section, we attempt to alleviate this shortcoming by examining asset valuation approaches to identify key drivers of shareholder value. These drivers – acceleration and enhancement of cash flows, reduction in the volatility and vulnerability of cash flows, and growth of residual value – are listed in the last column in Figure 1.

Asset Valuation Methods and Drivers of Shareholder Value

The valuation of assets is controversial. A variety of financial and accounting approaches has been proposed, each with its own set of problems. One way to value assets is on the basis of their costs. For example, the *book value* of a firm is based on the accounting value (costs less depreciation) associated with creating the firm's assets. But historical costs associated with creating businesses do not reflect true costs today, leading some financial accountants to argue that the value of a firm should be based on the *replacement value* of the assets it owns. Unfortunately, replacement costs are notoriously hard to estimate, especially for intangible assets, such as intellectual property, brand names, and customer relationships. Consequently, book values and replacement values typically ignore the value of intangibles.

In recent years, it has become accepted widely that the difference between the book value and the market value of the firm is accounted for by intangible assets that are not recognized by today's standard accounting practices (Lowenstein 1996; Rappaport 1986). To the extent that the market value of a firm is greater than the book or replacement values, the differences can be attributed to intangible assets not captured by current accounting practices (Lane and Jacobsen 1995; Simon and Sullivan 1993). With 'market-to-book' ratios averaging 3.5 and 'market-to-replacement cost' ratios (or Q-ratios) averaging approximately 1.9 for the *Fortune* 500, it is clear that a substantial portion of a firm's market value is in intangible assets (Capraro and Srivastava 1997).

That financial markets are willing to pay price premiums in excess of book values for most firms leads to the question of how intangible assets are valued. According to Lane and Jacobsen (1995), intangible assets, such as brand names, enhance the ability of the firm to create earnings beyond those generated by tangible assets alone. In the paradigm of financial valuation based on present value of future earnings, firms with intangible strengths, such as well-known brand names, channel dominance, or an ability to innovate, should have higher net present values because of incremental earnings beyond those associated with tangible assets alone. The need to value intangible assets and the difficulties of doing so is reflected in the plethora of approaches that have been advocated in the past few years. These approaches include price premium, earnings valuation, and royalty payments (cf. Tollington 1995); determining the value of intangible assets as part of the value of intellectual capital (Simon and Sullivan 1993; Smith and Parr 1997); cost, market, and income approach methodologies (Reilly 1994); determination of brand 'multiples' (Murphy 1990); and the use of momentum accounting to measure brand assets (Farquhar, Han, and Ijiri 1991).

Perhaps the most widely used basis for a brand-valuation approach is the 'Price–Earnings (PE) Multiple' approach used by the InterBrand Group (Penrose 1989), in which the value of brands is estimated on the basis of incremental earnings associated with brand names multiplied by a PE multiple based on brand strength and product category attractiveness (higher for strong brands in more desirable categories). Intuitively, PE multiples and thus valuation of today's earnings increase with mitigation of risk and enhancement of future growth potential.

Although the PE Multiple is an often-quoted valuation measure, it has the problems associated with a reliance on earnings – an accrual accounting measure of firm performance (Fisher and McGowan 1983). Although the literature has yet to resolve which is the best measure of firm performance, there is a shift in recent years to use cash flows (Kerin, Mahajan, and Varadarajan 1990). Scholars in the finance area have argued that the market value of a firm is the net present value of all future cash flows expected to accrue to the firm (cf. Rappaport

1986). Thus, the 'share-holder value' approach, based on discounted cash flow analysis, is becoming increasingly important in strategic decision making for purposes of resource allocation among options that offer growth but are inherently risky. The importance of this perspective is underscored by the fact that a large proportion of the value of firms is based on perceived growth potential and associated risks, that is, value is based on expectations of future performance. The implications of this for the marketing profession are immense. If resources allocated to marketing strategies are not viewed as investments that create assets that can be leveraged to enhance future performance, provide potential for growth, or reduce risk, then contributions by marketers are likely to be perceived as marginal by corporate decision makers. The challenge then is to demonstrate and measure the value created or driven by marketing investments and strategies.

The shareholder value-planning approach proposed by Rappaport (1986) is based on several 'value drivers' (Kim, Mahajan, and Srivastava 1995). Because shareholder value is composed of the present value of (1) cash flows during the value growth period and (2) the long-term, residual value of the product/business at the end of the value growth period (for a detailed description of the approach, see Day and Fahey 1988), the value of any strategy is inherently driven by[3]

1 An acceleration of cash flows (earlier cash flows are preferred because risk and time adjustments reduce the value of later cash flows);
2 An increase in the level of cash flows (e.g., higher revenues and/or lower costs, working capital, and fixed investments);
3 A reduction in risk associated with cash flows (e.g., through reduction in both volatility and vulnerability of future cash flows) and hence, indirectly, the firm's cost of capital; and
4 The residual value of the business (long-term value can be enhanced, for example, by increasing the size of the customer base).

Market-based Assets and Shareholder Value

We turn now to a discussion of how market-based assets influence the four drivers of shareholder value identified in the previous section. We first discuss the influence of market-based assets on the acceleration of cash flows or the receipt of cash flows sooner than otherwise. We then examine how market-based assets enhance the level of cash flows. Next, we discuss how market-based assets lower the volatility and vulnerability of cash flows. Finally, we assess how market-based assets influence the residual value of cash flows. Although each market-based asset potentially can influence every driver of shareholder value, for reasons of brevity we discuss a select few of all the possible linkages. The goal is to illustrate rather than provide an exhaustive assessment of the influence of market-based assets on the drivers of shareholder value.

It also should be noted that there may be trade-offs on synergies involved in the influence of market-based assets on the four drivers of shareholder value. For example, it is possible that marketing activities to speed up cash flows also could have the effect of increasing the volatility of cash flows. Conversely, it is also possible that marketing activities to speed up cash flows simultaneously could increase the residual value of cash flows. Therefore, the criteria for choosing between investment opportunities in market-based assets must include the impact of the proposed marketing investments on all the drivers of shareholder value.

Market-based assets: influence on accelerating cash flows

Market-based assets can enhance shareholder value by enabling the firm to accelerate the receipt of cash flows or generating cash flows sooner than otherwise. As depicted in Figure 2, the faster the receipt of cash flows, the higher their net present value. To the extent that market-based assets can help accelerate the receipt of cash flows, such assets can influence positively the shareholder value of the firm.

There is considerable evidence in the marketing literature that market-based assets can accelerate cash flows by increasing the responsiveness of the marketplace to marketing activity. For example, Keller (1993) argues that brand equity can be captured in the differential effects of brand knowledge on consumer response to how the brand is marketed. Thus, if brand awareness and brand attitude are positive, customers are likely to respond with greater speed to the marketing efforts of the brand. Therefore, when exposed to a brand of which they are aware and to which they are disposed positively, customers are more likely to try the brand, adopt the brand, and begin to refer the brand to others sooner than otherwise.

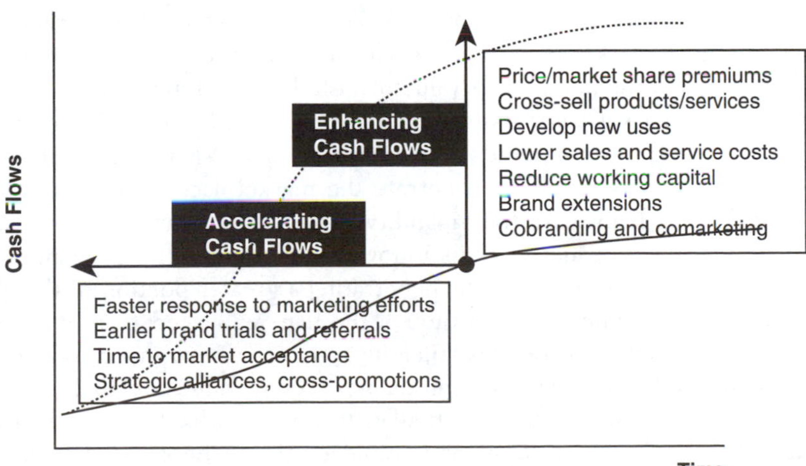

Figure 2 Accelerating and enhancing cash flows

Empirical evidence from industry studies also suggests that the more positive the brand attitude, the quicker the response of customers to new products. Zandan (1992) finds that brands with the strongest images in the personal computer industry, such as IBM, Compaq, and Hewlett-Packard, typically can expect customers to adopt their next-generation products three to six months sooner than brands with weaker images. Furthermore, his study also suggests that customers generally are willing to refer these brands to others three to six months sooner than they are for weaker brands. Therefore, customers with whom the firm has developed stronger long-term relational bonds through brand-and loyalty-building investments are likely to respond faster to marketing programs designed to stimulate earlier purchases and faster referrals, which leads to the acceleration of cash flows and thus greater shareholder value.

There is increasing recognition in the marketing and new product development literature that speed to market is a crucial variable. However, Robertson (1993) highlights that though there is a tremendous focus on speeding the new product development cycle, relatively little attention has been paid to achieving reductions in time-to-market acceptance for new products. Consequently, Robertson (1993) argues that being quick to market with a new product is only half the battle, the other half being the ability of the firm to penetrate the market quickly with the new product or reduce the market penetration cycle time. Jain, Mahajan, and Muller (1995) demonstrate that 'seeding' the market (i.e., using promotions to establish an installed base) and then leveraging these early adopters to facilitate word-of-mouth advertising can speed up product life cycles and therefore cash flows. Recent research on network externalities demonstrates the importance of the installed base (and buyers' expectations of the future installed base) in driving the adoption process. Network externalities lead to 'increasing returns' with the growth of the installed base and have been used to justify marketing activities that focus on licensing and standardization as a way of developing and leveraging the buyer installed base (Besen and Farrell 1994; Conner 1995). In the framework of network externalities, both clones and unauthorized (pirated) copies lead to the development of de facto standards (Conner and Rumelt 1991; Takeyama 1994). To the extent that market-based assets help reduce market penetration cycle time, the receipt of cash flows will be accelerated, and the net present value of cash flows will increase.

In addition, market-based assets also have network-level effects on market penetration cycle times. Strategic partnerships can help a firm reduce the speed with which products are able to penetrate the marketplace. Robertson (1993) points out that few firms have the capability to penetrate all markets around the world before a new product loses its innovative advantage. If so, alliances with partners can accelerate cash flows by penetrating a greater portion of the global market in the same time frame. Although the firm will need to part with the margins that are needed to create partnerships, the lower margins could be more than compensated for by the increase in the net present value of cash flows due to the acceleration of cash flows. In particular, this is more likely to be the case if the pace of technology development is rapid or the technology pioneer has a short window in which to establish the product.

The appropriate use of partnerships also enables firms to respond more quickly to market needs by taking advantage of existing networks. For example, a recent trend in the fast-food industry is to seek new locations in institutional markets, such as airports, gas stations, retail stores, and universities. Thus, McDonald's has an arrangement with Wal-Mart to place restaurants in the new Wal-Mart Supercenters, which enables McDonald's to penetrate new markets with greater speed, albeit at the cost of sharing margins with Wal-Mart.

Marketers traditionally have focused on financial metrics such as sales volume, market share, gross margin, and so forth. As such, marketing expenditures that are aimed at accelerating cash flows by shortening the market penetration cycle time are difficult to justify in the context of resource allocation within a firm. To the extent that the impact of marketing investments on shareholder value can include the additional value created by the acceleration of cash flows, the value of marketing activities such as brand building, product sampling, and comarketing alliances will be understood better and valued more appropriately by senior management and other functional executives.

Market-based assets: influence on enhancing cash flows

Market-based assets can increase shareholder value by enhancing the level of cash flows or generating cash flows that are higher than otherwise. As shown in Figure 2, higher cash flows translate into higher shareholder value. Cash flows can be enhanced by (1) generating higher revenues, (2) lowering costs, (3) lowering working capital requirements, and (4) lowering fixed capital requirements. Although the first two have been discussed in the marketing literature (Glazer 1991), the impact of marketing activities on the fixed and working capital requirements of the firm, though it has received some attention lately, generally is not well understood.

Although great care must be taken not to overextend brands, a great deal of evidence in the marketing literature suggests that brand extensions are important mechanisms for enhancing revenues (cf. Aaker 1991: Srivastava and Shocker 1991). Well-established and differentiated brands can charge a price premium on the basis of their monopolistic power attributable to customer switching costs and loyalty (Boulding, Lee, and Staelin 1994; Farquhar 1989). Brand equity also is associated with a customer base that is more responsive to advertising and promotions (Keller 1993). Therefore, the marginal costs of sales and marketing are lower for higher equity brands. Brand extensions enable firms to fill out their product lines, expand into related markets, and increase revenues by licensing brand names for use in other product categories. Furthermore, Smith and Park (1992) demonstrate the positive impact of brand extensions on market share and advertising efficiency and present evidence for how brand extensions help lower costs. Although brand extensions give rise to the danger of diluting brand equity, Dacin and Smith (1994) show that the number of products associated with a brand can even strengthen the brand, provided a consistency in quality is maintained across all products associated with the brand. Indeed, Wernerfelt (1988) argues that brand extensions can be interpreted as a firm's use of its accumulated investment in the brand, and future cash flows from other products affiliated with the brand as a 'bond' or collateral for the quality of the extension, which signals to customers the firm's faith in the brand extension.

There is a growing recognition in the literature that customer relationships enhance cash flows by reducing the level of working capital and fixed investments. The trend toward relationship marketing has created, in many instances, closer relationships between suppliers and customers (cf. Sheth and Parvatiyar 1995; Weitz and Jap 1995). These relationships have enabled both parties to achieve efficiencies by linking their supply chains. For example, the relationship between Procter & Gamble and Wal-Mart has resulted in efficiencies in managing order placement, order processing, cross-docking, and inventory holding that have provided both firms with cost savings. In the absence of strong supplier–customer relationships, the ability of either party to create partnerships that lead to the more efficient use of working capital and fixed assets, such as manufacturing capacity and warehouses, is extremely limited. Thus, strong relationships make it possible for firms to conceive and implement new policies and programs that otherwise would be nearly impossible.

Networked market-based assets also influence shareholder value by positively affecting cash flows. Anderson and Narus (1996) highlight how channel members can collaborate to help provide superior service to customers that otherwise would not have been possible. Thus, by pooling inventories at the network level, each member of the channel can promise and deliver improved customer service levels while lowering the investment required in inventories by each member of the network. Anderson and Narus (1996) cite inventory reductions of 15–20% and improved customer service as a result of better utilization of channel relationships.

In addition, cooperative ventures, such as cobranding and comarketing alliances, also enable firms to enhance cash flows (Bucklin and Sengupta 1993). The essence of cobranding and component branding is that both partners gain access to the other's customer base. Cooperation that involves sharing brands and customer relationships enables firms to (1) lower the cost of doing business by leveraging others' already existing resources, (2) increase revenues by reaching new markets or making available others' products, and (3) avoid the fixed investment of creating a new brand altogether or of establishing or extending the customer base.

Although researchers in marketing have addressed the issue of how marketing activities lower costs and enhance revenues, they have paid little attention to how market-based assets help reduce working capital and fixed investment needs. A notable exception is the recent literature on relationship marketing, which has brought to the fore issues such as the ability of partnerships to create efficiencies in the use of capital. If such a recognition has occurred, the willingness to invest in customer and partner relationship-building activities is apparent. However, the vast majority of marketing practitioners and top managers have yet to develop an appreciation for the role of marketing in influencing the capital needs of the business.

Market-based assets: influence on the vulnerability and volatility of cash flows

Market-based assets also can increase shareholder value by lowering the vulnerability and volatility of cash flows. Lower volatility and vulnerability reduce the risk associated with cash flows, which results in a lower cost of capital or discount rate. Thus, cash flows that are more stable and predictable will have a higher net present value and consequently create more shareholder value. Therefore, the capability of market-based assets to reduce the volatility and vulnerability of cash flows has a strong influence on the creation of shareholder value (see Figure 3).

The vulnerability of cash flows is reduced when customer satisfaction, loyalty, and retention are increased. When the firm has a satisfied and loyal base of customers, the cash flow from these customers is less susceptible to competitive activity. As a relatively rare and inimitable asset, the loyalty of the installed base represents a significant entry barrier to competition and makes the firm's cash flow less vulnerable. A variety of marketing programs are geared toward increasing customer loyalty and switching costs by increasing benefits (e.g., American Airlines' AAdvantage program) and reducing risks (e.g., through unconditional money-back guarantees) to more loyal customers. Furthermore, research from the services industry demonstrates that customer switching behavior is attributable more often to inadequate and indifferent customer service than to better products or prices (Reichheld 1996). This suggests that experiential as opposed to search attributes are more important for facilitating customer retention and loyalty. In addition, cross-selling of multiple products and services – and therefore increasing the number of bonds between firms and their customers – can increase switching costs.

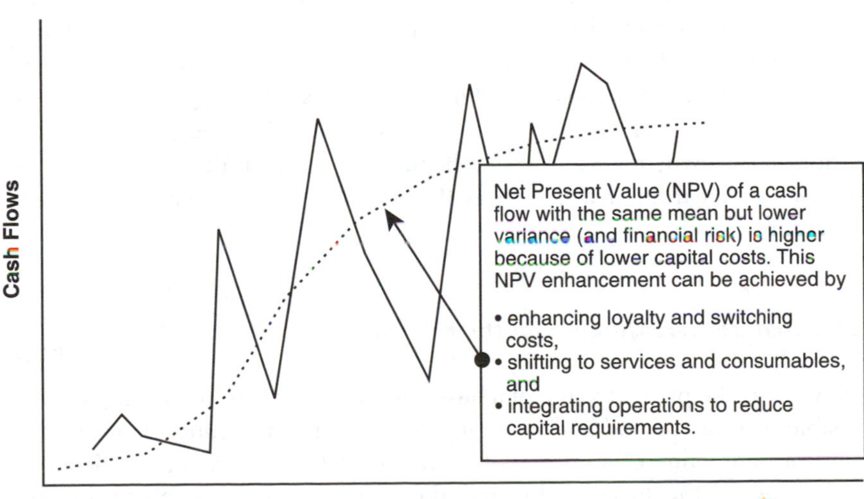

Figure 3 Reducing volatility in cash flows

Although marketers do focus on how to generate customer loyalty, they often fail to communicate its value. One way to do this could be by looking at the consequences of disloyalty. For example, the average retention rate in the automobile insurance industry is 80%. San Antonio-based USAA has a retention rate of more than 99%. So whereas the average insurance company must replace approximately 50% of its customers after three years, USAA must replace less than 3%. With customer acquisition costs running at least five times retention costs, the mathematical justification of a marketing focus on customer loyalty and retention is not difficult (for detailed analyses and arguments, see Reichheld 1996).

The volatility of cash flows is reduced when the firm's relationship with customers and channel partners is arranged in a manner that promotes stability in operations. This is, in part, the motivation for packaged goods manufacturers as they attempt to forge relationships with retailers that create operations that result in fewer and smaller peaks and valleys in sales. Customer and partner relationships enable firms to coordinate activities across the value chain, which enhances the ability of all members of the value chain to make their cash flows more stable. Thus, customer and channel partnerships that lead to greater sharing of information, automatic ordering and replenishment, and lower inventories can help reduce the unpredictability of cash flows. Volatility also is reduced when the firm is able to retain a large proportion of customers, as the cost of retaining customers is likely to be more predictable than the cost of acquiring new customers. Finally, companies such as General Electric and Kodak have followed the approach pioneered by Xerox – leasing imaging and medical equipment and generating stable cash flows from consumables and services that are then less vulnerable to competitive actions.

Although marketing activities can be structured to reduce the volatility and vulnerability of cash flows, such assessments of market strategy are rare. Indeed, traditional marketing activities often can be faulted for increasing the volatility and vulnerability of cash flows by using promotion and pricing strategies that encourage customers and channel partners to buy more unevenly than they otherwise would. Only in the past few years, as is so aptly illustrated by the current problems of America Online, have marketers begun to recognize the impact of their actions on the level of volatility in their businesses. As this recognition has grown, marketers have begun to look at measures beyond the level of sales and market share, such as the volatility and vulnerability of sales volume and market share.

Market-based assets: influence on the residual value of cash flows

Residual value is the present value of a business attributable to the period beyond a reasonable forecast period and generally accounts for a significant proportion of the net present value of a business (Rappaport 1986). As such, it reflects the expected value of the business beyond the planning horizon. Naturally, this expectation is linked to sources of expected cash flow in the future. As Figure 4 depicts, a strong case can be made for the link between market-based assets and

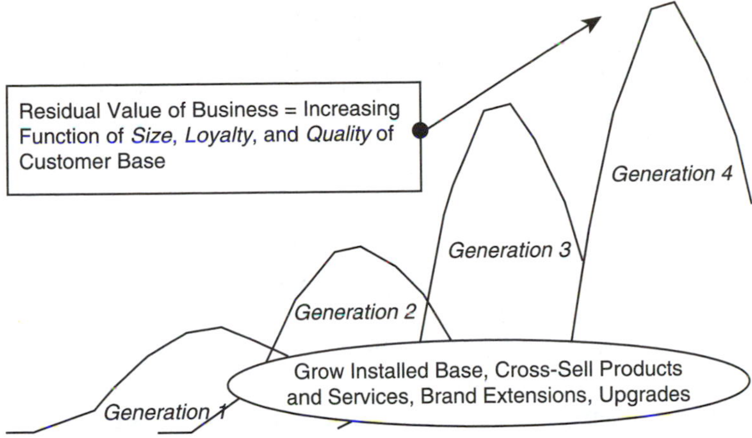

Figure 4 Enhancing the residual value of cash flows

residual value. For example, users of earlier versions of products and/or services not only can buy later versions but also can buy related products and services and brand extensions. More important, they contribute to growth by also referring these products and services to other potential users and therefore aid the adoption process. In many industries in which cash flows can be linked directly to customers (e.g., magazine subscriptions, cable television, cellular telephone services), the residual value of the business is linked closely to the size and quality of the customer base (Kim, Mahajan, and Srivastava 1995).

Some of the same factors that contribute to enhancing cash flows and reducing volatility and vulnerability also lead to higher residual values. For example, the larger the customer base and the higher the quality of the customer base (as measured by usage volume, willingness to pay a price premium, lower sales and service costs, and so on), the higher the loyalty (and therefore the lower the risk or vulnerability) and the residual value. This understanding is important because to create shareholder value, companies not only must grow the customer base but also must refine it (i.e., eliminate less profitable customers). Furthermore, a long-term goal of less vulnerable cash flows suggests a higher priority for customer retention versus acquisition, because customer loyalty is associated with higher revenue, lower sales and service costs, and lower risk. Finally, it is important to recognize that sustained, long-term customer loyalty results in more stable businesses and therefore a lower cost of capital. This further enhances the residual value of businesses.

Research on customer satisfaction, retention, and loyalty demonstrates the impact of marketing on the size and quality of the customer base of a business (cf. Anderson and Sullivan 1993; Johnson, Anderson, and Fornell 1995; Oliver 1980: Yi 1990). Satisfied customers are more loyal. Satisfied customers also extend their relationships with vendors to include other products and services. Finally, satisfied customers also are willing to pay higher prices. Furthermore, the possession of a large and loyal customer base confers a degree of legitimacy on the organization that is difficult for competitors to emulate. As a socially complex, difficult-to-imitate, and relatively rare asset, the customer base creates barriers for competition and thus increases the residual value of a business.

Discussion

Although the assertion that marketing activities create financial value is well accepted, marketing practitioners historically have found it difficult to measure and communicate to other functional executives and top management the value created by investments in marketing activity. Prior frameworks that assess the value of marketing activities typically have addressed the issue of customer value, but relatively little has been said about how marketing creates shareholder value. It is this gap that we hope to address by developing a conceptual framework that links marketing activities to the creation of shareholder value. In this discussion, we focus on the potential impact of the framework on marketing theory development, empirical research, and the teaching and practice of marketing.

Implications for marketing theory

As a multifaceted discipline, marketing lacks a single, integrating theory (cf. Hunt 1983). What is clear is that as the practice of marketing evolves, as the influence of marketing increases within organizations, and as the need for greater integration of marketing with other disciplines such as finance and manufacturing becomes necessary, marketing theory has not kept pace. In the absence of development of its underlying theory, marketing as an academic field of inquiry cannot avoid further intellectual disintegration (cf. Day 1992), and as a field of practice, it is likely to lose influence within organizations in the battle for managerial attention.

Although it is not offered as a solution to these ills, a significant contribution of the framework presented in this article is its potential to influence the development of theory in marketing. Fundamentally, the framework is a powerful tool to help understand the changing contours of marketing: what it is and what it is not, how and why it is evolving in specific directions (as suggested by the changing assumptions about marketing noted at the beginning of the article), and the role of marketing in broader business issues and contexts. Specific to this article is the contention that theories of marketing must be extended and broadened to include developments in finance, as indeed, theories of finance must be extended and broadened to include recent developments in marketing.

In at least one respect, the framework presented here represents a paradigm shift of modest proportions in the domain of marketing theory. If theory is the stipulation of cause and effect, given particular conditions, then marketing theory must incorporate more explicitly market-based assets as an input to marketing strategy choices that affects financial performance measures such as cash flows. Although we have made an attempt to define and delineate carefully the concept of market-based assets, we are far from developing a theory that refines the concept of market-based assets, identifies the range and extent of such assets, and develops sets of indicators to measure their stock and flow. Moreover, theory development in this area must address the trade-offs and synergies involved in accelcruting cash flows, increasing cash flows, lowering the volatility and vulnerability of cash flows, and increasing the residual value of cash flows. Without such theory development, critical distinctions among types of market-based assets are likely to remain far too coarse-grained. We hope this article stimulates such theorizing.

Implications for empirical research in marketing

By adding shareholder value-based criteria to assess the effectiveness of marketing activities, the framework has the potential to influence empirical research on the value of marketing by (1) highlighting under-researched variables in marketing and (2) examining hitherto unexplored paths among existing variables.

Under-researched variables. Cash flow is a relatively underutilized variable in marketing theory and research. Prior research has examined the impact of marketing on variables such as brand loyalty and customer satisfaction. Many studies also have examined the influence of marketing activities on financial measures, such as return on sales, return on assets, and return on equity. However, these are accrual accounting variables and as such are not always the most appropriate measures of firm performance (Rappaport 1983, 1986). Among the problems with accrual accounting measures of firm performance are that (1) they reflect previous performance and are not forward looking, (2) they are not adjusted for risk, and (3) they can be distorted by accounting laws and conventions (Bharadwaj and Bharadwaj 1997; Fisher and McGowan 1983; Montgomery and Wernerfelt 1988). Although the debate on the pros and cons of alternative measures of firm performance is far from resolved, cash flow is viewed increasingly as less susceptible to the problems associated with accrual accounting measures (Day and Fahey 1988). Thus, the inclusion of cash flow as a variable in marketing studies will help marketers better understand the influence of marketing activities on shareholder value.

Yet another variable that has received limited attention in marketing is speed. With the exception of the new product development literature, speed has not been a popular variable in marketing research. A focus on speed as a variable of interest undoubtedly will alter the focus of marketing activities and reframe research questions around the influence of marketing variables in attaining more rapid market penetration and hence greater shareholder value. In particular, the effect of speed on the capability of a firm to increase the net present value of cash flows is an interesting area that remains unexplored.

Unexplored relationships. The framework also has the potential to highlight some relationships that remain unexplored in the marketing literature. For example, the link between customer loyalty and the reduction of the vulnerability and volatility of cash flows as of yet has not been understood adequately. Likewise, the linkage between marketing strategies and the capital requirements of the firm remains relatively less understood. Further research in these areas will help sharpen marketers' understanding of the impact of marketing activities on shareholder value.

By considering hitherto underutilized variables and understanding these unexplored relationships, the current framework has the potential to influence the nature, content, and tone of the marketing conversation. Traditionally, studied variables, such as market share, market orientation, customer satisfaction and loyalty, and brand equity, must be linked to their influence on cash flows as research in marketing increasingly focuses on the creation of shareholder value.

Implications for teaching marketing

The framework also has implications for how marketing is taught. First, it enables marketing academics to provide a coordinated treatment of concepts from the marketing, finance, and accounting disciplines. Second, it also allows for the development of course materials to aid in the team teaching of courses that integrate marketing, finance, and accounting perspectives. Given the demands placed on business schools to develop integrated courses that prepare students to work more effectively in cross-functional environments, this framework and others like it can serve a valuable role in guiding the way the nature, scope, and value of marketing activities are taught in the future.

Implications for marketing practice

A critical implication of this article is that both the input and output dimensions of many practitioners' mental models of what marketing is might need to be amended radically. An appreciation of market-based assets, shareholder value parameters, and, more important, the linkages between them could lead to nothing short of a paradigm shift in how many marketing managers understand the scope and content of marketing, its role in the organization, and how to communicate with managers in the top echelon and other functional areas. Although the change in marketing assumptions enumerated at the beginning of this article suggests that this paradigm shift is at least in the early stages in some organizations, the thrust of the managerial implications suggested here is that it must occur on a grander scale and at a considerably more rapid rate.

A fundamentally new challenge for many marketing managers at the strategy input end is the identification of the market-based assets they now possess. This involves nothing short of cataloging each relational and intellectual asset. In the spirit of the marketing – finance framework presented here, cross-functional teams can aid in both listing such assets and affording an opportunity to begin the necessary dialogue across organizational boundaries about market-based assets and their impact on financial performance.

The market-based assets an organization possesses may not be those it needs Using current and potential marketing strategies as a guide, managers should ask what relational and intellectual assets would be required ideally to attract, win, and retain customers. Such judgments would compel managers to think in terms of market-based assets. Managers then must make assessments about asset stocks (that is, how much of each asset they possess) and flows (that is, whether each asset is augmenting or atrophying). The challenge here is to determine relevant stock and flow parameters. Some organizations might be unaware of market-based asset parameters they already possess, such as customer and channel surveys, third-party reports, and managers' own judgments that are contained in their reports of visits to customers, channels, and other strategic partners. Articulating and measuring such parameters, however crude they may be, will familiarize managers with the notion of market-based assets.

The central managerial challenge is how to leveraged market-based assets for marketplace success. Consideration of how intellectual and relational assets might be leveraged in developing new products or solutions, reaching new customer sets, and establishing new modes of differentiation could lead managers to identify new opportunities or ways to exploit existing opportunities better. Managers can ask whether the stock of each asset is being exploited fully. For example, some organizations will discover that their strong relationships with specific channels are underutilized, the channel could take more throughput, or they could do a better job of detailing and pushing the firm's products to customers. At a minimum, assessing how such assets can be leveraged will give managers a greater appreciation of their role and importance in developing and executing marketing strategy.

At the output end, managers must assess, even if they only do so crudely to begin with, how leveraging these assets affects cash flows. Again, learning both the analysis methodology and the underlying thought process, as articulated here, is essential. For example, marketing managers must assimilate and use the concepts and vocabulary now second nature to financial and accounting managers. In many organizations, it also will necessitate reconfiguring the core of marketing decision analysis: The output or performance measures now will include financial as well as marketplace parameters. Managers can begin by carefully identifying how a marketing strategy or individual marketing programs, such as a sales promotion program or a new advertising campaign, might affect cash flows. Indeed, the few organizations that do leverage their market-based assets well provide excellent guidelines for how other firms also can create and use market-based assets. At a minimum, additional marketing decision levers will be added to the arsenal of marketing managers.

Conclusion

The focus of this article is to enhance the understanding of the marketing-finance interface by developing a framework that captures the linkages between marketing activities and the creation of shareholder value. The framework proposes that marketing is concerned with the task of developing and managing market-based assets, or assets that arise from the commingling of the firm with entities in its external environment. Examples of market-based assets include customer relationships, channel relationships, and partner relationships. Market-based assets, in turn, influence shareholder value by accelerating and enhancing cash flows, lowering the volatility and vulnerability of cash flows, and increasing the residual value of cash flows. It is our hope that this framework will influence the nature, content, and tone of the marketing conversation and enable marketing professionals to assess and communicate the value of marketing activities to other disciplines.

Notes

1 In addition, a substantial body of literature links marketing constructs, such as customer satisfaction, brand equity, and quality, to various accrual accounting measures of business performance, such as profits and return on investment (cf. Anderson, Fornell, and Lehmann 1994; Rust, Zahorik, and Keiningham 1995). However, these studies stop short of linking marketing variables to the creation of shareholder value.

2 Our focus in the article is on marketing activities and not on the marketing department. This is consistent with the work on market orientation by Kohli and Jaworski (1990) and Narver and Slater (1990). As they do, we focus on marketing activities regardless of where in the organization they take place and who in the organization performs them.

3 Prior attempts in the marketing literature to develop a conceptual framework of the value of intangible assets such as information typically have stopped short of shareholder value. Glazer's (1991) influential work on the value of information describes value as arising from the capability of the information to (1) generate revenues from transactions higher than otherwise, (2) make cost of future transactions lower than otherwise, and (3) generate revenues from the information itself. The present framework extends Glazer's work in three ways. First, it adds new components of value, such as the capability to accelerate cash flows and lower their vulnerability and volatility. Second, it describes the four components of higher cash flow (i.e., higher revenues, lower costs, lower working capital levels, and lower levels of fixed investment). Third, it includes the value of relationships, or relational assets, and not just the value of information and knowledge.

References

Aaker, David A. (1991), *Managing Brand Equity: Capitalizing on the Value of a Brand Name.* New York: The Free Press.

—— and Robert Jacobsen (1994), 'The Financial Information Content of Perceived Quality,' *Journal of Marketing Research*. 31 (May), 191–201.

Agrawal, Jagdish and Wagner Kamakura (1995), 'The Economic Worth of Celebrity Endorsers: An Event Study Analysis,' *Journal of Marketing*, 59 (July), 56–62.

Amit, R. and P. J. H. Schoemaker (1993), 'Strategic Assets and Organizational Rent,' *Strategic Management Journal*, 14 (1), 33–46.

Anderson, Eugene W. Claes Fornell, and Donald R. Lehmann (1994), 'Customer Satisfaction. Market Share and Profitability: Findings from Sweden,' *Journal of Marketing*, 58 (July), 53–66.

—— and Mary W. Sullivan (1993), 'The Antecedents and Consequences of Customer Satisfaction for Firms.' *Marketing Science*, 12 (Spring), 125–43.

Anderson, James C. and James A. Narus (1996), 'Rethinking Distribution: Adaptive Channels,' *Harvad Business Review*, 74 (July/August), 112–22.

Anderson, Paul (1979), 'The Marketing Management/Finance Interface.' *American Marketing Association Educators' Conference Proceedings*. Neil Beckwith et al., eds. Chicago: American Marketing Association, 325–29.

—— (1981), 'Marketing Investment Analysis,' in *Research in Marketing*, Vol. 4, Jagdish N. Sheth, ed. Greenwich, CT: JAI Press, 1–37.

—— (1982), 'Marketing Planning and the Theory of the Firm.' *Journal of Marketing*, 46 (Spring), 15–26.

Badaracco, Joseph L. (1991), *The Knowledge Link: How Firms Compete Through Strategic Alliances*. Boston: Harvard Business School Press.

Barney, Jay (1991), 'Firm Resources and Sustained Competitive Advantage,' *Journal of Management*, 17 (1), 99–120.

—— and William Ouchi (1986), *Organizational Economics: Toward a New Paradigm for Studying and Understanding Organizations*. San Francisco: Jossey-Bass Publishers.

Barwise, Patrick, Paul R. Marsh, and Robin Wensley (1989), 'Must Finance and Strategy Clash?' *Harvard Business Review*, 67 (September/October), 85–90.

Besen, Stanley M. and Joseph Farrell (1994), Choosing How to Compete: Strategies and Tactics in Standardization.' *Journal of Economic Perspectives*, 8 (Spring), 117–31.

Bharadwaj, Anandhi S. and Sundar G. Bharadwaj (1997), 'Information Technology Effects on Firm Performance as Measured by Tobin's q.' working paper, Goizueta Business School. Emory University.

Boulding, William, Eunkyu Lee, and Richard Staelin (1994), 'Mastering the Mix: Do Advertising, Promotion, and Sales Force Activities Lead to Differentiation?' *Journal of Marketing Research*, 31 (May), 159–72.

Bucklin, Louis P. and Sanjit Sengupta (1993), 'Organizing Successful Co-Marketing Alliances,' *Journal of Marketing*, 57 (April), 32–46.

Capraro, Anthony J. and Rajendra K. Srivastava (1997), 'Has the Influence of Financial Performance on Reputation Measures Been Overstated?' *Corporate Reputation Review*, 1 (1), 86–93.

Chaney, Paul, Timothy Devinney, and Russell Winer (1991), 'The Impact of New Product Introductions on the Market Valuation of Firms,' *Journal of Business*, 64 (4), 573–610.

Conner, Kathleen R. (1991), 'Historical Comparison of Resource-Based Theory and Five Schools of Thought within Industrial Organization Economics: Do We Have a New Theory of the Firm?' *Journal of Management*, 17, 121–54.

—— (1995), 'Obtaining Strategic Advantage from Being Imitated: When Can Encouraging "Clones" Pay?' *Management Science*, 41 (February), 209–25.

—— and Richard P. Rumelt (1991), 'Software Piracy: An Analysis of Protection Strategies,' *Management Science*, 37 (February), 125–39.

Constantin, James A. and Robert F. Lusch (1994), *Understanding Resource Management*. Oxford, OH: The Planning Forum.

Dacin, Peter A. and Daniel C. Smith (1994), 'The Effect of Brand Portfolio Characteristics on Consumer Evaluations of Brand Extensions.' *Journal of Marketing Research*, 31 (May), 229–42.

Day, George (1992), 'Marketing's Contribution to the Strategy Dialogue,' *Journal of the Academy of Marketing Science*, 20 (Fall), 323–30.

—— (1994), 'The Capabilities of Market-Driven Organizations,' *Journal of Marketing*, 59 (October), 37–52.

—— and Liam Fahey (1988), 'Valuing Market Strategies,' *Journal of Marketing*, 52 (July), 45–57.

Drucker, Peter (1993), *Post-Capitalist Society*. New York: Harper Business.

Fama, Eugene and Merton Miller (1972), *The Theory of Finance*. New York: Holt, Rinehart and Winston.

Farquhar, Peter H. (1989), 'Managing Brand Equity,' *Marketing Research*, 1 (September), 24–33.

——. Julia Y. Han, and Yuji Ijiri (1991), 'Recognizing and Measuring Brand Assets.' Report No. 91–119. Cambridge, MA: Marketing Science Institute.

Fisher, Franklin and John McGowan (1983), 'On the Misuse of Accounting Rates of Return to Infer Monopoly Profits,' *American Economic Review*, 73, 82–97.

Glazer, Rashi (1991), 'Marketing in an Information-Intensive Environment: Strategic Implications of Knowledge as an Asset.' *Journal of Marketing*, 55 (October), 1–19.

Grant, Robert M. (1991), 'The Resource-Based Theory of Competitive Advantage: Implications for Strategy Formulation.' *California Management Review*, 33 (Spring), 114–35.

Hall, Richard (1992), 'The Strategic Analysis of Intangible Resources.' *Strategic Management Journal*, 13 (2), 135–44.

—— (1993), 'A Framework Linking Intangible Resources and Capabilities to Sustainable Competitive Advantage.' *Strategic Management Journal*, 14 (8), 607–18.

Horsky, Dan and Patrick Swyngedouw (1987), 'Does It Pay to Change Your Company's Name? A Stock Market Perspective.' *Marketing Science*, 6 (Fall), 320–35.

Hunt, Shelby D. (1983), *Marketing Theory: The Philosophy of Marketing Science*. Homewood. IL: Richard D. Irwin.

—— and Robert M. Morgan (1995), 'The Comparative Advantage Theory of Competition.' *Journal of Marketing*, 59 (April), 1–15.

Itami, Hiroyuki (1987), *Mobilizing Invisible Assets*. Cambridge. MA: Harvard University Press.

Jain, Dipak. Vijay Mahajan, and Eitan Muller (1995), 'An Approach for Determining Optimal Product Sampling for the Diffusion of a New Product,' *Journal of Product Innovation Management*, 12 (March), 29–37.

Johnson, Michael D., Eugene W. Anderson, and Claes Fornell (1995), 'Rational and Adaptive Performance Expectations in a Customer Satisfaction Framework.' *Journal of Consumer Research*, 21 (March), 695–707.

Kamakura, Wagner A. and Gary J. Russell (1994), 'Understanding Brand Competition Using Micro and Macro Scanner Data.' *Journal of Marketing Research*, 31 (May), 289–303.

Kaplan. Robert S. and David P. Norton (1992), 'The Balanced Scorecard – Measures That Drive Performance,' *Harvard Business Review*, 70 (January/February), 71–79.

—— and —— (1993), 'Putting the Balanced Scorecard to Work,' *Harvard Business Review*. 71 (September/October), 134–47.

Keller, Kevin L. (1993), 'Conceptualizing. Measuring and Managing Customer-Based Brand Equity,' *Journal of Marketing*, 57 (January), 1–22.

—— and David A. Aaker (1992), 'The Effects of Sequential Introductions of Brand Extensions.' *Journal of Marketing Research*, 29 (February), 35–50.

Kerin, Roger, Vijay Mahajan, and P. Rajan Varadarajan (1990), *Contemporary Perspectives on Strategic Market Planning*. Boston: Allyn and Bacon.

——, P. Rajan Varadarajan, and Robert A. Peterson (1992), 'First-Mover Advantage: A Synthesis, Conceptual Framework, and Research Propositions,' *Journal of Marketing*, 56 (October), 33–52.

Kim, Namwoon, Vijay Mahajan, and Rajendra K. Srivastava (1995), 'Determining the Going Value of a Business in an Emerging Information Technology Industry: The Case for Cellular Communications Industry.' *Technological Forecasting and Social Change*, 49 (July), 257–79.

Kohli, Ajay K. and Bernard Jaworski (1990), 'Market Orientation: The Construct, Research Propositions, and Managerial Implications.' *Journal of Marketing*, 54 (April), 1–18.

Lane, Vicki and Robert Jacobsen (1995), 'Stock Market Reactions to Brand Extension Announcements: The Effects of Brand Attitude and Familiarity,' *Journal of Marketing*, 59 (January), 63–77.

Leonard–Barton, Dorothy (1995), *Wellsprings of Knowledge: Building and Sustaining the Sources of Innovation*. Boston: Harvard Business School Press.

Lowenstein, Roger F. (1996), 'The "Q": When Is a Burger Not a Burger?' *The Wall Street Journal*, (May 30), Cl.

Lusch, Robert F. and Michael G. Harvey (1994), 'Opinion: The Case for an Off-Balance-Sheet Controller,' *Sloan Management Review*: 35 (Winter). 101–5.

Mahoney, Joseph T. and J. Rajendran Pandian (1992), 'The Resource-Based View Within the Conversation of Strategic Management.' *Strategic Management Journal*, 13 (5), 363–80.

Montgomery, Cynthia and Birgor Wernerfelt (1988), 'Diversification. Ricardian Rents, and Tobin's q.' *Rand Journal of Economics*, 19 (Winter), 623–32.

Murphy, John M. (1990), *Brand Strategy*. New York: Prentice Hall.

Narver, John C. and Stanley F. Slater (1990), 'The Effect of a Marketing Orientation on Business Performance.' *Journal of Marketing*. 54 (October), 20–35.

Nonaka, Ikujiro and Hiro Tukcuchi (1995), *The Knowledge Creating Company*. New York: Oxford University Press.

Oliver, Richard L. (1980), 'A Cognitive Model of the Antecedents and Consequences of Satisfaction Decisions,' *Journal of Marketing Research*, 17 (November), 460–69.

Penrose, Noel (1989), 'Valuation of Brand Names and Trademarks,' in *Brand Valuation: Establishing a True and Fair View*, John Murphy, ed. London: The Interbrand Group. 32–46.

Pessemier, Edgar and H. Paul Root (1973), 'The Dimensions of New Product Planning,' *Journal of Marketing*, 37 (January), 10–18.

Peteraf, Margaret (1993), 'The Cornerstone of Competitive Advantage: A Resource-Based View,' *Strategic Management Journal*, 14 (3), 179–91.

Pine, Joseph B., II (1993), *Mass Customization: The New Frontier in Business Competition*. Boston: Harvard Business School Press.

Quinn, James Brian (1992), *The Intelligent Enterprise*. New York: The Free Press.

Rappaport, Alfred (1983), 'Corporate Performance Standards and Shareholder Value,' *Journal of Business Strategy*, 4 (Spring). 28–38.

—— (1986), *Creating Shareholder Value*. New York: The Free Press.

Reichheld, Frederick F. (1996), *The Loyalty Effect*. Boston: Harvard Business School Press.

—— and Earl W. Sasser (1990), 'Zero Defections: Quality Comes to Services.' *Harvard Business Review*, 68 (September/October), 105–11.

Reilly, Robert F. (1994), 'Valuation of Intangible Assets for Bankruptcy and Reorganization Purposes,' *The Ohio CPA Journal*, 53 (4), 25–30.

Robertson, Thomas S. (1993), 'How to Reduce Market Penetration Cycle Times.' *Sloan Management Review*, 35 (Fall), 87–96.

Rust, Roland, Anthony J. Zahorik, and Timothy L. Keiningham (1995), 'Return on Quality (ROQ): Making Service Quality Financially Accountable.' *Journal of Marketing*, 58 (April), 58–70.

Senge, Peter (1990), *The Fifth Discipline: The Art and Practice of the Learning Organization*. New York: Doubleday-Currency.

Sharp, Byron (1995), 'Brand Equity and Market-Based Assets of Professional Service Firms,' *Journal of Professional Services Marketing*, 13 (1), 3–13.

Sheth, Jagdish N. and Atul Parvatiyar (1995), 'Relationship Marketing in Consumer Markets: Antecedents and Consequences.' *Journal of the Academy of Marketing Science*, 23 (Fall), 255–71.

Shocker, Allan D., Rajendra K. Srivastava, and Robert W. Ruekert (1994), 'Challenges and Opportunities Facing Brand Management: An Introduction to the Special Issue.' *Journal of Marketing Research*, 31 (May), 149–58.

Simon, Carol J. and Mary Sullivan (1993), 'The Measurement and Determinants of Brand Equity; A Financial Approach,' *Marketing Science*, 12 (Winter), 28–52.

Smith, Daniel C. and C. Whan Park (1992), 'The Effects of Brand Extensions on Market Share and Advertising Efficiency,' *Journal of Marketing Research*, 29 (August). 296–313.

Smith, Gordon V. and Russell L. Parr (1997), *Valuation of Intellectual Property and Intangible Assets*, 2d ed., 1997 Cumulative Supplement. New York: John Wiley & Sons.

Srivastava, Rajendra K. and Allan D. Shocker (1991), 'Brand Equity; A Perspective on Its Meaning and Measurement.' Report No. 91–124. Cambridge, MA: Marketing Science Institute.

Stein, Jeremy C. (1989), 'Efficient Capital Markets, Inefficient Firms: A Model of Myopic Corporate Behavior,' *Quarterly Journal of Economics*, 103 (November), 655–69.

Takeyama, Lisa N. (1994), 'The Welfare Implications of Unauthorized Reproduction of Intellectual Property in the Presence of Demand Externalities,' *The Journal of Industrial Economics*, 42 (June), 155–66.

Tollington, Anthony (1995), 'Brand Accounting and the Marketing Interface,' *Management Accounting*, 73 (July/August), 58–59.

Treacy, Michael and Fred Wiersema (1995), *The Discipline of Market Leaders*. Reading, MA: Addison–Wesley.

Van der Hijden, Kees (1996), *The Art of Strategic Conversation*, New York: John Wiley & Sons.

Webster, Frederick E. (1981), 'Top Management's Concerns About Marketing: Issues for the 1980's.' *Journal of Marketing*, 45 (July), 9–16.

—— (1992), 'The Changing Role of Marketing in the Corporation.' *Journal of Marketing*, 56 (October), 1–17.

Weitz, Barton A. and Sandy Jap (1995), 'Relationship Marketing and Distribution Channels,' *Journal of the Academy of Marketing Science*, 23 (Fall), 305–20.

Wernerfelt, Birger (1988), 'Umbrella Branding as a Signal of New Product Quality: An Example of Signaling by Posting a Bond, *Rand Journal of Economics*, 19 (Autumn), 458–66.

Yi, Youjae (1990), 'A Critical Review of Customer Satisfaction.' in *Review of Marketing*. Valarie Zeithaml, ed. Chicago: American Marketing Association, 68–123.

Zandan, Peter (1992), 'Brand Equity in Technology Product-Markets,' presentation slides. Intelliquest Inc., Austin. TX.

Questions

1 Why, in your opinion, did it take marketing managers nearly a century to move from a psychological measurement base, that is, changes in awareness, recognition, intent to purchase, and the like, to a financial view of marketing results? Why do you suppose the change did not occur sooner?

2 Srivastava and his colleagues argue that increases in shareholder value are the critical ingredient in determining the impact and effect of marketing programmes. Further, they believe these should be directly related to customer income flows. Do you agree that only financial values are important in marketing metrics? Shouldn't marketing be concerned with other values, such as society, the environment, culture and the like?

3 Using the financial measures and metrics proposed in the article would seem to require better training in accounting and finance among marketing managers. How would you include these concepts in a typical MBA course of study?

4 A major intangible asset of the firm is the brand or brands the organization owns or controls. The focus in this article revolves almost entirely around cash flows. How can this management of cash flows concept be related to or combined with some type of 'brand-as-corporate-asset' view?

5 As cited by the authors, Hunt (1983) argues that marketing, as a multi-faceted discipline, lacks a single, integrating theory. Do you think this article helps to build a single integrated marketing theory? If so, in what ways is that done? If not, what suggestions do you have for developing a single integrating theory of marketing that seems to be needed?

6 The idea of 'residual market value' is advanced by Srivastava et al. in this article. They suggest that residual value is the present value of a business that can be attributed to the time beyond a reasonable forecast period. As marketplace changes become more rapid, customers and consumer behaviour more dynamic, and management focus increasingly on the short term, does the idea of 'residual value' of marketing have much face value in the twenty-first-century organization. If so, what is that value and how might one go about measuring it?

Vignette

Expanding the Market-based Assets Concept

Perhaps the greatest verification of the importance of the concepts articulated by Srivastava et al. through the concept of market-based assets is the large number of academics, researchers and practitioners who have expanded, extended and enhanced the basic concepts of the original article. A brief look at the current literature shows three basic streams of thought, work and process based directly on or in concert with the Srivastava et al. concepts.

Value-based marketing

Value-based marketing, as articulated by Professor Peter Doyle, University of Warwick Business School in the UK, has provided many useful tools to improve marketing measurement. In his groundbreaking book, *Value-based Marketing: Marketing Strategies for Corporate Growth and Shareholder Value* (2000) Doyle develops the concepts and approaches that turn the Srivastava et al. models into practical, hands-on management tools.

As a start, he proposes a new definition of marketing: 'Marketing is the process that seeks to maximize returns to shareholders by developing and implementing strategies to build relationships of trust with high-value customers and to create a sustainable differential advantage' (*ibid.*). In Doyle's framework, he identifies three basic Drivers of Value in the firm, i.e. organizational, marketing and financial. He then identifies eighteen specific value drivers that are involved in the creation of shareholder value which are comprised of dividends and capital growth. The value drivers he relates to marketing include marketing knowledge, strong brands, customer loyalty, strategic relationships, market selection and differential advantage. Thus it is clear that there is great similarity between the approach proposed by Srivastava and his colleagues and Doyle. Students and practitioners will find the Doyle approach to value-based marketing a very useful tool to implement the recommendations of Srivastava et al.

Customer-based brand equity

Customer-based equity has been developed by Blattberg, Getz and Thomas in their book *Customer Equity: Building and Managing Relationships as Valuable Assets* (2001). Where Srivastava et al. and Doyle approach the creation of cash flows from a financial and accounting level, Blattberg and his associates argue that it is the creation and management of customer income flows over time that really define the success of the firm. It is the management of these customer income flows (cash, in the view of Srivastava et al. and Doyle) that ultimately define shareholder value.

The management of customer relationships to increase or maintain customer lifetime value is the key ingredient in their approach. They propose three basic marketing strategies be used: customer acquisition, customer retention and customer add-on selling.

Thus they have operationalized the Srivastava et al. approach in a more traditional direct marketing sense. Students and practitioners will find the approach

Blattberg et al. use quite helpful if the firm has direct contact and relationships with its customers.

Return on marketing investment (ROI)

Lenskold (2003), Schultz and others (Schultz and Walters 1997) have developed specific methodologies and approaches to tie marketing investments to marketing returns. For the most part, these approaches have focused primarily on the measurement of short-term, incremental returns on marketing activities. Using a range of methodologies such as correlation analysis, marketing mix modelling and return on customer investment (ROCI), these authors and consultants have used the concepts articulated by Srivastava et al. in a number of ways. All, however, tie back to the basic premise that the measurement of the change in value of market-based assets, primarily in the form of cash flows, is the marketing metric of today and tomorrow.

References

Aaker, David A. (1991) *Managing Brand Equity*, New York: Free Press.

Ambler, Tim (2003) *Marketing and the Bottom Line*, 2nd edn, London: Pearson.

Blattberg, Robert C., Getz, Gary and Thomas, Jacquelyn S. (2001) *Customer Equity: Building and Managing Relationships as Valuable Assets*, Boston, MA: Harvard Business School Press.

Day, George and Fahey, Liam (1998) 'Valuing Market Strategies', *Journal of Marketing* 52: 45–57.

Doyle, Peter (2000) *Value-based Marketing: Marketing Strategies for Corporate Growth and Shareholder Value*, Chichester: Wiley.

Haigh, David (2003) 'An Introduction to Brand Equity: How to Understand and Appreciate Brand Value and the Economic Impact of Brand Investment', *Interactive Marketing*, 5 (1).

Keller, Kevin L. (2002) *Strategic Brand Management*, 2nd edn, Englewood Cliffs, NJ: Prentice Hall.

Kotler, Philip (2003) *Marketing Management*, 11th edn, Upper Saddle River, NJ: Pearson.

Lenskold, James (2003) *Marketing Return on Investment*, New York: McGraw-Hill.

McCarthy, Jerome E. (1975) *Basic Marketing: a Managerial Approach*, 5th edn, Homewood, IL: Irwin.

McDonald, Malcolm, Martin, Christopher, Knox, Simon and Payne, Adrian (2000) *Creating a Company for Customers*, London: Pearson.

Schultz, Don E. and Jeffrey S. Walters, *Measuring Brand Communication Return on Investment*, New York: Association of National Advertisers.

Srivastava, Rajendra K., Shervani, Tasadduq A., and Fahey, Liam (1998) 'Market-based Assets and Shareholder Value: a Framework for Analysis', *Journal of Marketing* 62: 2–18.

Chapter 12

Philip J. Kitchen

CONCLUSION

THIS READER HAS PROVIDED an overview of issues considered important in the field of marketing communications as it is located with the domain of marketing – a fundamental necessity of most any business and management practice. As we have shown in the previous pages, the *study* of marketing communications can be, and often is, *different* from the practice! Yet *study* is a prelude to practice. Too often, managers are so busy sawing away at a particular marketing or communication problem, they take no time to continuously sharpen their saw.

Just in order to orchestrate the components of the promotional mix (i.e. advertising, sales promotion etc), one first has to explore the dynamics of the served market. These dynamics often result in answers to questions. What? Why? When? How? Where? Who? And with what calculable effect?

Integration involves an outside-in approach to marketing communications, where customers, consumers and prospects drive the communication process. This is the direct opposite of the business attempting to force perhaps unwanted messages into the minds of sophoric semi-resistant receivers. It also involves gathering information and building databases of customers' needs, wants and behaviours. Databases which must be regularly updated with fresh information, and databases that provide the technological and informational infrastructure to measure behavioural, as opposed to attitudinal, outcomes. Integrated communications programmes, which can and should be on-going, need to be underpinned by detailed analysis and careful planning, before being carefully implemented, and monitored to ensure that effectiveness results (see chapters 1, 2 and 11).

Communication programmes may involve one or several elements of marketing communications or the promotional mix in order which enables the building of relationships of trust with customers and consumers (see chapter 10). Successful marketing communication programmes are generally built around and rely upon:

- Advertising
- Sales promotion
- Direct marketing
- Marketing PR
- Sponsorship
- Personal selling
- Internet and the World Wide Web

Each of these elements has its own form, characteristics, dynamics, history and measures of success or evaluation. Obviously marketing communications can be built around or use any of these individually or in combination, contingent upon the communication task. In this book, the special articles the editors selected illustrate some or all these criteria. In a sense, we have chosen those articles that seem to most critically reflect upon, integrate and make sense of the developments in each domain.

The old iceberg analogy comes to mind. What we have discussed in each chapter is like the tip of the iceberg. The massive and incalculable human energy devoted to each topic lies below the surface. Isaac Newton once said:

> to myself I seem to have been only like a boy playing on the seashore, and diverting myself in now and then finding a smoother pebble or a prettier shell than ordinary, whilst the great ocean of truth lay all undiscovered before me.

While we cannot legitimately liken marketing communications to the realm of 'truth' it seems evident that there is a whole *ocean* of material which can be accessed in relation to each conceptual subject area discussed in this book. Moreover, we stress that the communications environment is extremely dynamic, with new media forms emerging and an increasing blurring between forms. For example blurring between advertising, editorial and entertainment such as 'advergames' and the increasing strategic and tactical use of product placements – coupled with the problem of how to measure effectiveness.

Nonetheless, we hope that this reader will act as a facilitator, or starting point, in developing your personal search for understanding. Yet there is a warning. Occasionally, a few dozen yards up the beach, you may find one of the editors, assiduously searching for greater depth of knowledge in these important areas. Enjoy the search . . .